Killing the Model Minority Stereotype: Asian American Counterstories and Complicity

Killing the Model Minority Stereotype: Asian American Counterstories and Complicity

Edited by

Nicholas D. Hartlep
Brad J. Porfilio

INFORMATION AGE PUBLISHING, INC.
Charlotte, NC • www.infoagepub.com

Library of Congress Cataloging-in-Publication Data

The CIP data for this book can be found on the Library of Congress website (loc.gov).

Paperback: 978-1-68123-110-5
Hardcover: 978-1-68123-111-2
eBook: 978-1-68123-112-9

CONTENTS

PART IV

CONSIDERATIONS WHEN CONDUCTING RESEARCH ON THE MODEL MINORITY STEREOTYPE

ADVANCE PRAISE

The contributors to this book demonstrate that the insidious model minority stereotype is alive and well. At the same time, the chapters carefully and powerfully examine ways to deconstruct and speak back to these misconceptions of Asian Americans. Hartlep and Porfilio pull together an important volume for anyone interested in how racial and ethnic stereotypes play out in the lives of people of color across various contexts.

— Vichet Chhuon, Ph.D.
Assistant Professor of Culture and Teaching,
University of Minnesota Twin Cities
Chair, Research on the Education of Asian Pacific Americans,
American Educational Research Association

Killing the Model Minority Stereotype: Asian American Counterstories and Complicity comprehensively explores the complex permutations of the model minority myth, exposing the ways in which stereotypes of Asian Americans operate in the service of racism. Through counter-narratives, critical analysis, and transnational perspectives, this volume connects to overarching projects of decolonization. A must read for social justice educators and practitioners engaged in understanding

Killing the Model Minority Stereotype: Asian American Counterstories and Complicity,
pages ix–x.

how the model minority myth functions to uphold white supremacy and the damaging impacts of our complicity in its perpetuation.

— Stefanie Smith, M.S.
Program Coordinator
Center for Intercultural Programs
DePaul University

This volume presents valuable additions to the model minority literature exploring narratives challenging stereotypes in a wide range of settings and providing helpful considerations for research and practice.

— David W. Chih, Ph.D.
Director, Asian American Cultural Center,
University of Illinois at Urbana-Champaign

Nicholas Hartlep and Brad Porfilio have put together a book that enhances the discourse around the model minority stereotype. Through exploration of the stereotype through counterstories, in non-U.S. spaces, and Asian American complicity, this volume is a welcome and timely contribution to the discussion around the model minority image.

— Teresa A. Mok, Ph.D.
Clinical Psychologist in Independent Practice

Asian Pacific Islander adolescents and young adults are especially impacted by the model minority stereotype, and this volume details the real-life consequences for them and for all communities of color. The contributors provide a wide-ranging critique and deconstruction of the stereotype by uncovering many of its manifestations, and they also take the additional step of outlining clear strategies to undo the stereotype and prevent its deleterious effects on API youth. *Killing the Model Minority Stereotype: Asian American Counterstories and Complicity* is an essential read for human service professionals, educators, therapists, and all allies of communities of color.

— Joseph R. Mills, LICSW
Clinical Social Worker and Coordinator of the
Southeast Asian Young Men's Group
Asian Counseling and Referral Service,
Seattle, WA

FOREWORD

Stacey J. Lee

Despite the significant body of scholarship critiquing the model minority stereotype, it does not appear to be going anywhere soon. Images of Asian Americans as
model minorities saturate popular culture and the mainstream press. The "model
minority" achievements of some Asian Americans continue to be used by conservative political forces in the fight against social justice. The persistence of the
model minority in the mainstream imagination maintains a racial hierarchy that
positions whites on top.

While the dominant society plays a central role in perpetuating the model minority image, we can't overlook the fact that some Asian Americans are complicit in its reification. Asian Americans in the California's San Gabriel Valley,
for example, embraced the rhetoric of the model minority stereotype to oppose
Senate Constitutional Amendment no. 5 (SCA-5), which would have repealed
portions of proposition 209 and would have allowed public universities to consider race in making admissions decisions. Advancing images of Asian Americans as model minorities, Asian American opponents of SCA-5 argued that the
amendment would punish their children for working hard to achieve the American
Dream (Vuong, 2014). Implicit in these narratives was the unspoken perspective
that other groups of color were somehow undeserving in comparison to Asian
Americans. Furthermore, opponents of SCA-5 failed to acknowledge that some
groups of Asian Americans struggle in our schools and might have benefited from

Killing the Model Minority Stereotype: Asian American Counterstories and Complicity,
pages xi–xii.
Copyright © 2015 by Information Age Publishing
xi

SCA-5. The voices of Asian Americans who opposed SCA-5 dominated the discussion, and ultimately the vocal opposition of a relatively small percentage of Asian Americans proved central in quashing SCA-5 for 2014. Significantly, the 2012 National Asian American Survey shows that the majority of Asian Americans actually support affirmative action, but mainstream media coverage often makes this fact invisible.

Why do some Asian Americans embrace the model minority image? What work does the model minority stereotype perform for Asian Americans who are complicit with the stereotype? There are doubtless many reasons that some Asian Americans consent to the hegemony of the model minority stereotype. I imagine that some Asian American supporters of the stereotype simply believe it to be true, and that others see it as being better than other stereotypes facing Asian Americans (i.e., yellow peril/perpetual foreigner). I also imagine that there are some who use the model minority image strategically for private gain. While Asian Americans who espouse model minority rhetoric often attract the attention of the mainstream media, the vast majority of Asian Americans are more critical of the stereotype, but our voices are often silenced. Asian Americans and others who are committed to social justice for all racial groups must continue to challenge model minority discourses through the telling of counter stories. We must continue to talk about the ways the stereotype hurts members of the Asian American community and other groups of color. *Killing the Model Minority Stereotype: Asian American Counterstories and Complicity* edited by Nicholas Hartlep and Bradley Porfilio continues the fight for racial justice.

REFERENCES

National Asian American Survey. Retrieved October 13, 2014, from http://www.naasurvey.com/reports/affirmative-action.html

Vuong, Z. (2014). Asians rally against SCA 5, call it revival of Affirmative Action. *Pasadena Star News*. Retrieved October 13, 2014, from http://www.pasadenastarnews.com/social-affairs/20140308/asians-rally-against-sca-5–call-it-revival-of-affirmative-action

ACKNOWLEDGMENTS AND DEDICATION

Nicholas and Brad would like to thank Lise Larocque of *Canadian Social Work Review* for the permission to reprint Gordon Pon's chapter. They would also would like to thank Nicholas Ozment for his excellent editorial assistance with the book manuscript. Any and all errors are theirs and theirs alone.

DEDICATION

Nicholas dedicates this book to his wife Stacey, and daughters Chloe, Avery, and Olivia. Brad dedicates this book to his wife, Shannon.

INTRODUCTION

Nicholas D. Hartlep and Brad J. Porfilio

This volume was edited during the height of the Tiger Mom Era (Chua, 2011). Amy Chua's *Battle Hymn* aroused the public's fascination and engagement with Asian American parents and Asian American student success. Interestingly, however, both scholars (Chang, 2011) and parent activists (Gym, 2011) have problematized the Tiger mother construction through critique and candor (also see Juang, Qin, and Park's "Tiger Parenting, Asian-Heritage Families, and Child/Adolescent Well-Being" special issue published in *Asian American Journal of Psychology*).

Linsanity—a parallel phenomenon originating in New York that swept across the United States—accents, if not punctuates, the Tiger Mom Era quite well. Jeremy Lin, now a basketball player on the Los Angeles Lakers, does not break the academic model minority mold of Asian Americans; he reinforces it. As an alumnus of Harvard with an economics degree, Lin's success on and off the basketball court complies with his own discrimination and further invisibility as an Asian American. Nowhere is this best exemplified than in the documentary *Linsanity* (2013), which was directed by Evan Leong. Lin's "Christian" identity also adds to the Eurocentric model minority construction (Schlosser, 2003). In an interview with African American *CNN* correspondent TJ Holmes, for instance, television viewers witness humility on Lin's part, and an overemphasis on Harvard on

Holmes's part.[1] This interview is consonant with the documentary: Lin is devoted to being humble and a hard worker.

However, Lin himself, perpetuates the model minority stereotype through satire, as evidenced in his 4–minute YouTube video "How to Get into Harvard," in which he lays out the following steps: (1) get glasses, (2) play an instrument (piano or violin), (3) improve test taking skills (play *Fruit Ninja* app on iPad and also bubble in scantrons), and (4) practice while you study (dribbling basketball in library) and study while you practice (respond to multiplication flashcards).[2] Lin's Christian identity emerges as the YouTube film comes to a conclusion: Proverbs 3:5–7 is displayed, which reads, "Trust in the Lord with all your heart, and do not lean on your own understanding. In all your ways acknowledge Him, and He will make straight your paths." It is interesting to us, the editors of this volume, that the original model minorities in the United States were not Christian (they were Jews), given that Christianity is a key element that marks Asian American model minorities (e.g., see Busto, 1996; Freedman, 2005; Kim, 2006).

STRUCTURE OF THE BOOK

The chapters in this volume are organized around three interrelated—so far as the editors perceive—phenomena, which are divided into three parts. Part I deals with model minority counterstories. Part II shares chapters written on the model minority in non-U.S. spaces, while Part III highlights Asian American complicity in perpetuating the Asian model minority stereotype.

In this volume *counterstories* refer to narratives that push against the model minority narrative, while *complicity* occurs any time an Asian American is involved or participates in an action that reinforces or reifies the model minority stereotype. It is an unfortunate fact that Asian Americans are sometimes guilty of perpetuating the model minority stereotype (either consciously or unconsciously), because this maintains whiteness (Jackson, 2006). Nevertheless, Asian American complicity is something that scholars have not explicitly explored, although Chang (1999) states the following: "To the extent that Asian Americans accept the model minority myth, we are *complicit* in the oppression of other racial minorities and poor Whites" (p. 58, italics added). We believe Chang is referring to the notion that Asian Americans who seemingly benefit from complying with the myth or who accept that meritocracy is real unwittingly cause harm to those minority groups that are compared to the Asian stereotype. This is something very important to consider because the model minority stereotype divides and conquers groups of people, rather than builds and supports an interracial understanding. As Kang (2014) points out, "Laudatory views of Asians can be invoked to discredit the claims of other minority groups and then revoked when Asians emerge as a potential threat to whites" (p. 92).

---

[1] This *CNN* interview is available on YouTube: http://www.youtube.com/watch?v=V_EWTMG0Yy8
[2] This YouTube video is available here: http://www.youtube.com/watch?v=-9yVnKQNj58

Why An Edited Volume on the Model Minority Stereotype and Why Now?

The chapters in this volume are critically important since they re-center the voices of Asian Americans, who, despite their status (at times being model minorities, at other times being yellow perils), continue to be overlooked by the wider academic and general population. Asian American counterstories are important anti-hegemonic tools because they counter stock stories. According to Bonilla-Silva (2010), stock stories are fundamentally problematic because they "make sense of the world but in ways that reinforce the status quo, serving particular interests without appearing to do so" (p. 75). This is one reason that the model minority stereotype is so hegemonic and why it needs to be deconstructed. Another reason a book like this is necessary now is because everyday language keeps the model minority stereotype discourse alive.

In her important book *The Everyday Language of White Racism,* Hill (2008) points out that many whites do not believe that they are racist because they don't consider their actions or their speech (such as mock Spanish) to be malicious or invidious. Consequently, racist gaffes are labeled errors of the head rather than of the heart, a "semantic move" (Bonilla-Silva, 2002) that Hill problematizes effectively well in her book. Notwithstanding, Hill's arguments and analyses would have been strengthened if she had looked at the fact that "mock" language extends beyond Spanish in the United States. Indeed, Asian language is frequently mocked, not only in the popular media but in the news media as well. The crash landing of *Asiana* Flight 214 is a prime example of everyday language being used to talk nasty about Asians in the United States without sounding racist (Hartlep, 2015a, 2015b). The pilots' names were reportedly (1) Captain Sum Ting Wong, (2) Wi Tu Lo, (3) Ho Lee Fuk, and (4) Bang Ding Ow (see Figure 1).

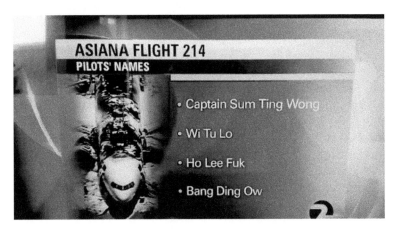

FIGURE 1.   Asiana Flight 214

Everyday language, as described by Hill (2008), is the primary reason this edited volume on the Asian model minority stereotype is sorely needed, especially since model minority stereotypical enthymemes are frequently used. According to Bitzer (1959),

> The enthymeme is a syllogism based on probabilities, signs, and examples, whose function is rhetorical persuasion. Its successful construction is accomplished through the joint efforts of speaker and audience, and this is its essential character. (p. 408)

Model minority enthymemes are part of the everyday language of racism. For instance, comments such as the following can be heard regularly in schools and mainstream middle-class white professional society: "Of course she will get into a top college—her mother is Chinese!" or "Those sisters are going to ace the exam; they come from a Korean family." The implied premise in the first statement is that all Chinese are top students because Chinese mothers parent in unique ways.[3] The implied premise in the second comment is that all Korean families produce studious test takers.[4]

CHAPTERS IN PART I

Chapter one, "Towards the Model Minority: Asian Americanization of Burmese Immigrants as a Model Minority in a High School," focuses on the model minority stereotype of Asian Americans in relation to the Asian Americanization of Burmese students at New High School. The first section of the chapter highlights the aspects of schooling at New High that contributes to the segmented assimilation of Burmese students away from mainstream America, while the second section describes the construction of the model minority stereotype for "good" Burmese immigrant students. In the concluding section, chapter contributor Gilbert C. Park highlights two ways that the model minority stereotype, as constructed at New High, affected the Americanization of Diane and David, two Burmese students at New High.

Chapter two, "New Starting Points: Becoming Asian Pacific Islander Educators in a Multiracial and Multicultural Society" written by Thomas M. Philip and Edward R. Curammeng (with contributions from Leslie Chanthaphasouk, Troy Keali'I Lau, Juliet Lee, Jeffrey Lieu, Sakiko Muranaka, Juliane Nguyen, Elizabeth Ul, and Kate Viernes), shares counterstories that attempt to move beyond the construct of the model minority stereotype by defining Asian Pacific Islanders within the increasingly complex and arguably less obvious relationships of power that racialize them in the 21st century. Building on an understanding of Asian Pacific Islander identity that honors its roots in struggles against racism and im-

---

[3] See Amy Chua's *Wall Street Journal* essay "Why Chinese Mothers Are Superior."
[4] See the book *Top of the Class: How Asian Parents Raise High Achievers—and How You Can Too* authored by two Korean sisters.

perialism, the contributors begin a dialogue about the relevance of this political/racial identity for Asian Pacific Islander educators today.

In chapter three, "Hapas in College: Multiracial Asian Identity and the Model Minority Myth," Amy L. Miller, Thai-Huy Nguyen, and Marybeth Gasman examine through a single, in-depth vignette how the model minority stereotype hampers student confidence and opportunities to connect with other students on campus. In their thoughtful analysis, Miller, Nguyen, and Gasman attempt to shine a light on the mixed-race Asian American community by making a case for why their stories are important in the overall landscape of educational research on Asian Americans and other non-dominant minority groups.

In chapter four, contributors Marissa S. Yenpasook, Annie Nguyen, Chia S. Her, and Valerie Ooka Pang, representing a group of four AAPI women—Pilipino-Thai-Chinese American, Vietnamese American, Hmong American, and Japanese American—share their diverse life stories. The contributors discuss their intersectionality and the roles it has in perpetuating stereotypes about AAPI women, as well as their experiences with and their relationships to the model minority stereotype. Their chapter is rightfully titled "Defiant: The Strength of Asian American and Pacific Islander Women," which in many ways is a counterstory to numerous societal stereotypes of AAPI women.

CHAPTERS IN PART II

The fifth chapter, "Importing the Asian Model Minority Discourse into Canada: Implications for Social Work and Education," is a reprint of Gordon Pon's article originally published in the *Canadian Social Work Review*. Pon analyzes the model minority discourse within a Canadian context. He explains that while there is a tremendous amount of literature on the model minority in the United States, there is a dearth of it in Canada. Pon argues that the model minority discourse has been imported into Canada from the United States and that the Canadian model minority discourse draws on the American model minority discourse in the context of Canadian multiculturalism.

The sixth chapter is an original chapter written by Grant Hannis, a professor at Massey University in New Zealand. "The Model Minority and Yellow Peril Stereotypes in New Zealand Journalism" considers the depiction of Chinese in the print media of New Zealand (a small country in the south Pacific whose dominant culture is white European). Hannis focuses on an analysis of the major influx of Chinese immigrants into the country in the early 2000s. He starts by looking at the history of Chinese immigration into New Zealand, and then considers how diversity is reported on in the New Zealand journalism industry. Using content analysis, the chapter explores how the Chinese were depicted in a major New Zealand newspaper and discusses the controversy that arose following the contemporaneous publication of an article on Chinese immigration in a major nationwide New Zealand magazine. Hannis's analysis reveals that the Yellow Peril stereotype was alive and well in New Zealand during the influx of new Chinese immigrants, and he provides an original contribution to scholarship on the model minority stereotype outside of the United States.

Rob Ho's (2014) *Studies on Asia* article is reprinted here as chapter seven, retitled "Model Minority Convergences in North America: Asian Parallels in Canada and the United States." Ho describes current manifestations of the Canadian model minority stereotype vis-à-vis the United States, examining their distinct historical trajectories and the concept's colonization into Canada. The stereotype's replication north of the American border has resulted in a racial framing of Asians that continues to sway mainstream public perceptions and policy. By analyzing two crucial incidents that received nationwide attention, Ho traces their effects and the similarities and differences with the U.S. situation, arguing that these racial assumptions continue to be as destructive and caustic to Asian Canadians as they are to other Asians worldwide.

"From Model Minorities to Disposable Models: The Delegitimization of Educational Success Through Discourses of Authenticity," the eighth chapter of this volume, is a reprint of Alice Bradbury's (2013) *Discourse: Studies in the Cultural Politics of Education* article in which she shares research on the model minority stereotype in a United Kingdom context. Bradbury uses data from qualitative research based in Primary (age 5–11) and Secondary (age 11–16) schools in London in order to illustrate the widening groups of students who may be intelligibly understood as model minorities, and the range of ways in which their educational successes are rendered inauthentic.

"Modern Em(body)ments of the Model Minority in South Korea," the ninth and final chapter in Part II, is a reprint of Nicholas D. Hartlep's (2014) *Studies on Asia* article in which he shares his analysis of how Korean culture perpetuates the stereotype through a specific, troubling practice: Korean women, responding to idealized Western beauty standards, internalize racism by undergoing body enhancement surgery. Hartlep concludes that the culture of South Korea is perpetuating the Asian model minority stereotype. According to his analysis, K-pop artists and Korean athletes like Yuna Kim (a world class figure skater) are buying into white standards of beauty. Making matters worse, says Hartlep, they are spreading the stereotype further through their music videos, promotional materials, and product advertisements.

CHAPTERS IN PART III

In chapter ten, "Korean Newcomer Youth's Experiences of Racial Marginalization and Internalization of the Model Minority Myth," contributors Yoonjung Choi and Jae Hoon Lim discuss Korean newcomers' inter/intra-racial relationships in U.S. schools and the detrimental effect of the model minority myth on their racial experiences. Their work presents how the myth is received, internalized, and reproduced by the Asian newcomer students, and how this process creates the vicious circle of racism within U.S. school culture. Choi and Lim call for more research through Asian Critical Race Theory on the reproduction of the model minority stereotype.

Chapter eleven contributor Vijay Pendakur conducted in-depth narrative inquiry interviews with nine college freshmen at a mid-sized urban, private, Catholic university in the Midwest. In "Primed to be Color-Blind: Asian American College Students, Racial Identity Development, and Color-Blind Racism" Pendakur shares his findings, which in the aggregate seem to indicate that the Asian American university students in his study internalized numerous aspects of model minority typology and its attendant mantle of honorary Whiteness. In his chapter Pendakur states that the narratives of the Asian American students that he interviewed appeared to reproduce the hegemonic logic of color-blind racism.

In chapter twelve, "Deconstructing Linsanity: Is Jeremy Lin a Model Minority Subject?", chapter contributor Nathan Kalman-Lamb uses discourse analysis of popular North American written electronic and print media to explore the ways in which National Basketball Association (NBA) player Jeremy Lin has been represented. In this insightful chapter, Nathan Kalman-Lamb argues that the model minority subject is often caught in-between—not quite reproducing the model minority myth, and not quite contesting it.

The thirteenth chapter, "Pleasing the 'Aunties': Navigating Community Expectations within the Model Minority both in the United States and in India," is based on a study conducted in the Southern United States at an elite public university. Contributor Amardeep K. Kahlon's hermeneutic, phenomenological study revealed the pressure some Asian Indian American students face when they deal with issues of family honor. Kahlon shares that there was an expectation from the parents that the students would uphold the family honor, both through their public behaviors as well as through their academic and professional accomplishments. Pleasing the "aunties" was very important to the parents and less important to the participants, thus generating intergenerational issues. An actual or perceived inability to live up to the high expectations of both parents and community, leads to further anxiety, thus perpetuating the cycle of high expectations and the resultant stress.

Sociologist Daisy Ball contributes chapter fourteen, "Perpetuating the Model Minority Stereotype in the Face of Highly Visible, and Highly Negative, External Events." In order to ascertain the experiences of Asian American undergraduates at Virginia Tech, professor Ball conducted in-depth interviews with 18 Korean and Chinese American students from May 2010 through May 2011. She wanted to learn about their experiences at Virginia Tech, and how (or if) those experiences had been impacted by the April 16, 2007 Virginia Tech shooting. Specifically, she was interested in learning if her Asian American interviewees experienced race-based prejudice and/or discrimination, as well as whether they perpetuated the model minority stereotype or worked actively to fight it. Interestingly, Ball notes that all of her respondents supported the idea of the model minority in their discussions of themselves as students.

In chapter fifteen, "A Few Good Asians: Unpacking Cultural Dimensions of the Model Minority Myth and Deconstructing Pathways to Complicity," Tien Ung, Shalini Tendulkar, and Jocelyn Chu discuss how the existing discourse about complicity requires a deeper understanding of the rhetoric associated with the model minority myth, and a deeper analysis of the meaning of complicity, especially as it pertains to identity and the politics of representation. Through in depth interviews with four Asian Americans, the authors present findings from a phenomenological study of the experiences of Asians in order to explore the cultural dimensions of the model minority myth that are often left unchallenged in popular rhetoric surrounding the stereotype. Given the magnitude and pervasiveness of the model minority myth, it is impossible to consider complicity among Asian American and Pacific Islanders (AAPIs) without considering the social, political, and economical epistemologies that underlie the experiences of AAPIs. To this end, complicit behavior among AAPIs is inextricable from the issue of migration and its influence on identity, values, and behavior. A critical examination of complicity among AAPIs therefore has to involve peering through the lenses of migration, politics, economics, and values together and not solely from the rhetoric of race and racial relations in the United States.

CHAPTERS IN PART IV

In chapter sixteen, "A primer on Research Validity for Conducting Quantitative Studies of the Model Minority Stereotype," Grant B. Morgan and Kari J. Hodge offer statistical insight into how best to define four types of research validity. This important chapter examines two types of research fallacies as well as sampling strategies and population inference that impact the model minority stereotype.

Grant B. Morgan and Kari J. Hodge also contribute chapter seventeen, "Statistical Procedures For Addressing Research Fallacies Such as the Model Minority Stereotype," which provides readers and researchers much-needed statistical information related to the model minority stereotype. They discuss two statistical modeling procedures that may allow researchers studying the model minority stereotype to more efficiently and effectively align their analysis with guiding research questions and/or a theoretical expectation.

In the eighteenth chapter, "The 'Model Minority' Myth: A Critical Race Theoretical Analysis of Asian Americans in America's Most Segregated City," professors Nicholas D. Hartlep and Antonio L. Ellis, using 1990, 2000, and 2010 data procured from the National Center for Education Statistics' (NCES) School District Demographic System (SDDS), share their findings based on a case study that investigated the residential loci of Asian American students in Milwaukee, Wisconsin. Through the use of Geographic Information Systems (GIS) mapping technology as their analytical tool, they found strong patterns demonstrating that the Asian American student population in Milwaukee continues to grow at a greater rate than other racial groups, and although a "White-belt" exists in certain areas of the greater-Milwaukee area, it has been "yellowing"—becoming more

Asian. They attribute this yellowing to factors such as the decompressed housing market—such as owners versus renters—and issues related to per capita income.

Chapter nineteen, the volume's concluding chapter, is authored by Nicholas D. Hartlep, Grant B. Morgan, and Kari J. Hodge. In "An Asian American Subgroup Analysis of the Restricted-Use ELS:2002 Dataset: Mixture Modeling as a Way to Problematize the Asian American 'Model Minority' Stereotype" the contributors share their analysis of restricted-use Educational Longitudinal Study of 2002 (ELS:2002) data. The researchers feel that the theoretical, methodological, and practical implications of their chapter are significant. For instance, they state that the use of finite mixture modeling (FMM) to analyze disaggregated Asian American high school students and their parents by subgroups reduced the likelihood of committing inferential errors. Another strength that they share regarding using FMM to problematize the Asian American model minority stereotype is that it allows readers to see real subgroup differences among the diverse and heterogeneous Asian American population.

CONCLUDING
INTRODUCTORY COMMENTS

Originally we sought to include a powerful model minority counterstory that situated Asian adoptees within the model minority stereotype. Although this important counterstory did not make it into the final book, while we were working on finalizing this volume we came across a study that revealed that those who were adopted were almost four times more likely to attempt suicide. According to Keyes et al.'s (2013) study "Risk of Suicide Attempt in Adopted and Non-adopted Offspring," published in *Pediatrics,* the odds for reported suicide attempt are elevated in individuals who are adopted relative to those who are not adopted. The sample of adoptees in Keyes et al.'s study was highly female (60%) and from South Korea (90%). This article reminded us as editors why model minority scholarship is relevant and important. We feel strongly that future scholarly work can and should be conducted on Asian American adoptees as racialized model minorities, and we hope that their counterstories will be included in future anti-model minority stereotype literature. In addition to the important research done by professor Eliza Noh on Asian American suicide, there remains a need for suicide research that is linked not only to impacted Asian Americans, but also to Asian American adoptees, since this sort of scholarship is lacking in the literature as well (Bhugra, 2004; Leong & Leach, 2008; Macdonald, 2007; Mayer, 2011).

Chapters 1–4, 6, and 11–18 are published here for the first time while chapters 5 and 7–10 are republished. The permissions and details of the original publication are provided in the beginning of the book for interested readers.

We hope that this book is of benefit to the reader.

—*Nicholas D. Hartlep and Brad J. Porfilio*

REFERENCES

Bhugra, D. (2004). *Culture and self-harm: Attempted suicide in South Asians in London.* New York: Psychology Press.

Bitzer, L. F. (1959). Aristotle's enthymeme revisited. *The Quarterly Journal of Speech, 45,* 399–408.

Bonilla-Silva, E. (2002). The linguistics of color blind racism: How to talk nasty about Blacks without sounding "racist." *Critical Sociology, 28*(1–2), 41–64.

Bonilla-Silva, E. (2010). *Racism without racists: Color-blind racism & racial inequality in contemporary America.* Lanham, MD: Rowman & Littlefield Publishers.

Bradbury, A. (2013). From model minorities to disposable models: the de-legitimisation of educational success through discourses of authenticity. *Discourse: Studies in the Cultural Politics of Education, 34*(4), 548–561.

Busto, R. V. (1996). The gospel according to the model minority?: Hazarding an interpretation of Asian American evangelical college students. *Amerasia Journal, 22*(1), 133–147.

Chang, M. J. (2011). Battle hymn of the model minority myth. *Amerasia Journal, 37*(2), 137–143.

Chang, R. S. (1999). *Disoriented: Asian Americans, law, and the nation-state.* New York: New York University Press.

Chua, A. (2011). *Battle hymn of the tiger mother.* New York: The Penguin Press.

Freedman, J. (2005). Transgressions of a model minority. *Shofar: An Interdisciplinary Journal of Jewish Studies, 23*(4), 69–97.

Gym, H. (2011, Summer). Tiger moms and the model minority myth. *Rethinking Schools, 25*(4), 34–35.

Hartlep, N. D. (2014). Modern em(body)ments of the model minority in South Korea. *Studies on Asia, 4*(1), 108–123. Retrieved April 1, 2014, from http://studiesonasia.illinoisstate.edu/seriesIV/documents/NDHartlep_studies_march14.pdf

Hartlep, N. D. (2015a). How to talk nasty about Asians without sounding racist. *TEDx Talk.* Retrieved January 1, 2014, from http://www.tedxnaperville.com/talks/nicholas-hartlep/

Hartlep, N. D. (Ed.). (2015b). *Modern societal impacts of the model minority stereotype.* Hershey, PA: IGI.

Hill, J. H. (2008). *The everyday language of White racism.* Chinchester, UK: Wiley-Blackwell.

Ho, R. (2014). Do all Asians look alike?: Asian Canadians as model minorities *Studies on Asia, 4*(2), 78–107. Retrieved December 20, 2014, from http://studiesonasia.illinoisstate.edu/seriesIV/documents/Ho_Studies_Fall14.pdf

Jackson, M. (2006). The enthymematic hegemony of whiteness: The enthymeme as antiracist rhetorical strategy. *JAC: A Journal of Rhetoric, Culture, and Politics, 26*(3–4), 601–641. Retrieved December 23, 2014, from http://www.jaconlinejournal.com/archives/vol26.3–4/jackson-enthymematic.pdf

Juang, L. P., Qin, B., & Park, I. J. K. (Eds.). (2013, March). Tiger parenting, Asian-heritage families, and child/adolescent well-Being). *Asian American Journal of Psychology, 4*(1), 1–78.

Kang, M. (2014). "I just put Koreans and nails together": Nail spas and the model minority. In N. D. Hartlep (Ed.), *The model minority stereotype reader: Critical and challenging readings for the 21st century* (pp. 89–114). San Diego, CA: Cognella.

Keyes, M. A., Malone, S. M., Sharma, A., Iacono, W. G., & McGue, M. (2013). Risk of suicide attempt in adopted and nonadopted offspring. *Pediatrics: Official Journal of the American Academy of Pediatrics, 132*(4), 1–8. Retrieved December 14, 2014, from http://pediatrics.aappublications.org/content/early/2013/09/04/peds.2012–3251.full.pdf

Kim, R. Y. (2006). *God's new whiz kids?: Korean American evangelicals on campus.* New York: New York University Press.

Leong, F. T. L., & Leach, M. M. (Eds.). (2008). *Suicide among racial and ethnic minority groups: Theory, research, and practice.* New York: Routledge.

Linsanity. (2013). The true life of Jeremy Lin: Linsanity. Retrieved December 14, 2014, from http://www.imdb.com/title/tt2359427/

Macdonald, C. J-H. (2007). *Uncultural behavior: An anthropological investigation of suicide in the Southern Philippines.* Honolulu, HI: University of Hawai'i Press.

Mayer, P. (2011). *Suicide and society in India.* New York: Routledge.

Schlosser, L. Z. (2003). Christian privilege: Breaking a sacred taboo. *Journal of Multicultural Counseling and Development, 31*(1), 44–51.

PART I

MODEL MINORITY COUNTERSTORIES

CHAPTER 1

TOWARDS THE MODEL MINORITY

Asian Americanization of Burmese Immigrants as a Model Minority in a High School

Gilbert C. Park

Immigrants have been arriving in the United States since its founding, and the flow of immigrants continues today as approximately fifty million residents in 2010 were either immigrants or their children (Camarota, 2012). Among them are over eighteen million immigrants from Asia who represent the fastest-growing immigrant population (Kieu, 2013). It has been assumed that these immigrants and their children will gradually become Americans over time, as it was with earlier immigrants from Europe who eventually became incorporated into the American mainstream. This straight-line *assimilationist* view on Americanization has been challenged by scholars like Roediger (2005), who complicated this process by focusing on the racial politics that allowed some to become a part of white America. Similarly, Portes and Rumbaut (2001) argue that today's immigrants of color are "undergoing a process of segmented assimilation where outcomes vary across immigrant minorities and where rapid integration and acceptance into the American mainstream represent just one possible alternative" (p. 45).

Killing the Model Minority Stereotype: Asian American Counterstories and Complicity,
pages 3–17.
Copyright © 2015 by Information Age Publishing

Other alternatives for today's immigrants of color include rapid assimilation into non-mainstream and oppositional cultures like the urban youth culture of African Americans (Neckerman, Carter, & Lee, 1999; Rumbaut, 1994; Waters, 1994). This chapter looks at the segmented Americanization of a group of Asian immigrants from Burma in a Midwestern public school. The specific focus is on the role of the model minority stereotype in guiding their Americanization towards Asian America. Through interviews and observation, the chapter reports three findings. First, the school's focus on rapid assimilation without critical conversations on race led the Burmese students away from mainstream America despite good intentions of the educators. Second, the model minority stereotype of Asian Americans served as the end goal of their Americanization as the Burmese students were expected to be a quiet and hardworking minority. Third, segmented assimilation towards the model minority at the school fostered a sense of disentitlement to challenge authority, as well as a sense of superiority over other racial minorities at the school.

SEGMENTED AMERICANIZATION IN SCHOOLS

Instead of serving as merely the context in which immigrants learn about America, Olneck (2004) posits that schools have sought to Americanize immigrants through both acculturation and accommodation. By acculturation, he is referring to the ways that schools sought to "incorporate culturally, ethnically, linguistically, racially, and religiously 'different' immigrants into mainstream America" (2004, p. 382). Development of common schooling, for instance, was, in part, a response to the American natives' perception of "moral" decay caused by the large influx of immigrants. In order to "Americanize" the immigrants to become more like them, schooling was a way to "reduce" the threat (Kaestle, 1983; Schultz, 1973). In pushing for rapid acculturation of immigrants, schools often overlook the resources that the students bring with them to the school (Lee, 2005; Valenzuela, 1999). Instead, some students learn that English fluency should be achieved even at the expense of losing their native language (Olsen, 1997; Valenzuela, 1999).

While accommodation also aims to acculturate the immigrants, schools sought to "acknowledge" and "accommodate" the demands of the immigrants through the so-called accommodation approach. Such was the case in small Midwest towns and large cities like Milwaukee and St. Louis with a large concentration of immigrants in much of the 19th century. In these communities, the bible was read without commentary for religious minorities like Catholic immigrants, and instructions were offered in the native languages of the immigrants. Olneck (2004) posits that the accommodation approach was supported by local politicians, who sought not to alienate the current and future votes of these immigrants, and by school officials, who desired to "entice immigrant children to come to 'Anglicanizing' public schools" (p. 384). Today, many more schools seek to facilitate the incorporation of immigrants into America using programs like English as Second Language (ESL) and transitional bilingual education to accommodate immigrants' development of English proficiency. This chapter adds to this body of literature by documenting how a Midwestern pubic school is acculturating and accommodating Burmese immigrant students.

MODEL MINORITY STEREOTYPE

Challenges to the model minority stereotype, which depicts Asian American students as quiet and uncomplaining academic superstars, have been one of the major themes in the literature on the topic of Asian American experiences. Among these challengers is Suzuki (1995), who explains that the stereotype is a myth that asserts Asian Americans have finally succeeded in becoming accepted into white, middle-class society through "hard work, uncomplaining perseverance, and quiet accommodation" (p. 113). In an effort to combat the myth, scholars (Chae, 2008; Chang, 2011; Lee, 2005; Louie, 2004; Wing, 2007) have sought to highlight the downside of the myth. For instance, Wing (2007) argues that the stereotype has been used to support the notion of meritocracy in schools by underlining the achievement gap in Asian American students. By pointing out Asian American school success, one's failure to succeed is constructed to be an individual failure. In the process, the blame is shifted away from the system, and the stereotype works to delegitimize claims by minorities who challenge the existing system. This negatively affects inter-racial relations of Asian American students with other students of color (Chao, Chiu, Chan, Mendoza-Denton, & Kwok, 2013; Lee, 2005; Wing, 2007).

Also, others (Hayashi, 2003; Inkelas, 2006; Lee, 2001; Lew, 2006; Park & Lee, 2010) explore the diversity of Asian Americans to counter the myth's portrayal of Asian Americans as a homogenous group who experience success. While some Asian Americans attain more education and earn higher income than other people of color, there are many Asian Americans who are illiterate and poor. Ignoring these subgroup differences, the Asian American students in need of service are less likely to receive the help they need. While the stereotype has been studied and contested as discussed above, relatively little attention has been paid to its impact on the Americanization of Asian immigrant students. With this in mind, this chapter looks at the role of the model minority stereotype in shaping particular trajectories of American identity development at school for recent Asian immigrants from Burma. The goals of this chapter are to 1) explore how those at the school construct the model minority stereotype and to 2) understand how the stereotype shapes the immigrants' understanding of their place in the racial hierarchy. In the process, it adds to the body of literature on the model minority stereotype and Asian American school experiences.

METHODS

Data for this chapter was generated as part of a larger ethnographic study that looked at the Americanization process of recent Burmese immigrant students in a Midwestern public high school, *New High School*. I use the words Burma and Burmese instead of Myanmar and Myanmarese since these were the terms of choice by the students themselves. New High is located in a small town that is adjacent to a larger urban city of roughly 250,000 residents. According to the 2010 Census, 93.2% of the small town's nearly 15,000 residents are White, with 3% African American. New High is located in the center of town surrounded by smaller, ranch-style, working middle-class homes. While the town is predominantly White, New High has undergone a sudden increase in students of color as a result of redistricting. The district office chose to close one of its high schools a year prior to the data gathering and sent many of its students of color to New High, which resulted in the school becoming more diverse than the town. Compared to the 93.2% White resident population, White students make up 81% of the 1,129 enrolled students. Approximately 2% of the student population were Asian Americans, many of whom were new Burmese immigrants during that academic year.

This portion of data was gathered while in attendance at the school each week during most of the spring semester in 2013. The specific ethnographic tools employed include observations and interviews. As an observer, the author observed the participants—teachers and students—in classes as a way to learn what it is like to be them. A particular focus was on the nature of social interactions of the participants with other students and school personnel. Both formal and informal interviews were used. Formal interviews consisted of a set of prepared questions with a focus on their ethnic and racial identity in the context of the school as well as larger society. Informal interviews were casual conversations with the participants. These interviews were taped whenever possible. Other times, notes were taken either during or after the interview. Pseudonyms were used for the names of the participants and the location in an effort to protect confidentiality and IRB approval was obtained.

The primary participants in this chapter were the principal of the school, three teachers, one resource staff, one translator employed by the district, and two Burmese immigrant students. Upon the initial meeting, Mr. Adam, the principal, introduced me to Ms. Jill, the only ESL teacher at New High, who worked closely with Burmese students. She helped with recruiting David and Diane in her advanced ESL class to participate in this study. Ms. Jill also helped me to recruit Mr. John, who teaches Algebra primarily to Burmese ESL students, as well as Ms. Jane, who teaches a remedial Social Studies class that included David and Diane. Ms. Sally managed a resource room to which teachers sent Burmese students with limited English proficiency to receive help with assignments during class. Ms. Sunnie came to New High on Fridays to facilitate communication between Burmese students and their families with limited English proficiency and the school.

The teachers and the school staff were initially guarded when I approached them for interviews and observation. The sudden increase in diversity—and the ensuing racial tension between the white students who live in town and the students of color who are bussed in—may have been one cause of caution when approached by an outsider from a university. Over time, they felt more comfortable with me as they learned that the research goal was not an analysis of the effectiveness of their teaching and that their identity would remain confidential. The Burmese students, including David and Diane, were very curious to see a Korean American adult in their school. Many of them initiated their first contact with me by saying hello and asking questions about my work and me. Initially, communication was a barrier to establishing rapport with recent Burmese immigrants as I did not speak Burmese and many of the Burmese students spoke limited English. More fluent English speakers like David and Diane often helped me by translating. Over time, it seemed that many of the students began to see me as a role model and a father figure from whom they would seek advice on academic and social matters because I was a college professor who looked liked them.

The following sections focus on the model minority stereotype of Asian Americans as the end goal for the Asian Americanization of Burmese students at New High School. The first section highlights the aspects of schooling at New High that contribute to segmented assimilation of Burmese away from mainstream America. The second section describes the construction of the model minority stereotype for Burmese immigrants as "good" students. The last section highlights two ways that the model minority stereotype, as constructed at New High, affected the Americanization of Diane and David. The discussion suggests some implications of this study to the educators of recent Asian immigrants.

SEGMENTED ASSIMILATION AT NEW HIGH

As discussed previously, Americanization of immigrants in schools occurs in two interdependent and non-sequential processes: acculturation and accommodation. At New High, Burmese students' needs were identified to mean linguistic and academic. The first is the limited English proficiency that hinders their ability to participate fully in the academic and social opportunities that New High offers. The other is the lack of an academic background for many Burmese students who did not receive any formal schooling prior to entering the United States. Well-meaning and dedicated teachers at New High sought to meet these needs by 1) developing their English proficiency with ESL instruction, 2) giving foundational knowledge in mathematics, and 3) providing resources to keep up in the mainstream classes. Despite the good intentions and dedication, however, I argue that the Burmese students were acculturated away from the American mainstream.

> I want them to learn about the United States and its culture. Learning English is one thing, but they also need to learn how things are here in the United States as well. (Ms. Jill, ESL)

Ms. Jill was highly praised by the principal on my first visit to New High, and I observed her to be very passionate and enthusiastic about her teaching. It was also visible that she took pride in helping newly immigrated students. She is one of the few teachers who worked with every one of the Burmese students at New High as an ESL teacher. The students spoke very fondly of her as a caring person both in and outside of the classroom.

For instance, Ms. Jill offered to give a ride to Diane and her friends to the prom when they were worried about transportation. After further conversation, Ms. Jill learned that the problem was more complicated as their parents did not want the girls to attend the prom. Diane told me later that her parents wanted to "protect" the reputation of their daughters as "good" Muslim girls by keeping them away from the "bad" American youth culture. So, the girls' plan was to tell their parents that they were going to the library, then change into prom dresses in Ms. Jill's car on the way. Instead of taking part in deceiving their parents, Ms. Jill offered to speak to their parents for them. When asked about why she offered to help the girls, she said, "It's about being a high school kid (in the United States)." Ms. Jill wanted the girls to experience American culture and tradition by attending prom.

Consistently, learning about the dominant American culture was a theme in Ms. Jill's ESL classes. In addition to literal meanings, she explained how words, phrases, and sentences are used in different contexts so that the students learned "how things are and work" in the U.S. It was not clear, however, what aspects of American culture the students were to learn. For instance, some scholars (Castagno, 2008; Perry, 2001) point to the invisibility of the dominant group as the key to normalizing their experiences as legitimate and authentic American ones. Among these scholars is Best (2000), who argues that prom—as a rite of passage in an adolescent's life—serves to celebrate as normal and natural the life experienced by white, middle-class, and heterosexual students. From this perspective, Ms. Jill and others who sought to help the Burmese students to learn American language and culture were actually teaching them to be more like white, middle-class, and heterosexual Americans. Conversely, authentic America is equated with white America, implying that the Burmese will become less than authentic Americans in the future because they are not white. This suggests that Burmese students may be en route to segmented assimilation away from American mainstream, unless they engage in a critical conversation on how race shapes power dynamics inside and outside of the school.

> My goal here is to give them a [mathematical] foundation. Many of my students here have a hard time with basics like addition and subtraction. I want them to master these skills. (Mr. John, Algebra)

Mr. John's Algebra class was filled with LEP (Limited English Proficient) students, most of whom are Burmese immigrants with a few exceptions. While the class is called Algebra, the students were actually working on lower level mathematics. For instance, the students were working on fraction problems found to be similar to fourth grade mathematics. This was one of the ways Mr. John accommodated the needs of his students who lacked mathematical foundations.

Other times, he would encourage the students to use calculators to understand the concept of the day rather than have their problems with adding and subtracting hold them back. His class was a lively one where students were free to use their language to communicate. For instance, the students were often allowed to work together to solve math problems. When they worked together, they would speak to each other in Burmese. When they were working independently, one student might translate Mr. John's instructions in Burmese for other limited English speakers to understand. Mr. John would walk around the classroom to talk to individual students and check up on their progress. Ms. Jill could also be found in this room, working on the sidelines with a handful of students who were struggling with the lesson and English.

Mr. John's class was a comfortable and safe learning environment where the Burmese students, many of whom were quiet elsewhere, were animated. Additionally, Mr. John allowed students to use their home language in the class, which was a way to use Burmese language and culture to promote academic success. However, such was not the case throughout the school, where English is understood to be the only language used and where Burmese should not be spoken. Except in Ms. Jill's and Mr. John's classrooms, Burmese students remained mostly invisible. When asked, the Burmese students often spoke about the fear of being teased for their heavy accent in English. It appeared that replacing Burmese with English fluency is not only desired but the required end goal of their Americanization. The efforts of Mr. John and Ms. Jill may not be enough to foster positive sense of selves for non-English speakers at New High.

> The teachers send them to me when they need help. Sometimes I don't have the answer to their questions, but I help them to find it. In a way, I am learning what they are learning too. …. [What I want them to get out of here is] for them to know that help is available, that we [New High] are here to help if they want to succeed. (Ms. Sally, Resource Room)

Many Burmese students with limited English proficiency come from families without someone to help them with schoolwork. Recognizing this social dynamic, New High arranged for Ms. Sally to manage a resource room where Burmese students can go to get assistance with assignments. In a typical period, the resource room would feature two to ten Burmese students sitting around Ms. Sally's desk. They would work mostly independently, but also as a group on occasions when they had a common assignment. When asked a question, Ms. Sally would explore the textbook together with the student for an answer. Other times, Ms. Sally would give detailed explanations on the questions asked using her own or the student's experience as context. Ms. Sally said she found her work rewarding since she feels that she's making "a difference." Indeed, the students spoke of how they were glad to have Ms. Sally to help them with their work.

While the resource room served as an important site for the students to get much needed help, some ways that the teachers used it were questionable. For instance, Burmese students were sent by teachers during class to get help from Ms. Sally. Sometimes, it was for Burmese students to make up missing assignments. Other times, it was because the class was working independently. In any case, the responsibility to teach Burmese students was shifted away from teachers to Ms. Sally this way. Furthermore, it fostered a sense of marginalization for Burmese students who were literally sent away from their classmates.

CONSTRUCTION OF BURMESE IMMIGRANTS AS MODEL MINORITY

While the model minority stereotype initially referred to a small group of Asian Americans (i.e. middle class Chinese and Japanese Americans), over time it has evolved into an image for the entire group over time. This evolution of the stereotype can be partially explained by the lumping effect that does not acknowledge the diversity within Asian America. Because of this effect, Burmese immigrants, many of whom are refugees with few resources or previous schooling before arriving, were lumped with other high achieving Asian Americans as a model minority. Instead of high achievement in school, however, the school staff pointed to behavioral traits like "quiet" and "hardworking" that are compatible with the stereotype. As a result, Burmese immigrants who were led away from the American mainstream were presented with the alternative as a hardworking and quiet model minority at New High.

> Diane is my favorite. I will miss her when she graduates this May. She is so sweet. She is shy. She doesn't talk a lot in the class [U.S. Government], but she always has a smile on her face. She takes her work seriously unlike some others [in the class]. (Ms. Jane, non-ESL Social Studies)

> You [the researcher] will notice that they [Burmese] are very different in regular [or non-ESL] classes. They are so quiet. They don't say a word. They keep their heads down and work [in other classes]! (Ms. Jill, ESL)

> These [Burmese immigrants] kids work hard. They come here to get help with assignments, and I like working with them. They work hard, you know. … . They come from difficult situations, but they come here [New High] to learn. There was this girl who graduated last year. She is now majoring in physics at [a local private college]. When she first came, she couldn't even write her own name [in English]. (Ms. Sally, Resource Room)

As found in the literature (Lee, 2005; Park & Lee, 2010; Suzuki, 1995; Tuan, 1998), behavioral traits in the classes like *honest, fair, hardworking, attentive,* and *respectful* are too often associated with the model minority stereotype of Asian Americans. Similarly, I also found that these same traits, like *hardworking* and *quiet,* were used when describing Diane, David, and other Burmese students by the New High staff.

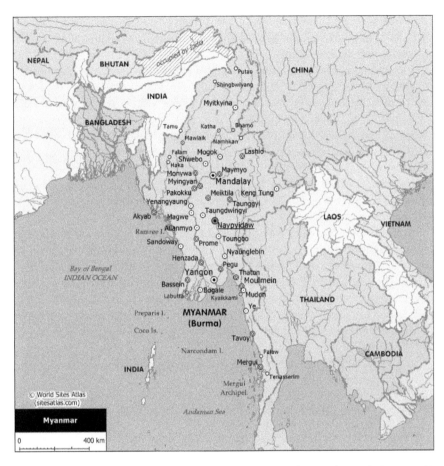

FIGURE 1.1. Map of Myanmar (Burma) Source: By Zeshan Mahmood (Own work) [CC BY-SA 3.0 (http://creativecommons.org/licenses/by-sa/3.0)], via Wikimedia Commons

Like many Burmese students at New High, both Diane and David are recent immigrants to the United States who arrived less than five years prior to the beginning of data collection. They represent the third wave of immigrants from what is now Myanmar, which is located between Bangladesh and Thailand on the western part of the Indochina peninsula. To be more accurate, all of the Burmese students that I spoke to had never been to Burma (see Figure 1.1) since they were born at a refugee camp in Thailand and remained in Thailand before arriving to the United States. Ms. Sunnie explained that the most of the Burmese students here at New High are ethnic and religious minorities as Muslims who, since the 1960s, have fled Burma to refugee camps in Thailand to escape the persecution from ethnic

Burmese, who are Buddhists. Like other Burmese refugees, Diane and David do not know their birthday, and their school placement was based on their parents' estimates of their age.

Life in the refugee camp is said to be difficult without modern amenities like running water or electricity, to name a couple. In addition to scarce jobs for the adults, which led to economic struggles, formal education was mostly inaccessible to Burmese children at the camp. As a result, New High was the first formal schooling Diane and David received, and they were considerably behind academically—as was the case with all of the Burmese immigrant students to whom I spoke. In fact, they were not only learning English as newcomers, they were also learning written language for the first time. Ms. Sunnie told me that many Burmese students were placed in the remedial track and faced academic difficulties in those classes.

In this respect, the narrative of the model minority stereotype is reconstructed at New High School through Burmese immigrant students. Diane and David are successful students who will earn a diploma. Diane will be the first in her family not only to graduate from high school but to pursue post-secondary education at a local two year college. David will also be the first in his family to graduate, alongside his older brother who had to spend an extra year in school due to inability to complete the state requirements in time. They are overcoming the odds to earn a high school diploma through quiet perseverance and hard work. Furthermore, their hard work is believed to be helpful in achieving the American dream by becoming a part of the American middle class.

MODEL MINORIFICATION OF DIANE AND DAVID

Literature on identity formation (Dhingra, 2003; Nagel, 1994; Park, 2011; Shelby, 2002) posits that one understands who he or she is as an individual and as a member of a group through conversation with the cultural and social context of the environment. Put differently, an American identity is a social construct that is context-specific, and how others view a person has bearing on how he or she sees him or herself. At New High, where Burmese immigrants are constructed as model minorities who are quiet, hardworking, and uncomplaining students, I found some Burmese students see themselves as such. Specifically, I found that the Burmese students are grateful recipients of American generosity and are not positioned to critique their benefactors. Also, some of them positioned themselves closer to other Asian Americans who are allegedly more traditional and respectful to authority and therefore "better" than other racial minorities.

> They [Burmese] are so grateful. They were allowed to come here [to the United States as refugees]. They get all these services including health care. They get a free ride to school and the school is free. I mean these kids never went to school! They appreciate all the things the school does for them too. (Ms. Sunnie, a translator for the district)

I am going to be a nurse. I will go to [a local community college]; I just got a pamphlet [she shows it to me excitedly]. I am so happy [to be here in the U.S.] … . America has been good to me and my family. …I learned a lot from New High. I like all the teachers. I am very thankful. (Diane)

Ms. Sunnie is a district employee who translates for Burmese students and their families, and she spends a day or two a week at New High. When the school staff does not need her, she spends her time in Ms. Sally's resource room helping Burmese students with schoolwork. During the interview, she talked about how Burmese students and their families are grateful for the opportunities in the United States away from the refugee camp in Thailand. American families and community organizations sponsored them to enter the United States as refugees. Upon their entry, sponsoring families and organizations helped them to find housing and locate employment as well. It appears that Diane extends this gratitude toward the sponsors to the United States in general and New High specifically. When asked about how her life was back in the camp, she said, after a long pause, that she didn't want to talk about it. Instead, she spent some time discussing how much she appreciated the opportunity she now has to graduate from high school. She specifically named Ms. Jill and Ms. Jane as her favorite teachers who helped her tremendously.

The other side of her gratitude was her sense of disentitlement to ask for more. Her response to my question regarding the possibility of bilingual education in Burmese or even a permanent translator at New High demonstrates the point. Diane's initial response was, "Can they [New High] do that?" She was not aware that bilingual education for Burmese students was a possibility. After much thought about it, Diane spoke from the position of the taxpayers that it would be too costly for the school to hire a bilingual educator for them, suggesting that they are not quite worthy. In general, Burmese students responded similarly. Some pointed to the high cost while others remarked that it would be difficult finding bilingual Burmese adults due to the recent immigrant history of their community. Literature (Lee, 2005; Park, 2011; etc.) on recent Asian immigrant students also found that many of them felt they were not in a position to make demands to improve their educational experiences. Instead, they waited for the change to come to them. It appears that the image of an uncomplaining minority who overcomes challenges through hard work alone has been internalized by Diane and other Burmese students, as expressed through their continuous show of appreciation.

David is a good student. He sometimes complains about the amount of work [in this class], but he does it. You know, those [Burmese] kids are pretty traditional. They respect adults. (Ms. Jane, U.S. Government.)

These are bad kids. They are so mean to Ms. Jane. I don't do that. We (Burmese) don't do that [talking back and yelling at teachers].… (David)

In addition to the sense of disentitlement, I found that some Burmese students, like David, view themselves as more traditional and better students than others. Ms. Jane's U.S. Government class serves as a case in point. Before I visited the class, other teachers told me that it is different than other classes at New High in that many students are unruly. As the students, many of whom are persons of color, filed into the class, they talked loudly to each other, often across the room. This continued well after the bell indicating that class had started. As Ms. Jane struggled to play a DVD for the class, occasional shouting interrupted the chatter. Even after the DVD started playing, a handful of boys made sarcastic comments about Ms. Jane that were followed by laughter from other students. It was not until a student was sent to the office that the students settled down a bit. While this was going on, Diane was working on an assignment quietly while David was playing with a school issued tablet and not taking part in the unruliness. Sometime later, Ms. Jane came over to me and apologetically explained that many of her students in the class are retaking it for a second or third time, as the state requires credit for this class for graduation. As if to excuse their behavioral issues, she also mentioned that about one third of them were special education students.

After identifying Diane and David among the few well-behaved students, Ms. Jane associated their good behavior with traditional values that respect authority, which, she noted, is missing from today's American young people. David seems to agree that Burmese kids are more respectful towards adults. When asked about how he felt about Ms. Jane's class, David said that he was angry about how others in the class are mistreating the teacher. He talked about how it is unimaginable for Burmese kids to talk back to the elders in the community. He then commented on what he said was negative about American mainstream culture—where kids are free to be disrespectful to adults—by generalizing the observed inappropriate interactions between teachers and the students in a remedial classroom to American mainstream culture in general. To David and Ms. Jane, showing respect is closely associated with a traditional value that is lost with American youth culture, and Burmese immigrants who do not challenge authority are holding on to this value; hence, they are model minority. In this way, the model minority stereotype, which positions Burmese students closer to lost traditional American values, fostered a sense of superiority over other students in Ms. Jane's class.

DISCUSSION

This chapter sought to contribute to the body of literature on the model minority stereotype and Asian American school experiences by exploring, through segmented assimilation theory, how the model minority stereotype affects the Americanization process of Burmese immigrants at New High. I found that the model minority stereotype was constructed to mean quiet, uncomplaining, and hardworking Asians and served as an alternative destination to mainstream America as the students were undergoing segmented assimilation. First, it discussed how well-meaning teachers led the students' Americanization process away from mainstream America. This was followed by the construction of the model minority stereotype at New High as behavioral, instead of achievement-based, because the Burmese refugees were without many resources to succeed academically. The last part looked at how the model minority stereotype shaped the social location of Diane and David. Diane was so grateful for the newly found opportunity in the U.S. that she thought it was not her place to make demands. One the other hand, David felt he was better than non-Burmese students of color in his class because Burmese kids showed respect to adults.

The chapter does not conclude that the Burmese immigrants have fully embraced the model minority stereotype or see themselves as Asian Americans. On the contrary, the Burmese students at New High displayed a strong sense of selves as Burmese apart from other Asian immigrants and Asian Americans; as they were quick to point out, their religion in Islam was different from other Asian Americans in the school. What the findings suggest is that construction of the model minority stereotype by the educators at New High is guiding a segmented Americanization process of the Burmese immigrants towards Asian America, along with the negative impacts of the stereotype felt by Asian Americans. This calls for a critical examination of the stereotype by educators and students alike.

Both educators and their students should be developing an understanding of race relations in the United States that positioned and continue to position Asian Americans as the model minority. This should be coupled with conversations on how the stereotype benefits the Whites in America when only they are validated as authentic Americans. Also, there should be a critical conversation about how one's assumptions and practices are contributing to the construction of the stereotype at the school. Exploring ways to challenge the stereotype should follow such a conversation. Challenges to the model minority stereotype may begin, for example, when one stops assuming that all people of Asian descent are quiet, hardworking, and successful. Active deconstruction of the stereotype may include candid conversations about how American identity is racially defined and how the stereotype, while seemingly positive, marginalizes Asian Americans away from the American mainstream as well as from other racial minorities as potential allies, as was the case with Diane and David.

Questions for Reflection

1. This study reports some of the negative effects of the model minority stereotype when it is constructed as the end goal of newer Asian immigrants' Americanization process. Is there an alternative to the stereotype as the end goal for them?
2. Are there ways that schools can use this Asian Americanization of newer Asian Americans to promote social justice? Explain.
3. How can educators empower newer Asian Americans to critique the segmented assimilation that guides them away from the American mainstream?

4. How do we convince White educators, many of whom do not fully recognize their racial privilege, that critical conversations on race are good for them as well?

5. How do we help educators to challenge recent Asian immigrants to critique the model minority stereotype?

REFERENCES

Best, A. L. (2000). *Prom night: Youth, schools and popular culture.* New York: Routledge.

Camarota, S. A. (2012). *Immigrants in the United States, 2010: A profile of America's foreign born population.* Center for Immigrant Studies. Retrieved December 1, 2014, from http://www.cis.org/2012–profile-of-americas-foreign-born-population

Castagno, A. (2008). "I don't want to hear that!": Legitimating whiteness through silence in schools. *Anthropology & Education Quarterly, 3*(3), 314–333.

Chae, Y. (2008). Cultural economies of model minority Creation. In Y. Chae, *Politicizing Asian American literature: Towards a critical multiculturalism* (pp. 19–30). New York: Routledge.

Chang, M. J. (2011). Battle hymn of the model minority myth. *Amerasia Journal, 37*(2), 137–143.

Chao, M. M., Chiu, C., Chan, W., Mendoza-Denton, R., & Kwok, C. (2013). The model minority as a shared reality and its implications for interracial perceptions. *Asian American Journal of Psychology, 4*(2), 87–92.

Dhingra, P. H. (2003). Being American between Black and White: Second-generation Asian American professionals' racial identities. *Journal of Asian American Studies, 6*(2), 117–147.

Kaestle, C. (1983). *Pillars of the republic: Common schools and American society, 1780–1860.* New York: Hill and Wang.

Kieu, T. (2013, May 28). *Why immigration is an Asian American issue.* Center for American Progress. Retrieved December 1, 2014, from http://www.americanprogress.org/issues/immigration/news/2013/05/28/64474/why-immigration-is-an-asian-american-issue/

Hayashi, M. C. (2003). *Far from home: Shattering the myth of the model minority.* Irving, TX: Tapestry Press.

Inkelas, K. K. (2006). *Racial attitudes and Asian Pacific Americans: Demystifying the model minority.* New York: Routledge.

Lee, S. J. (2001). More than "model minorities" or "delinquents": A look at Hmong American high school students. *Harvard Educational Review, 71*(3), 505–528.

Lee, S. J. (2005). *Up against whiteness: Race, school, and immigrant youth.* New York: Teachers College Press.

Lew, J. (2006). Burden of acting neither white nor black: Asian American identities and achievement in urban schools. *The Urban Review, 38*(5), 335–352.

Louie, V. (2004). *Compelled to excel: Immigration, education and opportunity among Chinese Americans.* Stanford, CA: Stanford University Press.

Nagel, J. (1994). Constructing ethnicity: Creating and recreating ethnic identity and culture. *Social Problems, 41*(1), 152–176.

Neckerman, K. M., Carter, P., & Lee, J. (1999). Segmented assimilation and minority cultures of mobility. *Ethnic and Racial Studies, 22*(6), 945–965.

Olneck, M. (2004). Immigrants and education in the U.S. In J. A. Banks & A. M. Cherry (Eds.), *Handbook of research on multicultural education* (2nd ed., pp. 381–404). San Francisco, CA: Jossey-Bass.

Olsen, L. (1997). *Made in America: Immigrant students in our public schools.* New York: The New Press.

Park, G. C. (2011). Becoming "model minority": Korean immigrants' acquisition, construction, and enactment of an American identity in an inner-city school. *The Urban Review, 43*(5), 620–635.

Park, G. C., & Lee, S. J. (2010). The model minority stereotype and the underachiever: Academic and social struggles of underachieving Korean immigrant high school students. In R. Saran & R, Diaz (Eds.), *Beyond stereotypes: Minority children of immigrants in urban Schools* (pp. 13–27). Rotterdam, Netherlands: Sense.

Perry, P. (2001). White means never having to say you're ethnic. *Journal of Contemporary Ethnography, 30*(2001), 56–91.

Portes, A., & Rumbaut, R. G. (2001). *Legacies: The story of the immigrant second generation.* London, UK: University of California Press.

Roediger, D. (2005). *Working toward whiteness: How America's immigrants became white.* New York: Basic Books.

Rumbaut, R. G. (1994). The crucible within: Ethnic identity, self-esteem, and segmented assimilation among children of immigrants. *International Migration Review, 27*(4), 748–794.

Schultz, S. (1973). *The culture factory: Boston public schools, 1789–1860.* New York: Oxford University Press.

Shelby, T. (2002). Foundations of Black solidarity: Collective identity or common oppression. *Ethnics, 112*(2), 231–266.

Suzuki, R. (1995). Education and socialization of Asian Americans: Revisionist analysis of the 'model minority' thesis. In D. T. Nakanishi & T. Y. Nishida (Eds.), *The Asian American educational experience: A source book for teachers and students* (pp. 113–145). New York: Routledge.

Tuan, M. (1998). *Forever foreigners or honorary whites: The Asian ethnic experience today.* New Brunswick, NJ: Rutgers University Press.

United States Census Bureau. (2010). *State & county quick facts* [Data file]. Retrieved December 1, 2014, from http://quickfacts.census.gov/qfd/states/18/1852992.html

Valenzuela, A. (1999). *Subtractive schooling: U.S.-Mexican youth and the politics of caring.* Albany, NY: State University of New York Press.

Waters, M. C. (1994). Ethnic and racial identities of second generation black immigrants in New York City. *International Migration Review, 28*(4), 795–820.

Wing, J. Y. (2007). Beyond black and white: The model minority myth and the invisibility of Asian American students. *The Urban Review, 39*(4), 455–487.

Zhou, M. (1997). Segmented assimilation: Issues, controversies, and recent research on the new second generation. *International Migration Review, 31*(4), 975–1008.

CHAPTER 2

NEW STARTING POINTS

Becoming Asian Pacific Islander Educators in a Multiracial and Multicultural Society

Thomas M. Philip and Edward R. Curammeng[1]

Our struggle to explore what it means to be an Asian Pacific Islander (API) educator in the United States started when a small group of us came together to envision
a class specifically designed for API educators. Four months later, history was
made, at least for us. A course conceptualized by API educators for API educators
was taught for the first time, as far as we know, at a major university in the United
States.

Of course, this is not the type of history that will make its way into textbooks.
Nor is it the type of history that more than a dozen or so people will remember.
But it was a historical moment for us precisely because we embarked on a jour-
ney that reminded us that "history is not the past; it is the stories we tell about the

---

[1] Contributors to this chapter include Leslie Chanthaphasouk, Troy Keali'i Lau, Juliet Lee, Jeffrey
Lieu, Sakiko Muranaka, Juliane Nguyen, Elizabeth Ul, and Kate Viernes. All the authors and contributors identify racially as API. Ethnically, we identify as Cambodian, Chinese, Filipin@, Indian, Lao,
Native Hawaiian, Japanese, and Vietnamese. We thank Brian Lin, Melody Liao, and Kathy Ng for
their participation in the course described in this chapter and for their contributions to our collective
growth as API educators.

Killing the Model Minority Stereotype: Asian American Counterstories and Complicity,
pages 19–39.
Copyright © 2015 by Information Age Publishing
19

past" (Lee Boggs, 2012, p. 79). It was a recognition that the stories we had told about our past, which seemed so simple and true, were often not our own. We began listening for the incongruities, the ambiguities. There were soon multiple storylines, rather than just one. Some tapered off, others rejoined. There were stories of solidarity, and there were stories of strife. There were stories of hope, and there were stories of pain. There were stories that brought clarity, and there were stories that seeded uncertainty. Ultimately, though, we realized that stories are not simply about remembering the past. They are also about understanding the present and charting the future. They are about becoming. So, we share our stories of becoming API educators.

The historical significance of the day we describe is not merely symbolic. It marks a day when we came together at UCLA in a graduate course entitled "API Educators in a Multiracial Society." There we began to grapple with a question that resisted clear answers over the course of our quarter together: "What does it mean to be an API educator in a multiracial and multicultural society?" We recognized that the space we were making together was unique, perhaps even "sacred" (Soto, Cervantes-Soon, Villarreal, & Campos, 2009). It quickly grew to be a "place of comfort and nurturance and … of building communities of resistance" (Solórzano & Bernal, 2001, p. 336, citing Haymes, 1995). Never had we gathered in a room of APIs to think about who *we* are as educators. But it was not always clear who *we* were, educators or not. We are shaped differently in our API identity as men and women, straight and gay, native and settler, "central" and "peripheral." We inherit diverse stories about our API identity through our parents, who were middle-class and poor, immigrant and refugee, "Westernized" and "traditional," college educated and not. Even the second attribute of the shared identity we were building was thorny. We were educators, in the broad sense of the word; however, the contexts, goals, and needs of our work were dissimilar. Some of us were prospective elementary and high-school teachers, others were soon to be social workers, and yet others were aspiring university faculty members and researchers. Also in this mix were a future student affairs administrator and a professor at a research university. Within this diversity of experience as API educators, our pursuit of defining our shared identity often led to more questions than answers, more openings than closures. Given our collective struggles and even exasperations with assigning meaning to this identity, we resist the temptation to erase these productive tensions and to converge on definitive conclusions. Instead, we share our stories, taken from our final writing for the course. We view these stories as ways to "help strengthen traditions of social, political, and cultural survival and resistance" (Solórzano & Yosso, 2002, p. 32). We share our narratives with the hope that they invite responses, more stories, and varied interpretations, all of which together will begin to render a more complete, nuanced, and complex portrait of what it can mean to be an API educator.

While our differences are real, we also coalesced around a set of shared stories. These are stories that now partially define us, convey our shared principles, and shape our actions going forward. The first of these is a (re)discovery of the origins of the Asian American movement and a (re)commitment to the fundamental belief that our API identity is inherently tied to a struggle against racism in the United States and against imperialism abroad (Aguirre & Lio, 2008; Maeda, 2012, Philip, 2014). We have also come to appreciate our changing API racializations as embedded within this nation's systems of power. This shared story, a (re)telling of who we are as APIs, leads to two more stories about our identity as API educators. The first captures our responsibility to engage in critical dialogue about inequity and injustice with other APIs (Omatsu, 2003) and to address historical wrongs and contemporary injustices within the API umbrella (Yamamoto, 2000). The second compels us to examine the realities of inter-racial conflict (ex. Park, 1996) and learn from examples of solidarity (Widener, 2008) in order to engage in the difficult and necessary work of inter-racial struggles for justice.

In our work as API educators, we are inevitably prompted to deeply engage the concept of the "model minority" (Hartlep, 2013, 2014; Lee, 2009; Li & Wang, 2008)—an invitation that we consciously resist here. The model minority stereotype is an ideological construct that sustains and reproduces "whiteness" and white supremacy (Hayes & Hartlep, 2013; Leonardo, 2009). It attributes the apparent success of certain groups of Asian Americans to their individual efforts or their presumed shared cultural values. By obscuring the historical, social, political, and economic processes that produced and continue to sustain racialized inequities in the United States, the stereotype is racially divisive and undermines the racial struggles of other people of color. Additionally, by creating tremendous pressure to live up to a problematic ideal, and by harshly blaming APIs who fall short of unreasonable expectations associated with the stereotype, the construct adversely affects APIs by constricting their range of presumably acceptable personal, professional, and academic trajectories (Hune, 2002; Lee, 2009; Nakanishi & Nishida, 1995).

Critiques of the model minority stereotype provide a lens through which we can begin to understand the diversity and complex relationships of power within the API community (Buenavista, Jayakumar, & Misa-Escalante, 2009; Hune, 2002; Nakanishi & Nishida, 1995; Teranishi, 2002). However, the critique's emphasis on difference within APIs also undermines the potential use of the API identity for political organizing and change—a focus that "reduces the chances of forming a coalition to challenge the existing structure of power in society" (Chan & Wang, 1991, p. 64). Our differences that stem from ethnicity, class, immigration, gender, and sexuality are real and consequential and must be acknowledged and addressed. However, highlighting these differences *without* addressing our shared legacy of political struggle against racism can unintentionally reproduce unjust power relationships that further sustain "whiteness" and white supremacy (Hayes & Hartlep, 2013; Leonardo, 2009). Such emphasis on diversity and difference within APIs is prone to dismiss our shared racialization in the United States. In a racialized society, we are inevitably seen as racialized beings and therefore must contest inequities and injustices that stem from racism as racialized beings. Particularly given the claims that we live in a "colorblind" and "post-racial" society (Bonilla-Silva, 2003), we must be doubly cautious of analyses that underemphasize our collective racialization or undermine our use of "strategic essentialism" (Lowe, 1996; Spivak, 1988) to combat racism.

We do not attempt to critique the construct of the model minority here; instead, we make an attempt to move beyond the construct and define ourselves more fully as API within the increasingly complex and arguably less obvious relationships of power that racialize us today. Scholarship on the model minority stereotype has contributed significantly to problematizing and disrupting the homogenization of APIs—a need that was pressing within the political context in which the critique emerged. Yet, in this effort, we fear that the legacy of our shared racialized struggles as APIs has been glossed over and undervalued. Externally imposed and self-defined meanings of race are inherited from the past, but are also negotiated anew in the present. Our realities as APIs are different than those of the radical visionaries who coalesced around an API identity in the 1960s and 1970s, and those who contested the model minority myth in the 1980s, 1990s, and 2000s. We thus attempt to renew our understanding of API identity for ourselves and for our contemporary political context while honoring the activist and scholarly positions of APIs who preceded us.

As Hall (1981) would argue, even in our critiques of the model minority stereotype or the conceptualizations of API as a racial-political identity, we are left constrained by the "terms of the argument," the "logic," and the "starting points" of the debate. We choose, therefore, to begin a conversation about what it means to be an API educator through our own counter-stories that reflect our experiences in this historical moment (Delgado & Stefancic, 2001; Matsuda, 1995; Solórzano & Yosso, 2002). In the tradition of counter-stories, our narratives attempt to disrupt dominant ideology. More specifically, they are also meant to move us beyond the restrictive terms of the model minority debate to a place where we more fully embrace our charge for racial justice in the "post-Civil Rights" era (Bonilla-Silva, 2003).

We first share our stories without additional commentary to inspire resonances and divergences from the reader—unique readings of our stories and, in turn, writings of new ones that will continue to shape what it has meant for us to become API educators.

BECOMING OURSELVES, BECOMING API—JULIANE

Today, Juliane identifies herself as a 25-year old Asian/Vietnamese American female from Southern California. She sees herself as a womanist, a full-time graduate student, sister, and daughter. She is the first-born child of two refugees, Thanh and Donna, and the oldest sister of Kim and Kenny. Juliane, Kim, and Kenny are second generation Asian/Vietnamese Americans, who are currently living their parents' "American Dream" of obtaining an education that may lead to a successful future.

Throughout elementary school, Juliane was categorized as a "Limited English Proficient" student; as for Kim, she was in the gifted program and was an "Advanced" English speaker. This may have been because Juliane started assimilating to American culture and, in turn, speaking English to Kim in their household. Thanh and Donna tried their best to make their daughters speak Vietnamese within their home because they started to notice that their daughters were forgetting how to speak their mother tongue. Thanh tried to make his daughters enroll in Vietnamese school, but Juliane and Kim both rebelled. Juliane and Kim were assimilating to the American lifestyle rapidly, while Thanh and Donna were trying to do their best to preserve their culture.

Although Thanh and Donna often shared their immigration story, their children were oblivious to race and life outside of Southern California. Juliane always thought of herself as an American because she was born in America and assumed that everyone went through the same experiences as her parents. She thought that anyone who lives in America is simply an American. She did not understand the concept of race until she had a brief encounter at age 7. Her friends—a Vietnamese boy and Mexican girl—got into a dispute. When Juliane sided with the girl, she was criticized for hanging out with Mexicans instead of her "own" people. Juliane was perplexed.

Realizing that she was not the typical "white" American, Juliane tried her best to assimilate into mainstream culture. She refused to speak Vietnamese and tried her best to "perfect" her English. She started becoming embarrassed of her culture. She refused to bring Vietnamese food to school and only wanted to eat American food. Her behavior influenced her younger siblings; Kim started forgetting Vietnamese, while Kenny grew up barely speaking Vietnamese.

During Juliane's sophomore year, Thanh went to her high school to speak with Juliane's academic counselor (who was also Vietnamese) and asked if the school offered Vietnamese classes. It did. Thanh shamed Juliane in front of her counselor about forgetting her Vietnamese roots and enrolled her in the class. At first, Juliane was very upset. Eventually, however, she began to learn a lot about her heritage and identity as well as the importance of being bilingual and bicultural. Thanh was pleased that his daughter was finally taking the time to learn about their family's culture and history.

Juliane entered college with the goal of pursuing a nursing career. A classmate recommended that she take an Asian American Studies course. In the Asian American Studies course, Juliane learned more about culture, politics, and ethnic disparities, and about how significantly these factors have affected her lifestyle and identity. Juliane became intrigued by research on underrepresented communities—people like her family.

Juliane informed her father that she wanted to go into ethnic health research and education. Her father was disappointed when he found out Juliane wanted to change career paths. Thanh was confused about what Juliane meant by research and, like many other Asian parents, wanted Juliane to pursue either a career in medicine or law. Today, Thanh is starting to understand Juliane's pursuit of knowledge for what she believes in. He often feels guilty that he cannot provide more for his children, but he remains a constant source of emotional support for them.

OUR MANY SELVES—*JEFF*

In just one minute, I learned about the many roles that my activity-partner must take on as an API woman, an educator, a daughter, and about the complications that come with being a minority, female, and API in this society. I learned more about her in that one minute than I had over the entire quarter. When she described herself through the word "role," she was essentially responding to the question, "Who are you?" And so, I do the same.

I am positioned in society along dimensions of socio-economic status, immigration status, gender, and more. I experience these identities differently in different contexts and also in ways that complicate each other. I am a teacher, and more specifically, an elementary school teacher. I am male, but gay. By virtue of who I am, I disrupt gender role expectations in a dominant Christian society. But, I am Chinese American in a white society. This complicates my identity of being LGBTQ and my experience of being a racial minority. My experience as a gay Chinese male also arises from the specific gender roles expected of me in my Chinese family, such as preserving the family name through male children, giving face to family and friends, and making my parents proud. My inability to meet these expectations further complicates the many roles I must play as a male, as a son, and as a person within society. And in all this, I am always a teacher.

UNLEARNING OURSELVES, RELEARNING API—*JULIET*

A number of my reflections addressed the learning and re-learning of history. That, to me, was one of the most powerful experiences during this year, if not in my life. At the beginning of the course, I was anxious to learn more about what it means to be an API educator. I thought I had some ideas of what this meant because I am API, and because I am an educator. I thought that being API—because of where my family is from, the language we speak, or our cultural practices—provided me with the insight I would need to begin to answer this question. Once I began to learn about the history of APIs, their challenges and struggles with whites, with other People of Color, and with each other, I realized that my understanding of API was extremely limited. At that moment, I felt *less* like an API than ever before. How could I engage in this work when I do not know or understand this history, the work that was done before me, and, therefore, how to move this work forward?

As the course progressed, I began to re-examine my own privilege, both within the API community and my larger context. Another source of reflection was the ongoing discussion about the general category of API. As a Chinese American, I am almost always included in the API category, and that was something I took for granted. I speak about the diversity within the API community and how that diversity is not recognized, yet I have the privilege of having people like me being included in the little research that does exist about APIs. I speak about the lack of research on API students and teachers, without considering the *nonexistence* of research on some API groups.

This class was the first time I was in the company of a group of APIs. Until now, I questioned my experiences, wondering if they were shared or if they were unique to me. I struggled through them alone, and grappled with them in the best way I knew how. Through the stories of other members of the class, I learned that there *is* a common experience among APIs, and having this understanding brought me closer to seeing myself as a member of the community. For the first time, I saw myself as an insider, and felt a connection to others in the class. Despite meeting many of the people for the first time, there was an unspoken understanding we had of each other based on shared experiences. Through the work we engaged in over the quarter, I began to feel more concerned about how we are represented in literature and various forms of media, and to feel more invested in contributing our stories to the field. I'd like to think that this is the beginning of developing agency. Agency, to me, comes from learning—learning from texts and learning from others. It means being motivated to change and motivating others for change.

As an *API educator*, I am only beginning to understand my role. Race identifies us to others, whether it is acknowledged or not. As much as I want to think of myself as a teacher, or a math teacher, I must also recognize that before any of those identities, I am an *API teacher*. I did not acknowledge my API identity with my students, and thought that because I ignored it, they would as well. Students want to know more about us, and our role, then, as API educators is to answer their questions. I did not always address their questions in the best way, and as I reflect now, I realize how critical those moments were.

This quarter has been for me one of learning in a very different way. It has been learning about myself, my role, and my responsibilities as both an API and as an API educator. Whereas I began this course based on my own personal interest, I now feel drawn to the work, wanting to learn more, to share my story, to hear others' stories, and to have others understand the importance of the API voice. I learned that if we want to have a voice, we have to *use* our voice. Though the course is over, the work, for me, has only begun. I recognize that there is much more for me to learn, and I look forward to continuing to explore these ideas and deepening my understanding of what it means to be an API educator.

SOLIDARITY WITH (IN)VISIBILITY?—*TROY*

Something deep within made me enroll in this class when I heard the title of the course. I did not know what to expect from the class, and I did not know what I wanted from it. The class seemed like it might be a safe place I could talk about issues that relate to my community, a space where I could share the pain I endure in the academy where I am racially and culturally unique, but most importantly, a space where I could master my narrative. My narrative is my testimony on life. It is my message, my call to action; it is the accumulation of life experience and academic reflection. This course has been a place for all of these things, and it has consistently asked the question "What does it meant to be an API educator?"

As with the term API, I understand that "Asian" is not a monolithic racial and ethnic identity. I also recognize that underrepresented Asian groups are likely underfunded for the same reasons as many Pacific Islanders. Thus, my concerns as a Pacific Islander are likely identical to those of certain Asian groups as well. However, my focus in this paper is to evaluate the inclusion of my community and my participation in the API identity. That is, does our inclusion benefit or disrupt the goals of my community? What does this mean for myself as an educator?

This invisibility has occurred even within the discourse of this class. Articles are entitled API, or Asian American/Pacific Islander, with barely a tribute to issues within the Pacific Islander community. From an academic perspective, it seems a paragraph on Pacific Islanders is all it takes to qualify as an API piece. Our discussions and presentations barely scratch the surface of what each of us is trying to accomplish within our own communities. What is the problem? What are the issues? What compelling stories move me to action? If I was meant to be the voice of Native Hawaiians and Pacific Islanders, then my 5–15 minute presentations failed to accomplish this goal. In failing to create a voice, I have failed to create true empathy and knowledge, and, thus, have failed to create what Yamamoto (2000) called race praxis.

The Yamamoto (2000) reading was the first to make me realize that there is political impotency around the API identity, and that it is created by a lack of shared knowledge, racial experience, and empathy. The article begins by describing the polemics of privilege, and the willingness of some Asian groups to take financial accountability for the benefit gained from the overthrow of the Hawaiian monarchy and the subsequent cultural genocide and economic destruction of the Native Hawaiians. But as Yamamoto emphasizes, other Asian groups failed to acknowledge the privilege and power they have accrued since these historical events. They ignore or dismiss the effects of settler colonialism (Trask, 2000) on the indigenous population—the acquisition of (neo)colonial roles by Asian settler groups who control significant aspects of economic and political power in Hawaii and who oppose the Kanaka Maoli (Native Hawaiian) sovereignty movement. How can Native Hawaiians exist under the panethnicity of Asian Pacific Islanders if the majority of that taxonomy fails to recognize the historical causality of contemporary issues? Should the call to action go out to all allies and dispense with the API identity?

In addition to the current community work I do on access, I would like to provide a space for Pacific Islanders that legitimizes our work, affirms our place in academia, and creates a learning space to further develop literary contributions to, and from, our community. By occupying theoretical spaces, I believe we empower ourselves and our community to name and define our own experiences, to validate our epistemologies and indigenous ways of knowing, and to share narratives from the indigenous perspective instead of those imposed by the dominant culture. As to the API identity, I believe it is plausible. I believe that it must be a political group of activists with a defined mission, defined goals, and a plan of action. I believe that this group must work hard to communicate (to speak, listen, and share) with each other to develop empathy and urgency. Through empathy we care about one another and desire equality and fairness of circumstance, but without urgency there can be no social justice. Urgency demands praxis; an understanding of critical knowledge that, upon reflection, creates action. Only in this way does membership to the API identity make any practical sense.

I'M NEVER "JUST A SOCIAL WORKER"—*KATE*

While others' expectations of me do not always result in a social consequence that is apparent, at other times they do. What comes to mind is a time recently, during my first-year Masters of Social Welfare internship at a social service agency for the homeless, when an African American client asked me, "Girl, why do you talk and act like a white person? Why don't you be yourself?"

His comment had an air of disappointment and spite to it. I calmly and quizzically responded, "I sort of think I am being myself... but what do you mean exactly?"

Shaking his head, he replied, "I can tell, based on your nationality, that you shouldn't be so perky. Just be yourself."

At the time, I was helping this man apply for social security benefits, in a manner I saw as professional and positive (and yes, probably somewhat energetic, which is part of my personality). To the client, however, his impression of my race clearly affected his expectations of how I should behave while I worked with him. He could tell I was some kind of Asian or Pacific Islander, and the result was that he interpreted my way of speaking and acting as somehow "wrong."

In a different scenario, race could potentially have affected this interaction in a more negative way (in spite of the client's opinion, he still accepted my assistance in applying for benefits). Nevertheless, this example demonstrates how my race immediately affects my power to provide a professional service. Presumably, white social workers would not have been questioned or criticized for providing such professional service as it would have been seen as compatible with their racial identity.

MULTIETHNIC SALUTATIONS TO
MULTIRACIAL SOLIDARITY—*ED*

To begin articulating, defining, and imagining what an API teacher identity is, one must critically reflect on the tensions associated with such a powerful identity marker. Throughout this quarter, we have collectively been engaged in the necessary reflexive work to name and define what it means to be API. This process, I would argue, has been productive, thoughtful, and encouraging in acknowledging just how difficult it is to define what it means to be an API educator. Never did I imagine that the contours of these discussions would manifest so rapidly and cathartically in an academic space.

I refer to the complexities attached to articulating what it means to be an API educator as an asset because through these complexities we are able to conceptualize our role as educators in ways that are unique to APIs, as people who have diverse and shared backgrounds, histories, and relationships to the United States as racialized beings. I choose to reframe a central theme of our course, "Being an API educator," to "Becoming," as it evokes a process—continual, challenging, and critical. When we imagine the possibilities of our education, API as a racial and political identity certainly offers reflections that are urgent and necessary to examine. As we move forward, having critically examined our positionalities as API educators, it is our duty to "pursue meaningful answers" (Spade, 2009) in our pursuit of a society that is equitable and more socially just.

A part of my becoming stems from my experiences as an undergraduate who worked with the Asian American community generally and the Filipina/o American community in particular. An example I alluded to in one of my reflections was how many of the multi-ethnic student organizations had offices on the same level of the student union. Looking back, a shortcoming of that experience was not seeing how much more powerful "affinity" would have been in organizing students beyond simply supporting (read: publicizing) one another's events. The Filipina/o American student organization I worked with rarely organized with other Asian American student organizations. Ironically, most students involved in ethnic-specific organizations are highly aware of the rich histories forged through the struggle for ethnic studies. Yet, in spite of this knowledge, interracial solidarity was not exercised as much as it could have been. For this reason, Hall's (1996) evocation of rearticulating the purpose of interethnic/interracial solidarity is productive and offers a point of reflection in the process of becoming an API educator. Understanding multi-ethnic and multi-racial solidarities can be a point of departure—one that can provide "meaningful answers" and that can be useful for API educators in relation to educators of similar backgrounds and experiences.

ACKNOWLEDGING OUR PASTS TO FIND OUR COMMONALITY—*LIZ*

My field placement for my Masters of Social Welfare program this school year was at an in-patient alcohol and drug dependency rehabilitation program for veterans. Service providers at the site also assist veterans in seeking permanent housing and employment so that they may function as civilians once they are discharged from the program after about four to six months.

This placement experience encouraged me to consider how age, gender, and ethnicity have significant impacts on my interactions with potential clients. My Cambodian American identity had always been burning right below the surface, but I feared telling veterans about my background because I did not know what their response would be. The majority of veterans at the site served during the Vietnam era, and my family's emigration history is tied to their military service. I was concerned that I would reawaken past trauma if I were to disclose information about my family. As social workers, we are taught to be very strategic about what parts of our identity we reveal in the therapeutic process.

In a documentary film called *Enemy of the People*, a Cambodian journalist who interviewed Nuon Chea, the second in command to the Khmer Rouge Regime, chose to withhold information regarding his family members being among the two million plus decimated at the hands of the Khmer Rouge. The journalist chose not to disclose his family history to Nuon Chea until many years of building rapport and trust. Like the journalist, it was not until my very last group facilitation that I was able to genuinely share my personal history and my identity as a daughter of Cambodian refugees affected by war. Some veterans even wept for me as I shared my own story with them. For many, it was the first time they had allowed themselves to be vulnerable and cry.

I wished on that last day that I had not waited so long to share my story. It was a powerful moment. If I had shared my story earlier, it might have encouraged the veterans to share their own stories. As an API Social Worker, I've learned about my racialization in higher education. Through this course, I've slowly started to verbalize and critically assess how my racialization plays out in my role as a social worker.

My experience at the site was invaluable. It was not a group that I chose to work with. In retrospect, I am grateful for the experience. I am aware that I initially held misconceptions about the veterans. I strongly believed that I shared very little in common with them. I thought, "How can I serve them if I don't share similar struggles?"

Similar to those who are racist or prejudiced, I was allowing my ignorance to create a false fear. However, with guidance from other social workers and exposure to these individuals in a therapeutic environment, I have a newfound respect and empathy for them. Simultaneously, I learned a lot about how I must confront and deal with gender and racial dynamics within myself in order to be an effective API social worker. In the process of working with the veterans, I implemented activities and tools that I've collected through my many years of working in community organizing and activism. I am excited to combine my two identities as an API social worker and API activist and turn theory into practice.

BRINGING "OUR OWN" INTO DIALOGUE—*SAKIKO*

A big question that came up for me in this course was how to bridge groups and cultures in a racialized society. Where do we intersect? How do we create solidarity regardless of our varied and disparate experiences?

A recent incident at my middle-school student-teaching placement prompted me to examine these questions and to consider my role and responsibility to engage other API educators in the discussion about positionality. My guiding instructor was an Asian American woman. During a class discussion about the disproportionate representation of Latinos and African Americans in the prison population, she explicitly told the male students in the class, who were all Latino or African American, that they needed to learn to control their tempers or they may end up in jail.

Her intent was not wrong, but it indicated to me that she did not see herself as "part of the struggle" against the dominant ideology. I shied from engaging her in a conversation about how she addressed the students. In hindsight, I now see the responsibility I have in initiating these kinds of difficult conversations with fellow API educators. Instead of simply criticizing her practices or ignoring them, I feel a heightened sense of responsibility to engage my guiding teacher in further conversations regarding the racialization of APIs. I can see the importance of understanding our own racialization as APIs because it shapes the way we see and understand racism in the United States, and, subsequently, how we engage our students in learning.

BLACKFACE AND ME—*LESLIE*

The Lambda Theta Delta Asian American fraternity at UC-Irvine gained media attention for using Blackface in a promotional video that was posted on YouTube and then went viral. These types of racial and ethnic incidents are issues on college campuses around the nation and will potentially affect my work as a student affairs administrator. The situation made me think about how I would react in that situation as an API student affairs professional and about how I would work towards racial reconciliation in this situation.

Drawing from Yamamoto's (2000) work on interracial justice, the fraternity's reaction to the incident fulfilled some but not all dimensions of interracial justice. First, the fraternity showed recognition and responsibility by immediately taking down the video after it prompted outrage from the Black Student Union and gained attention from several media outlets. They also issued a formal apology that detailed certain actions that members will undertake, such as a self-suspension from campus activities, participation in educational programs and community dialogues addressing race and stereotyping, and the creation of new recruitment and pledge processes that include cultural awareness and respect (Brenner, 2013). Though these actions temporarily absolve the fraternity from the harm they created, many of these resolutions only address the current issue and fail to resolve the more systemic anti-black issues that pervade the university as a whole. While the Black Student Union continues to demand institutional changes such as the departmentalization of the African American Studies program and the institution of a zero-tolerance policy against discrimination and violence, the Asian American fraternity essentially falls off the radar (Ricks, 2013). As a student affairs professional, I wonder how much more successful (and meaningful from an inter-racial solidarity perspective) the Black Student Union's push would be if members of the Asian American fraternity were able to collaborate and organize for those demands to be met and for institutional change to occur. In this case, I foresee that the apology "will not change the relationship structure enough to bring about enduring forgiveness" (Yamamoto, 2000, p. 195). Rather, further action needs to be taken to ensure the appropriate reparation and reconciliation for Black students at UC-Irvine.

Though the fraternity took responsibility for their actions, what responsibility do they have to fight for justice beyond their own self-imposed sanctions? One of the most important things underlying interracial justice is the idea of responsibility, both individual and collective. Having knowledge and recognizing power and agency mean nothing without the feeling of responsibility to motivate collective action. One of the pieces that resonated with me early on in the course was the discussion of W.E.B. Du Bois' philosophy on black empowerment. According to Spring (2010), "What was most important for Du Bois was to educate blacks to be discontent with their social position in the South. Unhappiness—not happiness—was his goal" (p. 62). The concept of being unhappy, I feel, underlies the responsibility piece; that is, if one is constantly led to be unhappy with the status quo, he or she will feel the need or responsibility to create the conditions for happiness, which translates into transformational change. I believe that in the UC-Irvine case, the fraternity was rather content with the self-imposed sanctions, and did not feel the need to advocate for further institutional action. In order for transformational change to occur, this mindset essentially has to change.

Personally, I relate to the idea of feeling unhappy, particularly for the Lao American and Southeast Asian communities. During my undergraduate career, I was unhappy with the lack of attention paid to issues facing the Lao community. Therefore, I started a Lao student organization, put on events to promote awareness of the Lao American experience, and helped co-chair an event to increase the number of Southeast Asians (and Lao) students who attend UCLA. Recently, however, I have been trying to look beyond my own community and am constantly educating myself on how to become an ally to other communities of color. Taking this course and participating in intergroup dialogue as both a participant and facilitator has opened my eyes to the struggles that affect not only my own community, but other communities as well. As I become more aware of the issues at hand, I hope I will find that "unhappiness" to transcend the communities that I self-identify with. Even more, I hope to be able to see myself reflected in the struggles of other communities and to eventually push forward in solidarity with these communities. Of course, I understand that this is an ongoing process, which takes a lot of time and experience. Thus, it is my responsibility to continue to move through this process through constant action, dialogue, and reflection. A starting point was participating in this course.

BEGINNING A DIALOGUE

In these concluding pages, we return to our stories to more explicitly draw out themes and insights that emerged from our own re-readings of our stories. We see these narratives, in part, as "a strategy and a means of resistance" for API educators (Solórzano & Yosso, 2002, p. 37). We share these collective reflections with the hope that they will seed a dialogue on what it means to become an API educator in a multiracial and multicultural society.

Understanding our Dynamic Identities

Juliane reminds us that our identities–how we tell the story of who we are–change over time. Jeff's piece complicates our identities further, highlighting how they are not only dynamic over the course of our lives, but across contexts. Some identities are, at times, more salient than others, and identities inevitably exist as intersecting, hybrid, and competing. Our work as API educators must identify, engage, and challenge the ways in which our racialized identity intersects with markers such as gender, sexuality, class, immigration status, education, and the linguistic repertoires to which we have access. Jeff's writing cautions us against a romanticized API identity that erases layered systems of oppression within it. He challenges us, as API educators, to confront sexism and heterosexism within our communities.

Understanding our Experiences as API Students

Juliane's piece pushes us to deeply engage with our racialized educational histories. Understanding our own journeys as we become educators requires us to consider ourselves in light of and in contrast to the diversity of API educational experiences. These experiences range from South Asian students who contend with the model-minority image (Asher, 2002), to poor Korean American youth who negotiate the intersection of race and class (Lew, 2006), from Sa'moan students who are racialized as Black (Vaught, 2012), to Southeast Asian youths who find themselves caught between the binary portrayals of being "hardworking, high achievers" and "dropouts, gangsters, and welfare dependents" (Ngo & Lee, 2007, p. 416). Within the dominant narrative, our stories as API learners are often constricted, and our diversity of experiences as racialized learners is erased. Our role as API educators requires us to delve into and share these distinct stories.

The Importance of Learning, Unlearning, and Re-learning about ourselves as API

Juliet reminds us that unlearning and relearning what it means to be API are essential dimensions of growth as API educators. Juliane traces her own process of unlearning and relearning in ethnic studies courses in high school and college. She highlights the inadvertent contradictions that arise when a rediscovery of radical roots, partially inspired by her parents, seeds choices that are at odds with their immigrant aspirations of the American Dream.

Juliet and Juliane's pieces prompt us not only to acknowledge our ignorance about our racialization in this country, but to critically examine how we have come to learn such ignorance. What histories do we learn about ourselves? To what extent do they include our politicized and radical histories? When is this ignorance taught by others? When does it stem from our own willful historical amnesia?

Recognizing and Addressing Representation within the API Community

Juliet and Troy's contributions speak directly to Spickard's (2007) analysis of the centrality and marginality of groups within the API umbrella. Juliet and Troy name, from different positions of privilege and peripheral status, the comfort of being unquestionably included as a Chinese American and the frustration of cursory inclusion as a Native Hawaiian. Being an API educator compels us to examine our own positionality, and its implications, within the API community.

The Need for "Sacred" Spaces

Borrowing from Soto et al. (2009), we have come to appreciate the importance of "sacred" spaces in our work—spaces that are "deliberately created with particular goals cultivated through ongoing communal exchange, maintained for the extension of the relationships built and the projects pursued, and protected from forces that might obliterate its core" (p. 756). We use this space, not to isolate ourselves, but to build the strength to work in solidarity with others. As Juliet explains, there was power being with APIs to consider the meaning of this identity. It was a cathartic space (Ed) and a space to "share our pains and master our narrative" (Troy). Particularly in light of the "overwhelming presence of whiteness" in professional programs (Sleeter, 2001), "sacred" spaces are essential as we understand our role as API educators in a multiracial and multicultural society.

Disrupting Invisible Norms of Whiteness Associated with Being a Professional

Closely tied to Sleeter's (2001) argument about the "overwhelming presence of whiteness" in teacher education, as API educators and social workers we enter professions that are disproportionately white—more than 4 out of 5 teachers and social workers in this country are white, while 1 or 2 in a 100 are API! As Kate describes, this results in the implicit racialization of our professions, where our professional identity is conflated with being middle-class and white. Our effort as API educators must therefore be twofold: 1) to disrupt images that conjoin our profession with whiteness, and 2) to critically reflect upon and challenge the invisible norms of being middle-class and white that we may have appropriated through our socialization into our professions.

Contending with the Sorrow, Anger, and Regret in our Racialization

Liz's contribution forces us to move beyond abstract discussions of our racializations. Her experience with the veterans, whose lives were so intricately tied into her own, provides a compelling example of how our shared racialized pasts have made us who we are today. As educators and social workers, the privilege and marginality of our students and clients as racialized beings are linked with our own. Contending with and addressing our shared histories and moments of strife and solidarity is not simply an intellectual act. Drawing on Yamamoto (2000), we remind ourselves that embracing and struggling with grief, pain, and resentment are essential steps in the process of becoming an API educator who works for interracial justice.

Naming and Addressing Contemporary Processes of Racism

As Ed reminds us, our very presence as API educators, if we critically examine our racialization, disrupts simplistic analyses of race, racism, and power. A first step in our process of becoming API educators is to make ourselves visible in these professional identities where we are extremely underrepresented. The necessary accompanying action is to name and contend with the complexities of our racializations. These steps are not as direct or effortless as one might assume. As Juliet expressed, we are prone to think of ourselves as "just a teacher" or "just a math teacher." We tend to dismiss the particularities of being an API educator—an identity through which our students and colleagues inevitably see us. By doing so, we implicitly resist the difficult questions, and the pain and power that Liz highlights, which arise with an acknowledgement of our racialization. As Juliet urges us, "If we want to have a voice, we have to *use* our voice."

Returning to the roots of the API movement, our role as API educators entails particular commitment and responsibility to API communities and other communities of color. As Troy argues, social justice requires urgency, and urgency demands praxis. If an API identity is truly a political identity for social justice, it demands that we address injustices within ourselves and that we struggle for each other's causes. These struggles might lead us to engage, as Troy proposes, with historically, socially, politically, and economically complex questions such as Asian settler colonialism in Hawaii. Or, it might prompt us to struggle with everyday, but still consequential, interactions with other API educators as described in Sakiko's reflection.

Ed and Leslie force us to confront the challenges and possibilities of living in a multiracial society stratified by the historical and contemporary power of whiteness. Reflecting on his own process of growth and change, Ed pushes us to move beyond superficial affirmations of people of color to true solidarity. While Ed emphasizes the importance of solidarity across organizations, Leslie highlights the significance of working, as APIs, for institutional amends.

COMMENCEMENT

Ed provocatively shifted our focus from "being an API educator" to "becoming an API educator," reminding us that we are engaged in a continual and communal process. It would only be proper, therefore, not to think of these last few sentences as a conclusion that brings resolution, but as a commencement to new questions, challenges, and possibilities. As Juliet emphasized, our process of more fully understanding our own racialization as teachers and students prompts new roles for us as API educators. The API movement emerged within the context of the Civil Rights Movement and the Vietnam War, struggles that gave it purpose. Over the last few decades, APIs who were invested in racial justice have worked to problematize the ideological construction of the model minority. Within the intricate and increasingly obscure relationships of power that racialize us today, we begin to re-define our role as APIs through our narratives. Our racialization, positionality, and responsibility as APIs are significantly different in this era of "colorblind racism" (Bonilla-Silva, 2003). It is perhaps filled with more ambiguity and contention. But understanding our role as API educators in a multiracial and multicultural society is an endeavor that we embrace, as we are reminded of Fanon (1963, p. 206) who wrote, "Each generation must out of relative obscurity discover its mission, fulfill it, or betray it," and Lee Boggs (as cited in Omatsu, 2003, p. 9) who echoed, "new situations bring new contradictions, requiring new visions."

Through our narratives, we drew attention to processes that supported us in our evolving definition of the role of API educators in a multiracial and multicultural society. Given significant shifts in public discourse about gender and sexuality, the increased visibility of persons who identify as multiracial, and the number of second and third generation APIs who continue to challenge social and professional boundaries, our *dynamic identities*, our *experiences as API students*, and our *learning, unlearning, and re-learning of API identities* look dramatically different than they would have in the past. New possibilities and tensions arise in spaces where we work and study, such as UCLA, where we comprise a plurality. What does our plurality in this setting, and its relative uniqueness, mean for *solidarity within the API community* and for *"sacred" spaces* in such contexts and beyond? We recognize our imperative to disrupt the *invisible norms of whiteness in the overwhelmingly white professions* that are becoming increasingly accessible to us. In such spaces where we still experience isolation, we must support each other in contending with the *sorrow, anger, and regret rooted in our racialization* that inevitably seep into our professional lives. Given the shifting discourses of race, we strive to *name and address contemporary processes of racism*, not just as APIs, not just as educators, but as API educators. We share our narratives and name these reflective processes with the hope that they will benefit others in continuing the ongoing dialogue that defines our collective and emerging role as API educators in a multiracial and multicultural society.

Questions for Reflection

1. What stories and counter-stories about race and racism do you hear in our society, which is often assumed to be "colorblind" and "post-racial"? How do these stories implicitly or explicitly involve APIs? How might you re-frame such stories as an API educator?

2. Consider the context in which you work. For instance, how might you describe your context in terms of: a) race, class, immigration, geography, politics, and histories? b) the dynamics that exist between and within its multiple and intersecting communities? c) the spoken and invisible norms of gender and sexuality? Given the complexity of your context and the intersectionality of your identities, what is your role as an API educator or as someone who supports API educators? What are some of the unique possibilities and challenges you see for yourself as an API educator, or as someone who supports API educators?

3. We have argued for APIs to root themselves in a common ideal, but also to consistently ask themselves what that ideal means in the present historical moment. Given the history of the API movement's domestic focus on racism and international emphasis on imperialism, how do you conceptualize and enact your commitment to API solidarity today? What do the domestic struggle against racism and the fight against globalized systems of oppression mean for APIs now? Consider how your response is shaped by the ethnic identities and the intersecting identities (such as gender, sexuality, immigration status, transracial adoption, interracial marriage, and multiracial identity) that put you in central and peripheral locations in the racialized category of API.

4. Learning to be an educator and learning about racialization are iterative—these processes intricately build on each other. How have your understandings about your role as an educator and your analyses of race, power, and privileges mutually shaped the other?

5. In a society that tenaciously and simultaneously holds on to contradictory images of "colorblindness" and the "perpetual foreigner," how do you emphasize the critical intersection between your API identity and your educator identity in ways that contest, and also transcend, the "starting points" of these discourses?

REFERENCES

Aguirre, A., & Lio, S. (2008). Spaces of mobilization: The Asian American/Pacific islander struggle for social justice. *Social Justice, 35*(2), 1–17.

Asher, N. (2002). Class acts: Indian American high school students negotiate professional and ethnic identities. *Urban Education, 37*(2), 267–295.

Bonilla-Silva, E. (2003). *Racism without racists: Color-blind racism and the persistence of racial inequality in the United States.* New York: Rowman & Littlefield.

Brenner, L. (2013, May 3). *UCI Asian-American fraternity imposes self-suspension over blackface video.* 89.3 KPCC Southern California Public Radio. Retrieved December 1, 2014, from http://www.scpr.org/blogs/news/2013/05/03/13530/uci-asian-american-fraternity-imposes-self-suspens/

Buenavista, T. L., Jayakumar, U. M., & Misa-Escalante, K. (2009). Contextualizing Asian American education through critical race theory: An example of US Filipino college student experiences. *New Directions for Institutional Research, 142*, 69–81.

Chan, S., & Wang, L. C. (1991). Racism and the model minority: Asian-Americans in higher education. In P. G. Altbach & K. Lomotey (Eds.), *The racial crisis in American higher education* (pp. 43–68). Albany, NY: State University of New York Press.

Delgado, R., & Stefancic, J. (2001). *Critical race theory: An introduction.* New York: New York University Press.

Fanon, F. (1963). *The wretched of the earth* (Constance Farrington, Trans.). New York: Grove. Retrieved December 1, 2014, from http://thebaluch.com/documents/0802150837%20–%20FRANTZ%20FANON%20–%20The%20Wretched%20of%20the%20Earth.pdf

Hall, S. (1981). The white of their eyes: Racist ideologies in the media. In G. Bridges & R. Brunt (Eds.), *Silver linings: Some strategies for the eighties* (pp. 28–52). London, UK: Lawrence and Wishart.

Hall, S. (1996). The problem of ideology: Marxism without guarantees. In D. Morley & K. Chen (Eds.), *Stuart Hall: Critical dialogues in cultural studies* (pp. 25–46). London, UK: Routledge.

Hartlep, N. D. (2013). *The model minority stereotype: Demystifying Asian American success.* Charlotte, NC: Information Age Publishing.

Hartlep, N. D. (Ed.). (2014). *The model minority stereotype reader: Critical and challenging readings for the 21st century.* San Diego, CA: Cognella.

Hayes, C., & Hartlep, N. D. (Eds.). (2013). *Unhooking from whiteness: The key to dismantling racism in the United States.* Boston, MA: Sense.

Haymes, S. (1995). *Race, culture, and the city: A pedagogy for Black urban struggle.* Albany, NY: State University of New York Press.

Hune, S. (2002). Demographics and diversity of Asian American college students. *New Directions for Student Services, 97*, 11–20.

Lee, S. J. (2009). *Unraveling the "model minority" stereotype: Listening to Asian American youth* (2nd ed.). New York: Teachers College Press.

Lee Boggs, G. (2012). *The next American revolution: Sustainable activism for the twenty-first century.* Berkeley, CA: University of California Press.

Leonardo, Z. (2009). *Race, whiteness, and education.* New York: Routledge.

Lew, J. (2006). Burden of acting neither White nor Black: Asian American identities and achievement in urban schools. *The Urban Review, 38*(5), 335–352.

Li, G., & Wang, L. (Eds.). (2008). *Model minority myth revisited: An interdisciplinary approach to demystifying Asian American educational experiences.* Charlotte, NC: Information Age.

Lowe, L. (1996). *Immigrant acts: On Asian American cultural politics.* Durham, NC: Duke University Press.

Maeda, D. J. (2012). *Rethinking the Asian American movement.* New York: Routledge.

Matsuda, M. (1995). Looking to the bottom: Critical legal studies and reparations. In K. Crenshaw, N. Gotanda, G. Peller, & K. Thomas (Eds.), *Critical race theory: The key writings that formed the movement* (pp. 63–79). New York: The New Press.

Nakanishi, D., & Nishida, T. (Eds.). (1995). *The Asian American educational experience: A sourcebook for teachers and students.* New York: Routledge.

Ngo, B., & Lee, S. J. (2007). Complicating the image of model minority success: A review of Southeast Asian American education. *Review of Educational Research, 77*(4), 415–453.

Omatsu, G. K. (2003). Freedom schooling: Reconceptualizing Asian American studies for our communities. *Amerasia Journal, 29*(2), 9–33.

Park, K. (1996). Use and abuse of race and culture: Black-Korean tension in America. *American Anthropologist, 98*(3), 492–499.

Philip, T. M. (2014). Asian American as a political-racial identity: Implications for teacher education. *Race Ethnicity and Education, 17*(2), 219–241. Retrieved December 1, 2014, from http://tmp.bol.ucla.edu/Philip_REE.pdf

Ricks, O. (2013, May 3). Despite apologies from racist frat, UC Irvine Black students stick to demands. *The Feminist Wire.* Retrieved December 1, 2014, from http://thefeministwire.com/2013/05/despite-apologies-from-racist-frat-uc-irvine-black-students-stick-to-demands/

Sleeter, C. (2001). Preparing teachers for culturally diverse schools: Research and the overwhelming presence of whiteness. *Journal of Teacher Education, 52*(2), 94–106.

Solórzano, D. G., & Bernal, D. D. (2001). Examining transformational resistance through a critical race and latcrit theory framework: Chicana and Chicano students in an urban context. *Urban Education, 36*(3), 308–342.

Solórzano, D. G., & Yosso, T. J. (2002). Critical race methodology: Counter-storytelling as an analytical framework for education research. *Qualitative inquiry, 8*(1), 23–44.

Soto, L. D., Cervantes-Soon, C. G., Villarreal, E., & Campos, E. E. (2009). The Xicana sacred space: A communal circle of compromiso for educational researchers. *Harvard Educational Review, 79*(4), 755–775.

Spade, D. (2009). Trans law and politics on a neoliberal landscape. *Temple Political and Civil Rights Law Review, 18*, 353–373.

Spickard, P. (2007). Whither the Asian American coalition. *Pacific Historical Review, 76*(4), 585–604.

Spivak, G. C. (1988). Subaltern studies: Deconstucting historiography. In R. Guha & G. C. Spivak (Eds.), *Selected subaltern studies* (pp. 3–32). Oxford, UK: Oxford University Press.

Spring, J. H. (2010). *Deculturalization and the struggle for equality: A brief history of the education of dominated cultures in the United States.* Boston, MA: McGraw-Hill Higher Education.

Teranishi, R. T. (2002). Asian Pacific Americans and critical race theory: An examination of school racial climate. *Equity & Excellence in Education, 35*(2), 144–154.

Trask, H. K. (2000). Settlers of color and "immigrant" hegemony: "Locals" in Hawai'i. *Amerasia Journal, 26*(2), 1–24.

Vaught, S. E. (2012). 'They might as well be Black': The racialization of Sa'moan high school students. *International Journal of Qualitative Studies in Education, 25*(5), 557–582.

Widener, D. (2008). Another city is possible: Interethnic organizing in contemporary Los Angeles. *Race/Ethnicity: Multidisciplinary Global Contexts, 1*(2), 189–219.

Yamamoto, E. K. (2000). *Interracial justice: Conflict & reconciliation in post-Civil Rights America.* New York: New York University Press.

CHAPTER 3

HAPAS IN COLLEGE

Multiracial Asian Identity and the Model Minority Myth

Amy L. Miller, Thai-Huy Nguyen, and Marybeth Gasman

There was like an absolute certainty that I was somewhere in between, that
my father and my mother were from different backgrounds.
—*A. L. Miller, personal communication, June 19, 2013.*

Within the Asian American narrative, one part that is regularly excluded is the
story of mixed race Asian Americans. Despite the fact that mixed race Asians,
also known as Hapas, make up 15% of the Asian American community and are
one of the largest subgroups according to Pew Research Center, they have not
been given an equal place in cultural organizations, community leadership, and
academic research (Pew Research Center, 2012). According to Beverly Yuen
Thompson (2000), "Within the 'Asian American experience' there is a great deal
of diversity that has thus far remained unexplored. Issues of interracial relationships, transracial adoptions, biracial identity, and queer identity have remained
marginalized and considered exceptions to an unspoken norm of Asian American
identity" (Yuen Thompson, 2000, p. 175). Since Asian Americans are defined by
a monolithic term and are viewed by American society as a single entity, any de-

Killing the Model Minority Stereotype: Asian American Counterstories and Complicity,
pages 41–60.

viations from this normative definition have been excluded (Espiritu, 1992). For many Hapa students in college, their cultural and racial differences have resulted in a general exclusion from Asian American and other single-race groups and harsher criticism under the model minority myth (MMM). Through a single, in-depth vignette, our chapter examines the influence of this exclusion and how the MMM operates to hamper student confidence and opportunities to connect with other students on campus, ultimately eroding the quality of the college experience. Additionally, it attempts to shine a light on the mixed race Asian American community and to make a case for why these stories are important in the overall landscape of educational research on Asian Americans and other non-dominant minority groups in general. A discussion of implications and recommendations for greater awareness and sensitivity to mixed-race students and their development in student programming and services as well as questions for further reflection follow. The following question guided our overall inquiry and analysis: What are the stories—perceived and experienced challenges—of those who identify as Hapa during college?

BACKGROUND

The 2000 US Census, which was the first to allow people to choose more than one race since the late 1800s, showed that 6,826,228 people or 2.4 percent of the population identified as mixed race (U.S. Census Bureau, 2001). In just ten years, the portion of mixed race individuals identifying as such on the 2010 U.S. Census increased by 32 percent to 2.9 percent of the American population, which is among the fastest rate of growth of any population in the United States. Within the mixed raced population, both Asians and Native Hawaiians/Pacific Islanders have the highest percentage of people reporting multiple races, representing a significant majority (see Figure 3.1). More specifically, in the mixed race Asian community, the numbers of Asian/White people in the United States grew by 87% or 750,000 people, and the Black/Asian populations increased by nearly 74% or 79,000 people between the 2000 and 2010 Censuses, now totaling approximately 1.8 million people (Gamble, 2009; Jones & Bullock, 2013). Furthermore, the rate of interracial marriage in the United States is at a historical high, as the percent of interracial marriages has doubled over the past three decades (Passel, Wang, & Taylor, 2010; Swarns, 2012; Wang, 2012). Since Asian Americans have the highest rate of interracial marriage, with nearly 30% of marriages being interracial, and because Asians were the fastest growing ethnic or racial group in the U.S. during 2012 due to immigration, evidence suggests the rate of growth of mixed race Asians could increase in the coming decades. More specifically, demographers estimate that the Asian American population will triple in size in the next thirty years to approximately 41 million by 2050 (Pew Research Center, 2012). And many estimate that the mixed race Asian community could grow to a third of the total Asian American population in that time, making it the largest subgroup of Asian Americans (Perez & Hirschman, 2009).

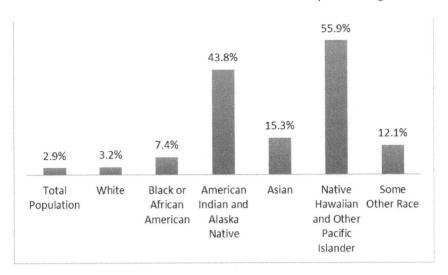

FIGURE 3.1.   Percentage of Major Race Groups, 2010. Source: U.S. Census Bureau, 2010 Census Redistricting Data (Public Law 94–171)Summary File, Table PI

For those mixed race individuals with Asian heritage, their narratives have been inextricably linked to the imperialist history of the United States military and of other colonial powers of the west (Chludzinski, 2009; Gamble, 2009; Taniguchi & Heindenreich, 2005). During and after World War II, the Vietnam War, and the Korean War, hundreds of thousands of mixed race Asian children were born to Asian women and U.S. servicemen (Laping, 2013; Williams-Leon & Nakashima, 2001). Officially termed by the U.S. government "Amerasian," these children were often discriminated against by both their Asian and American communities since they were thought to be the offspring of illegitimate unions with "bar girls" or prostitutes (Laping, 2013; Valverde, 1992; Williams, 1992). As a result of both societies' negative image of these Amerasian children, mixed Asian identity was not viewed as a positive aspect of one's life but rather was viewed as a deficit or liability (Gamble, 2009; Williams, 1992).

Despite significant legal and legislative victories such as the Supreme Court's ruling in the *Loving vs. Virginia* case in 1967, which deemed anti-miscegenation laws unconstitutional, and the Amerasian Act of 1982, which provided immigration status to children who were born after December 31, 1950 and before October 22, 1982 of an American father and an Asian mother from Cambodia, Korea, Laos, Thailand, or Vietnam, the historic legacy of the early mixed race experience still persists in our culture today (Laping, 2013). Still seen by many as illegitimate and uncouth, the onus to prove their authenticity as Americans and as legitimate members of the Asian American community falls on the mixed raced person. However, in reality, the culture of the U.S. military not only contributed to the rate at which these children were born but—even more shockingly—to the rate at which these children were abandoned and left without fathers. In the case of Jimmy Edwards, then 22 years old in 1974, the seaman fell in love with and impregnated a young Filipino woman while deployed overseas but was ultimately not permitted to marry her by his commanding officer, whose consent was required (Laping, 2013).

To this day mixed race Asian American people from Japan and the Philippines are omitted from the Amerasian Act, despite the fact that tens of thousands of mixed race children were born of American men during their military service in those countries. The U.S. government continues to ignore these children, as they have done for decades, leaving them to fend for themselves in environments that are commonly unwelcoming, economically disadvantaged, and even overtly hostile, especially for those with African American heritage ("America's forgotten children", 2011; Laping, 2013). When the Amerasian Act was originally enacted, the appearance of western features was enough to be granted a visa, whereas now applicants are required to submit evidence in the form of letters, photos, or DNA, ostensibly furthering the notion of perpetual foreigner that many Asian Americans endure ("America's forgotten children", 2011). Although recently deceased Senator Daniel Inouye of Hawaii repeatedly attempted introduce a bill to amend the Act, the Senate Judiciary Committee routinely rejected the proposal because they claimed these children were not a product of war, that they were not victims of discrimination in their countries, and that they were the product of relations with prostitutes, again furthering the false narratives for mixed race Asians (Laping, 2013).

Conversely, there is a growing movement of mixed race Asian people who have embraced their pluralistic racial identity and have formed affinity groups with other people who share their cultural mix or with other mixed race people generally (Gamble, 2009; Williams, 2003). Although many from both the majority and from monoracial minority groups frequently doubt the existence or the legitimacy of a mixed race community, these communities exist and are growing in size and political prominence. Progress, according to Adriane Gamble, is "prompted in large part by student organizing" from which "the mixed race community has begun to gain legitimacy in the past decade" (2009, p. 15). Starting in the 1990s, Hapa student and community groups have provided "a reference group, a group consciousness, role models, and terminology for identification" (Gamble, 2009, p. 15). Changing perceptions of mixed-raced people—brought about by the efforts of grass roots organizations, the institutionalization of new terms, and new ways of conceptualizing the complicated nature of race, especially in the U.S.—have given those who identify as mixed-race a platform on which to advocate for the inclusion of their experiences in both national and institutional policies. For the first time in history, mixed race Asians have a positive lens through which to view their identity; they have strong role models and terms that do not have a western imperialism connotation or deficient orientation.

REVIEW OF THE LITERATURE

According to Solórzano, Ceja, and Yosso (2000), "microaggressions are subtle insults (verbal, nonverbal and/or visual) directed toward people of color, often automatically or unconsciously" (p. 60). Persistent microaggressions are often the impetus for the development of student services or student organizations for mixed race students on campus (Renn, 2004). As such, it is not surprising that Hapa movements emerge from within the academy (Gamble, 2009). From the proliferation of courses and research on multiracial people to the founding of seminal mixed race organizations like the Mavin Foundation, which was started by a student at Wesleyan University, colleges and universities are uniquely positioned not only to support their individual mixed race students but to promote and support the mixed community on a larger scale (Mavin Foundation, 2011).

However, several studies have illustrated that many mixed race college students experience feelings of being pulled between groups, isolation and invisibility, and difficulty navigating social and physical spaces on campus (Kellogg & Lidell, 2012; King, 2008; Museus, Yee, & Lambe, 2011; Ozaki & Johnston, 2008). From insensitive faculty and administration to lack of inclusion in curriculum and student services, biracial and multiracial students often face additional challenges "fitting in" or finding their place in their university communities, which are particularly problematic considering the rate at which this population is growing (Jourdan, 2006; King, 2011).

Not only do many colleges and universities lack specific student services for multiracial students or courses that are reflective of their identities, but also most schools have not even kept accurate data on mixed students. Even though the United States Office of Management and Budget released new guidelines for racial and ethnic data to include the option for multiracial people to select more than one race in 1997, most universities did not immediately change their data collection method because they had not been obligated to do so by the National Center for Education Statistics (Renn & Lunceford, 2004). A full decade later, in 2007, the Department of Education disseminated guiding principles on collecting data on race and gave institutions another three to four years to implement such changes (Kellogg & Niskode, 2008). The way institutions of higher education have dragged their feet instead of leading the charge on more inclusive data collection has the potential of sending nonverbal signals to these students about how the institution values or does not value them as members of their community (Strange & Banning, 2001). Since the populations of students entering college in the coming years and decades will only become more and more diverse, truly understanding the demographics of a student body will be essential for institutions to efficiently track access and completion rates, allocate resources, and sufficiently support and nurture these students' development (Kellog & Niskode, 2008; Renn & Lunceford, 2004).

On the other hand, in the most fundamental area of higher education—curriculum—there is an increasing number of courses related to multiracial issues on course rosters across the country. From general survey courses such as "Multiracial America" at Rice University and "Mixed Race Studies: A Comparative Focus" at San Francisco State University to courses on subcategories of the mixed race community such as "Multiracial Asian Pacific American Issues" at University of California Davis, academic discourse and research is more accessible than ever before (MixedRaceStudies.org, 2013). "Such courses can help students challenge fixed and rigid racial categories and provide the language, theory and cognitive tools to understand the complexity of race" (Kellogg & Niskode, 2008, p. 98). For numerous mixed race students, college is the first time they have been able to directly study about their own history and their own community. It is the first time they are presented with resources and common language to express their identities, which can be empowering and can result in better academic outcomes (Kellog & Niskode, 2008; Renn, 2004). Students who see their identities reflected in the campus culture and who have strong cultural support through social groups are more likely to persist towards graduation (Kuh & Love, 2000; Strange & Banning, 2001). More specifically, "Cognitive development, perspective-taking, critical thinking, academic achievement and problem-solving skills are among the outcomes that researches have consistently noted in studies about the effects of inclusive pedagogy and curricula" (Quaye & Harper, 2007, p. 34).

For many mixed-race Asian Americans, there is also an overemphasis on physical appearance (Bradshaw, 1992). Since they may not physically represent their cultural heritages, many people question the legitimacy of their membership in a particular community or their loyalty to their ethnic/racial cultures. Terms like "exotic, interesting, fascinating" may sound innocuous, but for mixed race Asian American women in particular they connote feelings of otherness and foreignness (Bradshaw, 1992; King, 2011). Additionally, many Hapa women are characterized as being overtly sexual, which has roots in how some Asian women were conceptualized during the 20th century in the media and fictional performances like *Miss Saigon, Madame Butterfly*, and countless others that depict Asian women as tragic, hypersexual, prostitutes, and merely the object of male sexual desires (Bradshaw, 1992; Shimizu, 2007, p. 24).

Furthermore, multiracial individuals are subject to overt forms of racism and discriminations just like their monoracial peers. Although there is little research in this area, Johnston and Nadal (2010) recently published a book chapter that looks at five common categories of microaggressions that multiracial people are subject to in their daily lives. These categories include the following:

1.   "Exclusion or isolation" in which a person is constantly asked to define their ethnicities. The multiracial person is not permitted to possess a dual identity and bears the onus to choose one or the other.
2.   "Exoticization and objectification," which can appear like a compliment but can also project the narrative of "other" or even non-human. The multiracial person is regularly asked "What are you?".

3. "Assumptions of monoracial identity" which are typically based on overall appearance and phenotypes. In these situations, a multiracial person may be exposed to prejudiced comments about their identity group because others do not perceive them to be a part of their ethnic group.

4. "Denial of mulitraciality," where others try to designate a mixed person's race as monoracial or which can result in the multiracial person being accused of trying to pass as White.

5. "Pathologizing of identity and experiences," which is when their experiences are deemed out of the ordinary or strange. Multiracial people are seen as a mistake or as confused (2010, p. 133).

These microaggressions combine to create environments and experiences for multiracial people that can lead to psychological stress and other developmental issues (Johnston & Nadal, 2010). Such racist sentiments also stem from and overlap with the very influence of the MMM.

Since the 1960s, the Model Minority Myth (Teranishi, 2010) has become the dominant narrative by which society has come to understand and make sense of Asian individuals. It has also been used to measure the past, present, and future social and economic achievement (or lack thereof) of all racial minorities in the U.S. (Chou & Feagin, 2008; Hartlep, 2013, 2014). The MMM reinforces a racial hierarchy that places White social mores as the benchmark for social and economic success, and it deems Asians to be the superior minority group to which all other minorities must defer as a model of successful assimilation and complicity to those very mores—to name a few: a belief in personal agency; communicating proficiently both verbally (by speaking proficient English) and non-verbally (by dressing and gesturing in ways popularized by White communities). In essence, the model minority myth creates the illusion of a universal success that homogenizes variation among Asian communities and erodes the struggles—rooted from issues of health, immigration, poverty, and language and education—faced by the very same on a daily basis.

According to Chou and Feagin (2008), the purpose of the model minority myth is to demonstrate the lack of barriers to social upward mobility on the part of White individuals. Within this illusion, society would ask: If Asians can achieve success, why cannot other racial minorities meet or exceed the same level of success? For the individual, the myth "creates stressful and unrealistic expectations, self- and externally imposed, that Asian Americans should succeed in fitting the stereotype or be deemed failures" and "unrealistic expectations within, and outside, Asian American communities that negatively impact all Asian Americans" (Chou & Feagin, 2008, p. 139). Do the expectations experienced by an individual of mixed-Asian race deviate from the commonly postulated norms of the myth? How are these norms received and conceptualized by mixed-Asian race students? How do these norms operate to constrain, or even to liberate mixed-Asian race students? Because the influence of the myth is heavily dependent upon physical appearance and its associated characteristics and personal self-identity, and the challenges faced by mixed-race individuals are quite distinct from monoracial individuals, we suggest that the myth operates in less linear ways. Indeed, the influence of this dominant narrative can be similarly damaging to mixed-race individuals, but the process in which the myth operates in their daily lives is situational and demands movement.

TERMINOLOGY

There is a great deal of debate within the academic community and the general public about terms used to describe people of mixed racial backgrounds, particularly for mixed race Asian Americans. Many argue that terms like Eurasian, Afroasian and Amerasian frame the person's identity in relation to western forces of colonization and imperialism (Gamble, 2009; Taniguchi & Heindenreich, 2005). "The term Eurasian dates to European colonies in Asia, and the term Amerasian was first coined to describe the offspring of American military men and Asian women during occupations of Japan, Korea, Vietnam, and the Philippines. The history of imperialism, and perceived illegitimacy of such unions resulted in extreme negative connotations for the terms" (Gamble, 2009, p. 10).

On the other hand, terms like mixed race Asian American or Hapa are more contemporary and are generally embraced by the individuals who own that identity; however, they too are not without controversy[1]. The term Hapa has its origins in the Hawaiian Islands from as early as the late 1700s. Hapa, which directly translates as "half" or "part," was originally used to describe people of half native Hawaiian descent. In the early 1990s, many mixed race organizations adopted the term for mixed race Asian Americans. However, this has faced intense resistance from many in the Hawaiian community, particularly those who are a part of the Hawaiian sovereignty movement, who feel that co-opting the term is a form of cultural colonization (Taniguchi & Heindenreich, 2005). Today it is used in Hawaii to describe anyone of mixed heritage (Taniguchi & Heindenreich, 2005). Additionally, some are critical of the ambiguity of the term since it is not clear if the word encompasses any mixed person with Asian heritage or if it is limited to Asian/Whites. Supporters of the Hapa identity argue that language is fluid, and it evolves, typically outside of the bounds or control of the culture of origin. They claim that the word is used in homage to the rich and unique multiracial society in Hawaii, which has a long history of blending cultures and traditions from other nations, as evidenced in their food, regional language, and cultural customs (Taniguchi & Heindenreich, 2005).

---

[1] For the purposes of this chapter, we use the terms mixed race Asian American and Hapa interchangeably. Additionally, in our use of the terms, we include anyone with mixed Asian heritage. While we understand and empathize with the controversy surrounding the term Hapa, we also support the notion that "speaking ones' name is an act of self-validation; choosing that name even more so" (Taniguchi & Heindenreich, 2005, p. 136).

THEORETICAL FRAMEWORK: IDENTITY DEVELOPMENT OF
MULTIRACIAL PEOPLE

In the 1920s and 1930s, well known University of Chicago sociologists Robert E. Park and his mentee Evert Stonequist hypothesized that mixed race people were likely to have an unstable character and to live permanently marginal lives, as they were never fully accepted and incorporated into either of their various ethnic groups (Stonequist, 1937). During the 1920s and 1930s, the American public was not only intolerant of mixed people but rather antagonistic. This was during the height of Jim Crow laws, which enforced the separation of Whites and Blacks.

In more contemporary research on mixed race identity, there is still a stage of development in which a person can live on the margins of society or between their cultures; however, it is not a fixed or permanent state like Stonequist suggested, but rather a period along the development continuum (Renn, 2004; Root, 2000). Each generation has brought about more inclusive models of multiracial identity development, including Carlos Poston's theory (1990), which proposed that biracial identity development was a unique experience and which expanded upon existing frameworks for people from one race to include phases of development specific to biracial individuals. In the same year, Root (1990) posited that societal racism impacts identity, taking into consideration the role of external forces on an individual's choice of racial identity classification. According to Bradshaw (1992), "As such, 'any complete understanding of the biracial experience must account for effects of social and institutionalized racism, false assumptions about racial purity and intrapersonal and familial factors that affect results of self-identity and racial identity" (p. 78).

Root (1990) also proposed a new category of "biracial" as an identity in and of itself and offered a fresh perspective that identity was fluid and could change over time and space. She also penned the "Bill of Rights for People of Mixed Heritage," which gave a voice to the multiracial experience and illustrated the external and internal conflicts that are common for this community, such as "I have the right not to justify my ethnic legitimacy" or "I have the right to have loyalties and identification with more than one group of people" (Root, 1996, p. 7).

Like Root, most recent theorists take into account the influence of societal values and the multiple layers of a person's social class, race, gender, and other affinity groups (Creswell, 2007; Renn, 2003, 2004). Building off of Root's model, Kris Renn established the five patterns of identity in mixed race students theory, which she developed using Bronfenbrenner's ecological "Person-Process-Context-Time" model because it is a useful frame to explore fluid concepts such as identity and can be used to explore the interactions of a person and their environment (Renn, 2004). The five patterns Renn (2000) identified include:

1. Student holds a monoracial identity, which means they identify themselves as belonging to one race.

2. Student holds multiple monoracial identities. These students have also been said to engage in "border crossings" where they shift from one culture to another.
3. Student holds a multiracial identity, which means that they identify with being mixed race.
4. Student holds an extra racial identity by deconstructing race or opting out of identification with U.S. racial categories.
5. Student holds a situation identity (Renn, 2008, p. 16). Typically, the environment and people in that environment dictate which identity is dominant.

It is important to note that these are not mutually exclusive categories; an individual can fit one or multiple patterns of identity and shift at several points throughout their lives. As such, we anchor the design of the study and the analysis of its results within Renn's modification of Bronfenbrenner's ecological model.

METHOD

We produced a life history in which members of the team interviewed the member of the team who identifies as a Hapa. This process allowed an individual to share her personal story and perspectives while simultaneously receiving feedback, reassurance, and exploration from members of the research team. The interview process was a rich conversation of sharing, challenging, and learning on the part of the team. According to Tierney (2013), life history can "offer a glimpse into one person's life and hopefully provoke questions and ideas about how that individual lives his or her life and makes sense of it" (p. 260).

The interview lasted two hours and featured the first author answering a multitude of questions that reflect Renn's (2000) five patterns for mixed race student theory and how these patterns of racial identification have influenced her personal and school life. Once the data were transcribed, each author conducted open coding to allow for the possibility of new themes, beyond what is explained in prior theories, to emerge (Creswell, 2007). We then came together to discuss and deliberate upon the following prominent themes that respond to our research questions.

FINDINGS AND DISCUSSIONS

Life history captured how identifying as Hapa unfolded in college and how the MMM worked to exacerbate the common struggles faced by mixed-race individuals. Our findings are structured around the two themes: (1) *One or the Other, Nothing in Between* and (2) *Border Crossing*.

One or the Other, Nothing in Between

Student experiences frequently include the participation in student organizations. Common among these organizations are race-based affinity groups. When

Amy first began college, she sought out community in relation to her ethnic identity. However, given the lack of diversity at her institution, the resources for minority students were bare and certainly did not include the histories and perspectives of students of mixed-race backgrounds. At best, Amy felt out of place, as if she did not belong.

> In the first weeks of my freshman year, I joined Asia Society, which was made up of about 20 Asian students from a range of countries. There were no other Korean Americans and one half Filipino and half White girl, who ended up being of my best friends a few years later. I think I only attended 2 or 3 meetings before I quit because I never felt like I belonged there. In fact, the student who ran the organization was very vocally anti-White people. She made lots of disparaging comments about the White students on campus, comments that were on the verge of bigotry such as "these rich white kids are so ignorant and stupid." I remember asking myself, "Does she realize I am white too? Is she trying to make me feel uncomfortable?"

Since the MMM defines the Asian American community as a singular entity without taking into account the diversity within the group, it precludes any deviations from that definition and, as a result, excludes mixed race Asian Americans. Student organizations at Ithaca College were developed on the notion of a mono-racial identity, constraining Amy's opportunities for a space that paid respect to her cultural background. However, colleges and universities can play an important role in encouraging students' identity development by creating dynamic environments where all students can explore who they are and see themselves reflected in the institution (Chickering & Reisser, 1993; Root, 2000; Strange & Banning, 2001). Although this claim is considered an established truth (King, 2008; Shang, 2008), the environment at Ithaca College, unfortunately, was inconsistent and insufficient to meet Amy's needs given the lack of a welcoming environment, peer groups, or mentors that reflected her identity group. Regrettably, this is too frequently the case for Hapas, as very few institutions of higher education in America have organizations specifically for students of mixed racial backgrounds (Renn, 2000). Moreover, a mono-racial identity also operated on an individual level. As described by Amy, the student leader used language that was exclusionary to non-Asians, making Amy, who identifies as Korean as well as White, feel like a minority.

It was not until her senior year that Amy felt there was an institutionally sanctioned place for her to explore her identity, and even then it was really the individual professor who made all the difference.

> In the second semester of my senior year, I took the first Asian American studies course that was offered during my time at Ithaca. It was called the Asian American Experience, and there were about 12 students in the class, and four of us were Hapa. As such, our professor emphasized issues related to Hapa identity such as interracial marriage and anti-miscegenation laws. It was the first time in my life that I had the opportunity to explore my identity from an academic perspective. Although I had

heard the term Hapa from the Internet, Professor Shinagawa, who hailed from UC Berkeley, taught us about its Hawaiian origins and of the evolution of the term. It was an incredibly eye opening and enriching experience. In retrospect, he was the only Asian professor I had in undergrad, and as far as I can remember he was the only visible Asian American faculty member or administrator on campus.

It is through the interaction with peers, college administrators, and faculty, that identity development occurs (Jourdan, 2006; Ozaki & Johnston, 2008; Renn, 2004). In Amy's case, the first opportunity to explore her mixed race identity in an academic setting came during her final semester at college. As a relatively young field, Asian American Studies (Wei, 1992) continues to develop to make sense of and institutionalize or build on theoretical frameworks to provide legitimacy to the experiences of Asians and Asian Americans, as well as Pacific Islanders and Native Hawaiians. For Amy, it gave her the language (i.e., Hapa) by which to understand how her life has unfolded and her current experiences as they relate to the U.S. However, formal research on mixed-race individuals in higher education is nearly non-existent. In Amy's case, the recognition and discourse of mixed-race individuals came under the umbrella of a field devoted primarily to the histories and experiences of monoracial communities. The exclusion of any group in curriculum, both formally and informally, may reinforce its continued invisibility and communicate a message of insignificance to the broader university community. Consequently, the majority of her collegiate years were spent struggling to find her place on campus and, ultimately, in the workplace. There were no administrators who looked like her who could serve as a reference point or mentor. And there were not enough mixed race students who openly identified as such, or were comfortable identifying as mixed, to create a specific organization to support multiracial students.

Border Crossings

Since Amy's institution lacked structures of support and safe spaces to explore her identity, she navigated her institution by engaging in "Border Crossings," where she held multiple monoracial identities depending on her environment (Renn, 2004).

My Freshman and Sophomore year, most of my close group of friends were white, but I also had many friends who were students of color too. Being mixed race gave me access to both communities, in a way that seemed to make others uncomfortable. For example, there was a TV room in the Student Union that was almost exclusively used by Students of Color. It was almost a sanctuary for Students of Color because White students were intimidated to enter, and there were no other options like a multicultural center at the time. Every time I walked by that room, I would stop by to see if any of my friends were there. I did get the occasional questioning look from people who didn't know me since I just look White to many people. But more strikingly, some of my White friends would ask, "What were you doing in the TV lounge?" as if I didn't belong there.

Like Amy, many students from a multiracial background live with the constant pressure to choose just one part of their identity because others may be uncomfortable with the ambiguity of their racial identity. Self-identifying as mixed-race, Amy could never satisfy the unspoken racial criteria set forth by each group. Physical ambiguity precluded Amy from truly accessing and deriving the benefits of developing meaningful relationships among her peers. As several researchers have noted with monoracial minorities, campus environments can have an impact, both positive and negative, on the experiences of college students (Brown, 2001; Gaskins, 1999; Harper & Quaye, 2007). The same holds true for mixed race students. Campuses with physical spaces and support structures lend themselves to a more healthy approach to multiracial identity. Those that are more polarized by White and monoracial minority groups, leave biracial students stuck in the middle (King, 2008; Renn 2004).

Since many biracial and multiracial students may appear physically ambiguous, they can feel out of place or unwelcome at monoracial cultural centers and among the students from the majority (King, 2008; Renn, 2004). In contrast, where there were individuals who identified as mixed-race, Amy's experience was quite different:

> In my junior year, I spent a semester on Ithaca's Los Angeles campus with about 100 other students from the Communications School. The group of friends I made in LA ended up being my primary social group for the rest of college; among them were 4 other mixed race students. I think part of the reason I ultimately chose them over my previous group of friends was due to the constant pressure to choose just one aspect of my identity and to switch between identities. It became really tiresome. With my LA friends, I found other people who understood that pressure and exactly what I was going through.

The expectations and norms commonly used to perceive and understand monoracial individuals were not at serious play in this situation. Because Amy's friends were also mixed-race, the regulations of the myth had little influence in this social circle. Research has demonstrated the importance of peer groups in the identity development process (Renn, 2000; Root, 2000). Students need to feel like they fit in and to feel connected to those around them. The opportunity to leave campus provided Amy with a chance to explore other social circles on campus, with whom she could be herself without question and without having to deal with the frequent microaggressions experienced by mixed race people.

Back on the main campus, Amy noted a common experience that defined her interactions among her college peers:

> Some people see me and see a White person. In those cases, it has no impact on my life. Some people see me as 100% Asian, and in those instances that comes with

all the expectations that are placed on Asians to succeed. And some other people, a rather small group in comparison, see me as Hapa. And in those instances, the external pressures placed on me are compounded.

Being of mixed-race, Amy is frequently bombarded and pushed and pulled across racial communities. Depending on the situation, Amy can come to experience varying degrees of the MMM, which can also compound and amplify to reinforce the consequences of overlapping racial categorization. Because of her mixed-race background, Amy became susceptible to stereotypes associated with both Whites and Asians. According to Amy:

> Not only am I expected to be smart, good at math, and a hard worker like my Asian half, but I am also expected to be a good communicator, able to access power and belong in mainstream culture like my White half. And because I am Hapa, I am expected to be attractive and more successful because I have the best of both worlds. People assume that we have the best traits of both cultures.

As Asian and White, Amy is expected to achieve and fail both academically *and* socially. These polarizing expectations stem from different monoracial individuals and their dependency on the idea of racial purity as a criterion for inclusion in their communities. In Amy's case, the expectation to achieve academically emerged from her White peers, who held the belief that being of Asian ancestry granted Amy inherent intelligence and the accomplishments commonly associated with it. In contrast, the expectation to be upwardly socially mobile is contingent upon identifying as White. Her Asian peers perceived the Whites as dominant in spaces of power. As mixed-race, Amy is perceived to be granted seamless access to these spaces and the opportunities that abound within them. Additionally, because Amy is mixed-race, the myth places her above those who solely identify as Asian:

> If Asians are considered the "best minority group" or the group that is closest to White, rather, then being half Asian and half white kind of makes me even more of a model minority based on that notion.

More recently, discourse and images around the beauty of mixed-race individuals have surfaced across magazines and the casting of characters in television and movies (Beltran, 2005). Hapa actresses like Olivia Munn, Maggie Q, and Kristin Kreuk feature prominently in prime time television, advertisements, and Men's magazines. Researchers have also begun to explore this phenomenon. Psychologists at the University of Western Australia found that both their white and Asian participants selected photos of mixed race Asians to be the most attractive (Adams, 2006). To be beautiful is to be racially mixed. Similar to the myth surrounding Asians as human calculators, these stereotypes can be detrimental for mixed-race individuals who may not be able to successfully conform to those stereotypes.

I think there is this idea that Hapas are more attractive than monoracial Asians, which is problematic because it is essentially saying that our White features make us that way. I have had other people have discussions about my appearance, where they deconstruct my features: "Oh you have really slanted eyes so I can see that you are part Asian, but your nose and lips are more White because they are more pronounced."

Being mixed race, Amy found it more difficult to navigate the MMM because of the uncertainty in how others perceive her identity. The MMM was only applicable in her life when people knew she was Asian or if they could identify her Asian features. In her experience, each situation was unique because of her racial ambiguity. How others applied the Model Minority Myth varied greatly from individual to individual.

During Amy's collegiate experience, the MMM exacerbated the challenges she faced in navigating social and academic spaces on campus. Since all Asian Americans students were seen as the same or as belonging to one group under the MMM—despite the fact that there is great variation in academic and economic success between various Asian ethnicities in America—she felt excluded from student organizations and social spaces intended for Asian Americans.

Unlike her Asian American peers, who can anticipate how to respond to other people's expectations of their success and what stereotypes exist in society related to their identity, Amy had to develop skills to recognize and respond to any number of expectations others placed on her based on their presumptions of her racial identity. By not knowing how an individual will perceive them, Hapas cannot anticipate the expectations and preconceived notions the individual is applying. Because the MMM has such varied outcomes for mixed individuals, that sporadic effect is predicated on the assumption that being mixed race is not an identity in itself. Not only does it force you to conform to certain stereotypes it precludes you from identifying as mixed race.

RECOMMENDATIONS AND REFLECTIONS

Depending on their physical appearance, family name, and language abilities, Hapas often experience the same pressures and expectations placed on Asian Americans to live up to the model minority stereotype. However, unlike their monoracial Asian counterparts, they also experience other challenges specifically because of the duality of their identity. They experience pressures from both of their ethnicities as well as society as a whole to choose one aspect of their identity. They experience pressure to demonstrate their loyalty to one particular group or to prove authenticity among various groups. Whether intentional or not, they often experience pressures from various constituencies on their college campuses. As such, it is important to note the role all campus staff, administrators, faculty, and student groups can play in creating more inclusive environments and fostering open dialogue around Hapa issues and issues of multiracial identity generally.

In a review of 35 institutions' student services for mixed race students, Wong and Buckner (2008) found that most colleges structured their programs in one of two ways, with dedicated professional staff and/or strong student leadership. Institutions like New York University, the University of California campuses, and several other notably diverse schools, are able to have stronger programs for mixed students due to the presence of a formal staff member who is responsible for supporting students and increasing awareness of multiracial issues in the campus community as a whole (Wong & Buckner, 2008). Additionally, having a full-time university employee supporting mixed student initiatives provides continuity in programming and historical knowledge. They can also help to foster dialogue between multiracial and monoracial minority organizations on campus, as these relationships can frequently be contentious (Ozaki & Johnston, 2008). And since most administrators who manage multiracial student services are themselves from more than one racial background, they are uniquely positioned to support and advise students, often from their own firsthand experiences living as a mixed person.

Given the scarce resources available for minorities, it may not be possible for some campuses to provide physical spaces or a dedicated staff member for mixed students. In these cases, it is even more crucial that all staff, but more specifically those who work in cultural/ethnic-based organizations, are provided with training and education on how to support multiracial students. College administrators, like anyone, can become accustomed and acculturated to the narratives surrounding mixed race people and can perpetuate outdated ideas, without understanding the negative consequences of their rhetoric. In a study on biracial and multiracial student services, an administrator who was responsible for African American student services was quoted as follows: "As far as I'm concerned, if you have a drop of Black in you, you're Black" (Literte, 2010, p. 128). And another high-level administrator responsible for Asian American student services questioned, "Is there really a biracial identity...I'm not sure. A person may identify with both sides but as far as there being a separate biracial identity, I think it's unclear whether there is one" (Literte, 2010, p. 129). Clearly, these administrators have their own biases related to race, but their comments deny these students' identities, an experience that is all too familiar in their lives. According to Banning and Whitt, "An inclusive campus community requires staff and students who are comfortable with people from any culture, and whose attitudes, language and behavior reflect awareness and sensitivity to other cultures and backgrounds" (as cited in Harper, 2008, p. 40). Consequently, colleges and universities should actively work to recruit more multiracial faculty and administrators to act as mentors to mixed students (King, 2008).

Beyond specific courses related to multiracial issues, all faculty members and university administrators can play a significant role in creating more hospitable spaces in their classrooms and campuses by not taking a binary approach to race and by including issues related to biracial and multiracial in course discussion, readings, and co-curricular programming (King, 2008). Instead of seeing multiracial people as marginal, it is time we in the higher education community begin to embrace the idea and the possibilities of mixed race groups to challenge and disarm existing theories on race like the MMM, and to advance the discourse about race beyond black vs. white to a more inclusive and realistic conversation.

Questions for Reflection

1. In what ways does the inclusion of Hapas in the Asian American narrative help to dispel the Model Minority Myth?
2. How do Hapas challenge the Model Minority Myth?
3. As a growing proportion of the Asian American population, what will be an impact of Hapas on the Asian American community in the coming years?
4. As educators, how can we be more inclusive in our practice towards mixed race Asian Americans and other multiracial students?
5. Hapas represent a complexity in the way race and ethnicity are conceptualized and used in research. How does this narrative bring to bear additional questions and criticisms about current research methods?

REFERENCES

Adams, W. L. (2006, January 1). Mixed race, pretty face? *Psychology Today.* Retrieved December 1, 2014, from http://www.psychologytoday.com/articles/200512/mixed-race-pretty-face

America's forgotten children [Video file]. (2011, September 13). Retrieved December 1, 2014, from http://stream.aljazeera.com/story/americas-forgotten-children

Beltràn, M. C. (2005). The new Hollywood racelessness: Only the fast, furious, (and multiracial)Will Survive. *Cinema Journal, 44*(2), 50–67.

Bradshaw, C. K. (1992). Beauty and the Beast: On racial ambiguity. In M. P. P. Root (Ed.), *Racially Mixed People in America* (pp. 77–90). Newbury Park, CA: Sage.

Brown, U. M. (2001). *The interracial experience: Growing up Black/White racially mixed in the United States.* Westport, CT: Praeger.

Chickering, A. W., & Reisser, L. (1993). *Education and identity* (2nd ed.). San Francisco, CA:Jossey-Bass.

Chludzinski, K. (2009). The fear of colonial miscegenation in the British Colonies of southeast Asia. *The Forum: Cal Poly's Journal of History, 1*(1), 54–64. Retrieved December 1, 2014, from http://digitalcommons.calpoly.edu/forum/vol1/iss1/8

Chou, R. S., & Feagin, J. R. (2008). *The myth of the model minority: Asian Americans facing racism.* Boulder, CO: Paradigm.

Creswell, J. W. (2007). *Qualitative inquiry and research design: Choosing among five approaches* (2nd ed.). Thousand Oaks, CA: Sage.

Espiritu, Y L. (1992). *Asian American panethnicity: Bridging institutions and identities.* Philadelphia, PA: Temple University Press.

Gaskins, P. F. (1999). *What are you?* New York: Holt.

Gamble, A. E. (2009). Hapas: Emerging identity, emerging terms and labels & the social construction of race. *Stanford Journal of Asian American Studies, 2*, 1–20.

Harper, S. R. (2008). *Creating inclusive campus environments for cross-cultural learning and student engagement*. Washington, DC: NASPA.

Harper, S. R., & Quaye, S. J. (2007). Student organizations as venues for Black identity expression and development among African American male student leaders. *Journal of College Student Development, 48*, 127–144.

Hartlep, N. D. (2013). *The model minority stereotype: Demystifying Asian American success*. Charlotte, NC: Information Age.

Hartlep, N. D. (Ed.). (2014). *The model minority stereotype reader: Critical and challenging readings for the 21st century*. San Diego, CA: Cognella Publishing.

Johnston , M. P., & Nadal , K. L. (2010). Multiracial microaggressions: Exposing monoracism in everyday life and clinical practice. In D. W. Sue (Ed.), *Microaggressions and marginality: Manifestation, dynamics, and impact* (pp. 123–144). New York, NY: John Wiley & Sons.

Jourdan, A. (2006). The impact of the family environment on the ethnic identity development of multiethnic college students. *Journal of Counseling and Development, 84*(3), 328–340.

Jones, N. A., & Bullock, J. J. (2013). Understanding who reported multiple races in the U.S. decennial census: Results from census 2000 and the 2010 Census. *Family Relations, 62*(1), 5–16.

Kellogg, A. H., & Lidell, D. L. (2012). "Not half but double": Exploring critical incidents in the racial identity of multiracial college students. *Journal of College Student Development, 53*(4), 524–541.

Kellogg, A., & Niskode, A. S. (2008). Student affairs and higher education policy issues related to multiracial students. *New Directions for Student Services, 123*, 93–102.

King, A. R. (2008). Student perspectives on multiracial identity. *New Directions for Student Services, 123*, 33–41.

King, A. R. (2011) Environmental influences on the development of female college students who identify as multiracial/biracial-bisexual/pansexual. *Journal of College Student Development, 54*(4), 440–455.

Kuh, G. D., & Love, P. G. (2000). A cultural perspective on student departure. In J. Braxton (Ed.), *Reworking the student departure puzzle* (pp. 196–212). Nashville, TN: Vanderbilt University Press.

Laping, C. M. (2013, May 27). The forgotten Amerasians. *The New York Times*. Retrieved December 1, 2014, from http://www.nytimes.com/2013/05/28/opinion/the-forgotten-amerasians.html

Literte, P. E. (2010). Revising race: How biracial students are changing and challenging student services. *Journal of College Student Development, 51*(2), 115–134.

Mavin Foundation. (2011). About Mavin. Retrieved December 1, 2014, from http://www.mavinfoundation.org/new/about/purpose/

Museus, S. D., Yee, A. L., & Lambe, S. A. (2011). Multiracial in a monoracial world: Student stories of racial dissolution on the colorblind campus. *About Campus, 16*(4), 20–25.

MixedRaceStudies.org. (2013). *Scholarly perspectives on the mixed race experience*. Retrieved December 1, 2014, from http://www.mixedracestudies.org/wordpress/?cat=1564

Ozaki, C. C., & Johnston, M. (2008). The space in between: Issues for multiracial student organizations and advising. *New Directions for Student Services, 123*, 53–61.

Passel, J. S., Wang, W., & Taylor, P. (2010, June 4). One-in-seven new U.S. marriages is interracial or interethnic, *Pew Research Center*. Retrieved December 1, 2014, from http://www.pewsocialtrends.org/2010/06/04/marrying-out/

Perez, A. D., & Hirschman, C. (2009). The changing racial and ethnic composition of the U.S. population: Emerging American identities. *Population and Development Review*, *35*(1), 1–51.

Pew Research Center. (2012). *The rise of Asian Americans*. Retrieved December 1, 2014, from http://www.pewsocialtrends.org/2012/06/19/the-rise-of-asianamericans/

Poston, W. S. C. (1990). The biracial identity development model: A needed addition. *Journal of Counseling and Development, 69*(2), 152–155.

Quaye, S. J., & Harper, S. R. (2007). Shifting the onus from racial/ethnic minority students to faculty: Accountability for culturally inclusive pedagogy and curricula. *Liberal Education, 92*(3), 32–39.

Renn, K. A. (2000). Patterns of situational identity among biracial and multiracial college students. *The Review of Higher Education, 23*(4), 399–420.

Renn, K. A. (2003). Understanding the identities of mixed race college students through a developmental ecology lens. *Journal of College Student Development, 44*(3), 383–403.

Renn, K. A. (2004). *Mixed race college student: The ecology of identity, race, and community on campus.* Albany, NY: State University of New York Press.

Renn, K. A. (2008). Research on bi- and multiracial identity development: Overview and synthesis. In K. A. Renn & P. Shang (Eds.), *Biracial and multiracial college students: Theory, research, and best practices in student affairs* (pp. 13–21). San Francisco, CA: Jossey-Bass.

Renn, K. A., & Lunceford, C. J. (2004). Because the numbers matter: Transforming postsecondary education data on student race and ethnicity to meet the challenges of a changing nation. *Education Policy, 18*(5), 752–783.

Root, M. P. P. (1990). Resolving 'other' status: identity development of biracial Individuals. *Women and Therapy, 9*(1–2), 185–205.

Root, M. P. P. (1996). A bill of rights for racially mixed people. In M. P. P. Root (Ed.), *The Multiracial experience: Racial borders as the new frontier* (pp. 3–14). Thousand Oaks, CA: Sage.

Root, M. P. P. (2000). Rethinking racial identity development: An ecological framework. In P. Spickard & J. Burroughs (Eds.) *We are a people: Narrative and multiplicity inconstructing ethnic identity* (pp. 205–220). Philadelphia, PA: Temple University Press.

Shang, P. (2008). An introduction to social and historical factors affecting multiracial college students. *New Directions for Student Services, 123*, 5–12.

Shimizu, C. P. (2007). *The Hypersexuality of race: Performing Asian/American women on screen and scene.* Durham, NC: Duke University Press.

Solórzano, D., Ceja, M., & Yosso, T. (2000). Critical race theory, racial microaggressions, and campus racial climate: The Experiences of African American college students. *The Journal of Negro Education, 69*(1/2), 60–73.

Stonequist, E. V. (1937). The *marginal man: A Study in personality and culture conflict.* New York, NY: Russell & Russell.

Strange, C. C. & Banning, J. H. (Ed). (2001). *Educating by design.* San Francisco, CA: Jossey-Bass.

Swarns, R. L. (2012, March 30). For Asian American couples, A tie that binds. *The New York Times*. Retrieved from http://www.nytimes.com/2012/04/01/fashion/more-asian-americans-marrying-within-their-race.html?pagewanted=all&_r=0

Taniguchi, A. S., & Heidenreich, L. (2005). Re-mix: Rethinking the use of 'Hapa' in mixed race Asian/Pacific Islander American community organizing. *WSU McNair Journal*, 135–146.

Teranishi, R. T. (2010). *Asians in the ivory tower: Dilemmas of racial inequality in American higher education*. New York, NY: Teachers College Press.

Tierney, W. G. (2013). Life history and identity. *The Review of Higher Education, 36*(2),255–282.

U.S. Census Bureau (2001). *Overview of race and Hispanic origin: Census 2000 Brief*. Retrieved December 1, 2014, from http://www.census.gov/prod/2001pubs/c2kbr01–1.pdf

U.S. Census Bureau (2010). *Overview of race and Hispanic origin: Census 2010 Briefs*. Retrieved December 1, 2014, from http://www.census.gov/prod/cen2010/briefs/c2010br-02

Valverde, K. L. C. (1992). From dust to gold: The Vietnamese Amerasian experience. In M. P. P. Root (Ed.), *Racially mixed people in America* (pp. 144–161). Newbury Park, CA: Sage.

Wang, W. (2012 February 16). The rise of intermarriage: Rates, characteristics vary by race and gender. Pew Research Center. Retrieved December 1, 2014, from http://www.pewsocialtrends.org/2012/02/16/the-rise-of-intermarriage/

Wei, W. (1992). *The Asian American movement*. Philadelphia, PA: Temple University Press.

Williams, T. K. (1992). Prism lives: Identity of binational Amerasians. In M. P. P. Root (Ed.), *Racially mixed people in America* (pp. 280–304). Newbury Park, CA: Sage.

Williams-Leon, T., & Nakashima, C. L. (2001). Reconfiguring race, rearticulating ethnicity. In T. Williams-Leon & C. L. Nakashima. (Eds.), *The sum of parts: Mixed-heritage Asian Americans* (pp. 3–13). Philadelphia, PA: Temple University Press.

Williams, K. M. (2003). From civil rights to the multiracial movement. In L. I. Winters & H. L. DeBose (Eds.), *New faces in a changing America: Multiracial identity in the twenty-first century* (pp. 85–97). Thousand Oaks, CA: Sage.

Wong, M. P., & Buckner, J. (2008). Multiracial student services come of age: The state of multiracial student services in higher education in the United States. *New Directions for Student Services, 123*, 43–51.

Yuen Thompson, B. (2000) Fence sitters, switch hitters, and bi-bi Girls: An exploration of hapa and bisexual girls. *Frontiers: A Journal of Women's Studies, 21*(1&2), 171–180.

CHAPTER 4

DEFIANT

The Strength of Asian American and Pacific Islander Women

Marissa S. Yenpasook, Annie Nguyen, Chia S. Her, and Valerie Ooka Pang

The purpose of this chapter is to discuss how Asian American and Pacific Islander (AAPI) women see themselves and how the roles they play in families and society arise out of strong cultural beliefs through the socialization process. We represent a group of four AAPI women (Pilipino-Thai-Chinese American, Vietnamese American, Hmong American, and Japanese American) who have come together to share our completely different life stories. In this chapter, we discuss our intersectionality and the roles it plays in perpetuating stereotypes about AAPI women as their experiences relate to the model minority stereotype.

Through our personal histories we will examine how our race, ethnicity, gender (female), class (lower to middle class income), and generation (1.5, second, and third generations) in the United States have had a profound effect on our development and behaviors. Our parents realized that racism is strong in U.S. society, and so we were taught that in order to be successful we must persevere through continual social oppression. Since education is seen as one of the major avenues to pursue upward social mobility, three of the four of us were expected to pursue

Killing the Model Minority Stereotype: Asian American Counterstories and Complicity,
pages 61–80.

advanced degrees. For one of us, education was not an expectation from parents. We may not have known how to get admitted to college or attain an university degree; however, through trial and resilience we find ourselves able to reflect on how the influences of our experiences oppose the model minority: we do not all earn National Science awards and then get into Harvard (Li & Wang, 2008).

CONCEPTUAL FRAMEWORK

Asian American and Pacific Islander (AAPI) women often find themselves influenced not only by their ethnic communities and families, but also by mainstream society. In order to understand the complexities that they are confronted with, we use Bronfenbrenner's (1994) ecology of human development to explain the range of environments and factors that contribute to the behaviors and values that AAPI women may exhibit. These behaviors may appear to be a form of the model minority stereotype, but in this chapter, we argue that the label is an outsider view that inaccurately labels AAPI women because much of what AAPI women do is based upon cultural values and a reaction to social oppression as explained by relative functionalism (Sue & Okazaki, 1990).

First, we present the theory of Bronfenbrenner and how various social systems and interactions influence the development of children (Pang, 2007). Bronfenbrenner initially identified four ecological systems; these will be discussed in this section.

Bronfenbrenner's (1994) theoretical framework describes the maturation of an individual and how the environment in which s/he develops shapes her/his growth. The ecological system explains that there is much overlap and interaction between layers, including the need to deal with social oppression in schools and society in general (Ngo & Lee, 2007). Below is a description of how an AAPI woman grows mature; diverse social systems shape her values and behaviors. For example, the traditional and rigid gender roles found in many AAPI families can also be reinforced by interactions and values found in the general society. The following four systems are seen as layers in the maturation of a person in this theory:

Microsystem—This environment includes daily interactions with people who are closest to the child and involves family members, peers, and teachers. For example, if a girl learns that women are to stay at home and take care of the dishes, laundry, and vacuuming, these are strong gender expectations that many AAPI women have been shaped by.

Mesosystem—As the spheres of influence increase, in this environment there are interactions between people within the microsystem. For example, teachers may speak with the parents of an AAPI daughter and explain how the individual is a good student and does not cause trouble in the classroom. The message is that AAPI girls are responsible and do not challenge authority. This powerful expectation is covertly exchanged.

Exosystem—The next ecological environment deals with influence of other settings that are part of the community. For example, if traditional gender roles and biases against Asian Americans and Pacific Islanders are present and reinforced in schools by the curriculum, then an individual can be shaped by her/his schooling experiences. AAPI women may even be told by teachers that they do not have the potential to be leaders.

Macrosystem—This encompasses the socio-cultural values of society that influence the development of a person. For example, the lack of AAPI role models in mainstream culture can be demonstrated by the number of AAPI women who are CEOs of major companies. The messages that AAPI women may receive is that they do not have the potential to be a leader of a multinational firm or corporation and therefore should adjust their career goals to "something more manageable." All the systems come together in this layer, and cultural and societal messages conveyed to women about traditional gender roles are so powerful that AAPI females internalize these beliefs.

Along with the Bronfenbrenner ecology of human development, this chapter also utilizes the construct of relative functionalism developed by Sue and Okazaki (1990). They posited that AAPIs have experienced extensive historical and personal oppression in society, and they believe that AAPIs have few avenues for social and economic advancement. Therefore, Sue and Okazaki believe that many AAPIs choose a pragmatic approach to success. We believe relative functionalism explains how many AAPI women see education as the most promising path towards their career advancement (Kao, 1995). Since education is also an important value for many AAPI families, then earning Masters and doctoral degrees follows that route.

Though we understand that, as children, AAPI women can be shaped by teachers, peers, families, and society who believe in the model minority stereotype, it is our belief that the actions of AAPIs are far more complex than the outsider viewpoint of this misconception (Kao, 1995; Pang, et al., 2011). We also believe that some AAPI families reinforce rigid, cultural gender roles and that those expectations may seem to advance the model minority stereotype, but the behaviors and values of many AAPI women are based on Sue and Okazaki's construct of relative functionalism.

Similar to the functionalist view of education, which encourages the familial transmission of cultural capital (Bourdieu, 1986), relative functionalism specifically speaks to the educational demands and expectations that many AAPIs encounter growing up, due to the correlation of academic success and upward mobility. To support characteristics of relative functionalism within the AAPI community, Nagasawa and Espinosa (1992) discuss Asian values such as hard work, discipline, and respect for authority.

However, McDonough (1997) claims, "For the student who is first in her family to go to college, the tasks of preparing and planning for college will be less well-defined than for the individual who has generations of college-going relatives" (p. 98). This claim emphasizes the inherent difficulties an individual must encounter who does not have the cultural capital that can inform her/him about how to successfully maneuver through the educational system or the college process, in contrast to the individual who has these crucial resources embedded in her or his habitus (Bourdieu, 1986). Furthermore, the female AAPI student who may come from a family where women are not encouraged to attend college might not develop the habitus early in life to prepare her for a STEM (Science, Technology, Engineering, Mathematics) education.

Stereotypical Gender Roles and Women

Women in the United States have made advances in many fields from Wall Street to politics, e.g., former presidential candidate Hillary Clinton. Yet discrimination still exists, and equality is still far from achieved. Stereotyped beliefs about the attributes of men and women are invasive and broadly shared. Furthermore, these stereotypical beliefs have proven resistant to change (Dodge, Gilroy, & Fenzel, 1995; Leuptow, Garovich, & Leuptow, 1995). Women are seen as more "communal" (selfless and concerned with others) and less "agentic" (self-assertive and achievement-oriented) than men (Bakan, 1966). Hence, men are characterized as aggressive, independent, and decisive, whereas women are characterized as kind, helpful, and sympathetic. Though these stereotypes are not necessarily negative traits for either women or men, the characteristics that describe women are more often seen in individuals who play supportive rather than leadership roles in society.

Perhaps one of the biggest gaps in equality among men and women continues to be reflected in work settings. Although more doors are open to women today, there seems to be a "glass ceiling," a level above which women do not rise. An explanation for this lies in the traditional stereotypes of men and women that predominate the work setting (Woo, 2000). Research has shown that even when women are represented in managerial roles, they are characterized as less assertive and goal-oriented than men (Heilman, Block, & Martell, 1995). Meanwhile, other researchers argue that most working women will never encounter the glass ceiling as they become stuck to the "sticky floor" in low-paying, low-mobility jobs instead of advancing to higher positions in their workplace (Berheide, 1992; Harlan & Berheide, 1994). Further research shows descriptions of nontraditional woman as evaluated less favorably than descriptions of more traditional women (Haddock & Zanna, 1994). Negative reactions are voiced when women exhibit behavior typically reserved for men. Consequently, women who present themselves in a self-promoting manner are not as well received as those who do not (Rudman, 1998). In addition, women tend to wait to be rewarded for their hard work and are often not taught to negotiate salary increases or promotions. When they do assertively pursue their own goals, women are quick to be labeled as "bitchy" or "pushy," perpetuating the belief that only men can be assertive while women should be nurturing (Babcock, Laschever, Gelfand, & Small, 2003).

In education, men were historically given the opportunities to achieve higher education and were therefore largely more educated. However, as times have changed, women are now afforded the same opportunities and access to educa-tion, but not without resistance. As girls' school performance and women's high school and college completion rates have risen above men's in the last few de-cades, many argued that it was at the expense of boys and men; that caused a "war on boys" and "boys' crisis" in America. However, data analyzed by the American Association of University Women (AAUW), which aimed to debunk the myth, demonstrated that though girls were outperforming boys in achievement scores and women outnumbered men on college campuses, boys' and men's high school college completion rates had in fact not declined at all (Corbett, Hill, & Rose, 2008). Despite the strides women have made in the 21st century, many obstacles continue to foil the acknowledgement of their successes and achievements, both in the work field and certain educational fields. This is reflected in the underrepre-sentation of women in STEM fields such as science, technology, engineering, and mathematics (Blickenstaff, 2005). The cultural reality is that traditional gender roles are greatly ingrained in our society and remain difficult to alter.

Gender Roles in AAPI Families

For many AAPI families, particularly immigrant families, hierarchies charac-terize the family structure, often with women in subordinate positions of author-ity compared to their male counterparts (Chow, 1987; Espiritu, 1999; Pyke & Johnson, 2003). Though we do not want to overgeneralize about gender roles in every family, embedded within the hierarchies of many AAPI communities are well-defined, traditional gender roles and expectations (Chow, 1987).

AAPI men are often in positions of authority and power within the family (Chow, 1987; Espiritu, 1999; Lee, 1997; Pyke & Johnson, 2003). Related to their position of authority, AAPI men are viewed as the family protector, the primary provider, and the decision maker (Chow, 1987). This position of authority for men is evident in different AAPI communities. Zhou and Bankston (2001) noted that in the Vietnamese community, fathers are the authority figures. Another example of heritage gender roles is in the Hmong community. Men are not only considered smarter and stronger, but they are also given the honor and privilege of carrying on traditional cultural rituals (Symonds, 2004). Since Hmong men perform the traditional rituals, Hmong women take on a more supportive role and therefore are dependent on Hmong men within the community (Lee, 1997).

The power and authority many AAPI men ultimately have within their fam-ilies appear to be bestowed on them at a young age. Young AAPI men enjoy greater personal freedom than young AAPI women (Pyke & Johnson, 2003; Zhou & Bankston, 2001). There also appears to be greater tolerance of young men's social behaviors. Zhou and Bankston (2001) pointed out that differences exist in terms of discipline between young Vietnamese men and Vietnamese women. While young Vietnamese women reported being punished, including corporal punishment, Zhou and Bankston (2001) noted that the young Vietnamese men in their study rarely reported being punished. Symonds (2004) also observed a young Hmong man challenging a mother's authority without consequences. The greater personal freedom and the differences in parental control through the use of disciplinary actions appear to perpetuate more rigid gender roles, inequality, and hierarchy within families.

While the gender roles for many AAPI men are characterized by power, the gender roles for many AAPI women are often characterized by obedience (Chow, 1987). The expectation to be obedient is evident throughout many AAPI women's lives as they mature from single, young adult females into married women who are wives and mothers. Any authority that AAPI women may have is restricted to the domestic domain. Zhou and Bankston (2001) noted that young, single Vietnamese females are expected to be obedient and assist their mothers with household duties. These same expectations are shared by young, single Hmong females (Symonds, 2004). As they marry and become wives and mothers, women are expected to be obedient wives who are responsible for the domestic duties (Chow, 1987). As mothers, many AAPI women, including Vietnamese, Asian Indian, and Hmong women are also responsible for raising children (Dasgupta, 1998; Symonds, 2004; Zhou & Bankston, 2001).

Through the act of raising children, women are essentially responsible for socializing the next generation (Dasgupta, 1998). While women are still expected to enforce family control that socializes young men and women into traditional gender roles (Dasgupta, 1998), many AAPI mothers are leading the charge towards gender equality. Zhou and Bankston (2001) found that while Vietnamese mothers expect their daughters to maintain traditional gender roles, they also want their daughters to obtain an education to elevate their daughters' status in the family structure. Hmong mothers view the role of education from a slightly different perspective. Hmong mothers and older female siblings are encouraging Hmong women to pursue education as a means to gain independence and to transform gender roles (Lee, 1997). Thus, although they are expected to continue to fulfill traditional gender roles, it is apparent that mothers are using their roles as mothers to socialize the next generation of women to the possibility of gender equality.

The imminent threat to the patriarchal structure of many AAPI families is not necessarily the socialization by mothers toward the idea of gender equality. Rather, the structure for many AAPIs is changing due to changes in economic demands and opportunities (Espiritu, 1999). Asian American and Pacific Islander women's economic contributions—and therefore power in the family—have increased while many AAPI men have experienced a loss in economic earning power due to discrimination and reduced opportunities (Espiritu, 1999). This change in economic contributions to family resources has challenged the patriarchal and power structures of many AAPI families (Espiritu, 1999). While the shift in earning power is potentially paving the way to gender equality, many AAPI women have continued to maintain some aspects of the traditional gender roles as a mechanism to support their families, due to the awareness that they cannot truly be independent so long as gender and racial oppression exist within the dominant society (Chow, 1987; Espiritu, 1999).

VIGNETTES: THE STORIES OF FOUR DIVERSE AAPI WOMEN

It has been argued in a multitude of different ways that the traditional approach to studying the model minority stereotype, which involves looking at AAPIs from a singular macrosystemic lens, neither thoroughly nor accurately takes into account the complexity of the varied experiences of individuals (Kao, 1995; Li &Wang, 2008). We continue to explore characteristics of the stereotype through analysis and discussion of the cultural and social factors assigned to the experiences of AAPI women via the model minority myth, a myth that was originally coined by William Petersen, a Euro-American male, in 1966 and used to describe the isolated experiences of Japanese-Americans persevering and overcoming societal challenges post-World War II (Li & Wang, 2008). While this term was originally used to highlight success, what it did and what it has continued to do for over five decades is dichotomize the AAPI community from other communities of color (Kiang, 2002; Pang, Han, & Pang, 2011).

Additionally, this myth has minimized the diverse, lived experiences of ethnic groups within the AAPI community, and more specifically, the experiences of AAPI women. Our accomplishments have not been celebrated; rather, they have been manipulated to reinforce the meritocracy myth of American society.

Our stories, however, show that we must overcome difficult financial and cultural odds (Hartlep & Eckrich, 2013), even though the general public often believes we are innately smart and hardworking, thereby pitting AAPIs against other groups of color (Hartlep, 2013).

Vignette #1: Negotiating the Role of Young AAPI Women, Chia S. Her

Since its inception, critics have argued that the model minority is more myth than reality (Hurh & Kim, 1989; Osajami, 1998; Suzuki, 1989). Researchers have focused on the diversity between AAPI groups to help debunk the model minority stereotype (Hartlep, 2014; Ngo & Lee, 2007; Pang, Han, & Pang, 2011; Teranishi, 2010). Equally important, however, is the importance of debunking the model minority stereotype by taking gender into consideration. For many AAPI communities, traditional gender roles are common. While socializing young adults to assume traditional gender roles transmits the cultural and ethnic identity of a group (Dasgupta, 1998), traditional gender roles can affect the educational opportunities of individuals (Lee, 2006). The following vignette examines a Hmong American woman's renegotiation of the traditional gender role and how it may appear to be an act of complicity in maintaining the model minority image. However, this story also illustrates the multitude of factors that should be taken into consideration in demystifying the model minority stereotype, namely gender, ethnicity, social class, migration status, generation, birth order, and cultural values.

The youngest daughter's perspective. I am the *ntxhais ntxawm*, the youngest daughter, in my family. Being the *ntxhais ntxawm* has its benefits because the youngest daughter oftentimes receives more recognition than the older daughters. This affinity for the *ntxhais ntxawm* is woven into the fabric of the Hmong culture as the female protagonist in many Hmong folk tales is simply named *Ntxawm*, a female name derived from the abbreviation of *ntxhais ntxawm.*

As the *ntxhais ntxawm* I learned early on that I had a little more personal freedom than my older sisters. My older sisters were expected to take the lead with the domestic duties while I could get by with just following along. When my sisters and I were tired or busy, we would sometimes tell my mother that the domestic duties would have to wait. My mother saw it as her responsibility to prepare her daughters to be a good *nyab*, a good daughter-in-law. She would frequently remind us that as a *nyab* we would never be able to say to our in-laws that we are busy or tired; the *nyab* is always expected to be the most industrious member of the household. The frequent reminders by my mother of how we would need to behave once we become a *nyab,* along with stories from other Hmong women about the challenges of being in a subordinate position as both a wife and a *nyab,* made me realize that the status, affection, and personal freedom I had as the *ntxhais ntxawm* was a temporary one.

Educational expectations. While my sisters and I were being socialized to be a good *nyab*, my brothers were being taught that their roles as Hmong men would involve a great deal of responsibility. They were expected to be familiar with traditional Hmong rituals because it is Hmong men, not Hmong women, who perform the sacred rituals. Additionally, my brothers were taught that Hmong sons are expected to eventually assume responsibility for all aspects of caring for the family, which includes helping support the family financially, taking care of aging parents, and making decisions for the family. To fulfill these expectations of the traditional role, education was impressed upon my brothers at a very young age. Since their responsibilities included financial support for the family, my brothers were expected to pursue a college education to help increase their economic opportunities.

In comparison, my sisters and I were encouraged to pursue a college education if we wanted to; however, unlike with my brothers, a college education was not an expectation. The expectation was that Hmong daughters would marry, move in with the husband and his family, and become members of the husband's family. When I was growing up, many of the Hmong girls were getting married even before they graduated from high school. Knowing the difficulty of obtaining employment without an education, my sisters and I were expected at least to graduate from high school so we could contribute financially to our new family once we were married.

In spite of the traditional gender roles expected of my siblings and me, my family's educational expectations were rather progressive given that we were recent refugees dropped into modern civilization from an agrarian and pre-literate society. I was only three years old when my family fled a war-torn Laos, a result of the Vietnam War, and resettled in the United States. Neither of my parents have a formal education. My father attended adult school and eventually learned a little bit of English. My mother never learned how to read or write in Hmong or English. We lived in a small, lower class community with many other Hmong families who were in similar situations. I vividly remember the financial and emotional strains of growing up in poverty.

Traditional gender roles via an alternative path. The combination of growing up in poverty and the recognition of gender inequality between Hmong men and women influenced my decision to not marry young. I had seen Hmong girls marry young and continue the cycle of poverty. My peers who married young talked about the loss of their personal freedoms and the struggle to balance their education with the traditional wife and *nyab* roles. I knew there would be personal sacrifices if I did not follow the same path, but I was not ready to give up the limited personal freedoms I had already received as the *ntxhais ntxawm* to assume the roles of wife and *nyab*.

The only other viable path for me was to pursue a higher education. I chose to pursue a college education and then eventually advanced degrees, not to fulfill the model minority stereotype of AAPIs, but as a result of the life choices I made. I had hoped to achieve social, economic, political, and gender equality, only to realize that these same inequalities exist within the mainstream society. Furthermore, the daunting task of climbing up the socioeconomic ladder by deviating from traditional gender expectations is often not recognized. Instead, because of my race and the perception of AAPIs as the model minority, my rebellious decision to pursue a higher education has mostly been diminished by mainstream society as a stereotypical AAPI act. In addition to upholding traditional gender roles, many AAPI women also carry the weight of fulfilling familial duties and obligations.

Vignette #2: Duty and Obligation: Family Comes First, Annie Nguyen

Deeply rooted in Confucian ideals, filial obligation and duty are greatly valued by various AAPI ethnic communities (Shon & Ja, 1982; Uba, 1994). This is particularly true for Vietnamese families as the values of family loyalty and responsibility are often instilled in their children (Caplan et al., 1989). Traditional Vietnamese culture values the role of the entire family, members of which tend to live in extended families or in households combining several families (Caplan et al., 1989). It is common that extended family members are taken care of personally since this is viewed as the responsibility of the family and not of the government (Locke, 1992). Filial obligation is a prominent value in the Vietnamese community (Zhou & Bankston, 1998). Financial resources tend to be put towards the education of the children with the understanding and expectation that the children will in turn grow up and take care of their older family members (Caplan et al., 1989). AAPI parents expect their children to be academically successful as the means for upward mobility. The following story illustrates how these values drive and shape one Vietnamese American woman's perception of how to navigate her world, particularly through education, while also juggling the at-times dichotomous nature of her own personal goals versus the obligations to her family.

A daughter's duty. "When you finish college and have a good job as a doctor you can buy me a house to live in." "You will have to take care of me when I'm old and can't take care of myself anymore." "Make sure you get a good job with a lot of money." These quotes are just a few examples of what was spoken to me repeatedly in Vietnamese by my mother since I was a child. They illustrate the basis of what education means to me, and why I continue to pursue obtaining more of it.

Growing up as the eldest daughter in a Vietnamese family, I was burdened with what seemed to be endless expectations and responsibilities. One expectation was that I must do well in school and go on to graduate from college. My mom expected straight A's from me, which to her disappointment I could not deliver during my high school years. She also expected complete obedience, which I again failed her as I adopted American cultural values and began rebelling as a teenager. I went from being a straight-A student to failing several courses in my freshman year of high school. I was ashamed and embarrassed, not because I felt that I did not meet some societal expectation of Asian American students, but because I felt I was letting my mother and family down. In addition, I was expected to help out with different chores at home such as cooking, washing dishes, and doing laundry to name a few. These chores may seem standard, but I was given these responsibilities at an early age, even taking the public bus across town to and from school as young as eight years old and becoming a caretaker for my younger siblings by the age of eleven. I was the translator for my mom since her English was not fluent, often going with her to various appointments and helping her fill out paperwork for taxes, government assistance, school forms, etc. I did what was necessary to help my family navigate resources in order to survive in America.

Caretaking at eleven years old. Looking back, I can see more clearly why I was dealt the cards I held. There were three major factors that fostered the circumstances of my upbringing: (1) I was a girl; (2) I struggled with balancing Vietnamese cultural values and American cultural values; and (3) I came from a working-class family. As a girl in my family, I was expected to do more around the house and to be more obedient than my brothers. My two older brothers ended up dropping out of high school, and though my mom appeared to be unhappy with them, she also seemed resigned to the fact that they were boys and could not be "tamed." I, on the other hand, received a never-ending wave of expectations that I internalized. I was socialized at a young age to take care of my younger siblings while my brothers were given the freedom to roam around the city with their friends. Filial obligation is prominent in the Vietnamese community, so I understood that it was expected of me to help around the house and be an obedient daughter, but my "American side" resented the fact that I was eleven years old coming home after school to care for my siblings rather than attending my friends' birthday parties or sleepovers. I was especially frustrated with the unfair gender role expectations that were different for my brothers.

The Vietnamese-American culture clash often became the main stressor on my relationship with my mother. Though I felt I adhered to many Vietnamese values by helping around the house, taking care of my siblings, and doing well in school, my mother had expectations too high and rigid for me to fulfill. I rebelled and talked back to my mother as part of my American upbringing, but my mother viewed my actions as unacceptable disobedience. Not only was I to assume the role of being the eldest daughter, but also I was to do so without complaining. Hence, my brothers were often claimed as "better" children to my mother because of their more traditionally respectful manners.

In spite of my at-times defiant ways, I continued to display some form of obedience through my pursuit of post-secondary education. I also realize that my duties as the eldest daughter in a Vietnamese family were amplified by our working-class status. Had my mother had more money, she may have hired a nanny instead of requiring me to be the secondary caregiver. My views on education and the opportunities it represents might then have been different, as I would not have the weight of having to provide for my family.

Personal success equals family success. The perpetuation of what others see as the model minority stereotype continues as I carry on my education into doctoral studies, but for me I am doing it because I am supposed to. Others may view education as an option, but I view education as the only means to any success—a value ingrained in me since I was a child. Some may find it taboo of me to admit that I began pursuing my degree out of a partial feeling of necessity and obligation, rather than purely on self-motivated desire, but some of the collectivist values I was raised with remain pertinent in me. This is not to say that I do not find personal value in my education to grow as a scholar, but to say that I am pursuing it solely for my own benefit would be a lie. My academic achievements are not to fulfill some model minority stereotype, but instead symbolize the possibility of raising my family's working-class status and providing a better life for my family and myself. Calling my accomplishments expected and typical because of my race is offensive and negates all the sacrifices and hardships that led me to my path to begin with.

Given the circumstances of my upbringing and the immense pressure to do well academically, I remain grateful to have lived my experiences. Yes, it felt like a burden at times, but those expectations were my main source of inspiration and are what led me to my graduate studies. My family did not have the resources, financial or educational, to guide me in my academic journey. What they did possess was their support in the form of expectations, albeit sometimes rigid, that were the only means to provide some form of guidance and management in my academic achievements. In addition to maintaining responsibilities dictated by the family, many AAPI women feel obligated to uphold family honor and respect. These values reflect the common collectivist views of AAPIs.

Vignette #3: Personal and Family Honor: Outsider's Misconceptions, Valerie Ooka Pang

Family honor and personal integrity are intimately woven in many AAPI families. These values are often core elements of the cultural capital of collectivism. The value of collectivism refers to the group having more importance than the individual (Pang & Cheng, 1998). In many cases the identity of an individual is tied to the family's honor or shame, especially in the Japanese American family discussed below (Kitano, 1976). Individuals have the duty to make sure that they demonstrate social responsibility (Miyamoto, 1984) because their actions represent more than an individual; their actions represent a large ethnic community and the individual's family.

Introduction. Recently I watched a movie about Ip Man, who was Bruce Lee's Kung Fu (Wing Chun) teacher. The story took place in China and Hong Kong after the Second Sino-Japanese War. Though there was a great deal of martial arts fighting in the story, the "honorable" characters never used their skills to murder or take the property of another. I watched with interest because I was surprised by the strong sense of personal and family honor of the warriors. The men and women in the movie had exceptional martial arts skills and used them to bring honor to themselves and their family.

My story. Though not glamorous like the movie, my story does have numerous twists and turns, from the internment of my mother, who was born in Seattle, Washington and removed to Minidoka, Idaho when she was 12 years old in 1942, to my father's election as one of three County Supervisors in Kittitas County in the State of Washington. My father is thought to be the first Japanese American who was elected to a public office in the state. Both of my parents were native-born U.S. citizens and second-generation Japanese Americans, but that did not mean they were treated as equals within our nation (Kitano, 1976).

They both encountered extensive racism as they grew up and raised their family of seven women in a rural town in Eastern Washington. Though most people were accepting, there were also those who were not and who reminded my parents that they were always to be seen as "foreigners" in their own country.

I have been an educator for over 40 years and have two grown children. I use the introductory story from a Chinese movie because I feel that the film exemplifies some of the values of my parents. My parents believed in family and personal honor. And for outsiders to view them as model minorities because they successfully raised seven daughters is a disturbing misconception. The model minority myth does not explain that AAPI success is often built upon struggles against continual and pervasive racism. Few AAPIs can triumph in their careers without fighting social oppression (Hartlep & Baylor, in press; Pang et al., 2011; Woo, 2000).

For many AAPIs, women and men, personal honor and self-respect are more important than any amount of money. This is in contrast to our highly capitalistic nation where individual merit is often measured by one's financial resources. My father never made more than $30,000 a year though all seven of his daughters graduated from college and two have advanced degrees.

Most often, children learn about family values and family honor through the modeling of their parents. My parents did believe in working hard and contributing to the community. I would like to share one incident that I remember growing up. My dad developed friendships with many business people in Kittitas County. The federal government was going to build a new freeway near our small town of Ellensburg, the county seat. He was told where the freeway was going to go in, and his friend suggested that he should purchase the land before real estate prices soared; his friend told him that the land would be worth a great deal. My dad wrestled with the ethics of this possible purchase. He had been given insider information, which would have made him a millionaire and wealthy member in the small town. We were a family of modest means. In fact, at that time my youngest sister had brought home a yellow form; if he signed the paper, my sister would be eligible for free lunch at the high school. He threw the paper across the room and refused to sign it. My dad was a proud man and would not take something that he felt his family did not need or had not earned. Though it may seem as if my dad's actions tie in with the model minority, mainstream people need to understand that traditional cultures of AAPI emphasize the importance of personal and society ethics. Having integrity is a strength and should not be seen as a weakness.

Legacy of family honor and personal integrity. Though my father died with few funds in the bank, he left a legacy of hard-working daughters and, now, grandchildren. During their lifetime, my father and mother never had much money; however, they did believe in family honor and personal integrity. If others want to see this as a weakness because individuals or families may not "bend" rules in order to become wealthy, then they do not understand the values behind my parents' behaviors. Individuals may have a strong sense of ethics, and the model minority myth does not delve into this aspect of AAPI cultures. Like Ip Man, my parents and sisters believe in personal and family honor. When others use the model minority to explain the successes of many AAPIs, then they do not understand underlying insider cultural values. This manipulation of cultural values of AAPIs to fit mainstream norms is not only erroneous, but also cultural exploitation.

For many AAPIs, career and personal success are about personal effort and skill and honoring one's ethics. AAPI females work diligently, but do not do so because of any belief in the model minority myth. Most see the misconception as a gross overgeneralization that stereotypes hard work and personal integrity. In addition, the model minority ignores societal and economic racism that many AAPI women and men continually face in a society that espouses equity in schools and society (Pang, et al., 2011). Despite the commonalities that AAPI communities share, there is no one typical AAPI family. In the case of growing up in two or three different AAPI ethnic groups, establishing one's own cultural identity can be a lonely task.

Vignette #4: Balancing Multiple Cultures, Marissa S. Yenpasook

To survive in mainstream society and within racial and ethnic communities, I required a substantial amount of awareness and recognition of my cultural history and experiences. Thornton (1996) references individuals like myself, who are of mixed ethnicity or mixed race, when he states that ethnic identity is a complex interaction between an individual's personal definition of self and society's definition. A balancing act occurs when one is expected to respond to or meet the expectations of multiple groups.

Darder (2012) discusses Valentine's bicultural model of human development in order to explain the navigation complexities involved in a bicultural or multicultural person's process to learn and practice ethnic culture(s) and mainstream culture, which sometimes involves stepping in and out of different cultures at various points throughout one's life. Thornton (1996) goes on to say, "Ethnic or group identity has two significant contributors: a thread of historical experience that each group member shares in and a sense of potency or strength inhering in the group" (Thornton, 1996, p. 104). Therefore, to begin to understand my experiences as an unbefitting captive of the model minority myth, I will illuminate my identity and experiences as a multiethnic, AAPI woman.

Family identity. I had no idea as a child that the culture in which I grew up and the position that I held in my family had such a huge impact on my concept of self. While my position as the middle child is a familiar role that people from many different cultural contexts can identify with, my cultural circumstances were unique. I grew up in a multiethnic household with a Pilipino mother, a Thai-Chinese father, and two siblings—an older sister and a younger brother. The cultural schemas that each of my immigrant parents brought to the United States aided in developing a third culture in our household—one in which assimilation, acculturation, and the consciousness of race and socioeconomic status were present.

Most of my life has been a balancing act of straddling the middle ground between familial and societal expectations. At a young age, I was expected to be attentive and responsible, heeding warnings of what not to do and reading cues from one parent indicating that I was doing the right thing and then deciphering a set of different cues from the other parent. There were common cultural experiences that my parents shared, such as placing high value on family and honor; however, due to the life experiences that each of them brought into their marriage, there were clear differences in how they each practiced these values.

Coming from different life experiences and cultural backgrounds, my parents first met in Chicago shortly after they immigrated to the United States in the early 1970s. At that time, many of my mother's family members were already in the

U.S. My mother was fortunate to have relatives in Chicago who offered her a stable home, so she could focus on her education while her parents and younger brothers established a home in San Francisco. Like many Pilipinos, my mother and her cousins were tracked into the educational path that led to the nursing profession. The free will that my mother was able to explore while she lived away from her parents allowed her to reject any possibility of being pigeonholed into pursuing a career she had no interest in. Therefore, she ended up pursuing respiratory therapy, a specialty that had not yet been popularized by the healthcare field. As the oldest of four children and as the only girl, she had endured her share of familial gender role expectations and limitations, which prompted the desire and tenacity to explore something different.

As an adult today, I fondly recall listening to my dad tell transformative and inspiring stories of his journey to the United States. Everything from country to climate was unfamiliar. My dad was the first of his nine siblings to venture to the United States looking for greater opportunity than what was available to him in Thailand. To him, success meant being able to send money home and to one day sponsor other family members to come to the U.S. So he and a friend made their way out to the Midwest knowing little English, having a limited support system, and carrying a little over twenty dollars in his pocket. Three months after my dad arrived in the U.S., his father passed away of lung cancer. In 1987, at the age of six, I traveled to Thailand with my sister and dad for the first time to meet my grandmother. It was the first and last time I would see my grandmother, because a couple of years later she passed away.

A culture of our own. With their common values and their differences, my parents created a third culture for our family. This culture did not meet all of the cultural and generational expectations that had been placed on each of them by their own families. Their shared value in the concepts of sacrifice, family honor, and humility guided what was passed down to us, although their transmission of these values varied. An example of what sacrifice looked like for my dad was his commitment to his family by supporting my mom in her professional aspirations. He put his own career aspirations on hold to raise my siblings and me. My father modeled characteristics of patience, empathy, humility, and respect. An expectation that he had of us was that we would be focused and successful in education and in our careers so that we could honor his and my mother's sacrifices. My mom worked long hours and multiple shifts at different hospitals to keep our family financially stable. She made many sacrifices for our family. She modeled the characteristics of assertiveness, tenacity, critical thinking, and independence. She was an activist at work, speaking out as an advocate for her patients and from her colleagues. Her strong voice sometimes alienated her from her colleagues, especially other AAPI females. My mom expected us to be self-sufficient, educated, and strong-willed. As a result of my parents' expectations, many of my life decisions have inherently been a direct reflection of their sacrifice, humility, and strength.

It wasn't until much later that I realized the world that my parents had created for my siblings and me consisted of ebbs and flows when integrated with mainstream society's expectations and presuppositions of me. I remember moments during my childhood when I felt conflicted about my ethnicity. Attending primary schools that had little racial diversity, where the only AAPIs represented were either Japanese or Chinese, sometimes made me feel unique but mostly I felt like I did not belong. In schools where people of color were few and far between, the anomaly that was my identity had little space to grow and blossom. Additionally, not knowing how to speak or understand either of my parents' native languages sometimes made me feel like an outcast at my family gatherings.

Expectations. For every part of my identity, there was an expectation placed on me. As a female, I had to be on my guard to protect myself from people who could potentially take advantage of me. I received messages from my mother telling me that I should trust no one. As the second born, I had to be aware of what mistakes my older sister made and make sure not to make the same ones. My sister paved the road for me in many regards. She made mistakes, as most people do; however, she often paid a large price for these mistakes. As an older sister to my little brother, I was expected to watch over him, help him with his homework, and guide his decisions. As a grandchild, I was expected to know my mother's native language, without ever being formally or informally taught it. As a student, I was expected to obey my teachers and excel in math and science because, based on the model minority myth, that's what other kids who looked like me did. Little did my teachers realize that I had to try three times harder than my peers to understand math. All of these expectations turned me into an obedient child, family mediator, and hardworking, independent female.

I will never really know what it's like to grow up with nine brothers and sisters. I will never know what it's like to be a child growing up in such extreme poverty that my siblings and I have to be split up. I will never know what it's like to be the oldest sister to three brothers. I will never know what it's like to leave my family and my homeland to come to a country in which the language, culture, and climate are so extremely different and to be welcomed by a society that assumes that I am quiet, submissive, and will do what is told of me. However, because I grew up multiethnic in a society that constantly wants to slap a generalized pan-ethnic identity on me, I do know how harmful, dismissive, and unfair the model minority myth has been to many AAPIs, including myself.

CONCLUSION

Our four stories represent the intersectionality of many human characteristics such as ethnicity, generation, age, migration patterns, and U.S. historical experiences. We share our narratives so that the reader understands the damage the model minority myth has done to silence AAPIs. The myth was created by non-AAPIs, and it shapes, interprets, and presents untrue images of our experiences. We believe that the AAPI cultural experiences of women are vast. Though we share similar cultural values such as filial piety, family honor, and personal resilience, our experiences are extremely complex and should be honored. One of the overarching similarities of our stories is that all of us came from poor families, families who struggled, but who "swam" upstream in order to gain the opportunity to go to school. We all fought prejudice from outsiders who considered us to be foreign and not belonging to the U.S. society. We also saw how much stress our own parents went through in order to survive and provide for us. They had, and have, great courage and strength.

The women and men from our AAPI communities have made and continue to make important contributions to our nation in areas such as civil rights, education, business, and politics. For example, Patsy Takemoto Mink, the first Asian American female and woman of color in Congress, fought for women's rights. She pushed back against racism and sexism and was one of the original authors of Title IX legislation, which called for equality for women in education and athletics. AAPI women are often overlooked or ignored for leadership training and positions of authority. They only make up a little more than one percent of the Fortune 500 corporate chairpersons. We believe AAPI women continually have to prove themselves even though they may have achieved higher levels of education and have many more years of experience than their peers.

AAPI women must balance their family lives, roles as women in their communities, and the expectations of American society. We believe our stories are evidence of the complicated social and cultural contexts in which we live. Expectations from the general patriarchal society, along with another layer of anticipated female behaviors from our families and communities, create psychological and emotional boundaries, which restricts our development. Yet at the same time, our cultural lives give us strength. Although our experiences lead outsiders to assume we have embraced the ideals of the model minority, our actions reflect belief in relative functionalism, a survival mechanism we adopted to overcome the continual discrimination AAPI communities face. We continue to be defiant because we believe in the cultural values that guide and sustain us.

Questions for Reflection

1. How are the experiences of the four AAPI women similar and/or different?
2. Why is the model minority such a powerful myth in U.S. society?
3. How are economic, cultural, and political boundaries created to restrict AAPI women's identity?
4. How can various factors, such as class, gender, etc., affect the self-image of AAPI women?
5. How can people of different cultural backgrounds work with the AAPI community to eradicate the model minority myth?

REFERENCES

Babcock, L., Laschever, S., Gelfand, M., & Small, D. (2003). Nice girls don't ask. *Harvard Business Review, 81*(10), 14–16.

Bakan, D. (1966). *The duality of human existence: An essay on psychology and religion.* Chicago, IL: Rand McNally.

Berheide, C. W. (1992, Fall). Women still 'stuck' in low-level jobs. *Women in Public Service, 3,* 1–4.

Blickenstaff, J. C. (2005). Women and science careers: Leaky pipeline or gender filter? *Gender and Education, 17*(4), 369–386.

Bourdieu, P. (1986). Forms of capital. In J. G. Richardson (Ed.), *Handbook of theory and research for the sociology of education* (pp. 241–258). New York: Greenwood.

Bronfenbrenner, U. (1994). Ecological models of human development. In *International encyclopedia of education* (Vol. 3, 2nd Ed.). Oxford: Elseiver. Reprinted in M. Gauvin & M. Cole (Eds.) *Readings in the development of children* (2nd ed., pp. 37–43). New York: Freeman.

Caplan, N. H., Whitmore, J. K., & Choy, M. H. (1989). *The boat people and achievement in America: A study of economic and educational success.* Ann Arbor, MI: University of Michigan Press.

Corbett, C., Hill, C., & St. Rose, A. (2008). *Where the girls are: The facts about gender equity in education.* Retrieved July 14, 2014, from http://www.aauw.org/research/where-the-girls-are/.

Chow, E. N. (1987). The development of feminist consciousness among Asian American women. *Gender and Society, 1*(3), 284–299. doi: 10.1177/089124387001003004

Darder, A. (2012). *Culture and power in the classroom: Educational foundations for the schooling of bicultural students.* Boulder, CO: Paradigm.

Dasgupta, S. D. (1998). Gender roles and cultural continuity in the Asian Indian immigrant community in the U.S. *Sex Roles, 38,* 11–12. doi: 10.1023/A:1018822525427

Dodge, K. A., Gilroy, F. D., & Fenzel, L. M. (1995). Requisite management characteristics revisited: Two decades later. *Journal of Social Behavior and Personality, 10*(6), 253–264.

Espiritu, Y. L. (1999). Gender and labor in Asian immigrant families. *American Behavioral Scientist, 42*(4), 628–647. doi: 10.1177/00027649921954390

Haddock, G., & Zanna, M. P. (1994). Preferring "housewives" to "feminists": Categorization and the favorability of attitudes toward women. *Psychology of Women Quarterly, 18,* 25–52. doi: 10.1111/j.1471–6402.1994.tb00295.x

Harlan, S. L., & Berheide, C. W. (1994). *Barriers to work place advancement experienced by women in low-paying occupations.* Washington, DC: U.S. Glass Ceiling Commission.

Hartlep, N. D. (2013). I refuse to be a pawn for whiteness: A Korean transracial adoptee speaks out. In C. Hayes & N. Hartlep (Eds.), *Unhooking from whiteness: The key to dismantling racism in the United States* (pp. 57–70). Boston, MA: Sense.

Hartlep, N. D. (Ed.). (2014). *The model minority stereotype reader: Critical and challenging readings for the 21st century.* San Diego, CA: Cognella.

Hartlep, N. D., & Baylor, A. (In-Press). Educational leadership: A critical, racial, and theoretical examination of the "we-need-more-leaders-of-color" discourse. In T. Marsh

& N. Croom (Eds.), *Envisioning a critical race praxis for leadership: Critical race counter-stories across the p-20 pipeline.* Charlotte, NC: Information Age.

Hartlep, N. D., & Eckrich, L. T. (2013). Ivory tower graduates in the red: The role of debt in higher education. *Workplace, 22,* 82–97. Retrieved July 14, 2014, from http:// ir.library.illinoisstate.edu/fped/9/

Heilman, M. E., Block, C. J., & Martell, R. (1995). Sex stereotypes: Do they influence perceptions of the managers? *Journal of Social Behavior and Personality, 10*(6), 237–252.

Hurh, W. M., & Kim, K. C. (1989). The 'success' image of Asian Americans: Its validity, and its practical and theoretical implications. *Ethnic and Racial Studies, 12*(4), 512–538. doi: 10.1080/01419870.1989.9993650

Kao, G. (1995). Asian Americans as model minorities? A look at their academic performance. *American Journal of Education, 103*(2), 121–159. doi: 10.1086/444094

Kiang, P. N. (2002). K–12 education and Asian Pacific American youth development. *Asian American Policy Review, 10,* 31–47.

Kitano, H. L. (1976). *Japanese Americans: Evolution of a subculture.* (2nd ed.). Englewood Cliffs, NJ: Prentice-Hall.

Lee, S. J. (1997). The road to college: Hmong American women's pursuit of higher education. *Harvard Educational Review, 67*(4), 803–828.

Lee, S. J. (2006). Additional complexities: social class, ethnicity, generation, and gender in Asian American student experiences. *Race Ethnicity and Education, 9*(1), 17–28. doi: 10.1080/13613320500490630

Leuptow, L. B., Garovich, L., & Leuptow, M. B. (1995). The persistence of gender stereotypes in the face of changing sex roles: Evidence contrary to the sociocultural model. *Ethology and Sociobiology, 16,* 509–530.

Li, G., & Wang, L. (Eds.). (2008). *Model minority myth revisited: An interdisciplinary approach to demystifying Asian American education experiences.* Charlotte, NC: Information Age.

Locke, D. C. (1992). *Increasing multicultural understanding.* Newbury Park, CA: Sage.

McDonough, P. M. (1997). *Choosing colleges: How social class and schools structure opportunity.* Albany, NY: State University of New York Press.

Miyamoto, F. (1984). *Social solidarity among the Japanese in Seattle* (3rd ed.). Seattle, WA: University of Washington Press.

Nagasawa, R., & Espinosa, D. J. (1992). Educational achievement and the adaptive strategy of Asian American college students: Fact, theory, and hypothesis. *Journal of College Student Development, 33,* 137–142.

Ngo, B., & Lee, S. J. (2007). Complicating the image of model minority success: A review of Southeast Asian American education. *Review of Educational Research, 77*(4), 415–453.

Osajima, K. (1998). Asian Americans as the model minority: An analysis of the popular press image in the 1960s and 1980s. In G. Y. Okihiro (Ed.), *Reflections on shattered windows: Promises and prospects for Asian American studies* (pp. 165–174). Pullman, WA: Washington State University Press.

Pang, V. O. (2007). Asian Pacific American cultural capital: Understanding diverse parents and students. In S. J. Paik & H. J. Walberg (Eds.), *Narrowing the achievement gap: Strategies for educating Latino, Black, and Asian students* (pp. 49–66). Kluwer

Academic/Springer/Plenum Publishers, University of Illinois at Chicago Series on Children and Youth.

Pang, V. O., & Cheng, L. L. (1998). *Struggling to be heard: The unmet needs of Asian Pacific American children.* Albany, NY: State University of New York Press.

Pang, V. O., Han, P. P., & Pang, J. M. (2011). Asian American and Pacific Islander students: Equity and the achievement gap. *Educational Researcher, 40*(7), 378–389.

Pyke, K. D., & Johnson, D. L. (2003). Asian American women and racialized femininities: "Doing" gender across cultural worlds. *Gender and Society, 17*(1), 33–53. doi: 10.1177/0891243202238977

Rudman, L. A. (1998). Self-promotion as a risk factor for women: The costs and benefits of counterstereotypical impression management. *Journal of Personality and Social Psychology, 74,* 629–645.

Shon, S. P., & Ja, D. Y. (1982). Asian families. In M. McGoldrick, J. K. Pearce, & J. Giordano (Eds.), *Ethnicity and family therapy* (pp. 208–228). New York: Guilford.

Sue, S., & Okazaki, S. (1990). Asian-American educational achievements: A phenomenon in search of an explanation. *American Psychologist, 45*(8), 913–920.

Suzuki, B. H. (1989). Asian Americans as the "model minority": Outdoing whites? Or media hype? *Change: The Magazine of Higher Learning, 21*(6), 13–19. doi: 10.1080/00091383.1989.9937601

Symonds, P. V. (2004). *Calling in the soul: Gender and the cycle of life in a Hmong village.* Seattle, WA: University of Washington Press.

Teranishi, R. T. (2010). *Asians in the ivory tower: Dilemmas of racial inequality in American higher education.* New York: Teachers College Press.

Thornton, M. (1996). Hidden agendas, identity theories, and multiracial people. In M. P. P. Root (Ed.), *The multiracial experience: Racial borders as the new frontier* (pp. 101–120). Thousand Oaks, CA: Sage.

Uba, L. (1994). *Asian Americans: Personality patterns, identity, and mental health.* New York: Guilford Press.

Woo, D. (2000). *Glass ceilings and Asian Americans.* Walnut Creek, CA: Altamira.

Zhou, M., & Bankston, C. L. (1998). *Growing up American: How Vietnamese children adapt to life in the United States.* New York: Russell Sage.

Zhou, M., & Bankston III, C. L. (2001). Family pressure and the educational experience of daughters of Vietnamese refugees. *International Migration, 39*(4), 133–151. doi: 10.1111/1468-2435.00165

PART II

THE MODEL MINORITY IN NON-U.S. SPACES

PART IV

CHAPTER 5

IMPORTING THE ASIAN MODEL MINORITY DISCOURSE INTO CANADA

Implications for Social Work and Education

Gordon Pon

One of the fastest growing immigrant groups in Canada consists of Chinese Canadians. Recent Chinese immigrants are generally younger, more educated, and more skilled than non-Chinese immigrants (Lo & Wang, 1997). In 1996 almost one third of the 921,585 persons in Canada who reported Chinese as their ethnic origin were under the age of 25, according to the Canada Census. Despite this rapidly expanding young population, there is a paucity of social research on Chinese Canadian youth, especially in relation to social work and education. The discourse depicting Asians as a "model minority" often leads to the exclusion of Chinese Canadians from discussions of human service provision since the discourse constructs Asians in general as a highly successful and well-adjusted population characterized by supportive and intact families that promote Confucian cultural values such as respect for education (Lee, 1996; Maclear, 1994). These essential-

Killing the Model Minority Stereotype: Asian American Counterstories and Complicity,
pages 83–95.
Copyright © 2015 by Information Age Publishing

ist notions of Asians in the diaspora as ostensibly unburdened by difficulties can often lead human service providers, including educators, to overlook the hetero-geneity that characterizes Chinese Canadian youth and their attendant struggles with issues such as poverty, racism, dislocation, sexuality, housing, employment, second-language acquisition, and intra-familial conflict.

When Chinese North Americans are discussed by social scientists, it is often in the context of a culture clash between purported Chinese collectivist values, which are influenced by Confucianism, and the rugged individualism of the West (Hoefstede, 1983; Hui & Triandis, 1986). Some of these studies have drawn im-portant attention to the limits of Eurocentric Western theories, which take as their starting point the assumption that individualism is both normative and universal and is therefore inadequate for application to more collectivist populations (Ho, 1979; Hoefstede, 1983; Lam, 1998). Pointing to the influence of Confucianism,[1] Ching Lam (1998) argues that in collectivist Chinese culture the individual is never perceived as a separate entity, but rather "he or she is always regarded as part of a social network with a specific role in relation to others" (p. 182). He contrasts this with the individualism of the West, in which the self is regarded as an analytic, monotheistic, materialistic, rationalistic, and autonomous entity. Lam observes that Western theories of adolescent development based on individualis-tic notions of the self thus often pathologize non-Western youth such as Canadian Chinese immigrants.

The relationship between contemporary Chinese cultures and Confucianism has been problematized by Aihwa Ong (1999), who calls attention to profound changes in Chinese society given the rise of global capitalism and the emergence of China as a nascent economic powerhouse. As a result, she argues, Asian so-cieties such as China are now more like the West than at any previous historical juncture, despite the fact that many Asian leaders are endearing themselves to re-surgent 19th-century discourses on civilization such as Orientalism (Said, 1979), in which the East is the symbolic obverse of the West. She argues that many Asian leaders are currently engaged in a game of one-upmanship with the West in which a purportedly Confucian-inspired, Asian-Pacific capitalism is heralded as more caring and less callous than the capitalism of the West. As Ong points out, how-

---

[1] Confucianism is a secular social theory that emphasizes the Five Cardinal Relations and the achieve-ment of a harmonious society. The Five Cardinal Relations are between sovereign and subject, father and son, husband and wife, elder brother and younger brother, and friend and friend (Lam, 1998). Confucianism asserts that social harmony can be attained if all abide by the corresponding duties and responsibilities that accrue from the proper functioning of these relations (Chan, 1983; Chang, 1957; Lam, 1998). Much feminist scholarship has critiqued the patriarchal and misogynist assumptions that underpin Confucianism. For instance, according to Confucian ideology, women occupied the lowest echelon of the Confucian hierarchy. Confucius (522–479 BC) classified women with slaves and small humans (*hsiao ngren*), earning him the name of the "eater of women" among many of those who fought against his social influence in Chinese society (Kristeva, 1974). Ling (1990) notes that, on the subject of women's education, Confucius wrote, "The purpose of female education is perfect submission."

ever, the "demarcation of Western individualism and Asian collectivism skirts the fact that capitalism itself is wedded to liberalism and that capitalism, as a dialectical process of endless production and destruction, is itself a source of profound social inequality" (p. 194). In summary, Ong alerts us to the dynamic, contingent, and hybrid nature of contemporary Chinese cultures in which essentialist notions of a Confucian collectivist self may be increasingly tenuous given the conditions of globalization.

Although a rich body of literature exists in the United States that critiques the Asian "model minority" discourse and its promotion of Confucian discourses (Lee, 1996; Lee, 1999; Lowe, 1996), relatively little such research exists in Canada. That is not to say that the "model minority" discourse, which is an American concept by origin, has not been imported into Canada. Rather, the Asian "model minority" discourse converges with Canadian discourses of multiculturalism to buttress Orientalist notions of Chinese Canadians on the one hand, and to discipline and punish insurgent challenges to liberal democracy on the other.

Lisa Lowe (1996) argues that the present ontology of liberal democratic nation-states such as the United States and Canada involves a "forgetting" of the history of racism and Western imperial projects that proved central to the formation of the nation-state. This ontology thereby accedes to a political fiction of equal rights and is inseparable from the present-day liberal democracy, which persists in asserting that Canada is a fair and tolerant society, despite the reality of pervasive inequity based on racism (Henry, Tator, Mattis, & Rees, 1995). Implicated in this ontology is the erasure of how the nation-state building project is inseparable from gender, race, and class relations that converged in the operation of racism and sexism to exploit and subordinate non-Whites in Canada (Ng, 1993).

In the 1960s the civil rights movement and others inspired by it, including the antiwar, New Left, and women's liberation movements, exposed the gap between the United States' image of itself and reality (Wei, 1993). It posited America not as the land of equality, where a person could achieve success through individual effort, but rather a land of inequality, where racism marginalized non-Whites (Wei, 1993). According to William Wei (1993), these movements forced the nation to examine its concept of liberal democracy and the attendant crisis of citizenship. The civil unrest called into question the fundamental contradiction embedded in liberal democracy's claim to protect the "rights of man" to equality, liberty, and property—that it excluded those who were imagined as "others," such as non-Whites, women, and gays and lesbians.

Out of this context of tremendous social upheaval in the United States, the Asian "model minority" discourse emerged to prominence in the 1960s as one means deployed by those in power to manage the crisis in citizenship. According to proponents of the discourse (Brand, 1987; Petersen, 1966), Asian Americans had achieved success due to Confucian cultural values, which promoted hard work, while not blaming structural and systematic racism as obstacles to their achievements. This discourse therefore implicitly blamed oppressed Blacks and other racial groups for supposedly having inferior cultural values and no hard work ethic. Despite the dearth of Canadian critiques of the "model minority" discourse, ample scholarship examines the Canadian policy of multiculturalism as a liberal democratic discourse that maintains and reproduces racism while actually proclaiming to combat it (Bramble, 2000; Dei, 1996; James & Schecter, 2000; Ng, Staton, & Scane, 1995; Walcott, 1997; Yon, 2000). If human service providers and educators are aware of the links between this rich scholarship on multiculturalism, the "model minority" discourse, and liberal democracy, they will be better positioned to work across cultures without reinforcing persistent stereotypes.

EMERGENCE OF THE "MODEL MINORITY" DISCOURSE

As a means to invalidate the strident demands made by African Americans for equality and justice, Asian Americans were heralded as outstanding citizens who epitomized equality of opportunity in America. This is evidenced in one of the first of such stories to appear in the *New York Times*: "By any criterion of good citizenship that we choose, the Japanese-Americans are better than any group in our society, including native-born whites…even in a country whose patron saint is the Horatio Alger hero, there is no parallel to this success story" (Petersen, 1966, p. 21). The emergent "model minority" characterization of Japanese Americans was quickly expanded to include the Chinese in America. Ong (1999) explains that Asians such as the Chinese were chosen to be the "models" since by the 1960s a notable middle-class Chinese American population had emerged and provided a contrast to the growth of a non-White "underclass," a term used mainly to refer to "inner-city" Blacks. This is evident in the following excerpt from an article that appeared in the *US World and News Report* in 1966: "At a time when it is being proposed that hundreds of billions be spent to uplift Negroes and other minorities, the nation's 300,000 Chinese Americans are moving ahead on their own—with no help from anyone else…In crime-ridden cities, Chinese districts turn up as islands of peace and stability" (p. 73).

This quote reveals how the "model minority" discourse is inseparable from a neo-liberal ideology that contrasts the imagined community (Anderson, 1993) of Asian Americans with African Americans, discounting the impact of racism on one hand and promoting fiscal self-reliance on the other. This dual aspect of the discourse is effected by what Bhabha (1994) describes as a "double narrative movement," which produces a slide between stated positions. This slipperiness is evidenced in how state denunciations of racism, through such acts as desegregation, co-exist with a contradictory heralding of a population (Asian Americans) that ostensibly "proves" that racism is not, however, such an obstacle. The "model minority" discourse thus reveals a contradiction in which racism is simultaneously acknowledged while, yet its material and social effects are downplayed. The double narrative asserts that one's station in life depends far more on individual effort than on race and racism. This move reveals that what is at stake in the "model minority" discourse is a mechanism of power aimed at silencing or at least modulating the demands for fundamental changes to liberal democracy.

The discourse's implicit assertion—that if one pulls oneself up by one's bootstraps, then one can succeed—attempts to discipline and contain civil unrest. As a mechanism or tactic to regulate this "unruly" population, the "model minority" discourse tries to steer the discursive field of racial and class oppression away from systemic and structural origins towards an individual's character, such as her or his work ethic. This discourse reinvents America as the land of opportunity by heralding Asians as proof, and it thereby places the blame on downtrodden individuals for their economic impoverishment. Therefore, what is also at stake in the discourse is its provision of "governmentality,"[2] a mechanism for managing fundamental contradictions between liberal democracy and racism.

More than 40 years removed from these inaugural images of Asian American "success," the discourse continues to flourish, especially among proponents of the New Right. For example, the New Right deploys the "model minority" with discourses such as meritocracy, to portray the Asian American population as "victimized over-achievers" who are hurt by employment equity policies (Omi & Takagi, 1996). Likewise, right-wing groups continue to uphold examples of Asian American success as evidence that minorities can succeed in the United States (Lee, 1996) and attribute this success to the "Asian American family," citing it as a model of "good," old-fashioned, tight-knit, Confucian families (Lee, 1999; Palumbo-Liu, 1999).

THE ASIAN "MODEL MINORITY" AND THE NEW RIGHT

Robert Lee (1999) argues that current notions of the mythic Asian American family that are celebrated by the New Right have been upheld as not only a model for groups such as Blacks and Latinos, but for working-class and middle-class Whites as well. That is to say that the "model minority" discourse is also staked in the current neo-liberal ideological demands of globalization, which emphasize productivity and self-reliance. On a global scale, beginning in the 1970s, liberal democratic governments, often termed the New Right, have increasingly adopted a rationality of rule referred to as neo-liberalism. Heralded by some as the "triumph of capitalism," neo-liberalism is an art of government that emphasizes free market mechanisms aimed at harmonizing the world of national capitals and nation-states, creating what Teeple (1995) calls a global system of internationalized capital and supranational institutions. This embrace of free market principles implies a form of social distribution of goods and services, through the exchange of private property, which is free of any mitigating morality (Teeple, 1995, p. 122). This market-driven sense of "economic justice" coincides with widespread loss of support for the Keynesian welfare state, which is now increasingly deemed by a variety of discourses to be ineffective, bureaucratically unwieldy, unaffordable, and a tremendous barrier to the free flow of transnational capitals (Teeple, 1995).

Neo-liberalism espouses an ethos of government marked by an unmistakable disdain for the Keynesian welfare state and a concomitant glorification of the concepts of individualism and market freedom. Attendant to this celebration of freedom, progress, and individualism is the concept of "citizenship," often defined as "the civic duty of individuals to reduce their burden on society and build up their own human capital" (Ong, 1996, p. 739). Colin Gordon (1991) contends that neo-liberal governmentality involves a notion of *homo economicus* in which that individual is an "entrepreneur of himself or herself" (Gordon, 1991, p. 44). This idea of one's life as the enterprise of oneself "implies that there is a sense in which one remains always continuously employed in (at least) one enterprise, and that it is a part of the preservation, reproduction, and reconstruction of one's own human capital" (Gordon, 1991, p. 44). In contradistinction to Keynesian welfare statism, *homo economicus* involves an emphasis not on "state provisions of security against ills and injuries, but a greater focus on an individual's civic obligation" to look after oneself by moderating "the burden of risk which he or she imposes on society" (Gordon, 1991, p. 45). Consistent with these neo-liberal demands is the discourse of the Asian "model minority," which constructs the Asian as an extraordinary *homo economicus* of sorts. This is evidenced in the New Right's lauding of Asian Americans' "persistence in overcoming language barriers, their superior disciplinary and motivational roles as parents, and their 'intact' families' success at savings" (Lee, 1999, p. 184).

IMPORTING THE "MODEL MINORITY" DISCOURSE TO CANADA

Despite the fact that Asian Americans have repeatedly contested the stereotype (Suzuki, 1995), the "model minority" discourse remains highly prevalent in the United States (Chun, 1995; Suzuki, 1995) and Canada (Maclear, 1994). Throughout the 1980s and 1990s, Canadian presses like the *Toronto Star*, *Fortune Magazine*, *Globe and Mail*, *Montreal Gazette*, and *Toronto Life* have championed the Chinese as the "model minority." These newspaper columnists continue to perpetuate the discourse of Asians as being "academic giants" (Mathews, 1988), "math whizzes" (Sheppard, 1992), and extremely wealthy (Gillmor, 1998).

The importation of what originated as an American discourse into the Canadian context is supported by these many Canadian journalists who draw on the plethora of American writings (both popular and erudite) that support the "model minority" myth. For example, in a *Globe and Mail* article, journalist Robert Sheppard (1992) discusses an essay in *Scientific American* that remarks on the striking success of Asian immigrants in America. Sheppard argues that Asians have achieved tremendous scholastic success due to family and cultural values that place a heavy emphasis on schooling for their children. Borrowing from a British Columbian university professor, Sheppard terms this the "breakfast table mentality" whereby Asian parents continually encourage their children to get more education than they did. He concludes by stating: "But here they [Asians] are at, or near, the top of the scholastic heap, not just in their own schools but in state wide testing. And showing that the present system can be made to work—providing we don't forget our family histories and the value of the kitchen table" (Sheppard, 1992, p. A11).

The Sheppard article is provocative for several reasons. First of all, it rehashes the "model minority" discourse of Asians as being uniformly successful in school and, like the New Right, locates the phenomenon as being primarily attributable to family values and parenting skills. Interestingly, Sheppard draws upon the case of Asian Americans and weaves it seamlessly into a Canadian context, thereby buttressing Canadian liberal democracy with an American discourse. In this manner an originally American discourse is now fully interspersed within the discursive field of Canadian liberal democracy and finds convergence with its ontology of forgetting.

THE ASIAN "MODEL MINORITY" AND MULTICULTURALISM DISCOURSES

The Asian "model minority" discourse also dovetails neatly with Canadian discourses of multiculturalism. In 1971 the federal government enacted a policy of multiculturalism, which "recognizes the importance of preserving and enhancing the multicultural heritage of Canadians… [and] the diversity of Canadians with regards to race, national or ethnic origin, colour and religion as a fundamental characteristic of Canadian society" (*The Canadian Multicultural Act*, 1988). Multicultural education has since emerged as a logical application of the federal policy. Multicultural education seeks to "foster sensitivity to, and respect for, ethno-cultural differences and to promote the integration of minority students within the dominant educational framework" (James & Schecter, 2000, p. 29).

Multicultural education has become deeply entrenched in Canadian school discourses and practices, as evidenced in its widespread emphasis on the need for students to study "foreign" cultures, participate in "multicultural days," or go on field trips to "cultural communities" and community centres (James, 1998). These activities are proposed to be pedagogical ways of recognizing and representing the "cultures" of the students within the schools. Moreover, proponents of multicultural education assert that these pedagogical practices serve to improve race relations. This belief stems from the policy's fundamental assumption that racial and ethnic group tensions are linked to ignorance and a lack of contact between individuals of various ethnic/racial groups. Hence, multicultural education is purported to heighten students' awareness and to counteract negative attitudes attendant to prejudice, ethnocentrism, racism, and xenophobia (James, 1998).

The multiculturalism policy and its educational ramifications have been critiqued for celebrating cultural difference while perpetuating racism (James & Schecter, 2000; Yon, 1999). For example, critics contend that multicultural education casts non-Whites in Canada as belonging outside the nation-state and therefore reinscribes the colonialist notion of White Anglophone and Francophone Canadians as constituting "real" Canadians (James, 1998; Ng et al., 1995; Walcott,

1997). This is evident in the fact that terms such as "cultural groups" and "other Canadians" do not appear to include those Canadians of Anglo and Celtic origin. According to these terms of debate, then, culture is understood to be found only in and displayed by people who come from somewhere foreign and whose primary language is not English or French (James & Schecter, 2000).

Multiculturalism has also been critiqued for equating race with ethnicity and culture. Central to this ethnicity paradigm is the belief that our society is characterized by equal opportunity, and the contemporary success of Eastern European immigrants in North America is often cited as proof. However, this obscures the fact that, in North America, inequality based on race is not only markedly different, but also significantly more acute than inequality based on ethnicity (Lee, 1996; Omi & Winant, 1993). Multicultural education's emphasis on culture reproduces the ethnicity paradigm and thereby perpetuates the widespread belief that problems faced by racial minority students are not linked to structural barriers attending such issues as racism, but instead to cultural differences. While it is important to recognize the influence of culture on the schooling experience of students, it is equally vital to note how the multicultural paradigm that equates race with ethnicity and culture overlooks the salience of skin colour as a negative impact on the educational experience of students (Dei, 1996).

In addition to precluding a critical grappling with racism in its multiple and structural forms, the notion of "culture" and "identity" embedded in multiculturalism and multicultural education is also highly problematic for its essentialism. The rudimentary notion of culture implicated in multicultural education not only constructs the "cultural Other" (James, 1998) but also ignores the tremendous heterogeneity within any given "cultural group." Essentialist or simplistic notions of culture elide the complex, ambiguous, heterogenous, contingent, temporal, and hybrid nature of cultures (James, 1999). James (1998) contends that culture within the multiculturalist framework is simply "understood as a set of information and observable items and practices that can be identified and communicated" (p. 7). This has often led to expressions of culture in terms of "ethnic" food, costume, art, dance, and making eye contact. The resultant net effect of this "tourist approach" to culture is that these cultural expressions are understood as coming from "elsewhere" outside Canada and thus as being exhibited by "foreign" bodies (James, 1998). This ultimately entrenches, within the discourse and practice of multicultural education, the long-standing notion of non-Whites as being "Other" to the Canadian nation-state.

Both the "model minority" and multiculturalism discourses essentialize a static and ahistorical notion of "Asian culture." This is evidenced in the "model minority" discourse by its idea of a Confucian-laden cultural upbringing that translates into academic success (Suzuki, 1995). Relatedly, multicultural expressions of "Chinese culture" tend to highlight dragon dances, martial arts, and Chinese calligraphy. These simplistic notions of Chinese culture remain frozen in time; remnants of a "foreign," mystical, and ancient Chinese society that is not only long past but ostensibly unattuned to the dynamics of globalization and the actual experiences and interests of today's Chinese Canadian youth.

Edward Said (1979) has referred to such Western stereotypical constructions of Eastern societies as Orientalism. In his seminal text titled *Orientalism*, Said showed how Western intellectuals imagined the geography and history of the "Orient" as the cultural polarity of the "Occident"—an imaginary construct both produced and sustained by the structures of imperialism. According to Said, the Orient is constructed as a mythical and exotic geopolitical region, which is also perverse, cruel, and ignorant vis-à-vis the West. The static and anachronistic notions of Asian culture subsumed within multicultural and "model minority" discourses invoke Orientalism and perpetuate the positioning of "Chinese culture" as something outside Canadian society. What is lost as a result is a grappling with the "Canadianness" of Chinese Canadian culture. According to multiculturalism and the "model minority" discourses, cultures are not seen as hybrid, dynamic, constantly "in the process of becoming" (Hall, 1988), and undergoing the inevitable diasporic processes of cultural fusion (Walcott, 1997).

The Asian "model minority" discourse also serves to reinforce the liberal belief that Canada and its institutions such as schools are accommodating, fair, and accessible to all those who work hard enough. By the same token, the multiculturalism discourse maintains the liberal myth that Canada is a welcoming land of opportunity for all newcomers:

> So while the specific narrative of the federal policy does not define multicultural as meaning non-white, discussions of the questions of immigration and education, for example, often tend to engage in the popular notion of multiculturalism as referring to "non-whites." These appropriations of the term are rife with the recurring myth of Canada as benevolent, caring, and tolerant country that adapts to "strangers" so that strangers do not have to adapt to it. (Walcott, 1997, p. 80)

By operating like two sides of the same coin, the "model minority" stereotype and multiculturalism discourse thus conveniently converge in liberalism and Orientalism. In a dialectical fashion, the "model minority" discourse, which has its roots in the United States, becomes seamlessly conjoined with the hegemonic Canadian discourse of multiculturalism. Together the "model minority" and multiculturalism discourses can be regarded not only as hegemonic devices that maintain White domination, but as mechanisms of control at the disposal of liberal democratic governmentality.

IMPLICATIONS FOR HUMAN SERVICE PROVISION AND EDUCATION

As noted earlier, Eurocentric notions of individualism, particularly in the context of theories of adolescent development, can indeed pathologize more collectively oriented non-Western youth, such as immigrant Canadian Chinese. Important scholarship that advocates grappling with the collectivist influences of Confucian philosophy on Chinese cultures and the interplay of migration factors such as trauma, dislocation, and adjusting to a host society (Lam, 1998) greatly augments better understanding of non-Western youth and more equitable provision of services.

The above discussion of the "model minority" and multicultural discourses, however, alerts us to the potential obstruction of equitable treatment of young Asian Canadians, since these discourses deploy aspects of Confucianism and Chinese collectivism in oppressive and stereotypical ways. For this reason, educators and social workers need to be continually cognizant of the importance of non-essentialist notions of culture that are attuned to the contemporary dynamics of global capitalism and neo-liberal ideologies. By being aware of hegemonic discourses such as "model minority" and multiculturalism in a global context, we make visible the fault lines implicit in static and anachronistic notions of Confucian-laden cultural values. These fault lines alert us to the dangers of reifying Orientalism and the "model minority" stereotype, as human service providers attempt to work across cultures in a just and equitable fashion.

Tension between the need to recognize the more collectivist values of some non-Western European cultures and the New Right's and liberal appropriations of such value systems presents us with a conundrum. One way out is what Daniel Yon (2000) calls the "duality of discourse." In his ethnographic study of students in a large urban high school in Toronto, Yon (1999) found that youths often invoke identities such as "Black" and "woman." Yet, these subjects assert these identities while refusing to be rendered mere objects of such categories. This is evidenced in the following statement made by a youth named Anne (A pseudonym):

> At one point I thought of myself as a Black person and that limits me because as a Black person there are things that I am suppose[d] to be. So I had to shed that. I am not just Black. I am a woman, and that limits me as well. [But]…if I think I am limited then I don't dare risk anything or try to do anything. So "bust" being Black and "bust" being a woman. (Yon, 1999, pp. 37–38)

Anne's pronouncement highlights the "duality of discourse" or what Yon (1999) describes as the young woman's ability to live "by the object that is made of oneself while working against the objectification at the same time" (p. 38). Bearing in mind this notion of the duality of discourse and how youths such as Anne negotiate identities, I suggest that human service providers might benefit from this young woman's insights. While recognizing the Confucian-influenced cultural values of some Chinese Canadians, human service providers must be alert, nonetheless, to the limitations of contemporary Confucian discourses. When human service providers are aware of these limitations, attention is called to the tenuous notion of Confucian-influenced Asian Canadian youth.

Duality of discourse for social work praxis might thus be understood as a certain wariness, a positive skepticism that human service providers might bring to bear upon the application of social categories such as "Asian" and "collectivist," especially if these are imagined as stable, unchanging, and outside contemporary global contexts. While recognizing that social categories premised on aspects of social difference such as race, gender, and culture do indeed have material effects, often deleterious ones, social workers who understand the duality of discourse can go further to grapple with how individuals are nonetheless continually engaged in complex ways of living with, and resisting, these representations, be they negative or positive (Yon, 2000). Most importantly, as Yon notes about African Canadian youth, "they also know how to discard them [representations] or to refuse their disciplinary effects" (p. 131). Similarly, Stacey Lee (1996) found, in her ethnography of a large suburban East Coast high school in America, that several Asian American youths, while critical of the "model minority" discourse, also enjoyed deploying it to their benefit. For example, some students jovially recounted stories about how, when accosted by teachers to explain why they had skipped classes, they would lie about having to help their families. Through their understanding of how the "model minority" discourse promoted popular beliefs about Confucian-inspired, Asian familial cohesion and collectivism, these youths highlight the duality of discourse. Indeed, the teachers readily accepted the youths' excuses, never questioning their veracity (Lee, 1996).

The implications of the duality of discourse for social workers and educators suggest the need to work continually with, but at the same time against, the limits of social categories. In this way a reliance on binary categories such as Eastern/Western, Asian/non-Asian, and collectivist/individualistic is kept in check as one strives for a sensitive, caring, and equitable cross-cultural provision of services to racially diverse groups of Canadian youth.

Questions for Reflection

1. Why does the Asian "model minority" discourse dovetail well with Canadian discourses of multiculturalism?
2. What Asian Canadian ethnic group is constructed to be a "model minority?"
3. How does the media support the stereotype that Asians in Canada are model minorities?
4. How does the model minority discourse operate as a "double narrative?"
5. What are the implications of the Asian Canadian model minority stereotype for education and social work?

REFERENCES

Anderson, B. (1993). *Imagined communities: Reflections on the origin and spread of nationalism.* London, UK: Verso.

Bhabha, H. (1994). *The location of culture.* London, UK: Routledge.

Bramble, M. (2000). Black education: Past, present, and future. In T. Goldstein & D. Selby (Eds.), *Weaving connections: Education for peace, environmental and social justice* (pp. 99–119). Toronto: Sumach Press.

Brand, D. (1987). The new whiz kids: Those Asian Americans. *Time 31*(August), 42–51.

The Canadian Multicultural Act. (1988). Retrieved from http://www.pier21.ca/research/immigration-history/canadian-multiculturalism-act-1988

Chan, A. (1983). *Gold mountain.* Vancouver: New Star Books.

Chang, C. (1957). *The development of Neo-Confucian thought.* New Haven, CT: United Printing Services.

Chun, K. (1995). The myth of Asian American success and its educational ramifications. In D. T. Nakinishi & T. Y. Nishida (Eds.), *The Asian American educational experience: A source book for teachers and students* (pp. 95–112). New York: Routledge.

Dei, G. S. (1996). *Anti-racism education: Theory and practice.* Halifax: Fernwood

Gillmor, D. (1998). Satellite city. *Toronto Life* (November), 146–150.

Gordon, C. (1991). Governmental rationality: An introduction. In G. Burchell, C. Gordon, & P. Miller, (Eds.), *The Foucault effect* (pp. 1–51). Chicago, IL: University of Chicago Press.

Hall, S. (1988). *New ethnicities, Black Film, British Cinema. ICA Document No. 7.* London, UK: ICA.

Henry, F., C. Tator, W. Mattis, & Rees, R. (1995). *The colour of democracy: Racism in Canadian society.* Toronto: Harcourt Brace.

Ho, D. Y. F. (1979). Psychological implications of collectivism: With special reference to the Chinese case and Maoist dialectics. In L. H. Eckensberger, W. J. Lonner, & Y. H Poortinga, (Eds.), *Cross cultural contributions to psychology* (pp. 143–150). Lisse, Netherlands: Swets & Zeitlinger.

Hoefstede, G. (1983). Dimensions of national cultures in fifty countries and three Regions. In J. B. Deregowski, S. Dziurawiec, & R. C. Annis, (Eds.), *Expectations in cross-cultural psychology* (pp. 335–355). Lisse, Netherlands; Swets & Zeitlinger.

Hui, C. H., & Triandis, H. C. (1986). Measurement in cross-cultural psychology: A review and comparison of strategies. *Journal of Cross-cultural Psychology, 16*(2), 131–152.

James, C. E. (1998). *Multiculturalism, diversity and education in the Canadian context: The search for an inclusive pedagogy.* Paper presented at the Annual Meeting of American Education Research Association, San Diego, California.

James, C. E. (1999). *Seeing ourselves: Exploring race, culture, and identity* (2nd ed.) Toronto: Thompson.

James, C. E, & Schecter, S. R. (2000). Mainstreaming and marginalization: Two national strategies in the circumscription of difference. *Pedagogy, Culture & Society, 8*(1), 23–41.

Kristeva, J. (1974). *About Chinese women.* New York: Urizen Books.

Lam, C. M. (1998). Adolescent development in the context of Canadian Chinese immigrant families. *Canadian Social Work Review, 15*(2), 177–191.

Lee, R. G. (1999). *Oriental: Asian Americans in popular culture.* Philadelphia, PA: Temple University Press.

Lee, S. (1996). *Unraveling the "model minority" stereotype: Listening to Asian American youth.* New York: Teachers College Press.

Ling, A. (1990). *Between worlds: Women writers of Chinese ancestry.* New York: Pergamon Press.

Lo, L., & Wang, S. (1997). Settlement patterns of Toronto's Chinese immigrants: Convergence or divergence? *Canadian Journal of Regional Science, 20*(1), 49–72.

Lowe, L. (1996). *Immigrant acts: On Asian American cultural politics*. Durham, NC: Duke University Press.

Maclear, K. (1994). The myth of the model minority: Rethinking the education of Asian Canadians. *Our Schools/Our Selves, 5*(3), 54–76.

Mathews, J. (1988). Asians make 'average' school academic giant." *Montreal Gazette* (June 15), A6.

Ng, R. (1993). Racism, sexism, and nation building in Canada. In C. McCarthy & W. Crichlow (Eds.), *Race, identity, and representation in education* (pp. 50–59). New York: Routledge.

Ng, R., Staton, P., & Scane, J. (1995). *Anti-racism, feminism, and critical approaches to education*. Toronto: OISE Press.

Omi, M., & Takagi, D. Y. (1996). Situating Asian Americans in the political discourse on affirmative action. *Representations* (Summer), 155–162.

Omi, M., & Winant, H. (1993). On the theoretical concept of race. In C. McCarthy & W. Crichlow (Eds.), *Race, identity, and representation in education* (pp. 3–10). New York: Routledge.

Ong, A. (1996). Cultural citizenship as subject-making: Immigrants negotiate racial and cultural boundaries in the United States. *Current Anthropology, 37*(5), 736–762.

Ong, A. (1999). *Flexible citizenship: The culture and logic of transnationality*. Durham, NC: Duke University Press.

Palumbo-Liu, D. (1999). *Asian/American: Historical crossings of a racial frontier*. Stanford, CA: Stanford University Press.

Petersen, W. (1966). Success story: Japanese-American style. *New York Times Magazine* (January 9), 21.

Said, E. W. (1979). *Orientalism*. London, UK: Penguin.

Sheppard, R. (1992). Kitchen table the key to success. *Globe and Mail* (February 3), A11.

Suzuki, B. H (1995). Education and the socialization of Asian Americans: A revisionist analysis of the 'model minority' thesis " In D. T. Nakinishi & T. Y. Nishida (Eds.), *The Asian American educational experience: A sourcebook for teachers and students* (pp. 113–132). New York: Routledge.

Teeple, G. (1995). *Globalization and the decline of social reform*. Toronto: Garamond Press.

Walcott, R. (1997). *Black like who*. Toronto: Insomniac Press.

Wei, W. (1993). *The Asian American movement*. Philadelphia, PA: Temple University Press.

Yon, D. (1999). The discursive space of schooling: On the theories of power and empowerment in multiculturalism and anti-racism. In A. Cheater (Ed.), *The anthropology of power* (pp. 28–41). New York: Routledge.

Yon, D. (2000). *Elusive culture: Schooling, race, and identity in global times*. New York: State University of New York Press.

CHAPTER 6

THE MODEL MINORITY AND YELLOW PERIL STEREOTYPES IN NEW ZEALAND JOURNALISM

Grant Hannis

This chapter considers the depiction of Chinese in the print media of New Zealand, a small country in the south Pacific whose dominant culture is white European. The analysis focuses on the major influx of Chinese immigrants into the country in the early 2000s. To set the context, we begin by looking at the history of Chinese immigration into New Zealand. The chapter goes on to consider the reporting on diversity in the New Zealand journalism industry. Using content analysis, we then examine how the Chinese were depicted in a major New Zealand newspaper and discuss the controversy that arose following the contemporaneous publication of an article on Chinese immigration in a major national New Zealand magazine. The chapter reveals that the Yellow Peril stereotype was alive and well in New Zealand during the influx of new Chinese immigrants.

The Chinese in New Zealand

The colonization of New Zealand by white settlers began in 1840 when representatives of Maori (New Zealand's indigenous people) and the British crown signed the Treaty of Waitangi. Following the subsequent major inflow of British

Killing the Model Minority Stereotype: Asian American Counterstories and Complicity,
pages 97–115.
Copyright © 2015 by Information Age Publishing
All rights of reproduction in any form reserved.

settlers, English-speaking white European culture has since become the country's dominant culture (King, 2003).

Chinese gold miners began to arrive in significant numbers in the colony in the 1860s (Ng, 1999; Te Ara, 2008a). Concerns over competition from Chinese workers for white employment led the government to enact laws to limit Chinese immigration. A poll tax on each new Chinese immigrant was first imposed in 1881, rising to £100 per head in 1896. The law was finally repealed in the 1940s.

The number of Chinese dramatically declined with the end of the gold rush era late in the 19th century. In the 1901 census, Europeans were overwhelmingly the largest ethnic group in the country, accounting for 94 percent of the country's population of 815,853. Most of the rest were Maori, with Chinese representing less than one percent of the population (Te Ara, 1966). Yet anti-Chinese sentiment actually intensified. Various anti-Chinese organizations were formed, and in 1908 the government passed the Immigration Restriction Act to consolidate laws impeding Chinese immigration.

The second wave of Chinese—and, more generally, Asian—immigration into New Zealand occurred beginning in 1987. This was prompted by uncertainty over the status of Hong Kong and a general sense among Chinese that New Zealand was a good place to start a new life. The influx was aided by the New Zealand government changing the immigration laws to permit equal access into New Zealand for all ethnic groups. These changes also coincided with a sharp increase in the number of Asian international students (Ng, 1999).

As a result, between 1991 and 2006 the proportion of Asians in the population trebled, from three percent of the population to nine percent, easily the largest increase for any single ethnic group over the period (Table 6.1). Most Asians settled in the country's cities, especially Auckland, the country's main commercial center. The only ethnic group to see a fall in its percentage share of the population was New Zealand Europeans, although they continued to be the dominant cultural group.

TABLE 6.1.   Percentage Distribution of the New Zealand Population by Ethnicity, 1991 and 2006

Ethnicity	1991	2006	% change
European	83.2	78.7	−5.4
Maori	13	14.6	12.3
Pacific	5	6.9	38
Asian	3	9.2	206.7
Other	0.2	0.9	350

Source: Statistics New Zealand (2008)
Note: Percentage totals may exceed 100%, as respondents could give multiple answers

A 2007 survey of New Zealanders' attitudes found that 81 percent believed Asians in New Zealand contributed to the economy, and 76 percent believed Asian immigrants brought valuable cultural diversity to the country. The New Zealand political climate was also generally favorable towards the Chinese. The government apologized for the anti-Chinese laws of the previous centuries (Clark, 2002; Wong, 2003). And when Dunedin, the city in the area that was once the center of much of the gold-rush activity, opened a Chinese garden, the city declared that it was "to commemorate the contribution the Chinese people have made, and continue to make, to the city" (City of Dunedin, 2008, para. 2). But some politicians have capitalized on lingering concerns among older white New Zealanders and conservative Maori about the influx of Chinese. Most notably, Winston Peters, the high-profile leader of political party New Zealand First, called for curbs on Asian immigration (Wong, 2003).

Reporting Diversity

Most new recruits in the New Zealand journalism industry are produced by the country's 10 journalism schools, based at universities and technical institutes. The schools typically teach modules on reporting on diversity, but the students are not themselves from a diverse range of ethnic backgrounds. Looking at figures for 2006 and 2007 for the four main ethnic groups in New Zealand, the proportions of ethnic groups among both journalism students and working journalists largely do not mirror that of the general New Zealand population (Figure 6.1). Whereas 79 percent of the New Zealand population was of European ethnicity, the figure for working journalists was higher (83 percent) and for students was essentially the same (78 percent). Clearly, journalists and journalism students were overwhelmingly from the dominant cultural voice.

By contrast, whereas 15 percent of the general population was Maori, only nine percent of journalists were Maori. Although the figure for journalism students was 16 percent, fractionally higher than in the general population, this was largely due to one journalism school, at the Waiariki Institute of Technology, having a large number of Maori students. If that school is removed from the figures, the percentage of Maori drops to nine percent.

There was a striking discrepancy in the Asian figures. Whereas nine percent of the general population was Asian, only two percent of journalists and journalism students were of this ethnicity.

Finally, whereas seven percent of the population was of Pacific Island ethnicity, only five percent of journalists and two percent of journalism students were of this ethnic background. So, although compared to the overall population the journalism workforce and journalism students generally had proportionately less people from the three main non-European New Zealand ethnic groups, the discrepancy was most pronounced for Asians.

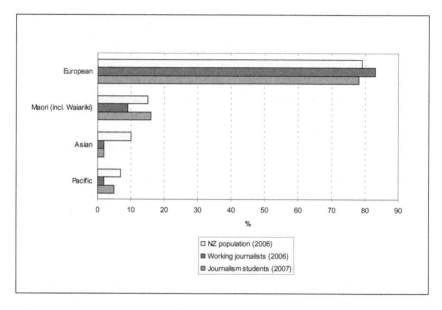

FIGURE 6.1. Percentage Ethnic Composition of the New Zealand Population, Journalism Workforce, and Total Journalism Students, 2006/2007. Source: Statistics NZ (2008), New Zealand Journalists Training Organisation (2006a), New Zealand Journalists Training Organisation (2006b).

Many educators and journalists were aware of the issue. In 2006 seven of the 10 journalism school heads in New Zealand reported that their classes had few students of Maori, Pacific Island, or Asian ethnicity (New Zealand Journalists Training Organisation, 2006a). Several reasons have been identified as to why few Asian students enter journalism schools, including the demanding English language requirements, the industry requirement that students master shorthand, the high level of general knowledge required, the fact that there are few Asian role models in journalism, and the perception among Asians that journalism offers fewer career prospects compared to, say, law and medicine (Tan, 2006; Asia New Zealand Foundation, 2008). Possible solutions could include promoting journalism in Asian communities as a career, providing intensive English courses for Asian journalism students, and fostering links between Asian and mainstream media (Tan, 2006).

About two-thirds of journalists in a 2006 survey said journalists from non-European New Zealand ethnic groups were under-represented in respondents' newsrooms (New Zealand Journalists Training Organisation, 2006b). When asked how to increase the number of journalists from non-European New Zealand ethnic groups in newsrooms, the single largest proportion of respondents (19 percent) said such people should be encouraged to train at journalism schools. This was followed by nine percent saying there should be active recruitment of people from such ethnic groups and eight percent saying there needed to be more Asian journalists.

Many respondents also noted resulting difficulties in covering non-European New Zealand ethnic group issues. Respondents were asked to rate their confidence in covering Maori, Asian, and Pacific Island issues. Whereas a third said they were "a bit uncertain" or "out of my depth" when covering Maori issues, virtually half the respondents said the same for covering Pacific Island and Asian issues (49 and 48 percent respectively).

Not all Asian journalists work in the mainstream media. There has been growth in Asian-specific media in New Zealand over recent years. In 2006, for instance, there were about 17 Chinese-language newspapers distributed as free newspapers in Auckland, Wellington, and Christchurch. However, many of these newspapers do not employ journalists, relying instead on contributions from readers and reprinting Internet news from China. Those newspapers that do hire journalists may also require them to find advertising for the newspaper and/or design the paper (Tan, 2006).

The Asia New Zealand Foundation, a not-for-profit organization that promotes links between Asia and New Zealand, has sought to promote better reporting of Asian issues in the mainstream media. Each year, the foundation offers a range of scholarships allowing journalism students and working journalists to travel and work in Asia. The foundations says such scholarships were designed

> to encourage interesting, considered, in-depth coverage of Asian issues that will give New Zealanders a context within which to develop greater understanding of the region, its economies, business environment, politics, cultures and peoples, and/ or New Zealand's relations with countries in the region (Asia New Zealand Foundation, 2008, para. 4).

Another mechanism whereby ethnic diversity can be better represented in the media is by the use of codes of ethics. For instance, responsible reporting on diversity is included in the 13 principles used by the print-journalism industry's self-regulatory body, the New Zealand Press Council. The majority of council members are drawn from outside the industry. If a complaint is upheld, the publication must print the substance of the council's decision. No fines can be imposed. The council hears complaints about newspapers, magazines, and periodicals, which it considers in light of its guiding principles (New Zealand Press Council, 2008a).

The council's Principle 1 centered on accuracy, and in the early 2000s read:

> Publications (newspapers and magazines) should be guided at all times by accuracy, fairness and balance, and should not deliberately mislead or misinform readers by commission, or omission (New Zealand Press Council, 2008b, para. 1).

The Press Council's Principle 6 included diversity:

Publications should not place gratuitous emphasis on gender, religion, minority groups, sexual orientation, age, race, colour or physical or mental disability. Nevertheless, where it is relevant and in the public interest, publications may report and express opinions in these areas (New Zealand Press Council, 2008b, para. 10).

Newspaper Coverage

The first piece of content analysis (Neuendorf, 2002; Swoboda, 1995) considers coverage of Chinese in New Zealand in the daily newspaper *The Evening Post*. This paper was published in Wellington, the country's capital, from 1865. In 2002 it merged with its morning rival, *The Dominion*, to become *The Dominion Post*. Analysis of this newspaper's coverage therefore reveals how the Chinese were portrayed in one of the country's leading newspapers and, since it is the only newspaper in Wellington that existed at the start of both the 20th and 21st centuries, allows a consideration of changes in coverage in the same newspaper over time.

The first period analyzed was 1 June 1906 to 31 May 1908 inclusive. This two-year period covered the public debate over the Immigration Restriction Act, thereby targeting the timeframe when the status of Chinese in New Zealand was a major journalistic topic. An online database of historical New Zealand newspapers, *Papers Past*, was used to obtain newspaper articles for this period, available at New Zealand's National Library (www.natlib.govt.nz).

The second period analyzed was 1 June 2006 to 31 May 2008 inclusive. Exactly 100 years later, this two-year period allowed an assessment of whether attitudes had changed after a century, following the second influx of Chinese that had commenced in the latter part of the 20th century. An online database of modern New Zealand newspapers, *Newztext*, was used to obtain newspaper articles for this second period, available at The Knowledge Basket (www.knowledge-basket.co.nz).

Searches were undertaken in both *Papers Past* and *Newztext* to obtain all articles on Chinese in New Zealand and Chinese immigration to New Zealand. The search produced 141 articles for the first period (42,939 cm^2) and 106 articles for the second (33,979 cm^2). Each line of copy in each article was coded by:

- Topic. The coding revealed five main topics in the coverage: Chinese immigration into New Zealand, Chinese activity in New Zealand, crime involving Chinese, Chinese protests over their treatment in New Zealand, and other.
- Tone. If the tone of a line of text painted Chinese in a favorable light, it was coded as positive. If the line's tone depicted the Chinese in a poor light, it was coded negative. The remainder was coded neutral.

- Voice. Any attribution of material in each line was coded as being either a Chinese or non-Chinese voice. The remainder was deemed to be the newspaper's voice, a non-Chinese source.

The content analysis was undertaken by two research assistants, with the author closely supervising the process. Ten percent of the articles were checked for inter-coder reliability, producing a robust score of 90 percent. The results are summarized in Table 6.2.

TABLE 6.2. The Evening Post/The Dominion Post coverage of Chinese in New Zealand, 1906–08 and 2006–08 (percentage of cm2).

Category	1906–08		2006–08	
	% of total reportage	% of category	% of total reportage	% of category
Topic				
Chinese immigration	42.1		9.0	
• Chinese unwanted		92.4		21.1
• Chinese wanted		1.9		72.2
• Other		5.7		6.7
Chinese activity in NZ	18.9		35.4	
• Business activity in NZ		38.1		29.1
• Other		61.9		70.9
Crime	18.5		36.4	
• Chinese committing crime		77.8		82.7
• Chinese victims of crime		22.2		17.3
Chinese protest their treatment in NZ	8.8		15.8	
Other	11.7		3.4	
Totals	100.0		100.0	
Voice and tone				
Non-Chinese	87.5		80.2	
• Non-Chinese negative		67.7		62.6
• Non-Chinese neutral		25.5		7.7
• Non-Chinese positive		6.9		29.7
Chinese	11.5		20.0	
• Chinese negative		7.0		50.0
• Chinese neutral		22.6		9.0
• Chinese positive		70.4		41.0
Totals	100.0		100.0	

Source: Content analysis
Note: Figures may not sum to 100 due to rounding.

TOPICS

Chinese Immigration

In the 1906–08 material, Chinese immigration to New Zealand was the main topic of reportage, accounting for 42 percent of all the material. This was nearly all (92 percent) reporting that Chinese were unwanted in New Zealand. A local anti-Chinese organization, the Anti-Asiatic League, said it "was unnecessary to go into the immorality of the Chinese; their ways were well known" (May 2, 1907, p. 2). The most senior politician in the country, Premier Joseph Ward, agreed, saying, "It was all important that the white inhabitants of Australasia should preserve their racial purity" (December 3, 1906, p. 7). The newspaper itself described Chinese as "undesirable immigrants" (November 14, 1907, p. 6) who threatened white men's jobs: "The Chinese is not a better worker, but he is a cheaper one" (June 22, 1907, p. 9). One item was headlined "THE YELLOW PERIL" (July 23, 1907, p. 2).

The 2006–08 material was in stark contrast, with Chinese immigration the smallest single topic area, accounting for only nine percent of reportage. About three-quarters focused on Chinese being wanted in New Zealand. While one might expect to see the model minority stereotype being used here, it is actually difficult to detect. One article profiled a young Chinese woman who had moved to Wellington: "It very well may be that the first word every Asian immigrant learns on coming to New Zealand is 'cool'. Si-Si says it a lot. And she is, actually" (January 2007, 17, p. 6). The government felt much the same, it was reported: "Skilled workers from India and China will find it easier to migrate to New Zealand when the Government relaxes restrictions to fill skill shortages" (July 1, 2006, p. 6).

There was a vestige of anti-Chinese feeling, with 21 percent of immigration coverage reporting on Chinese not being wanted in New Zealand. This included hate crimes—"a Chinese student was assaulted by three men in a racially motivated attack" (December 11, 2007, p. 4)—and a New Zealand First politician saying that increased immigration would cause "division, friction and resentment" in New Zealand (April 3, 2008, p. 1).

Chinese Activity in New Zealand

In the earlier period, Chinese activity in New Zealand comprised, at 19 percent, the second-equal largest topic area. The single largest portion of this coverage was Chinese business activity, comprising 38 percent, nearly all of which (91 percent) was reporting on Chinese market gardeners. The newspaper was concerned about the economic threat of such activity:

> The main interest in the fruit struggle is a European attack on the Chinese monopolists…John [i.e., John Chinaman, a racial epithet] is heavily fortified; he has barricaded himself behind his towers of apples, peaches, and oranges (March 30, 1907, p. 5).

In the later period, Chinese activity also figured significantly, at 35 percent of all reportage. Again, the largest single sub-category was Chinese business activity in New Zealand (29 percent), including the opening of an Asian supermarket (May 12, 2007, p. 10), the sale of a well-known Chinese restaurant (May 22, 2007, p. 6), and a profile of a high-profile Chinese New Zealand lawyer (December 12, 2007, p. 4). The reportage contained no suggestions that this Chinese activity was crowding out whites' economic interests. A broad range of other activities was also reported, including Chinese cultural events and international students in New Zealand (for instance, May 30, 2007, p. 7; August 26, 2006, p. 13).

Crime

The second-equal large category in the 1906–08 material was crime coverage (19 percent). About three-quarters reported on Chinese committing crimes, although these were not violent crimes. Instead, we learn of Chinese shops staying open after shops run by white New Zealanders had closed and Chinese smoking opium and gambling (for instance, July 30, 1907, p. 6; November 30, 1907, p. 9). Such activities were ostensibly illegal at the time (Te Ara, 2008b).

Of the 22 percent of material reporting Chinese being the victims of crime, two-thirds concerned violent crime, often hate crimes committed by whites. To take one example, four men entered Wellington's Chinese district and "assaulted every Chinese who passed them. They threw stones and even a piece of iron" (July 20, 1907, p. 4).

In the latter period, crime accounted for 36 percent of all coverage, making it the single most commonly reported Chinese news in the period. 83 percent of this coverage was of Chinese committing crime, including violent crimes. This included reports on Nai Yin Xue, who murdered his wife Anan Liu in Auckland, abandoned their daughter in Australia, and fled to the United States:

> Anan Liu, was murdered, her body stuffed in a car boot, and American authorities are hunting for Qian's father, Nai Yin Xue, in Los Angeles (September 24, 2007, p. 3).

Other crimes included the kidnapping and murder of a Chinese student by three fellow Chinese students, as well as drugs offenses (for instance, 5 September 5, 2007, p. 5; September 14, 2007, p. 12).

Seventeen percent of coverage involved Chinese as the victims of crime, about three-quarters of which involved violence. These included a woman punching a Chinese woman for speaking in her own language (June 29, 2006, p. 6) and Chinese attacking others in the Chinese community, such as the kidnapping and murder of a Chinese student mentioned above (for instance, September 5, 2007, p. 5).

Chinese Protest their Treatment in New Zealand

Nine percent of coverage in the earlier period was about Chinese protesting their treatment in New Zealand. This primarily concerned an organization Chinese themselves set up to oppose the proposed further restriction of Chinese immigration into New Zealand. In a letter to King Edward VII, the organization wrote:

> Chinese residents of the Dominion [ie, New Zealand] are peaceful, hard-working, and law-abiding. The proportion of law-breakers among them is considerably smaller than among European residents, and practically all offences committed by them are of a minor character (March 4, 1908, p. 2).

This topic was more significant in the 2006–08 material, accounting for 16 percent of the coverage. Most reports were of the group Falun Gong complaining that the Wellington City Council was preventing it from taking part in city festivals. To take one example: "Falun Gong is taking action against Wellington City Council to challenge a ban on taking part in street parades" (November 1, 2007, p. 7).

VOICE AND TONE

Non-Chinese Voice

The overwhelming majority of the 1906–08 material (88 percent) was in a non-Chinese voice. About two-thirds of this voice was in a negative tone. Half of all the negatively toned coverage was from the newspaper itself, a quarter from community leaders and professionals (such as lawyers and judges), 16 percent from politicians, and the remainder from anti-Chinese organizations. Clearly, anti-Chinese feeling was widespread in the community. Bluntly racist language was frequently used. The *Post* said Chinese lived in "hovels," that "Their jowls are sleek, their slant eyes twinkle" (June 22, 1907, p. 9), and that they break into "the inscrutable, mirthless smile of the East" (July 29, 1907, p. 3).

Positively toned material accounted for only seven percent of the non-Chinese voiced material. About 60 percent of this was the newspaper, such as when it described a Chinese child adopted by a New Zealand missionary: "Pih is aged five years, and she is a bright, intelligent-looking, ruddy-cheeked girl" (February 7, 1908, p. 3). Community leaders and professionals comprised most of the rest (26 percent).

In the later period, non-Chinese voices also dominated—80 percent—although a slightly smaller proportion of that (63 percent) was negative. This was primarily the newspaper (72 percent), with most of the remainder being community leaders and professionals (23 percent). The newspaper did not employ racist or derogatory terms, but its propensity for crime reporting meant the tone of the coverage still had a negative tone:

> Retired Chinese couple Ena and Hok Lai Dung were trying to help a younger friend fuel her drug addiction when they agreed to take part in an elaborate scam to get supplies of the painkiller pethidine (September 18, 2007, p. 6).

Far more of the non-Chinese voice was positive, 30 percent, compared to the earlier period. This was also mostly the newspaper (71 percent). For example, one of the newspaper's editorials said a New Zealand First politician's criticism of Asian immigration was "a distasteful attempt to revive his party's flagging fortunes by singling out a minority distinguished by its skin colour" (April 4, 2008, p. 4). Another 23 percent were community leaders and professionals.

Chinese Voice

Twelve percent of the 1906–08 material was in a Chinese voice. Of this, 70 percent was positively toned, primarily Chinese protesting New Zealand's anti-Chinese laws, as discussed above. Seven percent of the Chinese-voice material was negative. This was local Chinese criticizing the activities of other Chinese, such as one complaining:

> No. Now b'long welly hard for Chinaman to come British subjee'. You make 'm more hard. You talkee Chinaman no good; bad man; no clean; tief, liar (November 30, 1907, p. 9).

It seems likely the newspaper reported the direct quotations in this way to mock the Chinese person.

In the later period, the Chinese voice accounted for a higher proportion of the reportage (20 percent). Half was negative, of which 59 percent came from community leaders and professionals. This coverage was frequently of disputes between local Chinese and representatives of the Chinese government. This included the Chinese Embassy accusing Falun Gong of brainwashing its followers (May 12, 2007, p. 4) and a local Chinese reporter complaining that a Chinese official had him ejected from an event (for instance, March 27, 2007, p. 2).

Forty-one percent of the Chinese voice was positive, of which 60 percent came from community leaders and professionals. When a Chinese New Zealander became manager of the Wellington hockey team, for instance, she commented, "I want to use my skills of being an elite individual athlete to add value to a team environment" (May 14, 2007, p. 2).

The "Asian Angst" Article

The monthly glossy current affairs magazine *North & South* is one of New Zealand's leading journalistic publications. In 2007 the magazine had a readership of 290,000, putting it among the top 20 magazines by readership in the country (AGB Nielsen Media Research, 2008).

In late 2006 *North & South* ran a major story on Chinese crime in New Zealand, advertised on the cover of the magazine as "Asian Angst: Is it time to send some back?" (Coddington, 2006). The article used the terms "Asian" and "Chinese" interchangeably and was primarily concerned with crimes committed by those with "a Chinese-sounding name" (p. 40).

The article was highly controversial and, following complaints it received on the article, the Press Council ruled it was inaccurate and discriminatory (New Zealand Press Council, 2007). (Declaration of interest: The author was one of those who complained to the Press Council). Table 6.3 summarizes a content analysis of the article, which comprised 1123.5 cm² of text. The content analysis was conducted by the present author, using the same approach as that for *The Evening Post/Dominion Post* material above.

TABLE 6.3. Content analysis of "Asian Angst" article text (1123.5 cm²)

Category	% of total reportage	% of category
Topic		
Crime	68.7	
• Chinese committing crime		88.4
• Chinese victims of crime		11.6
Chinese immigration	18.0	
• Chinese unwanted		19.1
• Chinese wanted		16.8
• Other		64.0
Other	13.3	
Total topic	100.0	
Voice and tone		
Non-Chinese		
• Negative	72.8	78.7
• Positive	3.8	4.1
• Neutral	15.9	17.2
Total non-Chinese	92.5	100.0
Chinese		
• Negative	4.2	56.5
• Positive	1.1	14.5
• Neutral	2.2	29.0
Total Chinese	7.5	100.0
Total voices	100.0	

Source: Content analysis

Topics

The single largest topic in the article was crime (69 percent). This was overwhelmingly comprised of Chinese committing crime (88 percent), including murder, kidnapping, drug-trafficking, and deception. Examples included: "Zeshen Zhou was jailed for 17 years after being found guilty of murdering his wife" (p. 47), "when sentencing a 25-year-old Chinese kidnapper" (p. 41), "Alex Kwong Wong...received a 17-year jail term for importing methamphetamine" (p. 41), "the commission prosecuted Jonathan Ken...for falsely labelling and selling ordinary honey" (p. 45).

The remaining material concerned Chinese as the victims of crime. But this material continued to emphasize the danger Chinese posed, by exclusively reporting on Chinese as the victims of *Chinese* crime. For instance: "Tam was nearly killed by his then wife, Jai Fong Zhou, when she whacked him 10 times with his own meat cleaver" (p. 41).

The second-largest topic, comprising 18 percent of the text, was Chinese immigration into New Zealand. Most of this material simply stated the immigration situation, but it created a sense of Yellow Peril panic by linking Chinese immigration with crime, as exemplified by the standfirst (the large text at the start of the article):

> In the past 15 years we've opened our borders to people from North Asia and all they needed was money and a clean bill of health.

But, as DEBORAH CODDINGTON reports, they also brought murder, extortion, kidnapping, assassinations and disease (p. 39).

The Yellow Peril motif can also be detected in the article's depiction of Asians as an other, in contrast with average (presumably white) New Zealand. The article says that, because of Asian crime, "disquiet grows in heartland New Zealand about the quality of migrants we're letting through the door" (p. 40). The article describes how such crime affects "the average New Zealander" (p. 40), the "Frustration about Asians' attitude to New Zealand law" (p. 41), and how Asians poach paua [a species of shellfish] when "New Zealanders regard paua as a national treasure" (p. 47).

VOICE AND TONE

Non-Chinese

The article overwhelmingly used non-Chinese voices (93 percent), most (79 percent) of which were negative in tone. About half of the negative non-Chinese voice was the magazine, which spoke of "the gathering crime tide" (p. 40), the "Asian menace" (p. 41), Asians criminals' "brazen pursuit of big money" (p. 42), and the "monotonous regularity" of Asian crime (p. 47). The next largest category was the police, who accounted for 29 percent of the non-Chinese negative material. For instance, one police officer said that "drug peddling was becoming the 'crime of choice' within the international student community" (p. 43). Another 14 percent was from community leaders and professional people, such as a district court judge stating, "Hardly a week goes by…without the kidnap of a Chinese student" (p. 42).

Only four percent of the non-Chinese voice was positive. 44 percent of this was community leaders and professional people, such as an immigration officer who observed that "the Asian reputation as a law-abiding community is still there" (p. 44). A further 25 percent were comments from politicians, such as the immigration minister noting that "he's seen no evidence Asian crime rates are higher than any other ethnic groups" (p. 47). A further 30 percent of the non-Chinese positive voice was the magazine, which stated near the start of the article that "the vast majority of Asians making New Zealand their new home are hard-working, focused on getting their children well educated, and ensuring they're not dependent on the state" (p. 40). This was the clearest example of model-minority commentary detected in any of the reportage considered in this chapter.

Eight percent of the text was in a Chinese voice. Just over half was negative in tone. This included a Chinese woman who had lived in New Zealand for many years and was "sad and angry at increasing criminality among recent Asian immigrants" (p. 46). Fifteen percent of the Chinese voice was positive, and was comprised of the same woman's comments on the descendants of 19th-century Chinese immigrants, who, she said, "went to universities and entered professions" (p. 46).

Critical Assessment of the Crime Statistics

Although the article focused on summarizing crime stories that had already appeared elsewhere in the news media, 10 percent of the article was statistical analysis, used to paint a picture of rising Asian crime. The article said,

> [F]rom 1996 to 2005, total offences committed by Asiatics (not including Indians) aged 17 to 50 rose 53 percent, from 1791 to 2751. Compare that with offences committed by Pacific Islanders, who make up 6.5 percent of the population. They certainly committed more offences—11,292 in the same decade—but their increase was only 2.9 percent (p. 44).

The standard statistical measure of the incidence of crime is the crime rate (Statistics New Zealand, 2006). This is the number of reported crimes divided by the relevant population and then multiplied by some number, often 10,000. The crime rate, which was not calculated in the article, is calculated here, using data for the time periods and populations used in the article (Figure 6.2).

As the article noted, in 1996 the number of Asian apprehensions (that is, arrests of Asians) was 1791. A national census was conducted in 1996, and the total population of Asians in New Zealand was 78,513. The Asian crime rate in 1996 was therefore 228.1 crimes per 10,000 Asians. In 2005 the number of crime ap-

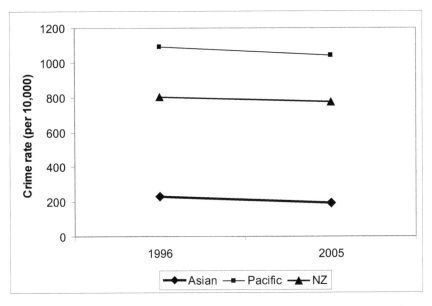

FIGURE 6.2. Asian, Pacific Island and New Zealand crime rates, 1996 (actual) and 2005 (estimate). *Source:* Derived by author from Statistics NZ data.

prehensions for Asians was 2752 (the article said 2751, presumably a typographical error). Using census data for 2001 and 2006, the author prepared a robust population estimate for the number of Asians for 2005 of 142,527. The crime rate was therefore 193.1 crimes per 10,000 Asians.

So the Asian crime rate *fell* by 15 percent between 1996 and 2005—the gathering tide of Asian crime that *North & South* identified did not exist. The number of arrests rose by 54 percent, but the Asian population rose by 82 percent. As a result, Asians were committing proportionately less crime, not more.

The article also said the rise in Asian crime was greater than for Pacific Islanders. But the crime rate was 1091.2 per 10,000 Pacific Islanders aged 17 to 50 in 1996, and 1041.3 in 2005. That is, in 2005 the Pacific Island crime rate was more than five times that for Asians. The Pacific Island crime rate did fall across the period, but by only five percent. The Asian crime rate fell by three times that.

For the entire New Zealand population, the crime rate was 801.9 per 10,000 New Zealanders aged 17 to 50 in 1996, and 772.4 in 2005. In other words, in 2005 the crime rate for all New Zealanders was four times that for Asians. Clearly, Asians were far more law-abiding than was the general population.

Reaction to the Article

The article created a storm of controversy, with *North & South* publishing 23 letters to the editor in the three months following publication. Eight letters supported the article, describing it, for example, as "a valuable insight into an underworld the public needs to be alert to" and "BRILLIANT" (Cullinane, 2007, p. 17; Laing, 2007, p. 13). The other 15 letters denounced the article, describing it, for instance, as "damaging" and "racist, xenophobic" (Howie, 2007, p. 14; Mabbett, 2007, p. 12). Another magazine, *New Zealand Listener*, published a critique of the article (Ng, 2006). But *North & South* was unrepentant. Editor Robyn Langwell declared that the article was an example of the magazine's desire to "highlight issues many New Zealanders are talking and anguishing about privately" (Langwell, 2007, p. 14).

The New Zealand Press Council received several complaints about the article. The complainants were a consortium of mostly Chinese academics, journalists, and community leaders led by Chinese social commentator Tze Ming Mok; the Asia New Zealand Foundation; and the current author (New Zealand Press Council, 2007).

The Press Council issued its decision in June 2007. It found the article breached the Council's principles of accuracy and discrimination. In terms of accuracy, the Council found that the Asian crime rate had decreased over the period and so to "talk of a gathering crime tide is therefore wrong" (New Zealand Press Council, 2007, para. 27). Regarding discrimination, the Council found the article's language to be "emotionally loaded" and that its failure to place the crime stories and negative commentary in the context "both of other sectors of New Zealand society and of the Asian communities as a whole, cannot but stigmatise a whole group" (New Zealand Press Council, 2007, paras. 30 and 31).

North & South was obliged to run the Council's decision (*North & South*, July 2007, p. 15). The Council's decision was widely reported in the mainstream news media (for instance, *The New Zealand Herald*, June 11, 2007 p. A4; *The Press*, June 11, 2007, p. 7; Radio New Zealand news broadcasts, June 10, 2007; Close-Up television programmer, 11 June, 2007) and the Asian news media (for instance, *Chinese Herald*, June 14, 2007, p. 1; *Oriental Times*, June 12, 2007, p. 1; *The Global Indian*, August 2007, p. 15).

By coincidence, both Langwell and Coddington left *North & South* soon afterwards. Langwell's departure was shrouded in secrecy, but it seems it was due to *North & South*'s failure to attract a younger readership and was unrelated to the Press Council decision (Drinnan, 2007). Langwell joined the staff of a newspaper and Coddington effectively left journalism. Coddington later declared:

I wish I'd never written that article. Not because I agree with all the criticism, but because I unwittingly pressed a button which unleashed the toxic nature of this country.

I am genuinely sorry for offending those members of the Asian community who are not engaged in criminal activity and who felt discriminated by the same stereotypical brush.

I never set out to upset them and I can't undo that hurt (Coddington, 2008, paras. 16–18).

CONCLUSION

This chapter has considered the depiction of Chinese in the New Zealand media. Two strong themes arise from our analysis. First, the mainstream media largely excluded Chinese voices, with most of the coverage written in a non-Chinese voice. This reflects the fact that New Zealand Europeans are the overwhelming dominant cultural voice in New Zealand society and New Zealand journalism.

Second, although the rampant Yellow Peril hysteria of the 1906–1908 newspaper coverage had largely disappeared from the paper 100 years later, nevertheless there continued to be a significant amount of negatively toned coverage. This was due to the high incidence of crime reporting, which continued to depict Chinese generally in a poor light. Rather than having gravitated to the model-minority stereotype, the Yellow Peril stereotype continued in modified form. This focus in the national media on crime reporting led to "Asian Angst," an article that largely summarized high-profile crimes involving Chinese. Although a small element of model minority mythmaking was detected in the article, it overwhelmingly depicted the Chinese as a Yellow Peril.

There have been no articles similar to "Asian Angst" published in the years since 2006. It is likely the Press Council's strong—and widely reported—condemnation of "Asian Angst" played a role in ensuring no similar articles appeared. Indeed, it seems likely that the stigma of having written the article will remain with its author for many years. But the news media continues to be dominated by white voices and continues regularly to report crimes, including those that occur in the Chinese community. It is therefore likely that, despite our more enlightened age, the New Zealand news media will continue to often depict Chinese as a potentially dangerous other.

Questions for Reflection

1. How did the newspaper and magazine benefit from depicting the Chinese as a Yellow Peril?
2. How did the newspaper and magazine suffer from depicting the Chinese as a Yellow Peril?
3. Why do you think the newspaper and magazine rarely employed the model-minority myth in its reportage?
4. How could *North & South* have avoided making errors in its statistical analysis of Chinese crime in New Zealand?
5. Deborah Coddington felt the negative reaction to her article revealed the toxic nature of New Zealand. Do you agree? Why or why not?

REFERENCES

AGB Nielsen Media Research. (2008). *National readership survey*. Retrieved December 1, 2014, from http://www.nielsenmedia.co.nz/MRI_pages.asp?MRIID=32

Asia New Zealand Foundation. (2008). *Grants and awards*. Retrieved December 1, 2014, from http://www.asianz.org.nz/grants

City of Dunedin. (2008). *Dunedin Chinese Garden set to open*. Retrieved December 1, 2014, from http://www.cityofdunedin.com/city/?page=feat-chinesegarden08

Clark, H. (2002). *Address to Chinese New Year celebrations*. Retrieved December 1, 2014, from www.beehive.govt.nz/speech/address+chinese+new+year+celebrations

Coddington, D. (2006, December). Asian angst. *North & South*, 38–47.

Coddington, D. (2008). *Deborah Coddington: I wish I hadn't written that Asian angst article*. Retrieved December 1, 2014, from http://www.nzherald.co.nz/nz/news/article.cfm?c_id=1&objectid=10530906

Cullinane, L. (2007, March). Immigration goulash [Letter to the editor]. *North & South*, p. 17.

Drinnan, J. (2007, May 8). End of a magazine era? *The New Zealand Herald*, C2.

Howie, M. (2007, January). Outbreak of fury [Letter to the editor]. *North & South*, p. 14.

King, M. (2003). *The Penguin history of New Zealand*. Auckland: Penguin.

Laing, C. (2007, January). Weasel words? [Letter to the editor]. *North & South*, pp. 13–14.

Langwell, R. (2007, January). Footnote. *North & South*. 14

Mabbett, C. (2007, January). The Asia New Zealand Foundation strikes back [Letter to the editor]. *North & South*, p. 12.

Neuendorf, K. (2002). *The content analysis guidebook*. Thousand Oaks: Sage.

New Zealand Journalists Training Organisation. (2006a). *Survey of NZ journalism schools*. Retrieved December 1, 2014, from http://www.journalismtraining.co.nz/publications/surveys/200608jtoreport.pdf

New Zealand Journalists Training Organisation. (2006b). *National survey of journalists*. Retrieved December 1, 2014, from http://www.journalismtraining.co.nz/publications/surveys/200608jtosurvey.pdf

New Zealand Press Council. (2007). *Case number: 1090 Tze Ming Mok and others against North & South*. Retrieved December 1, 2014, from http://www.presscouncil.org.nz/display_ruling.asp?casenumber=1090

New Zealand Press Council. (2008a). *Main*. Retrieved December 1, 2014, from http://www.presscouncil.org.nz

New Zealand Press Council. (2008b). *Principles*. Retrieved December 1, 2014, from http://www.presscouncil.org.nz/principles_2.html

Ng, J. (1999). *Chinese settlement in New Zealand*. Christchurch: New Zealand Centre for Chinese Studies.

Ng, K. (2006, December 2). Damned statistics. *New Zealand Listener*, 26.

Statistics New Zealand. (2006). *Crime in New Zealand: 1996–2005*. Wellington: Statistics New Zealand.

Statistics New Zealand. (2008). *Census*. Retrieved December 1, 2014, from http://www.stats.govt.nz/census/default.htm

Swoboda, D. (1995). Accuracy and accountability in reporting local government budget activities: Evidence from the newsroom and from newsmakers. *Public Budgeting and Finance, 15*, 74–90.

Tan, L. (2006). *There's scope for more Asian involvement in the mainstream media.* Retrieved December 1, 2014, from http://www.journalismtraining.co.nz/d200607.html

Te Ara. (1966). *Population.* Retrieved December 1, 2014, from www.teara.govt.nz/1966/P/Population

Te Ara. (2008a). *Chinese.* Retrieved December 1, 2014, from http://www.teara.govt.nz/NewZealanders/NewZealandPeoples/Chinese/en

Te Ara. (2008b). *Anti-Chinese legislation.* Retrieved December 1, 2014, from www.teara.govt.nz/NewZealanders/NewZealandPeoples/Chinese/3/en

Wong, G. (2003). "Is saying sorry enough?" In M. Ip (Ed.), *Unfolding history, evolving identity: The Chinese in New Zealand* (pp. 258–279). Auckland: Auckland University Press.

CHAPTER 7

MODEL MINORITY CONVERGENCES IN NORTH AMERICA

Asian Parallels in Canada and the United States

Rob Ho

There are rich Chinese and Koreans in Los Angeles. But many others are doing menial jobs for low pay. For the most part, the Chinese you see in California are not the typical ones you see in Vancouver (Canada), the ones who are buying up the big houses.

—*Edward Yang, a dual U.S.-Canadian citizen, on the income disparities between Asian Americans and Asian Canadians*

INTRODUCTION

This quotation distinguishing well-off Asians in Vancouver, BC from the apparent greater income discrepancies in Los Angeles, CA comes from an August 2013 *Vancouver Sun* newspaper article that featured a story on "The Asian experience in America: New study outlines some of the successes and challenges faced in

Killing the Model Minority Stereotype: Asian American Counterstories and Complicity,
pages 117–132.
Copyright © 2015 by Information Age Publishing

Canada and the U.S." (Todd, 2013). The piece discussed the controversial findings from the 2012 Pew Center Report "The Rise of Asian Americans" and attempted to apply its results to the Canadian context. Despite the report's widespread criticism amongst various Asian American and Pacific Islander (AAPI)
groups, scholars, and activists in the U.S. as being one-dimensional portrayals of
AAPIs as model minorities with the highest income and educational attainment
among racial groups, the *Vancouver Sun* author nevertheless characterized Asian
Canadians as similarly successful. In fact, citing statistics that proportionately
three times as many ethnic Asians reside in Canada than south of the border (i.e.
almost 15% of Canadians have Asian ancestry compared to just 5.8% of Americans), the article implies that the Pew study has even greater implications for
Canada—that their larger representation and their unbridled achievements have
a profound effect on everything from housing prices and unemployment rates to
university admissions.

That Asian Canadians are feigned to be such "model minorities" in public discourse whose issues have warranted such underwhelming national attention unsurprisingly speaks to a collective paucity of available model minority literature
in a country that is commonly regarded as one of the most accepting, tolerant, and
multicultural societies in the world. As ostensibly uber-successful, affluent, and
high achieving, Asians in Canada are ascribed the same inherent high status as
their U.S. counterparts.

This article examines how the model minority myth influences Canada and the
insidious effects it has on Asian Canadians. It will discuss the concept's colonization outside US borders and its continued reproduction in Canada that sways public policy and discourse. By tracing its historical development and examining two
pivotal examples of how this issue has received national attention, it will provide
a better understanding of how these racial assumptions remain as destructive and
oppressive to Asian Canadians as they do to other Asians worldwide. Analyzing
the parallels and divergences with the U.S. situation will help to further complicate our current assumptions and parochial understandings of how the model
minority myth operates across nations.

The Legacy of the Model Minority Myth

As a growing body of literature demonstrates, perhaps the most challenging
ideological problem afflicting Asian American and Pacific Islanders is the notion
of the "model minority myth," the erroneous assumption that AAPIs are a monolithic group who are highly successful in all of their endeavors (including education, work, and in political and social pursuits). Although an in-depth analysis of
the concept will not be provided here[1], it is useful to review some of its central te-

---

[1] For a more detailed discussion of the model minority stereotype in the U.S., see Rosalind Chou and
Joe R. Feagin (2008) *The Myth of the Model Minority: Asian Americans Facing Racism*; Karen K.
Inkelas (2006) *Racial Attitudes and Asian Pacific Americans: Demystifying the Model Minority*;

nets before discussing its applicability to Canada (*cf.* chapter five in this volume). The idea that Asian Americans (the original term used did not include Pacific Islanders) have been a successful minority in the U.S. through a combination of hard work and determination emerged as a popular depiction in the mid-1960s (Chun, 1995). After a century of negative stereotypes as "unassimilable foreigners" and "Yellow Peril," this group found themselves placed in an increasingly positive light by the mainstream media who depicted Asian Americans (AAs) as a model minority group that had triumphed over racial obstacles to reach economic, educational, and professional success – the quintessential American Dream. The image was widely embraced and was perpetuated through media as well as the social science literature (Chun, 1995). Since the 1960s, the model minority stereotype has not only survived, but has arguably flourished. High profile politicians, prominent commentators, and news media continue to praise AAs for their educational and economic success (Chou & Feagin, 2008). As a result, the model minority image of AAs has been firmly ensconced in the American public's mind, and, despite much criticism and protest, is still prevalent today.

The model minority myth is based on statistical data on the overall educational, economic, and social achievements of AAs, though this concept has been criticized as overly simplistic, masking extreme inequalities within and between different Asian American groups, as well as diverting public attention from the existence of discrimination (Woo, 2000). In fact, opponents of this stereotype argue that contrary to widespread opinion, AAs face an ever-growing list of problems: growing poor and working-poor populations, considerable numbers of students who fail in school, and the adversities and family issues that small business owners who are unsuccessful in American society must cope with (Omatsu, 2010). The myth is also critiqued as a politically divisive tool that pits AAs against other minority groups (Chou & Feagin, 2008; Chun, 1995).

The stereotype also contains contradictory themes. On the one hand, AAs are supposed to embody traits of determination and resourcefulness that allow them to transcend racial barriers and structural inequalities. On the other hand, they are also viewed as polite conformists who are politically and socially passive. That is, AAs are presumed to be good, law-abiding minorities who know their place within society and do not challenge their place in it. This is particularly evident when comparing the historical pitting of AAs against African Americans and the emergence of Black Power in the 1960s that conflated Black representations with activism in the Civil Rights Movement while concomitantly characterizing AAs as political wallflowers.

Samuel D. Museus, Dina C. Maramba, and Robert T. Teranishi (2013) *The Misrepresented Minority: New Insights on Asian Americans and Pacific Islanders, and the Implications for Higher Education*; Stacey J. Lee (2009) *Unraveling the "Model Minority" Stereotype: Listening to Asian American Youth*; and Guofang Li and Lihshing Wang (2008) *Model Minority Myth Revisited: An Interdisciplinary Approach to Demystifying Asian American Educational Experiences.*

With this construction of the AA subject as universally successful, how does it affect their educational experiences? AAs have traditionally seen education as a way to reduce the effects of racism and racial discrimination and to achieve personal success (Chang, 2007). This view helped to increase the number of AAs in schools and is used by AA researchers to explain their large numbers (Hune & Chan, 2000). Ongoing racial discrimination has continued to motivate scholars to problematize the structural and institutional barriers this group faces in educational settings.

AAs have long been viewed as well-behaved, diligent, high achievers who attain success despite socio-economic and language obstacles; in effect, they are "whiz kids"—super achievers with soaring GPAs who spend hours on homework. They also make narrow academic choices specializing in mathematics, sciences, and engineering (Hune & Chan, 2000). Of course, many AA students do not fit this image.

The model minority stereotype often causes more harm than good. If students fail to live up to the stereotype, teachers may become frustrated and blame the students for their poor performance. This may lead students to internalize these stereotypes, feel unworthy, and begin to think that they are unintelligent (Young, 1998). Commonly, many AA children feel pressured to achieve academic excellence or risk losing face or shaming the family. Other minority groups who are viewed as less successful are held responsible for their failures, and this pits AAs against other racial minorities. Those who accept the stereotype therefore underestimate the discrimination that AAs face, since it is seen as easily conquered through determination and perseverance.

However, the model minority myth causes other problems in education. As Hune (1998) has noted, in higher education AAs are both highly visible and invisible. They are highly visible in their record numbers on U.S. campuses when flaunted as the model minority, while simultaneously they are frequently invisible in campus policies and programs as well as in administrative positions. Their over-representation at many highly-selective college campuses has antagonized and angered many non-Asian students, who blame them for "stealing" all the spots at highly selective schools.

But this blame is nothing new. AAs have long been criticized for taking over U.S. higher education for a litany of reasons. However, a 2008 National Commission on Asian American and Pacific Islander Research in Education (CARE) report argues that Asian American and Pacific Islander students parallel comparable increases that other student populations have experienced and that the AAPI student population is concentrated in only a small percentage of institutions, giving the fake impression of high enrollment in post-secondary education overall.

Furthermore, this same report also dispels the myth that AAPIs are concentrated only in highly selective four-year universities. In actuality, AAPI students are evenly distributed in two-year and four-year institutions, with most attending public institutions. AAPIs have a wide array of standardized test scores, which allows different levels of eligibility and competitiveness in selective admissions. AAPI enrollment in public two-year community colleges is increasing at a faster rate than their enrollment in four-year colleges, and AAPI community college enrollment is growing fastest in the Midwest and the South (CARE, 2008).

A couple of other issues in higher education are currently emerging, though these issues are what are known as "hidden indicators"—issues that usually lack sufficient data to warrant attention or resources—that have significant implications for policy, practice, and future research (CARE, 2008). The first is the effect of selective college admissions and affirmative action. AAs and Pacific Islanders have historically been excluded from discourse on affirmative action, equal opportunity, and college admissions. They are seen as the biggest benefactors of schools without affirmative action. This allows AAPIs to "become 'racial mascots' to camouflage an agenda that, if presented by Whites on their own behalf, would look too much like self-interest" (CARE, 2008). In other words, they are positioned as middlemen in the cost-benefit analysis of wins and losses in the affirmative action debate.

Secondly, cultural competency and mentorship is also an emerging issue. In short, there is a dearth of attention paid to the issues related to AAPI faculty, staff, and administrators (what Hune again calls an "invisible" existence). With such a large focus on AAPI college students in higher education, there is little questioning of the AAPI presence in other parts of the academic community. Sadly, few faculty and administrators come from this racial background and therefore do not take part in important decision-making processes. For instance, AAPI women are the most underrepresented group of college presidents with only 13 female presidents in all of the U.S. compared to 768 White women, 87 African American women, and 58 Hispanic women in 2004. It is crucial that AAPI role models and mentors exist at every level of a student's school experience (from elementary to post-secondary education) in order to properly train and encourage the next generation of leaders.

As the burgeoning critical literature in Asian American Studies attests, the model minority myth has had a long and far-reaching effect since its inception in the late 1960s. William Petersen's 1966 *New York Times Magazine* article had unknowingly launched an international cascade of racist Asian depictions that reached far beyond American borders and has adversely framed the Asian diaspora worldwide with damaging stereotypes and misrepresentations. The U.S.-born concept started gaining traction through popular American publications, including *Time* magazine and *Newsweek*. By the 1990s, it had become so entrenched within mainstream media that the depictions of AAs and Pacific Islanders became inextricably linked to notions of over-achieving, overly successful, and ultimately prosperous racialized people (Chen, 2004; G. Li & Wang, 2008).

Asian Canadians as Model Minorities

With Canada's close relationship to the United States through trade, interrelated economies, and mass media, it is no surprise that the concept of the model minority has traversed north of the border. As the U.S.'s largest trading partner and due to its close geographic proximity, Canada has held a longstanding inter-connectedness with its southern neighbor since the formation of the country. Hence, the notion of the model minority myth as a colonizing force dominating discussions about Asians in Canada is not a surprising one.

Though contestation of the model minority concept in the U.S. has been consistent since its inception in the 1960s, awareness and resistance to it in Canada has historically been more muted and limited. The absence of research and literature on the topic has been a surprising mainstay in Canadian academia (Maclear, 1994; Pon, 2000), despite highly transformative immigration patterns that have resulted in huge waves of Asian migrants moving and settling in the nation post-1967 (when the 1967 *Immigration Act* admitted immigrants based on a points system). Throughout the 1980s and 1990s, major newspapers and magazines including the *Toronto Star*, *Globe and Mail*, *Montreal Gazette*, *Fortune Magazine*, and *Toronto Life* continued to depict Asian Canadians as model minorities, including the use of such expressions as "math whizzes," "academic giants," and "extremely wealthy" citizens (Pon, 2000). The issue continued, for the most part, to escape widespread recognition as being problematic, and generally continued down a linear path that excluded its importance in the national spotlight, save for two major critical incidents: the 1979 "Campus Giveaway" and the 2010 "Too Asian?" article.

"Campus Giveaway": The Beginning of an Asian Canadian Movement?

There are two pivotal historic moments that elevated the awareness of Canadian model minority issues. The first is a 1979 feature on a television program called *W5*, which reports on the "who," "what," "where," "why," and "when" (hence *W5*) of issues that are deemed of importance to citizens across the country. Aired by the Canadian Television Network (CTV), the show still airs its weekly current affairs broadcast from coast to coast (it has been running since 1966). On September 30, 1979, the program televised a report called "Campus Giveaway," which accused foreign students from China of occupying a large number of Canadian university spots. Among the many misguided claims, it selectively displayed Chinese faces as representing all foreign students and gave distorted statistics to demonize Chinese students as taking over "Canadian" institutions (a claim similar to historic discourses of "yellow peril" and "Asian invasion") (Wai, 1998). The show attempted to affirm that the federal government was subsidizing their education and disavowing (white) "Canadian" students the opportunity to attend post-secondary institutions. Further, their footage at a University of Toronto campus that claimed to show that almost all of the students in a pharmacy class were

Chinese international students was simply incorrect; every one of the students was a (Chinese) Canadian citizen since no foreign students were allowed admission to the pharmacy program. This shoddy journalism with such disparaging accusations of the displacement of white students from the program was irrefutably unsubstantiated and clearly racist.

Amidst the slew of controversy and outrage came a rallying point for Asian Canadians: student groups wrote protest letters and were joined by vocal Chinese and Asian community leaders to denounce CTV's inaccurate and racist portrayals. Within the next few months, momentum built and vocal demonstrations became more prominent. Of significance was the support and coalition building across various racial and ethnic groups eager to challenge the discernably offensive television programming. Such growing opposition across Canada became a watershed moment in the nation's history—its own civil rights moment, which signaled a racial awakening and a call to action. Eventually, under mounting pressure, CTV ultimately issued an apology and fired the producer responsible for the transgressions.

Though *W5* had caused much racial tension and incensed anti-racist activists, the national campaign resulted in the creation of the Chinese Canadian National Council (CCNC), a Toronto-based organization that to this day continues to be a champion of the equality of all Chinese Canadians and other minority groups across the country. The activism of the Chinese Canadians, along with other groups, produced a strong sense of collective organization and racial identity and proved to be the most politically significant event in Chinese Canadian history (A. B. Chan, 1983).

"Too Asian?"

The second pivotal moment in Canadian history to spark national consciousness about the model minority myth occurred over three decades later. In the fall of 2010, Canada's leading national magazine *Maclean's* published the highly-controversial article "Too Asian?", which explored how the nation's top universities were being inundated with an invasion of industrious Asian students with their proclivity for studying and eschewing socializing. The article demonized these students for their reputation as high-achieving hard workers who, unlike their white peers, had a penchant for academic success at the cost of fraternizing and partying (Gilmour, Bhandar, Heer, & Ma, 2012). The authors, Stephanie Findlay and Nicholas Köhler (2010), focused on apparent racial imbalances on Canadian campuses and the predicaments of privileged "white" private school students who shunned applying to particular Canadian schools for their "reputation of being Asian."

There were numerous erroneous assumptions and stereotypes perpetuated in the "Too Asian?" article. True to the tenets of the model minority stereotype, the "Asians" referred to were of East Asian descent (Chinese, Japanese, Korean) and not South, Southeast, or other Asian nationalities. They were not differentiated based on generational status, citizenship, or as international students. The homogenizing effect therefore implied that all Asians are monolithic, share similar characteristics, and lack diversity. Of course, in over 150 years of Asian migration to Canada, there is a multiplicity of immigration patterns and types of Asian diasporic settlers who have come to this country under different immigration laws and restrictions. The notion of common characteristics as a collective racial group makes little sense, as each Asian ethnic group is highly affected by gender, race, and class in addition to their transnational forays and engagement in global economies.

If casting all Asian Canadians as a uniform group was not repugnant enough, the authors proceeded to categorize all white students as party-loving youth who seemingly would only attend universities in which they can fraternize and socialize unfettered by the presence of Asian students who would not facilitate their penchants for having a good time. Using upper-middle and upper-class youth as the norm frames exclusionary discourses of who is really "Canadian" and who is not (Heer, 2012).

The controversy received nationwide attention, sparked heated debates, and became a catalyst to re-examine the racist depictions of Asian Canadians in the mainstream public arena. These types of repeated misrepresentations in mass media throughout the past three decades have reified them as wealthy citizens, math geniuses, and academic superstars (Maclear, 1994; Pon, 2000).

Since 2010, cities from across Canada, including Toronto, Vancouver, Victoria, Markham, and Richmond Hill, all successfully passed motions denouncing the piece and calling for the magazine to make an official apology. However, despite much negative publicity, Rogers Communications—the parent company of *Maclean's* magazine—has consistently refused to apologize for the xenophobic article and claims that it was never offensive from the outset. Online debates continued to occur, with several conservative journalists and pundits openly supporting the magazine (Heer, 2010). Even though community groups, academics, and politicians spoke out against the discriminatory piece, Rogers would only revise the content, make clarifications about the article, and modify the online title. The title was changed from "Too Asian?" to "The enrollment controversy: Worries that efforts in the U.S. to limit enrollment of Asian students in top universities may migrate to Canada."

Both the "Campus Giveaway" and "Too Asian?" incidents, despite being separated historically by 31 years (1979 to 2010), exhibit a remarkable series of commonalities characterized by model minority stereotypes and rooted in xenophobic and anti-Asian racist sentiment. As "perpetual foreigners" whose demarcated outsider status has excluded them from inclusion in the nation state, Asian Canadians have always been a marginalized and invisible community in Canadian society (Anderson, 1991; P. S. Li, 1998; Roy, 1989). In the next section, I will explore how this exclusion compares to the AAs and Pacific Islanders south of the border and how the model minority concept is differentiated in Canada.

Do All Asians Look Alike? Cross-Border Similarities and Differences of the Model Minority Myth

The remainder of this article will focus on Canada/U.S. comparisons in how the model minority myth affects Asian Canadians versus AAPIs. As we have seen, there are many similarities in how the notion gets played out in both countries: Asians are mostly viewed as smart, ultra-successful, highly educated, wealthy, and highly accomplished; they are nerdy, quiet, shy, and obedient. The educational, economic, and social achievements of Asian Americans and Pacific Islanders and Asian Canadians have been lauded as the ideal to which all minorities should strive, regardless of social-economic status, immigration history, length of time in North America, or personal background. As proof of the results of hard work, determination, and strong work ethic, the Asian subject is seen as the ultimate success story that should be emulated by all racial minority groups. Taken as a whole, even though the intent and meaning of the model minority myth originated in the U.S., the construct ultimately retains most of the same meanings and has little variation in Canada, particularly as we have seen with the *W5* and "Too Asian?" examples.

However, I argue that there are four main lenses we can use to analyze AAPI and Asian Canadian model minority usage. The first involves disparities in state integration strategies between the U.S. and Canada. In other words, American *melting pot* ideology—the longstanding national strategy that posits that immigrants to the U.S. must "melt together" to form a common culture—has been the official approach to assimilate members of the minority group into the dominant mainstream (Healey, 2011; Reitz & Breton, 1994). Under this approach, the traditional cultural heritages that minorities have are deliberately supposed to be supplanted (or "melted away") in favor of prevailing American values and customs.

This contrasts greatly with Canadian multiculturalism, an official state policy that guarantees that all citizens can keep their identities, cherish their cultural ancestries, and maintain a sense of belonging. Canada's policy of multiculturalism promotes the preservation of one's cultural heritage concomitantly with full participation and acceptance in the larger society (Banting & Kymlicka, 2010; James, 1995; Noels & Berry, 2006). The rationale behind such an approach is that by feeling accepted to the nation-state Canadians are, in turn, more receptive to diverse cultures, thereby boosting racial and ethnic harmony and cross-cultural awareness.

As a pioneer in multiculturalism policy and the first country in the world to adopt this approach, Canada has since 1971 been a leader and a model for nations to emulate. Though not without its own problems and controversies (Banting & Kymlicka, 2010; Derouin, 2004; Stroink & Lalonde, 2009), this approach has been hailed as arguably the most successful integrationist strategy of immigrants to a new country (Kymlicka, 2010). Without the pressures to assimilate and renounce their culture, their individual rights are protected and they are free to identify with their specific ethnic/racial group if they so choose. Not surprisingly, then, Canada has become a major destination of choice for immigrants who seek to escape the anxieties and difficulties of moving to less tolerant countries. Accordingly, as Derouin (2004) points out, there is evidence to show that Asians from a variety of ethnic ancestries feel a strong attachment to Canada.

Although these two distinct strategies seem to have separate consequences for ethnic and racial minorities who choose to migrate to the U.S. and Canada, when it comes to the model minority myth, both countries suffer very similar outcomes. Asians on both sides of the border are racially framed and stereotyped in such parallel, sinister ways that they are almost indistinguishable from each other in their treatment by the dominant group. Despite highly divergent state integration policies, the fact that there are such analogous stereotypes of Asian Americans/Canadians is a disturbing and troublesome finding. The implication is that the model minority concept can traverse national boundaries and still have the same destructive effects; this provides little comfort in the supposed benefits of multiculturalism and its perceived advantages over a melting pot ideology. With the highly globalized and integrated world in which we live, mass media, social media, and technology are often used as vehicles to spread these ideas. If neither multiculturalism nor melting pot strategies are effective in minimizing the harms of the stereotype, then are there other national approaches left that can prevent this myth from encroaching upon state borders?

The second way we can analyze the U.S./Canada model minority usage involves immigration policies and migration patterns. It is not surprising that the ways in which America and Canada act as receiving countries for immigrants differ, as their immigration policies to accept foreign nationals are highly dependent upon state desires for economic growth, monetary capital, highly trained and educated workers, and the creation of jobs by both transnational and independent companies. For instance, until February 2014, Canada's Investor Class Immigrant Program had become a convenient way for immigrants to be accepted into the country, since under the program applicants with a net worth at least $1.6 million (all figures in Canadian dollars) could lend $800,000 for five years in return for permanent residency. This underpricing compared favorably to other countries, which usually required more capital investing and had greater restrictions to obtain a legal pathway to citizenship (DeVoretz, 2013). The relatively low costs of the program over the years have resulted in it becoming one of the most successful immigration programs in the world and created a backlog of tens of thousands of applicants (Marlow, 2014). Such success has subsequently led to a national public backlash from many concerned about an easy pathway to Canadian permanent residency; the criticism resulted in the federal government cancelling the Investor Class program by the summer of 2014 (Marlow, 2014).

One of the consequences of investor-class immigration over the past few years was its elevated numbers of mainland Chinese and other Asian applicants (Ley, 2013; Wang & Lo, 2005), which, to qualify under the program, necessitated their wealthy backgrounds and access to high levels of financial capital (transnationals that Aihwa Ong [1999] famously calls "flexible citizens"). Of course, it is unsurprising then that their presence in Canada as affluent one-percenters helped to reify Asian immigrants' status as model minorities, displaying levels of economic prosperity relatively few Canadians could attain. Under such an immigration program, the encouragement of the wealthy Asian migrant helped to further entrench stereotypes of model minorities in Canada. Therefore, instead of seeing a diversity of Asian immigrants come to Canada from numerous socio-economic backgrounds (including from family reunification and refugee-class programs), the affluent became the *de facto* face of many of the migrants from the Pacific Rim.

The third type of analysis we can apply to our understanding of the model minority myth involves Canada's lack of disaggregated, ethnic-specific data collection about Asian Canadians and Asian immigrants. Because only in occasional cases do federal and provincial bodies collect this specific type of data, researchers have few datasets in which they can determine race, ethnicity, gender, class, generational status, religious affiliation, sexuality, and levels of disability for people of Asian descent. For instance, as a general rule, universities and colleges in Canada do not collect or request their student applicants' particular racial/ethnic background, how long their families have been in the country, or other social variables. This shortcoming obfuscates concrete and empirical ways in which to debunk the model minority myth, making it extremely difficult, for instance, to change public policy, create/reinforce/fund student affairs initiatives, and generally make the case that Asian Canadians have unique sets of needs that require attention and social supports. In short, despite numerically being a major presence within Canada, Asians in Canada are consigned to the peripheries of research and scholarly attention, especially in the field of education (Coloma, 2012).

We can contrast this greatly with the United States, which has a long and impressive history of researchers who often use specific disaggregated datasets to study their Asian American and Pacific Islander subjects. Many scholars have deconstructed, analyzed, and tested the model minority myth in great detail, using data focused on particular AAPI groups and not just general AAPI groups. Samuel Museus (2014), Robert Teranishi (2010), Stacey Lee (2009), and Nicholas Hartlep (2013, 2014) are but a few of the leading scholars in recent years exposing and demystifying the stereotype. This work is even more impressive given the sheer volume of robust scholarship that they have produced even within the last half a decade alone using solid data collection, literature reviews, and strong theoretical/conceptual analyses to thoroughly debunk the myth. Sadly, access to similar levels of empirical evidence and critical scholarship on the topic north of the border has severely limited the effectiveness of countering—both in academic circles as well as in public discourse (e.g. *W5* and *Maclean's*)—the destructive nature of the concept and the propagation of its harmful messages.

Finally, we can analyze model minority myth usage in both countries through the lens of the politics of resistance. Resistance to oppression can take on many forms, and the different routes that have been adopted throughout both nations' histories have embodied myriad practices and formations. Perhaps one of the most pivotal distinctions in dealing with racial problems has been the establishment and proliferation of U.S. ethnic and Asian American Studies departments in higher education institutions nationwide. Born out of the Civil Rights Movement in the 1960s and 1970s, the Asian American Movement helped spark the institutionalization of academic departments and programs specifically targeted to deal with Asian American and Pacific Islander history and experiences (S. Chan, 2005; Omatsu, 2010). They precipitated generations of students and graduates with the racial consciousness to challenge their own oppression, provide racial and ethnic solidarity, and to deconstruct and critique anti-Asian sentiments (Osajima, 2007).

In contrast, similar Asian Canadian Studies departments have failed to materialize in the same manner as in the US. The only institutionalized departments in Canada to offer minor degree programs for undergraduate students have been Simon Fraser University's Asia-Canada Program and the more recent additions (within the last two years) of Asian Canadian Studies minors at the University of British Columbia and the University of Toronto. These minors have helped to address racial issues, and while commendable and important, their presence can be viewed as "late" (C. Lee, 2007) and do not yet match the sheer breadth and comprehensiveness of their American counterparts. The lack of such vital programs in Canada helps to constrain widespread social activism and scholarship during nationwide struggles against racism and serves to limit coalition-building amongst various racial and ethnic minority groups (Goellnicht, 2013). Of course, this is not to claim that resistance to racism need only be institutionalized as a formal program of study at a university or college, but their absence in the Canadian context prohibits certain collective and targeted ways to address these issues.

It is important to note, however, that Canadian politics of resistance vis-à-vis the model minority myth historically did not necessarily originate from critiques of the stereotype itself but rather from broader racial/ethnic relations within the country, including the state policy of multiculturalism and related integration strategies. Indeed, there has been and continues to be a coterie of Asian Canadian scholars in numerous academic fields who question the racial formation (Omi & Winant, 1994) and racialization of immigrant, naturalized, and domestically-born Asians in Canada that does not necessarily specify a targeted model minority construct. In fact, we should also be mindful, then, not to decree the U.S. as the normative standard that defines activism and resistance, while rendering Asian Canadians as apolitical and lacking opposition to oppressive forces. Grassroots struggles across the nation have for decades continued to work to disrupt state and social power.

Perhaps, with this analysis in mind, it is more precise to refer to the model minority myth or stereotype as more of a "model minority discourse," which more accurately reflects the social, historical, and political breadth of model minority dynamics in Canada and the U.S. (Pon, 2000). This terminology better captures the contradictory and fluid nature of the issue while being more encompassing and inclusive than a "myth" or "stereotype."

The model minority concept has long been an insidious construct that has perpetuated harmful stereotypes on AAPIs since the 1960s. Its expansion through mass media, popular culture, and social media throughout the decades has spilled into Canada to essentially reproduce similar outcomes for Asian Canadians. As a result, Asians in Canada suffer particular forms of racialization that essentialize them as being over-achieving, widely successful, and highly intelligent perpetual foreigners. The stereotype's export from the U.S. has demonstrated that the notion's migration north of the 49th parallel can be seen as what I refer to as a "conceptual colonialism" that dominates discussions about Asians in Canada, thereby leaving behind a trail of collateral damage that Canadians are still attempting to address and redress.

Questions for Reflection

1. In what ways does the model minority myth in Canada parallel the U.S. situation?
2. What important distinctions can be made between the Canadian and American versions of the myth?
3. What strategies can be used to prevent the spread of the model minority myth in Canada given that nation's close ties to the U.S.?
4. Recent immigration trends have firmly established the strong presence of mainland Chinese migrants to Canada, the U.S., Australia, and several other international destinations. What role does this particular group have in perpetuating the stereotype?
5. How would you refute someone who insists that the model minority stereotype is positive and therefore beneficial for Asians?

REFERENCES

Anderson, K. J. (1991). *Vancouver's Chinatown: Racial discourse in Canada, 1875–1980.* Montreal, QC: McGill-Queen's University Press.

Banting, K., & Kymlicka, W. (2010). Canadian multiculturalism: Global anxieties and local debates. *British Journal of Canadian Studies, 23*(1), 43–72.

CARE (National Commission on Asian American and Pacific Islander Research in Education). (2008). *Asian Americans and Pacific Islanders – Facts, not fiction: Setting the record straight.* The Asian/Pacific/American Institute at New York University, The College Board, and The Steinhardt Institute for Higher Education Policy at New York University.

Chan, A. B. (1983). *Gold Mountain: The Chinese in the new world.* Vancouver, BC: New Star Books.

Chan, S. (2005). *In defense of Asian American Studies: The politics of teaching and program building.* Chicago, IL: University of Illinois Press.

Chang, T. (2007). Factors affecting Asian American students choosing a college major. In C. C. Park (Ed.), *Asian American education: Acculturation, literacy development, and learning* (pp. 197–213). Charlotte, NC: Information Age.

Chen, C. H. (2004). "Outwhiting the Whites": An examination of the persistence of Asian American model minority discourse. In R. A. Lind (Ed.), *Race, gender, media: Considering diversity across audiences, content, and producers* (pp. 146–153). Boston, MA: Allyn and Bacon.

Chou, R., & Feagin, J. R. (2008). *The myth of the model minority: Asian Americans facing racism*. Boulder, CO: Paradigm Publishers.

Chun, K.-T. (1995). The myth of Asian American success and its educational ramifications. In D. T. Nakanishi & T. Y. Nishida (Eds.), *The Asian American educational experience: A sourcebook for teachers and students* (pp. 95–112). New York: Routledge.

Coloma, R. S. (2012). Theorizing Asian Canada, reframing differences. In N. Ng-A-Fook & J. Rottman (Eds.), *Reconsidering Canadian curriculum studies: Provoking historical, present, and future perspectives* (pp. 119–135). New York: Palgrave MacMillan.

Derouin, J. (2004). Asians and multiculturalism in Canada's three major cities: Some evidence from the Ethnic Diversity Survey. In C. Andrew (Ed.), *Our diverse cities* (Vol. 1, pp. 58–62). Ottawa, ON: Metropolis.

DeVoretz, D. J. (2013). The economics of immigrant citizenship ascension. In K. F. Zimmermann & A. F. Constant (Eds.), *International handbook on the economics of migration* (pp. 470–488). Cheltenham, UK: Edward Elgar.

Findlay, S., & Köhler, N. (2010). Too Asian? *Maclean's*, 76–81.

Gilmour, R. J., Bhandar, D., Heer, J., & Ma, M. C. K. (2012). *"Too Asian?": Racism, privilege, and post-secondary education*. Toronto, ON: Between the Lines.

Goellnicht, D. (2013). Outside the U.S. frame: Asian Canadian perspectives. *Concentric: Literacy & Cultural Studies, 39*(2), 83–100.

Hartlep, N. D. (2013). *The model minority stereotype: Demystifying Asian American success*. Charlotte, NC: Information Age.

Hartlep, N. D. (Ed.). (2014). *The model minority stereotype reader: Critical and challenging readings for the 21st century*. San Diego, CA: Cognella.

Healey, J. F. (2011). *Diversity and society: Race, ethnicity, and gender, 2011/2012 update*. Newbury Park, CA: Pine Forge Press.

Heer, J. (2010, November 24). Too brazen: Maclean's Margaret Wente, and the Canadian media's inarticulacy about race. *The Walrus*. Retrieved December 1, 2014, from http://walrusmagazine.com/blogs/2010/11/24/too-brazen/

Heer, J. (2012). Introduction. In R. J. Gilmour, M. C. K. Ma, D. Bhandar, & J. Heer (Eds.), *"Too Asian?": Racism, privilege, and post-secondary education* (pp. 1–13). Toronto, ON: Between the Lines.

Hune, S. (1998). *Asian Pacific American women in higher education: Claiming visibility & voice*. Washington, DC: Association of American Colleges and Universities, Program on the Status and Education of Women.

Hune, S., & Chan, K. (2000). Educating Asian Pacific Americans: Struggles in progress. In T. Fong & L. Shinagawa (Eds.), *Asian Americans: Experiences and perspectives* (pp. 141–168). Upper Saddle River, NJ: Prentice-Hall.

Inkelas, K. K. (2006). *Racial attitudes and Asian Pacific Americans: Demystifying the model minority*. New York: Routledge.

James, C. E. (1995). Multicultural and anti-racism education in Canada. *Race, Gender & Class, 2*(3), 31–48.

Kymlicka, W. (2010). The rise and fall of multiculturalism? New debates on inclusion and accommodation in diverse societies. *International Social Science Journal, 61*(199), 97–112.

Lee, C. (2007). The lateness of Asian Canadian Studies. *Amerasia Journal, 33*(2), 1–18.

Lee, S. J. (2009). *Unraveling the "model minority" stereotype: Listening to Asian American youth*. New York: Teachers College Press.

Ley, D. (2013). Does transnationalism trump immigrant integration? Evidence from Canada's links with East Asia. *Journal of Ethnic and Migration Studies, 39*(6), 921–938.

Li, G., & Wang, L. (2008). *Model minority myth revisited: An interdisciplinary approach to demystifying Asian American educational experiences*. Charlotte, NC: Information Age.

Li, P. S. (1998). *The Chinese in Canada*. Toronto, ON: Oxford University Press.

Maclear, K. (1994). The myth of the 'model minority': Re-thinking the education of Asian-Canadians. *Our Schools/Our Selves, 5*(3), 54–76.

Marlow, I. (2014, June 28). Chinese investors' immigration cases fail. *The Globe and Mail*. Retrieved December 1, 2014, from http://www.theglobeandmail.com/news/british-columbia/chinese-investors-immigration-cases-fail/article19383810/

Museus, S. (2014). *Asian American students in higher education*. New York: Routledge.

Museus, S. D., Maramba, D. C., & Teranishi, R. T. (2013). *The misrepresented minority: New insights on Asian Americans and Pacific Islanders, and the implications for higher education*. Sterling, VA: Stylus.

Noels, K. A., & Berry, J. W. (2006). Acculturation in Canada. In J. W. Berry, D. Sam, & A. Rogers (Eds.), *Cambridge handbook of acculturation psychology* (pp. 274–293). Cambridge, UK: Cambridge University Press.

Omatsu, G. (2010). The "Four Prisons" and the movements of liberation. In J. Y.-W. S. Wu, T. C. Chen, J. Wu, R. Lee, & G. Okhiro (Eds.), *Asian American Studies now: A critical reader* (pp. 298–333). New Brunswick, NJ: Rutgers University Press.

Omi, M., & Winant, H. (1994). *Racial formation in the United States: From the 1960s to the 1990s*. New York: Routledge.

Ong, A. (1999). *Flexible citizenship: The cultural logics of transnationality*. Durham, NC: Duke University Press.

Osajima, K. (2007). Replenishing the ranks: Raising critical consciousness among Asian Americans. *Journal of Asian American Studies, 10*(1), 59–83.

Pon, G. (2000). Importing the Asian model minority discourse into Canada: Implications for social work and education. *Canadian Social Work Review, 17*(2), 277–291.

Reitz, J. G., & Breton, R. (1994). *The illusion of difference: Realities of ethnicity in Canada and the United States*. Toronto, ON: C. D. Howe Institute.

Roy, P. E. (1989). *A white man's province: British Columbia politicians and Chinese and Japanese immigrants, 1858–1914*. Vancouver, BC: University of British Columbia Press.

Stroink, M. L., & Lalonde, R. N. (2009). Bicultural identity conflict in second-generation Asian Canadians. *Journal of Social Psychology, 149*(1), 44–65.

Teranishi, R. T. (2010). *Asians in the ivory tower: Dilemmas of racial inequality in American higher education*. New York: Teachers College Press.

Todd, D. (2013, August 24). The Asian experience in America: New study outlines some of the successes and challenges faced in Canada and the U.S. *The Vancouver Sun*. Retrieved December 1, 2014, from http://www.canada.com/vancouversun/news/westcoastnews/story.html?id=f1a22ff5–602d-4cd2–9f6e-323ddc6bc419

Wai, H. Y. (1998). Vancouver Chinatown 1960–1980: A community perspective. *New Scholars – New Visions in Canadian Studies, 3*(1), 2–45.

Wang, S., & Lo, L. (2005). Chinese immigrants in Canada: Their changing composition and economic performance. *International Migration, 43*(3), 35–71.

Woo, D. (2000). *Glass ceilings and Asian Americans: The new face of workplace barriers*. Walnut Creek, CA: Altamira Press.

Young, R. L. (1998). Becoming American: Coping strategies of Asian Pacific American children. In V. O. Pang & L.-R. L. Cheng (Eds.), *Struggling to be heard: The unmet needs of Asian Pacific American children* (pp. 61–73). Albany, NY: State University of New York Press.

CHAPTER 8

FROM MODEL MINORITIES TO DISPOSABLE MODELS

The Delegitimization of Educational Success Through Discourses of Authenticity

Alice Bradbury

INTRODUCTION

This chapter aims to develop two related discussions in the field of race and education concerning the constitution of some groups as model minorities and the use of discourses of authenticity to dismiss minoritized students' attainment. This discussion is motivated by the need to examine in more detail the limits of model minority status and to emphasize the multiplicity of ways in which the attainment of minoritized students can be rendered illegitimate. This is a combination of effects that, it is argued, allows for the continued idealization of White students and their successes and the maintenance of the status quo in terms of disparities in educational attainment. Data from qualitative research based in Primary (age 5–11) and Secondary (age 11–16) schools in London is used to illustrate the widening groups of students who may be intelligibly understood as "model minorities," and the range of ways in which their educational successes are rendered inauthentic.

Killing the Model Minority Stereotype: Asian American Counterstories and Complicity,
pages 133–149.

The analysis is informed by tools offered by Critical Race Theory (CRT), which illuminate how changing classroom discourses can work at a systematic level to maintain long-standing racial disparities.

The chapter begins with a discussion of *model minority* discourses and the related issue of authenticity based on research in the U.K. and international educational contexts. A second section examines the theoretical tools offered by CRT and their use in this discussion, before a description of the research studies that gave rise to the data used. The following sections are organized around the two main arguments proposed: first, that *model minority* status is fluid and has, in the English context, expanded to include smaller minoritized groups identified as having a good "education ethic"; and second, that all forms of *model minority* status are accompanied by multiple concurrent dismissals of educational success in the form of discourses of inauthenticity. A final section examines the role of this partial and precarious recognition of some minoritized groups' high attainment in the continuation of White dominance in education, and the lessons for those who wish to challenge this state of affairs.

"MODEL MINORITIES"

The discussion of model minorities in this chapter builds on David Gillborn's (2008) examination of this concept, which has origins in the United States, in the U.K. context in his book *Racism and Education: Coincidence or conspiracy?* Of particular relevance is his argument that there is "a disposable character to model minorities" (2008, p. 146); a fluidity in which groups of pupils can be intelligible as "model." Gillborn argues that some groups may no longer be seen as *model* when they "no longer serve the interests of powerholders"; following this argument, this chapter considers as to who may be added to the list of model minorities when this serves some purpose.

The term *model minority* has a longer history in the U.S. than the U.K., and is usually applied there to "Asian Americans," particularly the Chinese and Japanese communities.[1] According to Li and Wang's history of the term, the first use dates back to a 1966 *New York Times Magazine* article on Japanese Americans (2008, p. 3). This was followed by a *U.S. News and World Report* article on the success of Chinese Americans (cited in Pang & Palmer, 2012, p. 1518), and a 1971 article in *Newsweek* discussing how some minority groups were "outwhiting the whites" (Li & Wang, 2008, p. 3). The emergence of this stereotype has to be seen within the changing racial dynamics of the Civil Rights era, and the historic and continued constitution of Asian-Americans as Other; as a *New York Times* commentator reminds us in a reflective piece on 30 years since the racist murder of Vincent Chin, "[H]istory … teaches us that before Asian-Americans were seen as model minorities, we were also perpetual foreigners" (Wu, 2012).

Within the *model minority* discourse, which has remained persistent into the twenty-first century, Asian Americans are stereotyped as displaying "proper behaviors and attitudes (e.g. uncomplaining and docile) and proper work ethics (e.g.

hardworking, persistent, diligent, and self-abnegating)" (Li, 2008, p. 216); students from this community are essentialized as "whiz kids" (Lee, 2008, p. ix). Chang and Au (2007) list the characteristics of the *model minority* student as "devoted, obedient to authority, respectful of teachers, smart, good at math and science, diligent, hard workers, cooperative, well behaved, docile, college-bound, quiet and opportunistic" (p. 15). This is an infantilizing discourse, which positions Asian-Americans—in school and beyond—as dependent on their parents and lacking in agency. The stereotype had been fueled, Min (2004) argues, by statistics showing that Asian Americans have a higher median family income than White Americans, although this is a flawed measure skewed by higher average family sizes (Chang & Au, 2007).

Although some Asian Americans have accepted and explored this *model* status, many scholars have rejected the term as "complimentary on its face" but "disingenuous at its heart" (Wu, 2002, cited in Li & Wang, 2008, p. 2). The term is a "bomb cloaked in sugar," as it positions Asian Americans as "perpetual foreigners and/or honorary whites" (Li & Wang, 2008, p. 5). Extensive scholarship in this area has shown that there are multiple negative consequences of being positioned as a model minority, including the invisibility of racism against Asian Americans and a dismissal of claims of prejudice. Yamada (1981, cited in Chang, 2000, p. 359) gives an example of how university students reacted angrily to an anthology of "outspoken Asian American writers," whom they saw as militant although they had been sympathetic to literature from other minoritized groups; for Asian Americans to complain of racism, it seemed, was going too far. The stereotype disguises structural inequalities suffered by Asian Americans; Min (2004) points out that although Asian Americans have higher levels of attainment overall, they do not receive equal rewards for their educational investments; their success in school does not necessarily translate into higher incomes or more rewarding careers.

At the same time, the status of Asian Americans as model can cause resentment from other minority communities and from the White majority, concerned that Asian Americans "crowd out places for Whites in the classroom and workplace" by winning scholarships and increasing grade averages (Li, 2008, p. 219). The consequences of this discourse can also be significant for those students who do not fit the stereotype, including those having special educational needs, whose barriers to learning may not be recognized (Li, 2008; Lo, 2008); as Guofang Li (2008) argues, "If we blindly measure students against the stereotypes, we run the risk of ignoring their needs and overlooking their strengths" (p. 228).

Furthermore, beyond the impact on the community under discussion, there is also an impact on wider discussions of racism and other minoritized groups, a topic which is discussed in more detail later on in this chapter. The construction of successful Asian Americans, Min argues, "legitimates the supposed openness of American society" (2004, p. 334), with consequences for other groups. Moreover, as Stacey Lee argues, there can be "no 'model minority' without the concomitant stereotype of the lazy and unintelligent Black or Brown other" (Lee, 2008, p. ix). Model minorities thus function as a discursive tool to deny accusations of racism and divert attention from continuing racial inequities.

In the U.K., and more specifically England, the term model minority has more recently been applied to different communities, namely the Indian and Chinese communities (Gillborn, 2008), due to their high levels of attainment in standardized national tests through the 1990s and 2000s. However, it would be wrong to suggest that the emergence of this discourse is due only to availability of statistics; it is based on far more complex understandings of the place of the Indian and Chinese communities within the multiplicity of migrant groups in the U.K. In the case of Indian students, educational success has been linked to the supposedly middle-class occupations of many migrants from India in the post-war period, through perceptions of an appropriate *education ethic*. There is certainly an important class dimension to this discourse—the proportion of students from these groups in receipt of free school meals are similar to the White British majority— although this is sometimes denied by those who seek to compare the Indian and Chinese students' success with other minoritized students' levels of attainment (Gillborn, 2008, p. 147). This class-based analysis of differential attainment is also recognizable in the academic literature; for example, the argument of Chang and Au (2007) that differences within the wide Asian-American group can be explained by "the first rule of educational inequality ... Class matters" (p. 16).

In England, pervasive discourses that link parental attitudes and students' home lives to inevitable paths of educational attainment or failure, both linked to and separate from class explanations, are powerful in the operation of the model minority discourse. Qualitative research on British Chinese students' experiences by Archer and Francis (2007) found that they were understood by teachers as hardworking and successful in education, but were also subject to racist discourses of "Chinese geeks." British Chinese families were seen as too "pushy," and students were homogenized through "oppressive expectation" and pathologized as too focused on school at the expense of other activities. Despite their successful learner identities, British Chinese students' stereotyped subservience and passivity were criticized by teachers, leading to a "negative positive," where teachers had high expectations based on racist assumptions (Archer & Francis, 2007). As in research in the U.S., there were consequences for the British Chinese students' experiences of education.

Other than Gillborn's CRT-informed analysis, there has been little academic discussion of the model minority discourse in education in England, despite its prevalence in discussions of racism in schools (Archer and Francis do not use the term in their research on British Chinese students). As Gillborn argues, the fact that Indian and Chinese students attain higher scores in exams at age 16 than White British students (the government's term) is frequently cited as evidence that the education system is not institutionally racist. This argument is predicated on the idea that *a system must be racist to all minority groups, or none at all*; it denies the fact that racist assumptions may work in contradictory ways, and may have different effects on different groups. It also suggests that if a system (or indeed an individual) is racist, then it must be so equally to all groups, when this is patently not the case. A system may discriminate against one minority group, while leaving another apparently unaffected. Underlying this "racist to all or none" argument, I would argue, is a persistent conception of racism as individual prejudice manifested in explicitly racist actions, which refuses to accept the impact of unwitting actions on minoritized groups' experiences and attainment. This denial of the idea that racism can be systematic without intention and, indeed, institutional is a major barrier to progress in anti-racist work in the U.K. This chapter seeks to open up discussion of the discourse of model minorities, by exploring the fluidity of who is constructed as model and emphasizing the negative elements of this status, particularly the denial of authenticity. In doing so, this aim is to further reduce the impact of the "racist to all or none" argument as a denial of institutional racism in education.

THE RESEARCH STUDIES

The data used in this chapter arose from two studies, both conducted in London in the period 2009–2011. First, I use data from an ESRC-funded research project involving long-term ethnographic studies of two Reception classrooms (children aged 4–5) in inner London. The schools, which I call Gatehouse and St Mary's primary schools, were located in an economically deprived area of London, and the majority of the children in these two classes were from minoritized communities. The study involved classroom observation over the course of a year and regular interviews with the Reception teachers; the overall findings are discussed in detail elsewhere (Bradbury, 2011, 2013a, 2013b). The second study, funded by the London Educational Research Unit at the Institute of Education, was a small pilot project exploring the experiences and attainment of students from the Afghan community in London. This involved background research on the community and semi-structured interviews with a primary school teacher (children aged 5–11) and a secondary teacher (ages 11–16) in schools with high numbers of Afghan pupils. These schools were located in a different area of London.

Data from both of these studies were coded using NVivo and analyzed using a theoretical framework influenced by CRT and also by post-structural theory, including Foucault's conception of discourse and Butler's use of performative identities (Butler, 1993, 2004). In particular, Butler's theories of recognizable identities are used to examine as to which discourses need to be deployed to allow particular groups of children to be intelligible as students, and in this case the "intelligible space" required for these students to be constituted as model minorities. Davies (2006), using Butler's work, argues that "[s]ubjects, and this includes school students, who are constituted as lying outside intelligibility are faced with the constitutive force of a language that grants them no intelligible space" (p. 434). This lack of intelligibility is a significant theme in the discussion of authenticity in the later section of this chapter. Drawing on CRT, I use the principle of interest convergence (Bell, 2003) to examine the purpose of model minorities in the continuance of white dominance. Simply put, this principle suggests that gains are only made when they serve white interests; this is a useful starting point for the consideration of why some groups become constituted as model. I also build upon on Gillborn's (2008) CRT-inspired discussion of "disposable minorities," who may only be temporarily constituted positively but serve some purpose.

THE FLUIDITY OF MODEL MINORITIES

One, the central ideas of CRT and much other literature on *race* is the historicity of the social construct of race—that racisms and racial terms are flexible and serve the political interests of the time. Omi and Winant's (2004) "racial formation" approach, which takes neither a "race as illusionary" nor a "racial objectivist" position, takes into account "the importance of historical context and contingency in the framing of racial categories and the social construction of racially defined experiences" (p. 11). Thus the relative positions of different groups within popular discourse are dependent on the expediencies of a particular time and place; the movement of different communities into and out of model minority status (a status which is entirely constructed rather than an actual phenomenon, I should emphasize) is further indication of the fluidity with which race-based stereotypes can operate to maintain the status quo. I argue, using data from London schools, how students from a number of smaller Muslim communities from Afghanistan, Iraq, Kosovo, and elsewhere have access to model minority status alongside their Indian and Chinese counterparts. I comment here only on the situation in the U.K., and only speculatively, given the scale of the data used; nonetheless, this data raises questions regarding the overall assumption that "Muslim" students are constituted negatively in schools in England (Shain, 2010), and the idea that model minority status is fixed.

Previous discussion of model minorities in England has included discussion of groups of students who temporarily move into model status, as mentioned. Gillborn's (2008) examination of the positioning of students from Montserrat, who arrived in the U.K. after being evacuated following a volcanic explosion, found these students were initially lauded in the national press as part of criticism of the school system. However, in using the work of Gertrude Shotte, a Montserratian head-teacher who researched the experiences of the students, Gillborn argues that in the long term, the educational experiences and attainment of the Montserratian students were low and that a disproportionate number were excluded from school (2008, p. 159). Gillborn's discussion of these "disposable models" also reminds us of the subjectivity of model minority status; his discussion is based on one *Mail on Sunday* newspaper article, which had an alternative agenda, and unfortunately there is little research on how the Montserratian students were received in schools initially. It may be that these students were never model to the schools involved and experienced racism from the very start of their time in the U.K. education system. Nonetheless, what this discussion emphasizes is the way in which the use of discourses of model students, however temporary, serves some interest other than that of the group itself. In this case, this interest is the denigration of the school system, but in wider terms, model minorities provide evidence of a supposed meritocratic system in which any student can achieve.

Model Minorities in Reception

The flexibility of the term model minorities was evident in the Reception classrooms of young children I researched in inner London. In these classrooms, some minoritized children, and girls in particular, were held up as model students and in turn their families and communities were positioned as model minorities (see also Bradbury, 2013b).[2] At one school, which I call Gatehouse, five students from the Afghan and Kosovan communities were the highest attaining girls in the teacher's assessment,[3] alongside a White working- class girl.[4] They were also held up as examples for the other students, and chosen for special tasks requiring sensible behavior. These students were constituted as hard- working, well-behaved, and conscientious. Their teacher described one Afghan girl, Khadija, as "amazing, kind of, just funny and 'how do you know that?' kind of girl." As with the research on Chinese students, this model status was linked explicitly and implicitly to their families' attitudes and aspirations.

In this fieldnote, the staff are discussing a new student, Farah, who would go on to become the highest attaining pupil in the class:

> The teachers are discussing a new pupil after a home visit: the new girl is described as "quite bright, quite a bit of English." They hope the new girl will be good model of English for the other children. She is described as Afghan and Pashto speaking. They discuss if there are any other Afghan children. The class teacher mentions that older children in the family have gone to university and says "obviously they have high aspirations." The family is also described as very "with it"; Dad took time off work to meet Farah's new teacher. (Fieldnotes, Gatehouse)

From the very beginning of her first year in school, before she even enters the classroom, Farah's nascent model identity and the link with her family are established. Similarly, discussions of Khadija, the student mentioned above as "amazing," included references to her father's job at a broadcasting organization, such as "obviously [he] talks about stuff at home." This link with children's families' attitudes toward education was also mentioned in the other Reception classroom, where the teacher commented on what he saw as a hierarchy of different groups in terms of their "education ethic":

> In my last school it was a lot of Kurdish children, who'd come from villages, whose parents didn't know what … They really weren't that interested in education to be honest, and so they did no work with them at home … Those children seriously didn't move the way that some of our Arab-speaking children from Baghdad, whose

parents have fled the country but are very highly educated, who can't speak much English, but they've got high education ethic. (Class teacher, St Mary's)

In this teacher's view, the children who had left the city of Baghdad during conflict were preferable to the Kurdish children from villages, because of the two communities' different parental attitudes; this is similar to the way in which the justification of Indian students' success is often the assumed middle-class origins of their families.

The data from the second project on Afghan pupils suggests that this model status and the connection with family attitudes is present in relation to this specific group more widely: the primary teacher interviewed made the following comments:

The pupils themselves are very keen; behavior is never really an issue. They're kind of wide-eyed and very respectful and very well behaved. They respond to the opportunities of school very well. We assume that … if they've managed to get out of a war-torn area like Afghanistan they must have the means and the wherewithal … They are aspirational for their children; they understand that education is going to be the key way out. (Primary Teacher)

As in the Reception classrooms in the first study, the Afghan students are constituted as model, well behaved, keen to learn, and eager to make the most of "the opportunities of school." This last phrase is also indicative of a neoliberal discourse of individual responsibility for success that, as much of the U.S. literature on model minorities points out, locates responsibility for differential success firmly with the student and family and not with the school system. Like the Reception teacher's comments on Iraqi families above, these children's assumed escape from a conflict zone is taken as an indication of both middle-classness and aspiration; their refugee status is seen as a barrier to be overcome through education, and the wider structural inequalities faced by these communities are ignored. The secondary teacher interviewed also commented positively on her teenage Afghan students' attitudes toward school, saying they were "pretty motivated, they all have that in common." She made explicit comparisons with the British Indian community in the school and commented that "that kind of cultural aspirational desire to achieve well academically is something throughout the school." Both teachers made comments that identified the Afghan students as (relatively) middle class. The primary teacher said, "They are probably middle class, whatever that means for the Afghan community," while the secondary teacher explained how an Afghan student had told her that it was "people with money, not necessarily the wealthiest in society, but you know people with access to money, [who] could afford to escape the country."

As I have explained, it is not clear whether students from the Afghan, Kosovan, and Iraqi communities are more widely constituted as model, and the lack of available data on the attainment levels of these students[5] (and more detailed qualitative research) makes such a claim only tentative. However, there is some purpose in considering how these students are intelligible as model to these teachers, and what this means for the operation of model minority discourses more widely. Using Butler's ideas of intelligible subjects who are constituted through discourse (Butler, 1993, 2004), and following Youdell's (2006) work on intelligible student-subjecthood, we can explore how some students can become recognizable as successful learners, albeit temporarily. I would argue that these students from smaller Muslim minority communities who originated in countries that have experienced recent conflicts are constituted as model through a web of discourses relating to good/bad migrants, assimilation, class, and religious moderation. Their assumed "middle classness" (not equivalent to White middle classness, however, as I discuss below) resonates with wider discourses relating to the connection between income levels and attainment, middle-class parenting styles and a positive education ethic. At the same time, neoliberal individualist discourses of responsibility with an emphasis for on "upward mobility," applied in the past and present to working- class children (Walkerdine, 2003), make the discourse of aspiration among minoritized communities more potent. Assimilationist discourses of "good migrants" who have aspirations and are hardworking and keen to adopt "Western" values, which are present in a policy context of "contemporary assimilationism" (Gillborn, 2008), position these families as acceptable minorities in general.

More specifically for the girls, discourses of "Asian" pupils as passive and obedient (Connolly, 1998; Shain, 2003) and of girls' success in the education system overall make their high attainment and good behavior intelligible within educational discourse. Furthermore, in a context of increased Islamophobia and the regular connection of Iraq and Afghanistan in particular with Muslim extremist violence in popular discourse, these families who have come to the U.K. are positioned as models of a kind of submissive, assimilating, liberal and Westernized Islam, which is acceptable and welcomed. This is an important final point, given the tendency in the U.K. to use a binary notion of *Asian* communities (a term which may or may not include some of the communities under discussion here) divided into "good" Indian/Hindu and "bad" Pakistani/Bangladeshi/Muslim (Archer & Francis, 2007, p. 42). Within the Muslim communities there is a wide variety of different groups (including those not included within an *Asian* category), and there is a danger that discussion of "Muslim students" homogenizes a wide array of students into a singular, negative identity. Thus, it is important to emphasize that not all Muslim students are understood negatively in schools. In fact, through this complex set of discourses, some Muslim children are intelligible as model-minoritized students.

A key element of the model minority discourse is the constitution of an entire community as successful, not just individuals within that perceived racial group. Although some of the data here do suggest this is the case, this is an argument requiring further research and exploration. Furthermore, some of these schools may be atypical in terms of the absence or small numbers of White students. However, these data suggest that there is some "intelligible space" for other groups of students to be constituted as model minorities in the current context in England. This is particularly the case where these groups provide a contrast to other minorities, who are seen to have less positive attitudes toward education or to have lower attainment. As I discuss further below, the fluidity of model minority status, although it may offer some benefit to some students who have access to high expectations and positions of success (however temporarily), principally serves to maintain the status quo in terms of White dominance in education. I now turn to what I see as the sharper side of the double-edged sword of model minority status: the dismissal of high attainment as inauthentic.

MULTIPLE DISCOURSES OF (IN)AUTHENTICITY

As in the U.S. literature on Asian Americans in schools, the research on British Chinese students has identified the notions of "pushy parents," overwork, and unnecessary pressure in teachers' perceptions. In Archer and Francis' (2007) study, British Chinese students' success was seen as having been "achieved in the wrong way," and their parents' enthusiasm for learning was described by teachers as "aggressive, producing the 'wrong sort' of learning, being too 'enclosed' and denying children individuality" (p. 42). This discourse of inappropriate parental pressure among Chinese communities is familiar in the public domain, and has more recently been discussed explicitly with the debate surrounding the publication of *Battle Hymn of the Tiger Mother* by Amy Chua, a guide to "ultra-strict" parenting (2011).

In the U.S., the model minority myth has led to the marketing of books revealing the "secrets" of Asian American parenting (Chang & Au, 2007). There are parallels between the discussion of British Chinese students and Youdell's research findings that Indian students were constituted as diligent and successful "but not intrinsically gifted" (Youdell, 2006, p. 143). In schools, I would argue, this discourse of success through mere hard work and as a result of parental pressure can be applied to a wider range of students, and works powerfully to render these young people's successes *inauthentic*. The idea that high attainment among some minoritized students is caused by "overwork" or external parental pressure has as its counterpoint the idea that White students' successes are caused by something innate and internal; a White normative ideal is implicit, I would argue, in this dismissal of some students' success as inauthentic.

I use the term authenticity as shorthand for this complex discourse, as it arises both in Archer and Francis' analysis and independently in the data I collected in Reception classrooms (see the quote below). This discussion builds upon previous work on teachers' descriptions of girls' learning styles, particularly in masculine subjects, as not the "proper way" (Walkerdine, 2003), although two decades on the associations of gender and success are perhaps altered (Renold & Allan, 2006). With regard to authenticity, Archer and Francis conclude:

The "ideal learner" is an inherently embodied discourse which always excludes minority ethnic pupils and denies them from inhabiting positions or identities of "success" with any sense of permanency or authenticity. (2007, p. 170)

For the British Chinese students in their study, the association of their success with overwork and parental pressure meant that although they were constituted as model, they could not be positioned as ideal authentic learners. A similar analysis applies to the successful children from range of minoritized communities in the Reception classes I observed. In both classrooms, discourses of authenticity were used to delegitimize the attainment of minoritized students; here, the class teacher at St Mary's is discussing "thinking skills":

They all, there are some children who are very good at repeating, and memorizing, but in terms of real thinking skills: not really there … So you get what I mean, there are a lot of children who have learned a lot, but they haven't intellectually got that thinking skills and problem solving … There are too many children coming out that are able to repeat things, like a parrot, or follow a writing frame … they'll do that but ask them to really truly do something authentic and they can't do it and I think that's a major problem. (Class teacher, St Mary's)

For this teacher, there is a clear distinction to be made (which he can identify) between repetition, memorizing or following a writing frame, and something "authentic." This discourse, which places the responsibility for assessing authenticity with the teacher, can work as a refusal to recognize educational success in various forms, for any student. In the other Reception classroom I studied, the same discourse of skills that were "not really there" was used to question the attainment of one of the model Afghan girls discussed earlier in this chapter, Khadija. Although her class teacher had described her as "amazing" earlier in the year, when it came to placing the children in groups based on "ability," Khadija was placed in the second group of five. When I discussed the groups with the class teacher, he explained that "[s]he's very vocal, but she's there for consolidation. I'm not sure it's all there." As I have discussed in more detail elsewhere (Bradbury, 2013b), this was part of a wider shift in Khadija's learner identity, a central part of which was the rendering of her success as inauthentic. She was not the only student to be dismissed in this way: another Afghan girl, Bilqis, was initially praised by the staff as the only child in the class who could read all the required "high frequency words," a list of words that the curriculum requires Reception children to recognize instantly. However, she remained in a lower "ability" group for reading because, her class teacher explained, "Her mum has been working flat out since she joined Reception" to teach her these words. This achievement, just like that of the British Chinese students, was deemed to be entirely due to parental pressure rather than an inherent skill.

This discourse of authenticity has its roots in a model of an ideal student, a subject that has occupied a range of literature (Becker, 1952; Gillborn, 1990; Youdell, 2006). The idea that some learning is *not* authentic cannot exist without the idea that some is authentic. The problem is that the authentic ideal appears to be possible and intelligible only for the White student, leaving the successes of minoritized students unrecognized. Furthermore, authenticity is not simply about academic achievement; it can be used to dismiss a wider range of "good student" characteristics. In the Reception classes I observed, discourses of authenticity also applied to behavior and attitudes: some children were seen as being naturally well behaved and others as putting on a show of good behavior. Some were seen as taking part in activities, because their enthusiasm for learning was a natural trait, while other children were seen as merely trying to please the teacher. Thus, perceptions of a "performance" of good learning could be used to demean students' wider attributes, beyond their academic attainment.

Authenticity discourses also have a complex relationship with ideas about innate intelligence and the organization of education on the basis of *ability*. On many occasions, as in the quote about repetition and memory above, authenticity is linked to innate intelligence and contrasted with a lack of inherited ability. But it is important to note that some students from minoritized communities *are* constituted as inherently "able" or intelligent; some teachers in Archer and Francis' study described their Chinese students as "clever," for example. But this intelligence is often described as being linked to the racial group; thus it becomes another essentializing characteristic based on biological notions of *race*, while simultaneously demeaning the achievement of the individual. At the same time, notions of achieving in the "right way" can continue to delegitimize attainment, even if students are seen as intelligent.

Thus far, this discussion has focused on discourses of authenticity based on parental pressure and attainment that is "not all there." In this final section I want to consider another facet of authenticity, which was deployed in discussions of teenage Afghan children's attainment. In an interview with a teacher in a London secondary school with a number of Afghan students, clear distinctions were made between the motivations of successful Indian students and successful Afghan students. Although, as mentioned, motivation was seen as something that all the students had in common, the teacher explained that for the Afghan students "motivation comes more from within themselves than from parental expectations." She went on to say:

> I think that kind of psychological impact of having to flee your country, essentially as a refugee, has kind of affected their identity in a way that for another student it may not have the same effect. (Secondary teacher)

Several of this teacher's Afghan students had come from Afghanistan without their families and/or in traumatic circumstances; this was linked, it appeared, to her sense of their motivation. I would argue that this explanation is another form of dismissal through inauthenticity. These students' motivation and success are attributed to being refugees and needing to use education as a "way out" (like the Afghan parents' views mentioned by the primary teacher). It is based on a kind of "refugee mentality" and not, implicitly, due to their intelligence. These students' success is delegitimized through a slightly romanticized notion of a lone teenage refugee struggling against the odds, which resonates with wider ideas about "good migrants" and their aspirations. I would argue, albeit tentatively given the limits of these data, that this is an alternative form of the authenticity discourse, which, instead of linking success to parental pressure, bases inauthenticity on a need for escape. Authenticity, being in the eye of the beholder, is a flexible concept, which can be re- deployed in multiple forms. This difference between the data from Reception and Primary classrooms and the Secondary teacher in relation to Afghan students—this "model Muslim" minority—is perhaps due to the age of the students involved. Nonetheless, what it does point to is the multiplicity and complexity of discourses of authenticity and how they can be deployed to dismiss minoritized attainment.

DISCUSSION

A central argument of this chapter is that, in the education system in England, discourses of model minorities and authenticity are flexible, and can be used to delegitimize the academic successes of minoritized communities. These two discourses are intertwined, and one works to resolve the other: model minorities are useful in denying claims of institutional racism based on "racist to all or none" assumptions, but their success is achieved in the "wrong way." If a wider range of minoritized groups including Afghan, Iraqi, and Kosovan students begin to be constituted as model (and again, I reiterate this is certainly not a universal or widely used discourse yet), discourses of inauthenticity based on parental pressure and a "refugee mentality" can be used to dismiss this. Furthermore, assumptions that certain minoritized families are "pushy" linked to inauthenticity are the basis for model minority status, which leads to the argument that the system cannot be racist. Together, these ideas work powerfully to maintain a White idealized norm and deflect attention from race disparities in attainment.

What this discussion has not considered is the wider picture, which includes the significant problem of the lower attainment of many minoritized groups. Using a CRT framework, I want to explore as to what purpose model minorities serve in the wider maintenance of White dominance in education. A well-used theoretical tool in CRT is Bell's principle of interest convergence (Bell, 2003), which argues that gains made by the Black community in the U.S. are only those that serve White interests. Bell argues that the *Brown versus Board of Education* decision to desegregate schools was motivated by foreign policy interests; there was a convergence of interests, not a desire to reduce racial inequality. Although the issue of model minorities and authenticity discussed here is not an example of interest convergence, some of the ideas have some resonance with the concept. There is a sense with model minorities of having given something up (White groups at the top of attainment statistics) for the continuation of the wider project of White dominance. But while something is lost, the fundamentals are maintained through dismissals based on authenticity; Whiteness is still idealized, associated with authentic intelligence and educational success. As in interest convergence, what is gained is only partial and only occurs when it serves White interests.

Based on this argument, why would additional groups gain access to model status? The concept of interest convergence suggests that the minimum is only ever conceded. Furthermore, as Gillborn notes, "it does not matter who provides the model as long as there is a model to point to" (2008, p. 157), and Chinese and Indian high attainment in England continues to provide this model. Even if their positions are not as prominent as these two communities (and are limited by the statistics available), why would other groups be intelligible as model? Perhaps there is some purpose in positioning some smaller Muslim minorities as model, while the majority Pakistani and Bangladeshi Muslim minorities continue to be pathologized in what Youdell (2003) in a different context has called a "hierarchy of the Other."

In a context of concern over Islamophobia, perhaps a version of the usual model minority argument, a "racist to all Muslim groups or none" position is useful in denying accusations of racism. There is a need for a good/bad binary in discussions of all groups: perhaps what we see in the positive descriptions of Afghan, Iraqi, and Kosovan students is the emergence of a "good Muslim/bad Muslim" division, similar to the division of British Asians into good Indian/Hindu and bad Pakistani/Bangladeshi/Muslim in the 1990s and 2000s. Research from the U.S. on Asian Americans has provided examples of a similar binary within the model Asian-American group: Lee has argued that in some contexts Asian-Americans are discursively divided into passive high-achieving "good kids" and "bad kids," who were "Americanized" among students who adopted a "hip hop style associated with urban youth of color" (Lee, 2005, cited in Li & Wang, 2008, p. 7), for example. What remains potent in all these possibilities, both in the U.K. and U.S., is the centrality of the White ideal, as the measure against which all groups will be compared. It is also important not to overstate the planned or intentional nature of shifting boundaries of model status, and to reiterate the difference between this case and examples of interest convergence from legal studies. However, there is some utility, I would argue, in considering how changing patterns of how to adapt Gillborn's phrase, "racism plays favorites" (Gillborn, 2008, p. 153), and to what ends, this serves.

The roles played by model minorities and discourses of authenticity serve as useful reminders of continued White dominance. For all minoritized students, model or not, these discourses continue to locate the source of disparities with students and families, not with the education system. Model minorities deflect attention from continued educational difference in the U.K. and elsewhere, while students from these communities continued to be subject to racist assumptions of inauthentic learning. One of the tensions in discussions of model minorities lies between the need to reduce the idea to the status of myth, and recognizing the very real impact of this myth on the lived experiences of both people from that minority and those from other minoritized groups. Although it may have its advantages, as Chang (2000) argues, to accept that some minorities are model is to be "complicitous in the oppression of other racial minorities and poor whites" (p. 361). But while it exists and becomes established—and the U.S. is a cautionary tale for the U.K. in this respect—it must be challenged and questioned.

Questions for Reflection

1. In the United Kingdom, how are the discourses of model minorities and authenticity flexible?
2. Why has the term model minority been applied to Indians and Chinese in the United Kingdom?
3. What does Bradbury mean by discourses of authenticity? How do these discourses apply to the model minority stereotype of Asians in the United Kingdom?
4. Are there similarities between the model minority stereotype in the United States and the United Kingdom? If so, what are they?
5. What purpose does the model minority stereotype play in the United Kingdom?

ENDNOTES

1. To clarify, I use the term Asian American (sometimes referred to Asian Pacific American) in the sense that it is used in the U.S.; the term "Asian" in the U.K. is usually used to refer to the Indian, Pakistani, and Bangladeshi communities, not the Chinese community. In reference to the U.K., I avoid the term, except when citing research that uses this terminology.
2. These classes included only two or three White students, and few or no students from the Chinese or Indian communities, which may be relevant here.
3. This teacher assessment, which is a standardized system across Reception classrooms in England, is conducted through observation, and, as I have argued elsewhere, is not a true measure of what children can or cannot do. It is, however, a measure of what a teacher expects a child to be able to do (within the constrictions of a performative accountability system), and therefore is an indication of these students' model status.
4. It is worth noting that some of the literature on Asian American students makes use of the concept of "honorary Whites"; which I do not use but may be relevant here. In particular, there is scope for further exploration (which I do not have space for here) of the status of Kosovan children, who are listed in official documents as White European, but are nonetheless a minoritized group in contrast to the White British majority.

5. The U.K. Department of Education publishes data by "ethnic group," but not in a form that allows the consideration of the attainment of these smaller groups.

REFERENCES

Archer, L., & Francis, B. (2007). *Understanding minority ethnic achievement: Debating race, gender, class and 'success'*. London, UK: Routledge.

Becker, H. S. (1952). Social-class variation in the teacher–pupil relationship. *Journal of Educational Sociology, 25*(8), 451–465. doi:10.2307/2263957

Bell, D. (2003). *The Derrick Bell reader*. New York, NY: New York University Press.

Bradbury, A. (2011). Rethinking assessment and inequality: The production of disparities in attainment in early years education. *Journal of Education Policy, 26*(5), 655–676. doi:10.1080/ 02680939.2011.569572

Bradbury, A. (2013a). Education policy and the 'ideal learner': Producing recognisable learner-subjects through assessment in the early years. British Journal of *Sociology of Education, 34*(1), 1–19. doi:10.1080/01425692.2012.692049

Bradbury, A. (2013b). Understanding early years inequality: Policy, assessment and young children's identities. London, UK: Routledge.

Butler, J. P. (1993). *Bodies that matter: On the discursive limits of 'sex'*. London, UK: Routledge.

Butler, J. P. (2004). *Undoing gender*. New York, NY: Routledge.

Chang, B., & Au, W. (2007). You're Asian, how could you fail math? Unmasking the myth of the model minority. *Rethinking Schools, 22*(2), 15–19.

Chang, R. (2000). Towards an Asian American legal scholarship: CRT, post-structuralism and narrative space. In R. Delgado & J. Stefancic (Eds.), *Critical race theory: The cutting edge* (2nd ed., pp. 354–368). Philadelphia, PA: Temple University Press.

Chua, A. (2011). *Battle hymn of the tiger mother*. London, UK: Bloomsbury.

Connolly, P. (1998). *Racism, gender identities and young children: Social relations in a multi-ethnic, inner-city primary school*. London, UK: Routledge.

Davies, B. (2006). Subjectification: The relevance of Butler's analysis for education. *British Journal of Sociology of Education, 27*(4), 425–438. doi:10.1080/01425690600802907

Gillborn, D. (1990). *'Race', ethnicity and education: Teaching and learning in multi-ethnic schools*. London, UK: Unwin Hyman. doi:10.4324/9780203400265

Gillborn, D. (2008). *Racism and education: Coincidence or conspiracy?* London, UK: Routledge.

Lee, S. (2008). Foreword. In G. Li, & L. Wang (Eds.), *Model minority myth revisited: An interdisciplinary approach to demystifying Asian American educational experiences* (pp. ix–xi). Charlotte, NC: Information Age.

Li, G. (2008). Other people's success: Impact of the model minority myth on underachieving Asian students in North America. In G. Li & L. Wang (Eds.), *Model minority myth revisited: An interdisciplinary approach to demystifying Asian American educational experiences* (pp. 213–231). Charlotte, NC: Information Age.

Li, G., & Wang, L. (Eds.). (2008). Model minority myth revisited: An interdisciplinary approach to demystifying Asian American educational experiences. Charlotte, NC: Information Age.

Lo, L. (2008). Interactions between Chinese parents and special education professionals in IEP meetings: Implications for the education of Chinese immigrant children with disabilities. In G. Li & L. Wang (Eds.), *Model minority myth revisited: An interdisciplinary approach to demystifying Asian American educational experiences* (pp. 195–212). Charlotte, NC: Information Age.

Min, P. G. (2004). Social science research on Asian Americans. In J. Banks & C. Banks (Eds.), *Handbook of research on multicultural education* (2nd ed., pp. 332–348). San Francisco, CA: Jossey-Bass.

Omi, M., & Winant, H. (2004). On the theoretical status of the concept of race. In G. Ladson-Billings & D. Gillborn (Eds.), *The RoutledgeFalmer reader in multicultural education: Critical perspectives on race, racism and education* (pp. 7–15). London, UK: RoutledgeFalmer.

Pang, V., & Palmer, J. (2012). Model minorities and the model minority myth. In J. Banks (Ed.), *Encyclopedia of diversity in education* (p. 1518). London, UK: Sage.

Renold, E., & Allan, A. (2006). Bright and beautiful: High achieving girls, ambivalent femininities, and the feminisation of success in the primary school. *Discourse: Studies in the Cultural Politics of Education, 27*(4), 457–473. doi:10.1080/01596300600988606

Shain, F. (2003). The schooling and identity of Asian girls. Stoke-on-Trent: Trentham Books.

Shain, F. (2010). The new folk devils: Muslim boys and education in England. Stoke-on-Trent: Trentham.

Walkerdine, V. (2003). Reclassifying upward mobility: Femininity and the neo-liberal subject. *Gender and Education, 15*(3), 237–248. doi:10.1080/09540250303864

Wu, H. (2012, June 22). Why Vincent Chin matters. *New York Times*. Retrieved from http://www. nytimes.com/2012/06/23/opinion/why-vincent-chin-matters.html?_r=0

Youdell, D. C. (2003). Identity traps or how black students fail: The interactions between biographical, sub-cultural and learner identities. British Journal of *Sociology of Education, 24*(1), 3–20. doi:10.1080/01425690301912

Youdell, D. C. (2006). *Impossible bodies, impossible selves: Exclusions and student subjectivities*. Dordrecht: Springer.

CHAPTER 9

MODERN EM(BODY)MENTS OF THE MODEL MINORITY IN SOUTH KOREA

Nicholas D. Hartlep

I know of no literature on the Asian model minority stereotype that exclusively examines, in a South Korean context, how Korean culture perpetuates the stereo-type through a specific, troubling practice: Korean women, responding to ideal-ized Western beauty standards, internalize racism by undergoing body enhance-ment surgery.[1] This chapter therefore acknowledges that there are two gaps in the South Korean model minority stereotype literature. The first gap is the shortage of research conducted within the borders of South Korea and/or published in South Korean journals.[2] The second gap is the lack of literature that examines how South Koreans have themselves contributed to the Asian model minority stereotype by

---

[1] While this chapter focuses on the fact that Korean women undergo body enhancement surgery, it acknowledges that Korean men also undergo similar procedures. See http://blogs.wsj.com/koreare-altime/2012/10/09/more-men-opt-for-plastic-surgery/

[2] One exception is Choi, H. (2002). Note: This article is from the Korean journal *Kukche, Chiyok Yon'gu*. (The English words for this title are *Review of International and Area Studies*). Unfortunate-ly, this article was never published in English: full articles are published in Korean with article titles and abstracts published in English.

Killing the Model Minority Stereotype: Asian American Counterstories and Complicity,
pages 151–161.

undergoing body enhancement surgical procedures. This last gap, Korean complicity in perpetuating the stereotype, is the primary focus of this chapter. It is, I believe, interrelated with the phenomenon of body enhancement among South Koreans, although not identical (e.g., see Holliday & Elfving-Hwang, 2012; Ja, 2000).

I first review the literature on the Asian model minority stereotype outside of the United States. Next, I share photographs that illustrate how mainstream heterosexual Korean culture has internalized Western idealized forms of beauty standards (larger breasts, whiter skin, and wider eyes). One unintended consequence of this perception is that an Asian model minority becomes constructed in the public square. I argue that this publicly accepted construction leaves Western visitors (mainly tourists) to Korea believing in a Eurocentric form of exotified "Korean" women.

Photographic evidence obtained from posters and advertisements in the Seoul, Korean subway is presented to theorize a conceptual framework that can be used to better understand internalized racism from a South Korean geopolitical and geospatial perspective. Not only does this chapter fill two lacunae in the Asian model minority stereotype literature, it also creates new knowledge by arguing that the Asian stereotype exists in countries outside the United States (where much of the model minority stereotype literature is concentrated).[3]

REVIEW OF THE LITERATURE

In previous work I have cataloged 489 pieces of model minority stereotype literature (e.g., see the "Model Minority Stereotype Project" and Hartlep, 2013, 2014b). Much of this literature noticeably is written by scholars and intellectuals who live and work in North America, and who approach the topic from a North American perspective. Contradistinctively, a much smaller amount of model minority stereotype research has been conducted in Asian countries.

Notable exceptions include Chung and Walkey (1988), Ip and Pang (2005), and Hannis (2009), who have all researched the Chinese as model minorities in New Zealand, and Fang (2008, 2009a, 2009b, 2009c, 2010a, 2010b), the only academic to research Koreans as model minorities in China.[4] All in all, there are only 11 pieces of model minority stereotype literature that fall outside of a North American geopolitical or geospatial context—the nine citations mentioned previously being among them (also see Dechamma, 2012; Ha, 2011). A thorough read of this literature reveals that little-to-no attention has been paid by researchers to how the Asian model minority stereotype functions within the Republic of Ko-

---

[3] The stereotype has also been documented in Jewish (Freedman, 2005) and German/Polish (Dolowy-Rybinska, 2011; Kamphoefner, 1996) societies.

[4] Scholarship on the model minority stereotype appears in Chinese academic journals and theses; however, most of this material is related to an Asian American conceptualization of the model minority stereotype (e.g., see Cheng, 2011; Huang, 2002; Liu & Yang, 2007; Qu, 2007; Sun, 2012; Yi, 2006).

rea, especially with regard to how it is perpetuated by South Korean culture and behavior, which exacerbates Korean women's internalized oppression by altering female beauty standards in deference to Western images of sexuality and attractiveness.[5]

The "Forgotten" War (1950–1953)

During the Korean War, which lasted from 1950–1953, many Korean women married United States soldiers. South Korea was fighting against North Korea, and the United States came to its defense. According to Yu (1987a), during and immediately following the Korean War, 6,423 Korean women married United States military servicemen. Historians refer to the Korean War as the "forgotten war" because it has been overshadowed by other wars and military conflicts. Part of this forgetfulness relates to Korean comfort women—women who slept with American soldiers. These interracial marriages and interracial sexual relations resulted in many biracial children being born in Korea immediately following the Korean War. And many of these bi-racial children would later be persecuted by their full-blooded Korean peers who saw them as "less-than," scoffing at and scorning their mixed-race identity and heritage. I believe that this history of South Korean interracial antagonism can form a somewhat useful socio-historical, socio-cultural, and socio-political backdrop for present day South Korean culture. For instance, the importance of Korean bloodlines and purity of blood continues today, evidenced in South Korean governmental documents/forms that request an individual's blood type. I feel it is vital to acknowledge that the land of the "Morning Calm," as Korea is referred to, has historically looked down upon blackness (in a racial sense) while revering whiteness (in a racial sense). It is also important we not forget about South Korean comfort women, and the Korean War in general.

Photographic Evidence from Present Day South Korea

When I visited Seoul for a conference on international education, I commuted on the city's subway system. Many Koreans in Seoul travel via subway in order to avoid congested streets above ground. As of 2012, South Korea is the tenth most densely populated country in the world (Maps of World, 2012). While commuting via Seoul's first-class subway system, I could not help but notice the prevalence of products and physicians that seemed to support the idea that South Korean women should undergo cosmetic and bodily surgery, something I have written about elsewhere (Hartlep, 2014a). This underground advertising is especially effective for the simple fact that subway riders are, literally, a captive audience. On average,

---

[5] This chapter does not examine males in South Korea mainly because, as in the United States, males in South Korea are in positions of power, while beauty is seen through a heteronormative lens. As Yu (1987b) points out, "Major institutions of [Korean] society work to perpetuate the notion of male superiority" (p. 24) and "The household registry (*hojeok*) system based on male lineage also helps perpetuate the long-held tradition of patriarchy in contemporary Korea" (p. 24).

FIGURE 9.1. Plastic Surgery Center

Koreans spend an hour or more on the subway at any given time, which ultimately amounts to a lot of exposure to posters, advertisements, and videos. I snapped the photographs below (Figures 9.1–9.5) during my trip in November of 2013.

It is worth noting that iterations of this trend can be observed in other Asian countries such as the Philippines, China, and Taiwan, and doesn't necessarily reflect a uniquely South Korean culture. Although a broader consideration of the Westernization of cultural beauty standards falls outside the boundaries of the

FIGURE 9.2. Reasonable Confidence

FIGURE 9.3.   Jewelry Plastic Surgery

FIGURE 9.4.   Breast Revisions "I Can Change Your Breasts"

FIGURE 9.5. No Incision Plastic Surgery to Make You Prettier

FIGURE 9.6. White Perfect

present chapter, I have included an advertisement below that a colleague emailed me after learning I was conducting research into this topic (see Figure 9.6). It is from the Philippines, but it would fit right in with the ads plastering the Seoul subways.

Judging by this advertising and its effectiveness in influencing behavior, a significant number of mainstream heterosexual Korean women have internalized Western idealized forms of beauty standards. Conformity to these standards visually reinforces the public construction of a "model minority." Incidentally, I qualify this demographic as heterosexual because homosexuality is looked down upon in Korean society (Kim & Hahn, 2006).

Despite the fact that South Korean society attempts to appear conservative—for instance, pornography is banned—South Korean culture remains highly sexualized. Although the national government censors sexual images on the Internet, South Korea's citizens spend 26 billion dollars per year on pornography—second only to China, where porn generates 27 billion in annual revenue from a significantly larger population (D'Orlando, 2011, p. 54).[6] Meanwhile, in ways comparable to Hollywood in the United States, the Gangnam District of Seoul is a bustling metropolis of female K-pop stars who appear to have "perfect(ed)" bodies and sell their products in an overly-sexualized fashion. Gangnam, like Beverly Hills, is rife with plastic surgery clinics, where many of these famous K-Pop stars have had their bodies surgically altered to attain an artificial standard of beauty (Stone, 2013).[7]

---

[6] Korea's 26 billion dwarfs the United States' 13 billion, despite the fact it is legal in the United States.
[7] One in five South Korean women has had some form of cosmetic surgery, compared to around one in 20 in the United States.

The Most Cosmetically Enhanced People in the World

Cain (2013) notes that Gangnam is "a neighborhood that amounts to the Beverly Hills of Seoul" (para 9), adding that "[p]lastic surgery is a lucrative trade in South Korea, with citizens edging out Greece, Italy and the US as the most cosmetically enhanced people in the world" (para 5). The photographs I have shared here attest to how Korean culture encourages advertisements for products and procedures that will make their female clients more attractive. All of the models in Figures 9.1–9.5 are women. The products and procedures target such features as breast size, skin tone/color, and facial features like nose shape, capitalizing on potential clients' insecurity about these aspects of their physical appearance. As a Korean university student said, "To be Korean is to get plastic surgery. You must do it, or young people will think you're weird" (as cited in Cain, 2013, para 24).

I believe that Korean women who undergo these procedures cause onlookers to evaluate their beauty and Korean identity in ways that are compatible with the Asian model minority stereotype. I also believe that this model minority stereotype construction causes Westerners (mainly tourists) who visit the country to leave believing in a form of "Korean" womanhood that is inauthentic and ahistorical. The historical reality is that Korean women were often treated as sex objects for the pleasure of male GIs. If Korean women have historically been treated as "less-than," and currently they are undergoing procedures to alter their bodies, what does this say about Korean contemporary society?

The 2012 Miss Korea Pageant contest provides a textbook case study of what I am arguing. Some observers described the contestants as "clones" because they all looked alike. Plastic surgery was a culprit, and many in the South Korean media pointed to the similarities in the facial features of the women. Indeed, the model minority stereotype serves to erase physical differences and homogenize them instead. The result is an archetype for female beauty perfection. The problem with these beauty standards, which compel—through venues like the beauty pageant—South Korean women to undergo cosmetic surgery, is that they are unattainable. The result is that the Korean woman internalizes feelings of inadequacy, perhaps driving her to undergo even more surgical procedures to again try to perfect her body. This is highly cyclical and oppressive.

Figure 9.7 below shares a conceptual framework for understanding Korean women who internalize Western beauty standards, a form of internalized racism.

Inside the rectangle you can see the 2012 Miss Korea Pageant contained in a circle. Surrounding the circle is the model minority stereotype, which leads to the homogenization of beauty standards. Unattainable beauty standards result in Korean women internalizing racism, which results in more plastic surgeries. The framework points out how problematic this phenomenon is because the standards of beauty are a moving target.

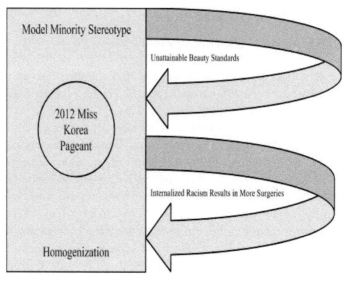

FIGURE 9.7. Conceptual Framework for Understanding Korean Women's Internalized Racism

CONCLUSION

The culture of South Korea is perpetuating the Asian model minority stereotype. K-pop artists and Korean athletes like Yuna Kim (a world class figure skater) are buying into white standards of beauty. Making matters worse, they are spreading it further through their music videos, promotional materials, and product advertisements (see Figure 9.8). Websites like Asian White Skin (http://www.asianwhiteskin.com/about.php) point to the need for more critiques of the model minority stereotype in Asian countries. Yuna Kim's Smoothie King poster, "Be White," is yet one more example of why more scholarship needs to be carried out that complicates the model minority stereotype in Asian countries.

Questions for Reflection

1. What does the 2012 Miss Korea Pageant illustrate regarding beauty standards in South Korea?
2. How have South Koreans contributed to the model minority stereotype?
3. One in five South Korean women has had some form of cosmetic surgery, compared to around one in 20 in the United States. What do you make of this statistic?
4. Why is plastic surgery so popular in South Korea?
5. In what ways does cosmetic surgery impact Korean womanhood?

FIGURE 9.8.   Yuna Kim, "Be White"

REFERENCES

Cain, G. (2013, February 26). *Plastic surgery 'Gangnam-style.'* Retrieved December 1, 2014, from http://www.globalpost.com/dispatch/news /regions/asia-pacific/south-korea/130221/plastic-surgery-gangnam-style-seoul　亚裔美国人公众形象转变研究_陈澄

Cheng, C. (2011). *A study on the change of Asian American public image-from yellow peril to model minority.* Unpublished thesis, East China Normal University, Shanghai, China.

Choi, H. (2002). Asian-Americans as a model minority: Myth of reality. *Review of International and Area Studies, 11*(4), 127–143.

Chung, R. C., & Walkey, F. H. (1988). From undesirable immigrant to model minority: The success story of Chinese in New Zealand. *Immigrants & Minorities, 7*(3), 308–313.

Dechamma, S. (2012). The model minority: Problematizing the representation of Kodavas in Kannada Cinema. *Inter-Asia Cultural Studies, 13*(1), 5–21.

Dolowy-Rybinska, N. (2011). A model minority. *Insight Academia, 30*(2), 48–49. Retrieved December 1, 2014, from http://www.english.pan.pl/im ages/stories/pliki/publikacje/academia/2011/2_2011_30/48–49_dolowy.pdf

D'Orlando, F. (2011). The demand for pornography. *Journal of Happiness Studies, 12*(1), 51–75. doi:10.1007/s10902–009–9175–0

Fang, G. (2008). What it means to be a model minority: Voices of ethnic Koreans in northeast China. *Asian Ethnicity, 9*(1), 55–67.

Fang, G. (2009a). Challenges of discourses on "Model Minority" and "South Korean Wind" for ethnic Koreans' schooling in northeast China. *Diaspora, Indigenous, and Minority Education, 3*(2), 119–130.

Fang, G. (2009b). Model minority, self-perception and schooling: Multiple voices of Korean students in China. *Asia Pacific Journal of Education, 29*(1), 17–27.

Fang, G. (2009c). Researching Korean children's schooling experience behind the model minority stereotype in China: An ethnographic approach. In C. Kwok-Bun, K. S. Agnes, C. Yin-Wah, & C. Wai-Wan (Eds.), *Social stratification in Chinese societies* (pp. 225–245). Leiden, Netherlands: Brill.

Fang, G. (2010a). A comparative analysis of the meaning of model minority among ethnic Koreans in China and the United States. *Comparative Education, 46*(2), 207–222.

Fang, G. (2010b). *Becoming a model minority: Schooling experiences of ethnic Koreans in China*. Lanham, MD: Rowan & Littlefield.

Freedman, J. (2005). Transgressions of a model minority. *Shofar: An Interdisciplinary Journal of Jewish Studies, 23*(4), 69–97.

Ha, J. (2011, Winter). A striking similarity: The stereotyping of Asian Americans in the U.S. media and the stereotyping of foreigners in the Korean media. *Situations: Cultural Studies in the Asian Context, 5*, 102–107.

Hannis, G. (2009). From yellow peril to model minority? A comparative analysis of a newspaper's depiction of the Chinese in New Zealand at the 20th and 21st centuries. *Asia Pacific Media Educator, 19*, 85–98.

Hartlep, N. D. (2013). *The model minority stereotype: Demystifying Asian American success*. Charlotte, NC: Information Age.

Hartlep, N. D. (2014a). Eyelid surgery among the Nacirema: Toward Asian American understanding. In D. T. Smith & T. E. Sabino (Eds.), *The impact of social factors on health* (pp. 139–154). San Diego, CA: Cognella.

Hartlep, N. D. (Ed.). (2014b). *The model minority stereotype reader: Critical and challenging readings for the 21st century.* San Diego, CA: Cognella.

Holliday, R., & Elfving-Hwang, J. (2012). Gender, globalization and aesthetic surgery in South Korea. *Body & Society, 18*(2), 58–81. doi:10.1177/1357034X12440828

Huang, J. (2002). The model minority thesis: Myth and reality. *Journal of Northeast Normal University, 6*(200), 51–59.

Ip, M., & Pang, D. (2005). New Zealand Chinese identity: Sojourners, model minority and multiple identities. In M. Ip & D. Pang (Eds.), *New Zealand identities: Departures and destinations* (pp. 174–190). Victoria, New Zealand: Victoria University Press.

Ja, W. K. (2000). The beauty complex and the cosmetic surgery industry. *Korea Journal, 44*(2), 52–82. Retrieved December 1, 2014, from http://www.ekoreajournal.net/sysLib/down.php?file=..%2FUPLOAD%2FT_articles%2FPDF4424

Kamphoefner, W. D. (1996). German Americans: Paradoxes of a "model minority." In S. Pedraza & R. G. Rumbaut (Eds.), *Origins and destinies: Immigration, race, and ethnicity in America* (pp. 152–160). Belmont, CA: Wadsworth Publishing Company.

Kim, Y., & Hahn, S. (2006). Homosexuality in ancient and modern Korea. *Culture, Health & Sexuality, 8*(1), 59–65. 解读_模范少数族裔_理论和多元文化主义思想的内在联系刘卓

Liu, Z., & Yang, D. (2007). Interpreting the intrinsic relationship between model minority and multiculturalism. *Journal of Liaoning University, 5*, 69–73.

Maps of World. (2012). *Most densely populated countries*. Retrieved December 1, 2014, from http://www.mapsofworld.com/world-top-ten/world-top-ten-most-densely-populated-countries-map.html

Model Minority Stereotype Project. (2014). Retrieved December 1, 2014, from http://my.ilstu.edu/blogs/ndhartl/ 模范少数族裔_形象对亚裔及其他少数族裔的负面影响_刘曲

Qu, L. (2007). *Model minority stereotype: A disservice to both Asian Americans and other minority groups in the U.S.* Unpublished thesis, China Foreign Affairs University Beijing, China.

Stone, Z. (2013, May 24). The K-pop plastic surgery obsession. *The Atlantic.* Retrieved December 1, 2014, from http://www.theatlantic.com/health /archive/2013/05/the-k-pop-plastic-surgery-obsession/2762 15/ 早期美国华裔文学作品中的_模范少数族裔_形象_孙冬苗

Sun, D. (2012). "Model minority" image in early America Chinese literature works. *Lovers of Literature, 4*, 92–93.

Yi, S. (2006). Asian American stereotypes in yellow peril and model minority myth. *Journal of Jiangsu Teachers University, 12*(1), 25–30.

Yu, E-Y. (1987a). Korean-American women: Demographic profiles and family roles. In E-Y. Yu & E. H. Phillips (Eds.), *Korean women in transition: At home and abroad* (pp. 183–197). Los Angeles, CA: Center for Korean-American and Korean Studies.

Yu, E-Y. (1987b). Women in traditional and modern Korea. In E-Y. Yu & E. H. Phillips (Eds.), *Korean women in transition: At home and abroad* (pp. 183–197). Los Angeles, CA: Center for Korean-American and Korean Studies.

PART III

ASIAN AMERICAN COMPLICITY IN PERPETUATION OF THE MODEL MINORITY MYTH

# CHAPTER 10

KOREAN NEWCOMER YOUTH'S EXPERIENCES OF RACIAL MARGINALIZATION AND INTERNALIZATION OF THE MODEL MINORITY MYTH

Yoonjung Choi and Jae Hoon Lim

BACKGROUND

The Korean population in the United States has been growing fast in recent years. There are approximately 1.7 million people of Korean descent residing in the United States, comprising 10 percent of the total Asian population in the U.S. (U.S. Census Bureau, 2012). This group contains a large proportion of newcomers. Over 25 percent of the Korean foreign-born immigrants arrived in 2000 or later. There were 1,030,691 foreigners from Korea residing in the U.S. in 2008, accounting for 2.7 percent of the country's 38 million immigrants (Terrazas & Batog, 2010). Between 2000 and 2008, the Korean immigrant population nearly

Killing the Model Minority Stereotype: Asian American Counterstories and Complicity, pages 165–183.

doubled in many states including New York, California, Georgia, and Virginia (Terrazas & Batog, 2010). Given the substantial inflow, Korean immigrants were the seventh largest immigrant group in the U.S. as of 2008.

The recent increase of the Korean student population in U.S. K–12 school contexts is also noteworthy. As the phrases "global awareness" and "global competitiveness" have become popular in many societal sectors, the number of pre-collegiate students who pursue tertiary education outside of their country of origin in their early years has increased significantly globally (UNESCO Institute of Statistics, 2009). Korean newcomer students who were enrolled in U.S. K–12 schools reached approximately 331,937 in 2006 according to the U.S. Census Bureau (2009), while Korean communities in the U.S. assume that the number is largely underestimated and should be more than doubled (Lee, 2010).

As of 2009, Korean newcomers accounted for the sixth largest body of English language learners in U.S. K–12 schools (Migration Policy Institute, 2010). While most of these students were found in large urban centers such as New York and Los Angeles metropolitan areas, many others are concentrated in smaller communities. This new trend of transnational migration accelerated the growth of the Korean population and diversified its communities in U.S. society and schools (Lim, Moon, Choi, Yoon, & An, 2011).

Korean students, frequently lumped under the label of Asians, are often viewed as the "model minority" within the public discourses of media, pop-culture, policy, and scholarship. Asian, especially East Asian, students reportedly perform much higher than other minority groups according to the published school report cards mandated by the No Child Left Behind Act, and score higher on the SAT and ACT, especially in math (Zhao & Qiu, 2009). Asians are overrepresented at America's most prestigious universities, for example, composing 46 percent of University of California at Berkeley's entering class in 2006 (Yang, 2011).

While much attention has been paid to the seemingly successful model minority's academic excellence for the past several decades, little attention has been given to Asian students' complex social, cultural, and educational experiences and relationships at schools beyond their academic achievement (Buenavista, Jayakumar, & Misa-Escalante, 2009; Yeh, Ma, Madan-Bahel, Hunter, Jung, Kim, Akitaya, & Sasaki, 2005). The oversimplifying, misleading racial stereotype, namely the model minority myth, disguises critical educational issues such as racism and mental health challenges that Asians, particularly those who do not fit into the stereotypical model images, encounter in school, thus concealing the contentious consequences of the myth (Choi, Lim, & An, 2011; Hartlep, 2013; Liu, 2009). Complicated schooling experiences of the highly diverse Asian students and the voices of their sub-racial, ethnic, cultural, linguistic, and religious groups have been homogenized by the monolithic model minority discourse (Ng, Lee, & Pak, 2007).

This study explores the destructive effect of the model minority myth on Korean newcomer youth's peer relations at school and their internalization of the racial stereotype. Drawing upon counter-storytelling as a theoretical and methodological framework of critical race theory, this multi-regional, mixed-method study traces the pretentious voices of 63 Korean newcomer students struggling to make sense of their experiences with racial marginalization and developing coping strategies. Shedding light on the Korean immigrant youth's sociocultural experiences of schooling and inter/intra-racial relationships, this study seeks to offer a unique glimpse of the ways the model minority myth operates and is perpetuated in the lives of Asian youth at school.

THEORETICAL FRAMEWORK

This study employs critical race theory (CRT) as a theoretical as well as methodological framework, focusing on its application to educational research and practice. This section explores CRT in education and its connection to the model minority myth and then reviews literature on the experiences of racism of Asians, particularly Korean newcomers.

Critical Race Theory (CRT) in Education

Originating as a counterweight to legal scholarship in the positivist and liberal legal traditions in civil rights, CRT embodies the belief that racism is an endemic facet of life in American society and continues to define the experiences of people of color (Taylor, Gillborn, & Ladson-Billings, 2009). The four central tents of CRT are as follows: (a) racism is enmeshed in the fabric of American social order; (b) CRT employs counter-storytelling to analyze the myths and presuppositions about racism; (c) CRT critiques liberalism for its slow process to gain equal rights for people of color; and (d) the dominant racial group develops the ideology of color-blind racism, which utilizes hidden codes to mask racist ideas and practices in order to maintain their privileges from the racial status quo (*cf.* Taylor et al., 2009).

Scholars in education have used CRT as a powerful explanatory tool for the sustained inequity that people of color experience in schools and for the color-blind racism in various segments of education (Ladson-Billings, 2003; Solórzano & Yosso, 2002). Extending the construct of CRT to further racial specificity and intersectionality of multiple aspects defining the experiences of people of color (e.g. ethnicity, immigration status, language, gender, class, etc.), this study posits CRT as a useful framework for investigating the racial marginalization of Korean newcomer youth, whose voices have been largely underrepresented in the educational scholarship, and their coping strategies for the model minority stereotype.

Research on Korean Newcomer Students' Racial Experiences in U.S. Schools

The image of Asians as the model minorities has become a shibboleth that posits Asians as hard-working, self-sufficient, and successful minorities who have reached the American dreams of economic and academic success (Ng, Lee, & Pak, 2007). It is true that a large number of Asians, who had been blamed for the yellow peril, initially welcomed this positive image and desired to live up to it (Takaki, 1989). They value education as a formal and serious process and work hard to achieve middle class socioeconomic positions in order to acculturate to the mainstream society (Lew, 2004). Asians reported the highest percentage of adults with academic degrees and highest median earnings of any racial group (U.S. Census Bureau, 2009).

However, this seemingly glowing stereotype overshadows the diversity of the Asian community, which is composed of over 25 different ethnic groups with diverse histories, languages, and cultures. It also masks critical educational concerns Asian students are facing (Zhao & Qiu, 2009). Those who do not fit into the successful image (e.g. newcomers, English language learners, low-income immigrants) have suffered from cultural maladjustment, academic failure, low self-esteem, and many other cultural, academic, or psychological problems while they have not received proper social, educational, and institutional help (Pang, Kiang, & Pak, 2004).

Although a growing body of research has examined the complex schooling experiences of students of Korean descent at K–12 schools, their unique voices of racial relations and experiences of racism have often been homogenized under the category of Asians, thus being undifferentiated in previous scholarship. Studies on Asian students reveal that direct/indirect forms of racism, often stemming from the false stereotypes, were a fact of life for Asian students (Hartlep, 2013; Wing, 2007). According to Alvarez, Juang, and Lian (2006), 98 percent of their 254 Asian student participants reported encountering a daily-life type of racism or microaggression, from verbal insults to racially motivated harassment to physical assault, at least once or twice a year. The experiences of racial discrimination negatively affect Asian students' psychological and behavioral well being, causing distress, feelings of helplessness, depression, violent behaviors, suicide risk, and so forth (Choi & Lahey, 2006; Whaley & Noel, 2013). Socially, Asian immigrant students frequently find themselves marginalized from English speaking mainstream peers and develop a sense of inferiority (Choi et al., 2011; Lee, 2009; Park, 2011)

Notably, Yeh's (2003) and Yeh et al.'s (2005) studies indicate that Korean immigrant youth were found to have higher levels of mental health symptoms in comparison to their other Asian counterparts. Korean newcomer adolescents, mostly early-study-abroad youth, were often overwhelmed by high expectations of academic excellence held by not only their immigrant parents but also by ethnic communities, schools, and peer groups. They experienced role conflicts within different racial, social, religious, and academic groups during the process of acculturation that caused them to feel caught between different cultures, to feel alienated, or to have interpersonal conflicts with whites.

Studies that paid close attention to Korean newcomer youth's racial experiences at K–12 schools, though few in number, similarly disclose the detrimental effect of the model minority myth on their making sense of racial marginalization and developing coping strategies (Palmer, 2007; Park, 2011). Having experienced racial hierarchy and associated racial stereotypes and discriminations from teachers, peers, and other school personnel, many Korean immigrant adolescents chose to live up to the model minority image in order to achieve "honorary white" status, at least, at the expense of their ethnic, cultural, and linguistic identities as Koreans (Lee, 2009; Park, 2011). The hard-working, never-complaining Asian newcomers often "looked fine"; thus, they did not need institutional support (Ngo & Lee, 2007). By illuminating Korean newcomer youth's experiences of racial marginalization within inter/intra-racial peer groups and their coping strategies, this study seeks to add to the currently limited body of knowledge on the racial experiences of Asians, particularly Korean newcomer students, and the influence of the model minority myth.

METHODOLOGY

This study employs critical race methodology, a theoretically grounded approach to research that foregrounds race and racism in all aspects of education (Solórzano & Yosso, 2002). Emphasizing racial experiences of students of color and valuing their voices as critical for knowledge of racism, CRT provides a solid methodological ground for this research. Using counter-storytelling, this study examines Korean newcomer students' peer relations at school, particularly focusing on their racial marginalization and coping strategies, with an eye toward understanding CRT and the model minority myths shaping their experiences.

Sixty-three Korean newcomer students between fifth and twelfth grade in four different states—two urban and two suburban/rural areas in the Northeast, Southeast, and Midwest—participated in this multi-regional, mixed-method study. The four research sites were selected based on their representations of the diversity of school and regional settings as well as accessibility to research data. Participants from the two urban areas attended schools that were located in culturally diverse immigrant communities and therefore served students from varying racial, ethnic, and linguistic backgrounds. Meanwhile, the other two suburban or rural locations had relatively smaller Korean populations; thus, most Korean newcomer youth in these areas attended predominantly white, culturally homogeneous schools. The majority of the participants were pre-collegiate study-abroad students whose average length of residence in the U.S. is 3.1 years. Detailed demographic characteristics of participants are described in Table 10.1.

Data sources include survey and in-depth interview. From 2010 to 2011, a survey including 28 questions was conducted in an effort to investigate participants' personal backgrounds and overall perceptions about their schooling experiences in the United States. Researchers conducted, on average, 40 to 60 minute to an hour long, in-depth interviews with each participant to understand the negative

TABLE 10.1.   Participant Demographics

	n (N=63)	%
Gender		
• Male	32	50.8
• Female	31	49.2
Regions		
• Urban Northeast	17	27.0
• Urban Southeast	17	27.0
• Suburban Southeast	14	22.2
• Rural Midwest	15	23.8
Grade Level		
• Elementary (1–5 grade)	5	7.9
• Middle (6–8 grade)	23	36.5
• Secondary (9–12 grade)	35	55.6
School Type		
• Public	39	61.9
• Private	24	38.1
Length of Residency in the U.S.		
• 0–2 years	28	44.4
• 3–5 years	25	39.7
• More than 5 years	8	12.7

influences of the model minority myth on their experiences of racial marginalization and coping strategies.

Data was analyzed both quantitatively and qualitatively. First, descriptive statistics and t-tests were used to investigate the background information of the participants and their peer relations at school based on survey results. To analyze in-depth interview data, this study employed inductive coding (Miles & Huberman, 1984) and constant comparative method (Strauss & Corbin, 1990) to identify patterns and themes in Korean newcomer youths' struggles to make sense of their experiences with racial marginalization and the influence of the model minority myth. Researchers first individually read, coded, and analyzed transcribed interview data, then consistently compared the two data sources and cross-checked each other's analytic results in order to ensure the credibility of findings of this study (Bogdan & Biklen, 2007). Through the axial coding process of interrelating categories and subcategories, the major findings of this study were generated.

FINDINGS

Korean newcomer youth in this study experienced multiple forms of racism, from racial microaggression characterized by a sense of distance and indifference to more explicit types of physical assault, in their peer relations at school. Fifty-two out of 63 Korean newcomers, almost 82.5 percent of the total participants, re-

TABLE 10.2. Korean Newcomer Youth's Experiences of Racism by Regions

Experiences of Racism	Yes (%)	No (%)	Total
Urban Northeast	15 (88%)	2 (12%)	17
Urban Southeast	17 (100%)	0 (0%)	17
Suburban Southeast	9 (60%)	5 (40%)	14
Rural Midwest	11 (73%)	4 (27%)	15
Total	52 (82%)	11 (18%)	63

ported having experienced varying degrees of racism, either directly or indirectly, from their school peers. Only the remaining 11 indicated that they had never noticed racial remarks against Asians or had never undergone racially discriminatory practices at school.

Regional difference was found in participants' racial experiences in their peer relations. Those enrolled in urban schools showed a higher percentage of racial marginalization experiences compared to their counterparts attending schools in suburban, rural areas (See Table 10.2).

To many of Korean newcomers in this study, unfriendly, racially-motivated verbal abuse and associated discriminatory behaviors by mainstream English-speaking peers were the major forms of racial marginalization. Groundless, yet pervasive racial stereotypes against Asians became major sources of their experience of racial marginalization, and functioned as significant barriers to their building of healthy inter/intra-racial relationships with peers. In the following section, we will explain how the misleading racial stereotypes against Asians, prevalent within K–12 school contexts, affected Korean newcomers' peer relations as well as how Korean students coped with their racial experiences.

Stereotype 1: "Perpetual Foreigners"

As previous studies on Asian immigrants have articulated, the major forms of anti-Asian racism faced by Korean immigrant youth reflected the stereotypical views of Asians as perpetual foreigners and considered their cultural heritages and customs as exotic (Sue, Bucceri, Lin, Nadal, & Torino, 2007). A number of Korean newcomer students in this study were subjected to degrading racial remarks such as "Chink" (a typical derogatory label against Asians, particularly Chinese) or were frequently called a "stupid Korean" by their mainstream peers. Many participants tended to consider the verbal assaults as sorts of hazing that newcomers have to undergo; some students felt insecure and distressed sensing the unwelcoming sociocultural atmosphere and unfriendly peer reactions in their new school.

Language was one of the major sources of racial assaults experienced by Korean newcomer students. A majority of them, at least once in a while, became laughingstocks and victims of bullying due to their limited English speaking skills. Dae-In, a 15–year-old boy, described his painful experiences of being bullied by other students who knew of his new immigrant status and lack of English proficiency. They repeatedly mocked his "incorrect accent" and "strange pronunciation," and threw food at him in the school cafeteria. Finding no other way to vent his frustration and anger, he shouted "Shut up!"—the only expression that he was able to think of—which only brought on even worse ridicule.

Other common reasons that Korean newcomers were bullied were their physical appearance, such as body figure, or foods they ate for lunch, as well as insubstantial prejudice and associated hatred, which they were not able to change or control. Lee, an eighth grader, had been disturbed by bullies who mocked his appearance almost every day on the school bus for the past two years. Jenny recollected the unpleasant days in her first American school where her classmates surrounded her and watched her like a "guinea pig" while frequently calling Asians "yellow" or "sleepy eyes." Another student, Bin, felt terrified when a girl in his class asserted that Asians are dirty and did not let him be around her. There was no one to stop her since she was a daughter of his homeroom teacher. This made it very difficult for Bin to handle the situation because he assumed no one would be on his side when he reported the incidents to other school personnel. Facing such racial prejudice and enduring racially insulting comments made by his peers, Bin came to believe that "Americans feel uncomfortable with those who have different ethnicity, and it is often expressed as xenophobia."

Korean newcomer youth understood that the prevalent racial stereotypes and discriminatory practices were partly rooted in their American peers' lack of understanding about the heterogeneity among Asians, fast-changing Asian regions, including Korea, and the global trend of increasing transnational migration. Participants noted that most of their mainstream peers perceived Asians as a homogeneous group, which was simply equated with Chinese, despite its national, linguistic, cultural, and religious diversity. A majority of them reportedly felt tired of receiving such questions as "Are you Chinese? Japanese? If not, what are you?" Seran, a 14–year-old girl, wondered, "Can't they just ask 'where are you from?'"

Likewise, most of the participants expressed their disappointment with other students' lack of understanding about contemporary Korean society as part of a rapidly-changing Asian economy and criticized their global unawareness. Jinsu, a high-performing high school senior complained that South Korea, especially its recent economic and industrial development, was barely known to his American peers, who undervalued the cultural heritage of the country of his origin. When his classmates laughed at an image of Korean laborers during the 1960s in a U.S. history textbook, Jinsu snapped at them: "Look at your cellphones! How many of you have Samsung and LG [Korean electronics brands] phones?"

"Are you from the North or the South?" is the question that a number of Korean newcomers felt most uncomfortable with or even offended by. Gary, a high school senior, expressed his frustration: "What kind of question is that?...I mean, don't they have to know better?" A large number of Korean students like Gary disliked the chance that mainstream peers might see them as communists or the poor from an underdeveloped country and consequently project negative images of North Korea on them.

It is noteworthy that a significant number of the Korean youth (21%) were legally American citizens or permanent residents. Several students (12%) were in the process of obtaining permanent resident status at the time of this study. The majority of the youth (57.4%) expected that they would attend college in the United States. Almost half of them envisioned that they would ultimately reside in the United States as their permanent home in the future (44%). However, these newcomers found themselves being perceived as perpetual "foreigners" by their school peers. They initially hoped to be fully integrated into American society by making close relationships with peers and other individuals who they believed were part of the mainstream American society. Yet, their peer relationships clearly showed to them that it was not a simple task to accomplish. As a result, they explored a different way to survive at their school as a member of the "perpetual foreigners." This will be explained in a later section.

Stereotype 2: "Model Minorities"

Given the pervasive model minority myth, Asian students are often considered successful minorities who are hard-working and high-achieving, especially in areas such as math, science, and engineering. As existing research on the model minority myth indicates, however, this apparently positive label could have a destructive impact on the academic choices, sociocultural relations, and mental health of Asian newcomers (Lee, 2009; Lim & Choi, 2013; Zhao & Qiu, 2009).

The stereotype of Asians as "math whiz kids" frequently appeared as the dominant form of the model minority myth. This view was widely held and frequently reinforced by school teachers, counselors, and peers of Korean newcomers. This stereotype, in fact, played mixed roles in shaping Korean newcomers' relations with peers at school. For example, Young, an eighth grader, shared her embarrassment when she was first faced with such a racial stereotype by peers instantly asking her, "So, you are good at math, right?" She had been in the U.S. for less than a year and was struggling with cultural adjustments and new language learning, so she was shocked when her classmates came to her during her first days in school to ask math problems, assuming she would be superior in math. Though it was surprising, she—who considered herself as a "math failure" previously in Korea—did not dislike the seemingly positive representation; rather, she became flattered by her peers' attention. Young worked hard exclusively in math to live up to their expectations. Her teacher soon placed her in honors math class and encouraged her academic success in math.

Meanwhile, the model minority label would also come into conflict with academic, social, and emotional needs of Korean newcomers. For those who did not meet the images of high achieving Asians, the model minority bias—by placing excessive academic pressure—increased their anxiety, lowered self-esteem, and evoked strong resentment toward the whole schooling system. Gary expressed his emotional distress and resentment toward peers who kept pressuring him to conform to the model minority stereotype. He complained:

> So it's more like sarcasm that they said "So you guys are all smart" or "How come can't you do this? You are Asian." They [classmates] said, "Asians must be good at this," and made me answer a quiz every day in math class…It's so much pressure, and I tried to avoid them…But if they do more, I think I will be aggressive.

Social isolation and self-blame are commonly found among the participants who were not able to live up to the model minority standards. Yunho, an academically struggling high school senior, confessed he often felt shameful not only of his failure to meet the model minority expectations of mainstream peers but also the expectations held by those who are of Korean descent. During the first couple of years after he came to the U.S., his legal guardian forced him to stay at home and to invest much of his time in schoolwork, which eliminated his chance of getting along with friends from his school. Surrounded by family, neighbors, and Korean newcomer friends frequently throwing comments at him like "Why can't you achieve high like other Asians?" either jokingly or seriously, Yunho seemed significantly isolated from both mainstream peers at school and Korean ethnic groups within the community.

Even high-achieving students who seemingly fit well into the stereotypical image found such high academic pressure hard to deal with. Sue, a straight-A student in the ninth grade, hated math because she always felt burdened by the "math genius" image from her peers. She was often confused and worried, thinking, "Why don't I like math since most other Asians like and are good at it?" During interviews, a number of participants who did not like or excel in math, including Sue, shared their feelings of self-condemnation, frustration, and dissatisfaction with schooling caused by the model minority myth.

Coping Strategy 1: Silence and Self-Blame

Facing racial prejudices and discriminatory practices of microaggression in their school, Korean immigrant students developed coping strategies, either voluntarily or involuntarily, as a way to counteract psychological stress and other negative consequences of being a victim of those racial biases (See Table 10.3). One of the major strategies utilized by Korean newcomer students was silencing their racial experience and/or self-blaming for the incident or situation. More than a half of 63 participants ignored or tried to avoid racially discriminatory practices and bullying targeted toward Asians. Twenty-five Korean newcomers chose to pretend that they did not hear the verbal racial remarks thrown upon them. They often forced a smile or innocent look in order to conceal their resentment and grief. Several Korean newcomers experiencing subtle types of racism did not

TABLE 10.3.   Korean Newcomer Youth's Coping Strategies to Racial Experience

Type of Coping Strategies	n (%)
No recognition/Denial	12 (23.1)
Passive Strategy	
No response/Ignorance/Silence	25 (48.1)
Active Strategy	
Reporting to School Authority	2 (3.8)
Verbal Confrontation to the Aggressor	5 (9.6)
Physical Confrontation to the Aggressor	2 (3.8)
Others	6 (11.5)
Total	52 (100)

want to overreact to such situations. Huang, a ninth grader who frequently became a scapegoat of racial bullying, suppressed his anger and urge to fight against repeated racial remarks from bullies around him. He was afraid that he would become more isolated from mainstream peer groups or disadvantaged if he openly reacted to the bullies. Therefore, those who worried of potential retaliatory acts or harsher physical assault censored their own experiences of racism and wished simply to avoid them.

Some Korean newcomer students kept silent about their racial marginalization in order to maintain trouble-free model minority reputations. Gary, who was subject to mainstream peers' ridicule on his low academic achievement throughout his schooling, still chose to censor his own experiences of racial bullying, instead of making troubles with it, because he did not want to tarnish Koreans' "model" reputation. The majority of the participants assumed, as expressed by Sora, that "Whites are mainstream in American society anyway" and having the model minority label is better than "lazy, lower-class images against other minorities like Hispanics."

However, there were some students who brought up the issue of their suffering from racism and openly acted upon it. Nine Korean newcomer adolescents were in this category, including five who gave either verbal warning or logical explanation of the unfairness of such practices to their peers, two who ended up having physical fights with their aggressor(s), and two who reported to school teachers. Unfortunately, the students who sought out help from school teachers did not receive adequate support and did not see much change after the reactions, which made those students much more intimidated, or sometimes worsened the situations. Yooni, a seventh grader, who complained of being harassed by offensive racial remarks from a classmate to her homeroom teacher, shared her pains as follows:

The teacher gave just a couple of warnings, and that's it! That didn't make any difference, and they are still doing the same things…The worst thing about American school is racism. And there is nothing good about it.

Repetitive racial harassment, lack of support, and worsening situations made Yooni have strong distrust about the whole school culture.

In the cases of the two students who had physical fights, one did not receive any involvement from school personnel who witnessed the brawl. The other student, Jinsu, received a week-long detention while his counterpart, who provoked the fight by throwing Jinsu's backpack into a locker, evaded it. Jinsu found that teachers refused to listen carefully to him and other newcomer friends who had observed the incident and instead pretended not to understand their explanation due to their limited English speaking skills. Upon the school's decision to give him a week-long detention, Jinsu trivialized the meaning of the unfair disciplinary act as "nothing but just sitting and studying, which is not that bad," despite the fact that he felt deeply "sad, really sad" over the whole situation. Being advised by his parents to "be extra careful," Jinsu decided to make friends with other international students who "share a similar background" and determined that he "would do even better [at school work] and show who [he] really [is]."

Those who suffered from negative racial experiences and received lack of institutional support seemed to put the blame on themselves: on their limited English skills, immigrant status, and low ethnoracial power. Surprisingly, there were only five students who viewed the issue of racism as a structural, institutional matter when they critiqued the prevalent racial biases and discriminations against people of color including themselves. The rest either had no idea or believed that racism might be a matter of individuals' actions, especially those few who are thoughtless—simply a distinction, rather than a hierarchy, among different racial groups, or a type of territoriality toward newcomers.

Experiencing anxiety, feelings of inferiority, and a sense of shame evoked by overt or subtle practices of racial prejudice and discrimination, the majority of Korean newcomers strived to preserve their self-worth by conforming to the stereotypical image of Asians as hard-working students concentrating on academic achievements. Huang chose to make more academic investment, hoping the racism would end when he became more academically successful and spoke English more fluently. Jongsoo added, "Once you speak English well, everything will be fine." Dongwoo decided not to hang out with Korean newcomers in order to improve his English skills in a short period of time, thus belonging to the mainstream group. Jinsu expressed a cynical, judgmental observation about his American peers as "rude, disrespectful, absolutely no basic etiquette, who surely deserve to be spanked to learn a lesson." As previous studies on Asian students have shown (*cf.* Lee, 2009; Zhao & Qiu, 2009), to those Korean newcomer students, focusing on academic success—thus consequently living up to the image of model minority—seemed to be the best, sometimes forced, strategy to survive in response to racism.

Coping Strategy 2: Ethnic Solidarity

To cope with racial marginalization and isolation within the mainstream school culture, a number of Korean youth chose to deepen peer relationships with non-mainstream groups. Only 10 out of 63 Korean newcomers claimed that they maintained close relationships with mainstream, mostly white English speaking students. Approximately 73 percent of total students *(n* = 48) found their comfort zone within non-mainstream international/immigrant peer groups. A majority of them, 33 students, built exclusively strong ethnic solidarity with other Korean newcomers. The remaining five either had no response or did not have close peer groups to which they belonged.

Korean newcomer students shared bonds of sympathy and empathy for difficulties associated with immigration experiences, for example, linguistic barriers, cultural adjustments, and racial discrimination against international and new immigrant students. Walter, an eleventh grader who had been in the U.S. for four years and felt a big cultural distance from his mainstream peers, mostly hung out with international students and felt intimacy with them. He felt safe and comfortable being part of the international group, which protected him from hearing derogatory racial remarks and feeling a sense of inferiority. He believed those international students, mostly newcomers, had higher morality and cared more about academic achievements at school than mainstream American peers. He liked the fact that he could share his academic concerns with his newly found friends and that they could learn diverse cultural perspectives from each other. This tendency—building a comfort zone with other international, immigrant students from diverse ethnoracial backgrounds rather than with mainstream students, was found across all five research sites, revealing the difficult racial climate and marginal status of the Korean newcomers in American school contexts.

However, some international peer groups were not a safe haven for the Korean newcomers. Ironically, the pervasive racial stereotypes and derogatory racial remarks that Korean newcomer students experienced within the mainstream groups continued, or were reinforced among some international students. Yoohee found that European immigrant students in her school, despite the same immigrant status, were more easily accepted by mainstream American peers, and then they tended to snub Asian newcomers who were not welcome by the mainstream peers. Sometimes, Korean newcomer students experienced obscure yet negative stereotypes against Koreans, for example, receiving hurtful comments about their physical/facial appearance or having negative images of North Korea imposed upon them by members of their own international peer groups. Those who made fun of Chang's small eyes and who persistently imposed North Korean communist images onto him were Filipino newcomers. Interestingly, a majority of the Korean newcomers, though puzzled and initially upset by receiving negative racial comments from peers in their international group, tended to consider such comments as friendly teasing rather than a hostile expression of racism.

Most disturbing was the finding that some, though not all, Korean newcomers accepted and co-constructed another layer of racial hierarchy by utilizing the model minority stereotype. These students eagerly accepted the stereotype, developed Korean supremacist notions by separating themselves from other ethnic groups, and acted as perpetrators of racial assaults at other international students. These Korean newcomers, being proud of their relative "model" status as high achievers over other minority groups, disregarded other international students, especially those who were from less economically affluent countries or who showed low academic performance at school and thus failed to live up to the model minority standards. They often reproduced the negative prejudices and discriminatory racial practices against other racial minority groups that they previously experienced in their interactions with their mainstream peers. Steve, a 15–year-old boy, often mocked his Muslim immigrant peers as terrorists or bomb-dealers, while he barely felt guilty about his racist assaults because "[e]verybody did so." Hyesoo, claiming Korean superiority, disliked the fact that she was often categorized as Asian with other "smelly" Asian ethnic groups.

Other Korean immigrants or Korean-American students who did not live up to the image of model minority were also the subject of their criticism and discriminatory practices. Daein said that he ignored and stayed away from another Korean-American student in his ESL class whom he evaluated as having "bad quality" and who "associated with bad students." Seunghwan, a high school student, reported a poorly performing Korean newcomer as one of his least compatible peers in his school life. It was unfortunate that some Korean newcomers like Steve and Hyesoo used the model minority label to position themselves on top of the racial minority hierarchy and to marginalize those who did not live up to the glowing image. In this case, the model minority myth turned into a destructive tool for the reproduction of racial bias among other racial minority immigrant groups as well as against those who did not fit the image of model minority.

Not surprisingly, a sizeable number of Korean newcomers maintained strong ethnic solidarity; therefore, they built exclusive peer communities of Korean newcomers. More than half of the participants expressed that they felt most comfortable being around others of Korean descent they had met in schools, churches, or local communities because of the cultural and linguistic homogeneity. As Kibria (2002), Lee (2009), and other researchers on Asian American studies have suggested, the strong ethnic solidary among the Korean students seemed to be a protective reaction to experiences with racism. Sharing similar academic, linguistic, social, and cultural difficulties in American schools, the students could relate to each other and build ethnic unity and sense of belonging within the ethnic group. In the meantime, they often claimed their ethnic superiority and elitism by separating themselves from other "non-model" ethnic minorities.

Regional difference was evident. Korean newcomers in urban areas appeared to form closer relationships with other Koreans compared to their counterparts in suburban/rural areas. Interview data indicate that those who were in urban areas

TABLE 10.4. Korean Newcomer Youth's Peer Group Association

	Urban Northeast	Urban Southeast	Suburban Southeast	Rural Midwest	Total (N=63)
Korean	9	13	3	8	33
Mainstream American	4	2	4	1	10
International	1	0	4	2	8
Regardless of Race	2	2	1	2	7
Nonresponse	1	0	2	2	5

with a larger Korean community were able to find peer groups with the same ethnic, language, and cultural backgrounds. Accordingly, they tended to build closed peer communities among Korean newcomers. Meanwhile, those who were in suburban/rural areas were not given many options to choose where they wanted to belong; thus, they decided to hang out with non-Korean international students (See Table 10.4).

DISCUSSION AND IMPLICATIONS

The model minority label and false racial representation of Asians contributed to Korean newcomer youths' painful experiences of racial marginalization and discrimination at school. The exotic, perpetual-foreigner image, pervasive in mainstream school culture, and associated hatred against Asians often made Korean students in this study to be viewed as an inassimilable non-English speaking group from an inferior country by their peers.

The model minority image seemed to be a benefiting stereotype, by portraying Korean newcomers as successful high-achievers in math. Indeed, the stereotype at some level provided positive academic motivations to some newcomer students, in particular those who experienced academic struggles while in South Korea, to succeed in math class, which helped them become accepted within mainstream groups. However, researchers wonder whether their excellence in math class could be a forced academic choice, given the model minority bias held by school personnel and peers, at the expense of their original academic interests and socio-cultural needs. The "model" image also caused a sense of helplessness, anxiety, and low self-esteem for those who did not fit into the label. Korean newcomers who did not show high academic performance, especially in math, began to doubt their ethno-racial identities. This finding is consistent with previous research indicating Asian students' academic achievement in math or related fields comes at the cost of other knowledge and skills that they need to acquire in other fields, as well as psychological problems they must deal with such as the burden of being a model minority (Choi et al., 2011). This study proposes that Asian immigrant students' difficulties in dealing with the misleading racial label need to be further explored and carefully identified so that the students can receive unbiased learning opportunities and build unprejudiced peer relations.

The model minority myth silenced the racism that Korean newcomer youth suffered from, and even promoted a blame-the-victim approach to the issues. In order not to be disadvantaged by making a disclosure of the prevalent racism and also not to harm the trouble-free model minority image, Korean newcomers decided to be silent about racially discriminatory assaults they experienced. Rather, they chose to become more invested in academic achievement and English-speaking skill development, hoping to be better accepted by mainstream friends. Such coping strategies were similarly examined in previous studies on Asian students' schooling experiences and identity developments (Sue & Okazaki, 2009; Zhao & Qiu, 2009). Sadly, Korean newcomers' self-silencing and self-blame coping strategies seemed only to solidify their uncomplaining, quiet, obedient, "nerdy" images. The danger of this result leads educators' attention away from real racial barriers that hinder Korea newcomers' positive peer relationship building and undermines the importance of institutional supports, rather than individual solutions, to tackle the matter (Lee, 2009; Pang et al., 2004; Taylor et al., 2009). Sleeter (2009) worried that the model minority myth authorizes flat denial of racism and structures of racial dominance. Indeed, some Korean students who were vocal about their suffering from racism reportedly failed to receive adequate support or fair action from school personnel. It is important that future research examines the complex effect of the model minority myth on Asian students' experiences of racism and the costs associated with it. This will prepare educators to better acknowledge the pervasive racial remarks and practices, including microaggressions, as structural rather than individual matters, and will provide more racially conscious and just educational support to the self-victimizing adolescents.

It is ironic that the pervasive racial stereotypes and racist remarks that Korean newcomer students experienced within the mainstream groups were repeated or even reinforced among international student groups in which most Korean newcomers found their comfort zones. Korean newcomer students were still teased, sometimes more harshly, with the model-minority and forever-foreigner stereotypes within the international peer communities. It was also surprising that some Korean newcomer youth who were the victims of racial bullying within the mainstream peer groups used the model minority image to claim their ethnic superiority, or acted as inflictors of racial bullying by distancing themselves from other "less-model" ethnic minority groups. This finding implies that Korean students consciously or unconsciously tended to internalize the racial bias that they critiqued and suffered from as a protective action to their experiences of racism (Kibria, 2002; Lee, 2009).

This finding also reveals that the model minority misperception contributed destructive effects to the vicious circle of racism within school culture. The model minority rhetoric, when it first emerged, was used to maintain the dominance of whites in the racial hierarchy by using Asians to set the standards of how minorities should behave within the black and white discourse on race (Lee, 2009). In this study, the rhetoric seemed to be used as a hegemonic tool that racial minority groups claimed for their sense of ethnic superiority and individual agency while reproducing the prevalent practices of racism among them. Due to the limited studies on the reproduction of the model minority myth by racial minority groups, it is difficult to know how the destructive myth is internalized and reproduced as a tool of racial discrimination within minority groups and what its consequences would be. This study calls for more research on the internalization and reproduction of the model minority myth, expanding the current CRT framework not only to native racial minorities but also to newcomers, thus adding a new dimension to the research on Asian studies in conjunction with CRT (Buenavista et al., 2009).

Questions for Reflection

1. How does the model minority myth affect Asian learners' academic choices and curriculum meaning making in the K–12 school setting?
2. What are the ways in which oppressive socialization is reproduced and internalized within immigrant groups of color?
3. How and why is the model minority myth imported and operated within transnational contexts?
4. What other theoretical lenses and knowledge sources can illuminate the dismal paradox of the model minority myth?
5. How could young students be informed about the causes and consequences of misleading racial stereotypes and discriminatory practices exiting in today's schools?

REFERENCES

Alvarez, A. N., Juang, L., & Lian, C. T. H. (2006). Asian Americans and racism: When bad things happen to "model minorities." *Cultural Diversity and Ethnic Minority Psychology, 12,* 477–492.

Bogdan, R. C., & Biklen, S. K. (2007). *Qualitative research for education: An introduction to theories and methods* (5th ed.). Boston: Allyn and Bacon.

Buenavista, T. L., Jayakumar, U. M., & Misa-Escalante, K. (2009). Contextualizing Asian American education through critical race theory: An example of U.S. Pilipino college student experiences. *New Directions for Institutional Research, 142,* 69–81.

Choi, Y., & Lahey, B. B. (2006). Testing the model minority stereotype: Youth behaviors across racial and ethnic groups. *Social Service Review, 80*(3), 419–452.

Choi, Y., Lim, J. H., & An, S. (2011). Marginalized students' uneasy learning: Korean immigrant students' experiences of learning social studies. *Social Studies Research and Practice, 6*(3), 1–17.

Hartlep, N. D. (2013*). The model minority myth: What 50 years of research does and does not tell us.* Retrieved December 11, 2014, from http://diverseeducation.com/52979/.

Kibria, N. (2002). *Becoming Asian American: Second-generation Chinese and Korean American identities.* Baltimore, MD: Johns Hopkins University Press.

Ladson-Billings, G. (Ed.). (2003). *Critical race theory perspectives on social studies: The profession, policies and curriculum.* Charlotte, NC: Information Age.

Lee, J. W. (2010, February 01). *The politics of Korean American and its population.* Retrieved December 11, 2014, from http://www.koreatimes.com/article/574585.

Lee, S. J. (2009). *Unraveling the model minority stereotype: Listening to Asian American youth* (2nd ed). New York: Teachers College Press.

Lew, J. (2004). The "other" story of model minorities: Korean American high school dropouts in an urban context. *Anthropology & Education Quarterly, 35*(3), 303–323.

Lim, J. H., & Choi, Y. (2013, April). *Korean transnational students' curriculum meaning-making and appropriation of academic identity in the American school context.* Paper presented to the Annual Meeting of American Educational Research Association, San Francisco, CA.

Lim, J. H., Moon, K., Choi, Y., Yoon, S. Y., & An, S. (2011). Analysis of economic, social and cultural capital among Korean-early-study-abroad students in America: A mixed-method study. *Proceedings of the 12th International Conference on Education Research, 12*, Seoul, Korea, 459–484.

Liu, A. (2009). Critical race theory, Asian Americans, and higher education: A review of research. *UCLA Journal of Education and Information Studies, 5*(2), 1–12.

Migration Policy Institute. (2010). *Top language spoken by English language learners nationally and by State.* Retrieved from http://www.migrationinformation.org/ellinfo/FactSheet_ELL3.pdf

Miles, M., & Huberman, A. (1984). *Qualitative data analysis: A sourcebook of new methods* (2nd ed.). Thousand Oaks, CA: Sage.

Ng, J.C., Lee, S. S., & Pak, Y.K. (2007). Contesting the model minority and perpetual foreigner stereotypes: A critical review of literature of Asian Americans in education. *Review of Research in Education, 31*(1), 95–130.

Ngo, B., & Lee, S. J. (2007). Complicating the image of model minority success: A review of Southeast Asian American education. *Review of Educational Research, 77*(4), 415–453.

Palmer, J. D. (2007). Who is the authentic Korean American? Korean-born Korean American high school students' negotiations of ascribed and achieved identities, *Journal of Language, Identity & Education, 6*(4), 277–298.

Pang, V. O., Kiang, P., & Pak, Y. (2004). Asian Pacific American students: Changing a biased educational system. In J. Banks, & C. Banks, (Eds.), *Handbook of research on multicultural education* (2nd ed., pp. 542–566). San Francisco, CA: Jossey-Bass.

Park, G. C. (2011). Becoming a "model minority": Acquisition, construction and enactment of American identity for Korean immigrant students. *Urban Review, 43*(5), 620–635.

Sleeter, C. (2009). Foreword. In S. J. Lee. *Unraveling the model minority stereotype: Listening to Asian American youth* (2nd ed., pp. vii-x). New York: Teachers College Press

Solórzano, D., & Yosso, T. (2002). A critical race theory counterstory of affirmative action in higher education. *Equity and Excellence in Education, 35*(2), 155–168.

Strauss, A., & Corbin, J. (1990). *Basics of qualitative research: Grounded theory procedures and techniques.* Newbury Park, CA: Sage.

Sue, D. W., Bucceri, J. M., Lin, A. I., Nadal, K. L., & Torino, G. C. (2007). Racial microaggressions and the Asian American experience. *Cultural Diversity and Ethnic Minority Psychology, 13*(1), 72–81.

Sue, S. & Okazaki, S. (2009). Asian-American educational achievements: A phenomenon in search of an explanation. *Asian American Journal of Psychology, S*(1), 45–55.

Takaki, R. (1989). *Strangers from a different shore: A history of Asian Americans.* New York: Penguin.

Taylor, E. Gillborn, D., & Ladson-Billings, G. (Eds) (2009). *Foundations of critical race theory in education.* New York: Routledge.

Terrazas, A., & Batog, C. (August, 2010). *Korean immigrants in the United States.* Retrieved December 11, 2014, from http://www.migrationinformation.org/usfocus/display.cfm?ID=793.

UNESCO Institute of Statistics. (2009). *Global education digest 2009.* UNESCO Publishing.

U.S. Census Bureau. (2009). *American community survey.* Retrieved December 11, 2014, from http://factfinder.census.gov/servlet/DatasetMainPageServlet?_ds_name=ACS_2008_3YR_G00_&_lang=en&_ts=306858868055.

U.S. Census Bureau. (2012). *The Asian population: 2010.* Retrieved December 11, 2014, from http://www.cen sus.gov/prod/cen2010/briefs/c2010br-11.pdf.

Whaley, A. L., & Noel, L. T. (2013). Academic achievement and behavioral health among Asian American and African American adolescents: Testing the model minority and inferior minority assumptions. *Social Psychology of Education, 16*(1), 23–43.

Wing, J. Y. (2007). Beyond black and white: The model minority myth and the invisibility of Asian American students. *The Urban Review, 39*(4), 455–487.

Yang, W. (2011, May 8). Paper tigers: What happens to all the Asian-American overachievers when the test-taking ends? *New York Magazine.*

Yeh, C. J. (2003). Age, acculturation, cultural adjustments, and mental health symptoms of Chinese, Korean, and Japanese immigrant youths. *Cultural Diversity and Ethnic Minority Psychology, 9*(1), 34–48.

Yeh, C. J., Ma, P., Madan-Bahel, A., Hunter, C. D., Jung, S., Kim, A. B., Akitaya, K., & Sasaki, K.(2005). The cultural negotiations of Korean immigrant youth. *Journal of Counseling and Development, 83*(2), 172–182.

Zhao, Y., & Qiu, W. (2009). How good are the Asians?: Refuting four myths about Asian-American academic achievement. *Phi Delta Kappan, 90*(5), 338–344.

CHAPTER 11

PRIMED TO BE COLOR-BLIND

Asian American College Students, Racial Identity Development, and Color-Blind Racism

Vijay Pendakur

INTRODUCTION

Vijay:	During high school, do you remember learning anything about your racial identity?
Charlotte:	Kind of. I mean I really don't feel any different than, you know, my white counterparts, because they're just people to me. For example, my boyfriend, Danny, is Caucasian. So one day we were like, oh yeah, we're an interracial couple, I didn't even realize that? And it was just kind of funny because like you know I'm so comfortable in my own brown skin and black hair, like around people who look very much different from me, that I really don't identify myself as being different. But the times when I do feel different, it's usually in a good way because then I'm like, oh, I'm unique.

Killing the Model Minority Stereotype: Asian American Counterstories and Complicity,
pages 185–202.
185

Charlotte is an Asian (Filipina) American college student at a mid-sized, urban university in the Midwest. She grew up in an upper middle-class Pilipino family in a predominantly White town and was excited to come to the big city for college. She was one of nine Asian American college freshmen who I interviewed for this research study. Charlotte shared numerous stories of being racialized and other-ized in her adolescent years. From being called a "golden Oreo"[1] by her high-school peers to being repeatedly asked "Where are you from?" by adults in her community, Charlotte's life experience appears to be profoundly Asian American (Ng, Lee & Pak, 2007). Charlotte, however, adheres to numerous elements of color-blind racist thinking, and her experiences with racism have not produced an Asian American race consciousness or an understanding of White racial hegemo-ny (Omi & Winant, 1994). Is it possible that Charlotte, by virtue of her positioning as a model minority, was primed to be color-blind?

This chapter emerges from research that I conducted on the relationship be-tween color-blind racism and the racial identity development of Asian American college freshmen. Over the course of my qualitative inquiry, I conducted in-depth narrative inquiry (Connelly & Clandinin, 1990; Reissman, 2008) interviews with nine college freshmen at a mid-sized urban, private, Catholic university in the Midwest. Each interview lasted between 90 minutes and two hours. Transcribed interviews were the data, which was coded using both open and axial coding schemas (Corbin & Strauss, 2007; Merriam, 2009). I found that my participants appeared to have internalized many aspects of model minority typology, including discursive positioning as "honorary Whites" (Alvarez, 2002; Junn, 2007). They also seemed to have internalized the logic of color-blind racism: that systemic racism is no longer a significant factor in American life and, as a result, race itself is not important (Bonilla-Silva, 2006).

This chapter is concerned with the positioning of Asian American subjects be-tween model minority archetypes and the hegemonic ideology of color-blind rac-ism. This chapter asks, "Are Asian Americans susceptible to becoming co-opted by color-blind racial logic because of their positioning as model minorities?"

I was motivated to carry out the present research because gaps in the literature exist. First, there is little written about Asian American college students (Museus & Kiang, 2009), or their racial identity development (Alvarez, 2002; Chen, LeP-huoc, Guzman, Rude, & Dodd, 2006; Kim, 2001, 2012; Kodama, McEwen, Li-ang, & Lee, 2002). This lack of research places Asian American college students at risk for being under-served during a crucial time in their lifetime development. Secondly, in the extant scholarship on the racial identity development of college students, there appears to be no acknowledgement that color-blind racism could be a central factor in mitigating Asian Americans' ability to form a healthy racial identity. This is deeply problematic to me, especially considering that color-blind

---

[1] Charlotte explained to me that her high school classmates used the term "Golden Oreo" to refer to someone who is "yellow on the outside but White on the inside."

racism has been the central hegemonic paradigm for managing race in America since the end of the Civil Rights era (Aleinikoff, 1991; Bonilla-Silva, 2006; Crenshaw, 1988; Forman, 2004; Gotanda, 1991; Neville, Lilly, Duran, Lee, & Browne, 2000; Smith, 2008). Finally, within the color-blind racism scholarship, the vast majority of the theoretical and application has been focused on how this form of modern racism affects white individuals and their communities (e.g. Gallagher, 2003). Because hegemony influences both dominant and subordinated group members, it is imperative that we understand the effects of color-blind racism on whites *and* people of color. Thus, it is my hope that this chapter will provoke a new research paradigm that focuses on the complex interplay between the hegemonic system of color-blind racism and the deeply under-studied process of Asian American racial identity development.

A BRIEF REVIEW OF THE RELEVANT LITERATURE

Defining Color-Blind Racism

Scholars attempting to map the contours of modern racism have generated a multitude of explanations for the shift from the overt, juridical racism of the Jim Crow era to the covert, *de facto* racism that remained after the 1964 Civil Rights Act (Guinier & Torres, 2003). For the majority of White Americans, however, the hard-won legal protections for race and ethnicity that Civil Rights activists in the late 1950s and 1960s gained marked the end of racism as a salient issue in American society (Bonilla-Silva, 2006). Indelibly, this shift gave rise to the notion that the public sphere was now truly egalitarian and meritocratic, and that people of color no longer had any excuses for not succeeding. In this new era, race no longer had the meaning once conferred by overt, legalized racism; hence, a corollary rhetoric of color-blindness emerged in the 1970s, supported by the logic that simply *not seeing race* will guarantee that *race does not matter* (Williams & Land, 2006; Wise, 2010). Ideologies that normalize this logic are often labeled color-blind attitudes, color-blind discourse, or color-blind politics (Neville, Spanierman, & Doan, 2006). Crucial to the focus of this chapter is an understanding that these pervasive ideologies buttress the current form of racial hegemony[2] in that they support the extant, racist, White power structure (Aleinikoff, 1991; Bonilla-Silva, 2006; Crenshaw, 1988; Forman, 2004; Gotanda, 1991; Smith, 2008).

---

[2] Omi and Winant (1994) draw from Gramsci to define hegemony as a system of control based on both coercion and consent. In a hegemonic system, the ruling elite incorporate key interests of subordinated groups to pacify resistance while also perpetuating a *common sense* ideology that leads subordinated group members to act in ways that enforce the rule of the elites. This complex interplay between incorporation, ideology, and resistance offers us a way to understand American racial rule, particularly in its shift from overt dominance to covert coercion and consent in the post-Civil Rights era.

Therefore, in this chapter I use the language of color-blind *racism* to indicate the hegemonic system that is informed and supported by color-blind ideologies.

In his seminal work, *Racism Without Racists: Color-blind Racism and the Persistence of Racial Inequality in the United States,* Bonilla-Silva (2006) breaks down the concept of color-blind racism into four dominant frames. Bonilla-Silva agrees with the broader consensus that color-blind racism is the racial discourse that supports the nuanced, covert institutional racism of the Post-Civil Rights Era. But Bonilla-Silva explains that racial ideology always has dominant frames through which information is disseminated, internalized, and reified. Bonilla-Silva developed his four frames from wide-scale interviews he conducted with college students from several different types of institutions and non-college students from the Detroit-area.

Abstract liberalism, Bonilla-Silva's first frame, combines key concepts from political liberalism, like meritocracy, with the tenets of economic liberalism, such as individual choice, to explain racial realities. Abstract liberalism supports color-blind racism by obscuring the role of the state and structure in producing and maintaining racial inequality.

Naturalization, the second frame, suggests that racial realities are the result of some sort of natural order – such as explaining urban racial segregation through the logic of "people like to live near others like themselves" (Bonilla-Silva, 2006, p. 28). Naturalization supports color-blind racism by shifting the locus of racial problems away from White hegemony and onto communities of color.

Cultural racism, Bonilla-Silva's third frame, asserts that the inequity found in communities of color is the result of cultural tendencies that negatively impact those communities. For example, the *cultural racism* frame is present when people conclude that Black people are often poor because they are (or Black *culture* is) prone to apathy and/or victimhood. Cultural racism, similar to naturalization, supports color-blind racism by shifting the etiology of racial inequity back onto people of color through the emphasis on *culture* over *history* or *structure*.

Minimization of racism, the fourth frame, asserts that racism is no longer an issue after the legal reforms of the Civil Rights Movement. Minimization supports color-blind racism by creating a discourse that directly contradicts, and often hides, the empirical reality of enduring systemic racism.

Bonilla-Silva's four frames are an important contribution to the definition of color-blind racism, as they add structure to the pathways through which a racist ideology exerts its influence in our society, and why its maintenance is so destructive to people of color.

Guinier and Torres (2003) explain that the color-blind racist framework that emerged after the passing of the Civil Rights Acts in 1964 and 1968, which banned overt discrimination based on race, religion, and national origin, generates the narrative that "after formal, state-sanctioned barriers to individual mobility are removed, any continuing inequality must result from the personal failure of individuals…" (p. 35). Through their use of CLS and CRT lenses, Guinier and

Torres (2003) are able to clearly explain how color-blind racism also works to problematize individuals of color while freeing the state from owning the burden of historical, as well as current, systemic racism.

Much like Bonilla-Silva (2006), Guinier and Torres (2003) attempt to boil down the complexities of color-blind racism to the essential components. Guinier and Torres argue that color-blind racism endorses three axioms: that (1) race is simply skin color; (2) the recognition of race is the invocation of fixed, biological notions of race; and (3) racism is now a personal problem. These three axioms work in concert simultaneously to strip race of its socio-historical context by reducing it to simply skin color. Furthermore, they silence any meaningful engagement with race by blaming those who wish to conduct serious discussions on race for contributing to the problem by keeping race alive. Guinier and Torres' scholarship on color-blind racism, in combination with Bonilla-Silva's (2006) work on the subject, provides scholars of color-blind racism with a many-faceted definition for this construct as well as a basic schema for how it works.

It must be noted that post-racial discourses—much like color-blind discourses— rely on the central proposition that American society has solved its enduring racial problems and, therefore, racial saliency is no longer valid. Critical scholarship (Barnes, 2009; Marshall, 2009) on post-racial politics takes note of the ways in which claims of post-raciality are used to destabilize social justice movements that invoke racial identity in their quest for equity. Post-racial discourses also fortify the key tenets of color-blind racism through the selective use of token characters such as celebrity Oprah Winfrey and President Barack Obama. Critical theorists such as Barnes (2009) and Marshall (2009) have been quick to point out that the post-racial frame is simply a new construction of color-blind racism. Therefore, I will use the term "color-blind racism" throughout this chapter to reference both color-blind racism and post-racial discourses.

Asian American Racial Identity Development

Asian American Critical Race Theorists (AsianCrits) often identify three central tropes when analyzing Asian American racial identity and the Asian American experience: (1) the Model Minority stereotype, (2) the Perpetual/Forever Foreigner stereotype, and (3) the homogenizing effect the "Asian American" panethnic label has on the population's subgroups (Alvarez, Juang, & Liang, 2006; Buenavista, Jayakumar, & Misa-Escalante, 2009; Chen, LePhuoc, Guzman, Rude, & Dodd, 2006; Junn, 2007; Kawai, 2005; Ng, Lee, & Pak, 2007).

The Model Minority Stereotype

Junn (2007), in her article "From Coolie to Model Minority: U.S. Immigration Policy and the Construction of Racial Identity," writes that the model minority stereotype is a sharp departure from the 19th century racialization of Asian American laborers as "coolies." Junn traces the movement of the dominant Asian American stereotype from coolie to model minority in the U.S. policy shift during the Cold War space race in the 1960s. In an attempt to compete with the Soviet Union in the science theater of the Cold War, the United States revised its long-standing ban on Asian immigration in the 1965 Immigration Act, allowing for Asians to once again enter America in large numbers. The model minority typology of Asians, however, was created by selective immigration criteria tied to the Immigration Act, which placed a preference on legal entry for Asians who possessed science, math, and medical degrees and could help the United States develop a powerful research and development base through which to compete with the Soviet Union. This selection criteria resulted in a community of post-1965 Asian Americans that, due to the broader socio-political circumstance, happened to be academically gifted, extremely hard working, focused on upward mobility, and ready to play "within the lines" of White-dominated society (Junn, 2007; Prashad, 2001). Junn's (2007) analysis, drawing on racial formation theory, labels the model minority stereotype as being a racial project that the nation state engineered to address specific domestic labor needs as well as to further foreign policy interests.

This historical background is imperative in understanding Asian American race theory, as the model minority stereotype is the dominant narrative that shapes Asian American college student experience (Ng, Lee, & Pak, 2007). Critical scholarship on the mode minority stereotype uncovers the various ways the trope supports White hegemony while simultaneously socializing and oppressing Asian American college/university students. An embedded narrative, within the model minority framework, is the idea that Asian Americans have "succeeded" on "their own." This assertion supports post-Civil Rights claims that America represents a meritocracy, which is a cornerstone master narrative of white hegemony and color-blind racism (Buenavista, Jayakumar, & Misa-Escalante, 2009; Kawai, 2005; Hartlep, 2014). Beyond supporting meritocratic mythologies, the model minority trope works as a wedge tool, positioning Asian Americans against other "unsuccessful" minority groups, who are constructed to have "failed to do it on their own" during the post-Civil Rights era. Ng, Lee, and Pak (2007) argue that this valorization of Asian Americans by the white state contributes to the marginalization and isolation of Asian Americans from other communities of color. This "wedge-tool" argument is important for understanding the way that Asian Americans have been used, discursively, to oppress other people of color, strengthen the neoliberal state, and extend white hegemony.

These politics of racial triangulation also have serious consequences for the way Asian Americans conceptualize their own racial identity (Kim, 2001, 2012). Junn (2007) notes that Asian Americans are, within the context of the black/white binary, offered an honorary whiteness that has resulted in higher levels of racial alienation for Asian Americans. Being positioned as *honorary* Whites helps people understand the racial experience of Asian American college students.

After several decades of enduring under the auspices of perceived honorary whiteness, Asian Americans also face many real barriers to developing strong racial group consciousness (Junn & Masuoka, 2008). By examining survey results on racial consciousness affinity and racial political identity, Junn and Masuoka (2008) offer the following list of factors that may lead Asian American group members to possess lower racial consciousness:

- The salience of ethnic group identity over racial identity;
- The ability to have more economic and social mobility in US society than Blacks or Latin@s (tied to model minority selection criteria);
- The connection between increased social mobility and the dissolution of ethnic enclave communities that can preserve racial consciousness;
- The relatively nascent nature of the Asian American community—most arrived after 1965 (again, due to U.S. immigration policy and the Asian Exclusion Acts), and this recent immigration cuts most of the Asian American community off of the legacy of overt racial oppression in the 19th century; and
- The more "positive" and individualistic framework of thinking of one's self offered by the model minority stereotype, which may lessen tendencies towards racial group consciousness.

One important theoretical consideration that must be made prior to concluding this section of the chapter is the dialectical tension and conceptual blurriness between ethnic identification and racial identification as it relates to Asian American identity development. Scholarship points to important linkages between individuals' ethnic identities and their racial identities (Junn & Masuoka, 2008). Scholarship on Asian American race and ethnic identity also indicates that, within the small body of scholarship on the subject, the majority of researchers have tended to focus on Asian American ethnic identity and acculturation processes rather than on race and racism, thereby downplaying the salience and relevance of these issues through omission (Alvarez, Juang, & Liang, 2006; Kim, 2012). As higher education moves toward developing a new research paradigm for studying Asian American identity development, it is important to consider why past scholars have focused on ethnicity more than race and how this emphasis might contribute to the politics of color-blind racism. Aspects of this tension will be addressed in the following sections of this chapter.

STUDY FINDINGS

As is often the case in qualitative research, the participants' narratives in this research contained complex, overlapping, contradictory elements that simultaneously spoke to the salience of race, an adherence to color-blind racism, and the powerful presence of model minority typology. As noted in the previous section of this chapter, Asian Americans have held a liminal position in the American racial landscape, where they have neither been regarded as "people of color" nor considered actually white (Buenavista, Jayakumar, & Misa-Escalante, 2009;

Junn, 2007). Asian Americans' liminal position on the color line in the United States has been termed "honorary Whiteness" or "discursive Whiteness" (Alvarez, 2002; Junn 2007).

The narratives of the participants I interviewed offer evidence that suggests their deep internalization of model minority status and the logic of honorary whiteness. My findings are supported by other research on Asian American internalization of model minority stereotyping (see Gupta, Szymanski, & Leong, 2011; Yoo, Burrola, & Steger, 2010). In the following section of this chapter, I choose to examine one participant's narrative that offers great depth and detail as it relates to the internalization of the model minority stereotype. By sharing Kelly's narrative, I hope to show how the landscape of model minority internalization is nuanced. Doing so helps everyone in higher education better understand how to intervene during this problematic process.

The Internalization of Model Minority Typology and Honorary Whiteness

The following example of internalization came from an interview with Kelly, an Indian American, Muslim woman who deeply desired to go to Midwest U (a pseudonym for the flagship state school in her home state), but was not offered sufficient funding to make it possible. While discussing this frustrating moment in her life, the subject of race and college admissions emerged as well as the effects of model minoritization and honorary Whiteness.

Vijay:	When you ended up not being able to attend Midwest U because of finances, how did it make you feel?
Kelly:	Oh, I hated it. I mean, like I felt like academically like going to school shouldn't be about like how much money you have or anything, it should just be if you have the academics to get in, like you should be able to get in without a problem. Because I knew people from my high school, a majority of the people went to Midwest U and there were people who were from Hispanic origin who definitely did not have like the academics that would have gave them like the huge scholarships that they got. Like they're basically going like for free.
Vijay:	Wow.
Kelly:	But it's because of their nationality that they're able to go, so that kind of really upset me about that.
	[A little bit later in the interview…]
Vijay:	Hmm. So um, do you think that ah South Asians are included in the minority group at Midwest U?
Kelly:	No, no.
Vijay:	How come?

Kelly:	I mean they're known as being like the smart ones who have like great jobs, so I, I feel like the minority groups that people consider for that are like Hispanic, African American, Native American.
Vijay:	Hmm.
Kelly:	They don't, I don't feel like they put Asians in that category.
Vijay:	How come?
Kelly:	There's a lot of them at Midwest U.
Vijay:	So there, that's the truth, there are a lot of them at Midwest U. Um, and you were saying that you feel like there's this rap around Asians that they're the successful ones?
Kelly:	Yeah, definitely.
Vijay:	What's that all about?
Kelly:	I mean I guess from like countries back home the schooling is different, they're more focused on books and doing well in class, so I guess when they come over to America they grab all the great jobs because they have like more experience and are more educated. So that just carries over to the whole stereotype that Asians are smarter and have better jobs, I guess.

Kelly's narrative demonstrates heavy internalization of model minority typology and aspects of honorary Whiteness. Her stance against affirmative action appears to be predicated on stories she has heard about "minorities" getting large scholarships even when they do not have the grades to merit such funding. This stance speaks to the erroneous positioning of Asian Americans as both model minorities and as *victims* in the politics of affirmative action. Wu (1995) explains:

> There are many fallacies in the affirmative action debate. One of them, increasingly prominent, is that Asian Americans somehow are the example that defeats affirmative action. To the contrary, the Asian-American experience should demonstrate the continuing importance of race and the necessity of remedial programs based on race... Again and again, claims are made that Asian Americans, like whites, suffer because of affirmative action for African Americans. By the rhetoric, it would almost seem as if Asian Americans, more than whites, have become the "innocent victims" of so-called "reverse discrimination"... The linkage of Asian Americans and affirmative action, however, is an intentional maneuver by conservative politicians to provide a response to charges of racism. (p. 225)

Kelly also locates Asian Americans as *non-minorities*, which reflects how Asian Americans have been positioned as discursive Whites, particularly in the national conversation on college access, affirmative action, and "negative action" (Kidder, 2006; Poon, 2009). Kelly's internalization of both model minority typology and elements of honorary Whiteness appears to position her in line with the neo-conservative agenda against affirmative action and race conscious college access programs.

As the interview continued, Kelly and I talked about the term "people of color." She shared that she believed only African Americans counted as people of color because, to be a person of color, your racial group has to have struggled against racism. According to her knowledge, Asian Americans have not had such a struggle. Her logic might be a result of the complex interplay between Asian Americans being viewed as "perpetual foreigners" (Kawai, 2005) and also being positioned as honorary Whites.

Kelly, like the rest of my research participants, was about halfway done with her first year of college and appeared to be struggling to understand her place in the world, in light of complex identity politics. While this is quite normal for someone who has just made a major life transition—from high school to college—her meaning-making process bears some alarming fruit. Kelly's narrative reflects heavy internalization of model minority archetypes and honorary whiteness. Out of my nine research participants, Kelly was not an outlier. Her meaning-making process is emblematic of my study participants as a whole. Taken together, my findings beg the question, "What are the outcomes of Asian Americans who internalize white hegemonic racial narratives?" In the following section of this chapter, I will share my findings on the presence of color-blind racial frames in my participants' meaning-making processes. I will then conclude the chapter with a discussion of the implications of these findings and areas for future research.

The Internalization of Color-Blind Racism

Over the course of my interviews with my nine study participants, I uncovered narratives from each participant that demonstrated a broad adherence to the tenets of color-blind racism. In the literature review section of this chapter, I reviewed numerous frames, or delivery mechanisms, of the hegemonic system of color-blind racism. Due to limitations in space, neither can I share evidence from all of my participants, nor can I share evidence for every frame of color-blind racism. In the following section, I will share typical examples of my participants' narratives to demonstrate the appearance of three frames in their meaning-making processes: (1) the minimization of racism, (2) cultural racism, and (3) racism-is-just-interpersonal.

Lina

In the following excerpt from my interview with Lina, an eighteen year-old Filipina from a mid-sized town in the upper Midwest, I was interested in hearing how she described her own cultural background; surprisingly, she launched into a disturbing account of her first-hand experiences with racism.

Vijay: Lina, how would you describe your cultural background?

Lina:	Well, back home it was predominantly white, so when I was in grade school, I was usually one of the only non-white people in school. And I wasn't really judged for that though. Sometimes it seems to be like maybe it was just coincidentally, but there was a girl who came in middle school and she was she was African American, and whenever we had to be put into groups I was always left with her.
	[A few minutes later in the interview…]
Lina:	And then one day I asked her [Lina's teacher] a question in class like during work time, and then she told me, "Wow, your English is really good," and I'm like, "Oh, umm, I was born here." And so it was kind of funny how it kind of made me laugh and it kind of annoyed me at the same time.

Under the logic of color-blind racism, minimizing the size and scope of present-day systemic racism is a key strategy in displacing the centrality of race and racism in modern American life (Bonilla-Silva, 2006). Lina's account begins with her stating that she grew up in a predominantly white environment, and then she immediately disclaims, "I wasn't really judged for that though." From the start of her narrative, she appears to be minimizing the salience of race and racism, while also sharing two stories that are profoundly racial. At the end of the exchange, Lina concludes by sharing how her teacher's racial microaggression made her laugh, but fundamentally how it annoyed her. The laughter and the annoyance capture the tension apparent in Lina's narrative as she works to minimize the salience of race while experiencing racism repeatedly.

Don

Don is an 18–year-old, working class, Indian American male from a large city. During my interview with Don, a powerful example of the cultural racism frame appeared in his narrative on anti-Asian American racism. Cultural racism, according to Bonilla-Silva (2006), is the sleight of hand that allows marginalized communities to be blamed for their struggles, by locating the cause of differential outcomes in the community of color's *culture* rather than in systemic racism.

Vijay:	Are Asian people affected by racism?
Don:	Not as much as others, I don't believe not as much as others.
Vijay:	How come?
Don:	Umm, I guess you don't hear much about like Asian people going, committing as much crime as other minorities, and I guess that plays an effect on the majority who are like, oh, these people are actually trying to do, trying to make, come up in this world, so they are a little lenient on us, a little lenient because they see we're trying to be hard working.

| **Vijay:** | So, just so I can understand, umm, your answer, so Asian peo-ple don't face as much racism because in our society they're perceived to be harder working? |
| **Don:** | Yeah. |

Don's reasoning is revelatory, not because it illustrates cultural racism, which we know exists broadly in American society, but because it is coming from a person of color. This frame has historically been associated with white individu-als and communities and, in Don's narrative, it appears to have been internalized fully by a non-white individual. It is important to note that Don's reasoning is problematic on two levels. First, it absolves systemic racism, shifting the blame on to marginalized communities. Secondly, it casts racism as white people's rea-sonable response to crime and laziness, rather than as a system of exploitation and oppression.

Sarah

The final example I will share comes from my interview with Sarah, an 18–year-old, middle-class, Indian American woman from a suburb of a large Mid-western city. During our conversation, Sarah's reflection on the future of racism in America revealed a third frame of color-blind racism: racism-is-just-interpersonal. Guinier and Torres (2003) explain that color-blind racism obscures the systemic realities of white racial hegemony by framing any remaining vestiges of racism as simply person-to-person unpleasantness. Sarah's response to my question, like most of my participants, appears to demonstrate this problematic understanding of racism.

| **Vijay:** | That's great. We've been talking a lot about racial identity and just race in the abstract. How about racism, you know, just as a force, right? Do you think racism exists anymore? |
| **Sarah:** | Yeah, I think it always will with certain people. It's just kind of you know, some people are just never going to change. |

Sarah, along with the majority of my study participants, seemed to think of racism as interpersonal, rather than systemic. Her conviction that "some people are just never going to change" actually works to minimize racism by locating it in the hearts and minds of a few misguided individuals (Hill, 2008). The broad internalization of this frame of color-blind racism for my participants is signifi-cant because misunderstanding racism as interpersonal rather than systemic leads to other false conclusions about the experience of people of color within white hegemony.

In conclusion, the examples I have shared from Lina, Don, and Sarah speak to my overall findings that my Asian American research participants appeared to have internalized numerous facets of color-blind racism. Furthermore, my participants' meaning-making process regarding their own experiences of race, and the role of systemic racism in our society, appears to have been powerfully shaped by this internalization. In the next section of this chapter, I will discuss the implications of my research findings before concluding this chapter.

PRIMED TO BE COLOR-BLIND?

In the aggregate, my qualitative research findings seem to indicate that the Asian American university students in my study have internalized numerous aspects of model minority typology and its attendant mantle of honorary Whiteness. Furthermore, their narratives appear to reproduce the hegemonic logic of color-blind racism, in its various frames. Keeping in mind the adage that correlation does not imply causation, I still think it is vital for scholars invested in the politics of race to understand these parallel processes. Over the course of my research, Asian American race consciousness, or a lack thereof, emerged repeatedly as a key factor in how the participants engaged with both model minority typology and color-blind racist frames. In the final section of this chapter, I will examine two scholarly frameworks that might help explain the tenuous relationship between the Asian American subjects in my research and Asian American race consciousness.

When considering processes of internalization, it is important to contextualize the complex relationship between individual group members, ethnic identity, and racial identity, as this has the potential to influence their complicity with model minority status and honorary whiteness. Using a socio-historical model to examine the relationship between racial formation and the hegemonic state, Omi and Winant (1994) argue that "[t]he dominant paradigm of race for the last half-century has been that of *ethnicity*" (p. 12). They explain that an ethnicity theory of race emerged in the early part of the 20th century as a Progressive Era response to biologistic, fixed notions of race that were deeply racist. Scholars such as Park (1950) and Kallen (1956) offered a contrasting formulation of race that explained identity through the frameworks of culture and descent. Omi and Winant (1994) offer the following definitions for these two key terms in the ethnicity paradigm:

> "Culture" in this formulation included such diverse factors as religion, language, "customs," nationality, and political identification. "Descent" involved heredity and a sense of group origins, thus suggesting that ethnicity was socially "primordial," if not biologically given, in character. (p. 15)

By rooting a notion of identity in social factors such as culture and descent, scholars of the ethnicity paradigm hoped to counter racist formulations of identity that offered fixed, biological explanations for various racial problems in American society at that time. Both the assimilationist and cultural pluralist paradigms, however, suffer from key issues when trying to explain *racial experiences* of non-white groups by using a framework built on a white, European norm.

My research participants relied heavily on the tools of the ethnicity paradigm, such as culture and descent, to try and describe and explain their *racial* experiences. Furthermore, they drew extensively from the broader liberal frameworks of assimilation and cultural pluralism in their values and opinions of American society. Taken as a whole, the *ethnicity* paradigm seemed to inform the way my participants thought of their *racial* identities, and this has serious implications for their ability to develop a race consciousness.

Adherence to an ethnic paradigm of race might facilitate the internalization of model minority typology in my participants in three ways. First, by supplanting a race consciousness with an ethnic identity, my participants appeared to emphasize individual experiences over collective racial experiences. Second, the role of the state in producing hegemonic whiteness along with structural racism was also noticeably absent from the narratives I collected, which can be attributed to the ethnicity paradigm's epistemic blind spot in matters of state power. Third, my participants placed enormous value on numerical diversity, heritage celebration, and cultural pluralism as a result of their adherence to the ethnicity paradigm. In summary, the three outcomes of the ethnicity paradigm of race mentioned above emphasize the individual over the collective, obscure state power, and center liberal multiculturalism.

My research suggests that the participants' adherence to the ethnicity paradigm serves as a barrier to investing in Asian American racial identity, opting instead for ethnic identification such as "Filipino" or "Indian." This low level of racial identity salience is immediately troubling when considering the research on race consciousness and resisting racism. Kim (2012), in her work on the Asian American Racial Identity Development model, writes, "Racial identity describes how people deal with the effects of racism, eventually disowning the dominant group's views of their own race and developing a positive self-definition and positive attitude towards their own group" (p. 139). All of the participants in my study recalled experiencing anti-Asian American racism, yet they held little to no race consciousness. Further research is necessary to determine whether Asian Americans might be more vulnerable to the deleterious effects of racism, particularly internalization, if they have low levels of racial identity salience.

In addition to raising critical questions about the cost of ethnic identification over racial identification, the participants' narratives also raise questions about honorary whiteness serving as a *barrier* to racial identification. Junn and Masuoka's (2008) article on the relationship between Asian American racial identification and political behavior compares Asian American and Black racial salience levels gathered from survey data. They conclude that Asian Americans have a much higher level of variance in their identification with their racial group when compared to African Americans and that this leads to much lower cohesion in their political behavior as a racial group. Junn and Masuoka (2008) write:

> The structural factors of racial categorization, immigration policy and racialized tropes help to construct Asian American group identity based on a shared racial

status. Rather than the clearly politicized racial identity of blacks, the contours of Asian American group consciousness take shape as latent solidarity. Like blacks, racial categorization for Asian Americans persists, and is readily identifiable on face value. In this sense, racial group membership is not a choice, and categorization as a race other than "white" will always be there and will always play a role. Yet, this racial distinction also means that the formation of Asian American racial group consciousness depends on the particular context. (p. 736)

The crucial role of context in the formation of Asian American race consciousness is a key factor for researchers and educators to take into account. In the current context of race and politics in American society, Asian American college students appear to be being denied their racial reality by the context of model minoritization and their positioning within political discourses, such as affirmative action. This triangulation between race consciousness, honorary whiteness (vis-à-vis model minoritization), and political discourses might actually serve as a primer that readies Asian American college students for the hegemonic framework of color-blind racism.

This nexus of risk and complicity calls for further research and immediate action. In the spirit of promoting both of these outcomes, I conclude my chapter with five questions for reflection that I hope will provoke critical inquiry and liberatory praxis.

Questions for Reflection

1. What are the psychological and emotional effects *for Asian Americans* being positioned as a wedge between people of color and as poster children for color-blind racism?

2. Some of the research on model minority typology indicates that Asian Americans who reject this label can feel a resulting distance from the Asian American racial identity. Alternately, this research suggests that Asian Americans who internalize the archetype might also possess low racial saliency, due to the deracinating effects of honorary Whiteness. How can we better account for Asian Americans who reject the trope and, in their rejection, move towards a deeper race consciousness as Asian Americans?

3. Research on ethnic identity affinity within Asian American communities suggests that ethnic identity might represent a survival strategy during processes of migration and acculturation. How can we offer Asian American communities a way to access their racial identity that serves this need? Can Asian American racial identification be shaped to serve as an asset in processes of migration and acculturation?

4. Currently, the existing models of Asian American racial identity development do not account for color-blind racism explicitly. Can we develop

a model for Asian American racial identity formation that takes color-blind racism into account from its foundation?

5. If the internalization of color-blind racism is a coping mechanism for Asian Americans to resist racial microaggressions, what are the available catalysts in producing race consciousness among Asian American subjects?

REFERENCES

Aleinikoff, T. A. (1991). A case for race consciousness. *Columbia Law Review, 91*(5), 1060–1125.

Alvarez, A. N. (2002). Racial identity and Asian Americans: Supports and challenges. In M. K. McEwen, C. M. Kodama, A. N. Alvarez, C. Liang, & S. Lee (Eds.), *Working with Asian American students: New direction for student services.* San Francisco, CA: Jossey-Bass.

Alvarez, A. N., Juang, L., Liang, C. T. (2006). Asian Americans and racism: When bad things happen to "model minorities." *Cultural Diversity and Ethnic Minority Psychology, 12*(3), 477–492.

Barnes, M. L. (2009). Reflection on a dream world: Race, post-race and the question of making it over. *Berkeley Journal of African-American Law & Policy, 11,* 6–18.

Bonilla-Silva, E. (2006). *Racism without racists: Color-blind racism and the persistence of racial inequality in the United States* (2nd ed.). Lanham, MD: Rowman & Little-field.

Buenavista, T. L., Jayakumar, U. M., & Misa-Escalante, K. (2009). Contextualizing Asian American education through critical race theory: An example of U.S. Pilipino college student experiences. *New Directions for Institutional Research 142,* 69–81.

Chen, G. A., LePhuoc, P., Guzman, M. R., Rude, S. S., & Dodd, B. G. (2006). Exploring Asian American racial identity. *Cultural Diversity and Ethnic Minority Psychology, 12*(3), 461–476.

Connelly, F. M., & Clandinin, D. J. (1990). *Stories of experience and narrative inquiry. Educational Researcher, 19*(5), 2–14.

Corbin, J., & Strauss, A. (2007). *Basics of qualitative research: Techniques and procedures for developing a grounded theory* (3rd ed.). Thousand Oakes, CA: Sage.

Crenshaw, K. W. (1988). Race, reform, and retrenchment: Transformation and legitimation in antidiscrimination law. *Harvard Law Review, 101*(7), 1331–1387.

Forman, T. A. (2004). Color-blind racism and racial indifference: The role of racial apathy in facilitating enduring inequalities. In M. Krysan & A. Lewis (Eds.), *The changing terrain of race & ethnicity* (pp. 43–66). New York: The Russell Sage Foundation.

Gallagher, C. A. (2003). Color-blind privilege: The social and political functions of erasing the color line in post race America. *Race, Gender & Class, 10*(4), 22–37.

Gotanda, N. (1991). A critique of "Our Constitution is Color-Blind." *Stanford Law Review, 44*(1), 1–68.

Guinier, L., & Torres, G. (2003). *The miner's canary: Enlisting race, resisting power, transforming democracy.* Cambridge, MA: Harvard University Press.

Gupta, A., Szymanski, D., & Leong, F. (2011). The "Model Minority Myth": Internalized racialism of positive stereotypes as correlates of psychological distress, and attitudes toward help-seeking. *Asian American Journal of Psychology, 22*(2), 101–114.

Hartlep, N. D. (Ed.). (2014). *The model minority stereotype reader: Critical and challenging readings for the 21st century.* San Diego, CA: Cognella.

Hill, J. H. (2008). *The everyday language of White racism.* Chincester, UK: Wiley-Blackwell.

Junn, J. (2007). From coolie to model minority: U.S. immigration policy and the construction of racial identity. *Du Bois Review 4*(2), 355–373.

Junn, J., & Masuoka, N. (2008). Asian American identity: Shared racial status and political context. *Perspectives on Politics, 6*(4), 729–740.

Kallen, H. M. (1956). *Cultural pluralism and the American idea: An essay in social philosophy.* Philadelphia, PA: University of Pennsylvania Press.

Kawai, Y. (2005). Stereotyping Asian Americans: The dialectic of the model minority and the yellow peril. *The Howard Journal of Communications, 16*(2), 109–130.

Kidder, W. C. (2006). Negative action versus affirmative action: Asian Pacific Americans are still caught in the crossfire. *Michigan Journal of Race & Law, 11*, 605–624.

Kim, J. (2001). Asian American identity development theory. In C. Wijeyesinghe & B. W. Jackson (Eds.), *New perspectives on racial identity development: A theoretical and practical anthology* (pp. 67–90). New York: NYU Press.

Kim, J. (2012). Asian American racial identity development theory. In C. Wijeyesinghe & B. W. Jackson (Eds.), *New perspectives on racial identity development: A theoretical and practical anthology* (2nd ed.) (pp. 138–160). New York: NYU Press.

Kodama, C. M., McEwen, M. K., Liang, C. T., & Lee, S. (2002). An Asian American perspective on psychosocial student development theory. *New Directions for Student Services, 97*, 45–59.

Marshall, P. L. (2009). Multicultural education in a post-race political age: Our movement at risk? *Multicultural Perspectives, 11*(4), 188–193.

Merriam, S. B. (2009). *Qualitative research: A guide to design and implementation.* San Francisco, CA: Jossey-Bass.

Museus, S. D., & Kiang, P. N. (2009). Deconstructing the model minority myth and how it contributes to the invisible minority reality in higher education research. *New Directions for Institutional Research, 142*, 5–15.

Neville, H. A., Lilly, R. L., Duran, G., Lee, R. M., & Browne, L. (2000). Construction and initial validation of the color-blind racial attitudes scale (CoBRAS). *Journal of Counseling Psychology, 47*(1), 59–70.

Neville, H., Spanierman, L., & Doan, B. (2006). Exploring the association between color-blind racial ideology and multicultural counseling competencies. *Cultural Diversity & Ethnic Minority Psychology, 12*(2), 275–290.

Ng, J. C., Lee, S. S., & Pak, Y. K. (2007). Contesting the model minority and perpetual foreigner stereotypes: A critical review of literature on Asian Americans in education. *Review of research in education, 31*, 95–130.

Omi, M., & Winant, H. (1994). *Racial formation in the United States: From the 1960s to the 1990s.* New York: Routledge.

Park, R. E. (1950). Negro race consciousness as reflected in race literature. In E. C. Hughes, C. S. Johnson, J. Masuoka, R. Redfield & L. Wirth (Eds.), *Race and culture, essays in the sociology of contemporary man* (pp. 284–300). Glencoe, IL: Free Press.

Prashad, V. (2001). *The karma of brown folk.* Minneapolis, MN: The University of Minnesota Press.

Poon, O. A. (2009). Haunted by negative action: Asian Americans, admissions, and race in the "color-blind era." *Harvard University Asian American Policy Review, 18*, 81–90.

Reissman, C. K. (2008). *Narrative methods for the human sciences*. Thousand Oaks, CA: Sage.

Smith, B. (2008). Far enough or back where we started: Race perception from Brown to Meredith. *Journal of Law & Education, 37*(2), 297–305.

Williams, D. G., & Land, R. R. (2006). The legitimation of black subordination: The impact of color-blind ideology on African American education. *Journal of Negro Education, 75*(4), 579–588.

Wise, T. J. (2010). *Colorblind: The rise of post-racial politics and the retreat from racial equity*. San Francisco, CA: City Lights Books.

Wu, F. H. (1995). Neither Black nor White: Asian Americans and affirmative action. *Boston College Third World Law Journal, 15*, 225–284.

Yoo, H. C., Burrola, K. S., & Steger, M. F. (2010). A preliminary report on a new measure: Internalization of the Model Minority Myth Measure (IM-4) and its psychological correlates among Asian American college students. *Journal of Counseling Psychology, 57*(1), 114–127.

CHAPTER 12

DECONSTRUCTING LINSANITY

Is Jeremy Lin a Model Minority Subject?

Nathan Kalman-Lamb

In this chapter I use discourse analysis of popular North American written electronic and print media in order to explore the ways in which National Basketball Association (NBA) player Jeremy Lin has been represented. As an elite professional athlete, Lin defies the stereotype that East Asians are academically rather than athletically accomplished. Yet, although Lin appears to be something of a trailblazer in countering the hegemonic myth of Asian American passivity and hyper-intellectualism, such a reading is overly simplistic. The representation of Lin by sports entertainment and media, in fact, serves to reproduce the myth of the model minority and disseminate it through one of the most popular forms of contemporary culture in America: sport. While Lin participates in a non-traditional occupation, he still comes to embody precisely the sort of attributes associated with the model minority: hard work, discipline, intelligence, Christian devotion, and a general acceptance of the prevailing norms of whiteness and capitalism. As such, he comes to serve a particularly useful disciplinary function for both hegemonic and subordinated groups in American society. For the white majority, Lin becomes an unthreatening face of non-white (im)migrant labor, making more palatable the pivotal role this labor plays in the U.S. political economy.

Killing the Model Minority Stereotype: Asian American Counterstories and Complicity,
pages 203–218.
Copyright © 2015 by Information Age Publishing
All rights of reproduction in any form reserved.

More insidious, for other non-white subjects, Lin models the mode of behavior required to achieve acceptance in U.S. society—the acceptable side of the good immigrant/bad immigrant binary. This chapter does not focus on the way in which Lin chooses to represent himself, nor will it hold him accountable for the ways in which he challenges or upholds the myth of the model minority. Rather, it will interrogate the ways in which the U.S. sports media has represented him in order to demonstrate the power of this hegemonic discourse.

In order to properly investigate the ways in which Jeremy Lin has been represented as a model minority subject, it is necessary to explore precisely what a model minority is, how Asian Americans specifically have been constructed as model minorities, and, finally, how the discourse of the model minority comes to operate through the bodies of exemplary racialized subjects.

Why Model Minorities?

In order to explain how the myth of the model minority operates, we must begin by examining the context within which the trope has currency. Model minority discourse functions in the context of multicultural societies, be they openly assimilative like the United States, or putatively celebratory of heterogeneity, such as Canada or Australia. Whether assimilationist or not, these multicultural societies have historically sought to retain white hegemony while managing considerable racialized populations that have provided and continue to provide a pool of labor available for exploitation, albeit in varying forms (slavery, indentureship, segregation, migrant labor) (Bolaria & Li, 1985; Hage, 2000; Mackey, 2002; Puar & Rai, 2004; Sharma 2006). Although the discourse of race tends to successfully legitimize the exploitation of non-whites, it simultaneously produces the spectre of a threat. Racial discourse dehumanizes non-white bodies, framing them as animal. There are multiple implications to this fact. Crucially, racial logic figures the racialized subject as hyper-physical and un-intellectual, which feeds into the perception that the non-white body is naturally predisposed for manual labor. At the same time, however, the trope of racialized body as animal also implies tendencies towards violence, criminality, and hyper-sexuality (Fanon, 2008). These are characteristics, unsurprisingly, viewed as less desirable to the white majority.

This split is the binarism at the heart of the way in which racialized subjects are represented in multicultural societies. Such representational binaries, of course, rely on simplicity, not complexity. That is, the non-white subject is not framed as simultaneously hard-working and threatening. Rather, two separate types or categories are produced (Dhamoon, 2009). The first is what I have been referring to as the model minority. This is the non-white subject who is diligent, hard-working, uncomplaining, and generally ideally suited to whatever form of labor the political economy demands of her or him. This racial other is ultimately presented as a boon to the nation, not a threat.

The second category functions quite differently. This is the threatening other, the bad immigrant, who poses a threat to the nation. The presence of the abject other is assumed to be the cause of most of the nation's problems (Abdel-Shehid, 2004). It serves as the justification for the constant surveillance and regulation of all non-white populations. In short, the model minority/bad immigrant binary allows hegemonic white nations to rationalize the presence of non-white others within national borders for the purposes of labor exploitation.

The efficacy of this binary is not limited to its impact on the perceptions of the white majority. On the contrary, the discourse of the model minority has an equally strong effect upon non-white populations themselves, for it demonstrates the ways in which it is permissible to act and the implications of transgressing these boundaries (Dhamoon, 2009). Popular representations of non-white people make it clear that it is possible to achieve a measure of acceptance and even approval so long as one comports oneself as a model minority subject (Abdel-Shehid, 2004; Kalman-Lamb, 2013). Conversely, it is equally evident that approbation accompanies any demonstration of abject characteristics. Thus, the model minority/bad immigrant binary serves as a form of representational discipline, enforcing a set of norms for what will and will not be tolerated. Indeed, it also serves as a reminder to those who do successfully embody the model minority subject that they are always at risk of slipping into the other category.

Up to this point, I have been making the assumption that all non-white subjects in multicultural societies experience the same relationship to the model minority/ bad immigrant binary. This is not the case. Indeed, the very term "model minority" emerges out of a *New York Times Magazine* article, which characterized particular racialized groups in their entirety as model minorities (Palumbo-Liu, 1994). Such a claim is a logical extension of the binary principle that underlies this mode of classification. Just as certain members of racialized populations can be valorized in contrast to others, so too can the same be said for groups writ large. In the history of the United States, blackness has long been associated with the animal. This began as a justification for slavery and persists as legitimation for discrimination, exploitation, and criminalization. Other racialized groups have historically come to be defined in the United States as model minorities in direct opposition to this portrayal of African Americans. Jews, South Asians, and East Asians all fit this designation (it should be noted that indigenous people are not included on this list, for they are generally, and of course erroneously, perceived to have disappeared from history altogether [Dua & Lawrence, 2005]). It is the latter of these groups that I will focus on here, as they have become the most visible and widely recognized and acknowledged model minority group in the United States.

Asian Americans and the Model Minority Myth

I have sketched out the underlying binary that governs the athletic model minority stereotype, but what remains is to see what it looks like in practice as it is applied to Asian Americans. Gao (2010) has written that the stereotype suggests Asians "have a passive, introverted personality style, which makes them unsuited for positions of leadership" (p. 216). Indeed, I would note that this is precisely the sort of personality expected of laborers since, again, the function of model minority discourse is inextricably linked to the demands of political economy. Kim (1999) has defined the characteristics ascribed to Asian Americans through the model minority stereotype as "diligence, family solidarity, respect for education, and self-sufficiency" (p. 18). Kibria (2002) has revealed some of the meanings associated with Asian American model minority-hood by conducting a series of interviews with Asian Americans. Many of the individuals interviewed clearly have interpellated the myth, and in the process provide another window into what it entails. A Korean-American corporate type remarked, "Then there's the whole idea of Asians being book smart, but not politically savvy, and hardworking but not aggressive" (p. 140). A Korean-American lawyer echoed this idea: "Asians are not seen as aggressive or outspoken enough. They don't speak loudly or whatever" (p. 142). A police officer defined the model minority myth by positioning himself as an anomaly: "I'm not one of those Asian kids with straight A's, the honors student who plays the violin. I was basically a jock who didn't care too much about school" (p. 138). Crucially, here we see an explicit statement of the fact that the athletic sphere ostensibly falls outside the purview of Asian Americans. To be a jock is to defy the model minority myth. This will be important to keep in mind as we move into a discussion of Jeremy Lin. One implication of the model minority myth is that it places inordinate pressure on Asian Americans to live up to it or risk being perceived a failure. A Korean-American who had just completed law school told Kibria, "Your mom and dad, who are probably immigrants, they're telling you to be the super-student, like, 'Get into Harvard.' Then because you're Asian and people have this idea that Asians are really smart, you feel like you have to live up to it" (p. 136).

Just as the model minority myth plays a central role in conditioning and shaping the lives and experiences of Asian American subjects, so too does it serve a pivotal function to the broader political economy of the United States. As discussed above, the figure of the model minority assumes its signification in part through a binary relation to a different other framed as abject. For Asian Americans, the position of binary opposition has been filled by African Americans. Kim (1999) suggests that if Asian Americans have been defined as disciplined, thrifty, moral, and self-sufficient, African Americans are seen as lazy, hedonistic, criminal, and dependent. There is nothing essential or trans-historical about this opposition. Lee (1996) explains that in early parts of the twentieth century, "Asian Americans had often been stereotyped as devious, inscrutable, unassimilable, and in other overtly negative ways" (1996, p. 6). The shift to the model minority paradigm is not an accident of history. Rather, Kim (1999) contends that this opposition has a very particular and historically contingent function: it subverts the gains made by African Americans through policies such as affirmative action and other political struggles for structural change by deflecting attention back to cultural characteristics. Economic success, according to the logic of the model minority myth, owes to the hard work and self-discipline of individuals (who belong to particular cultural groups that value these traits). This logic obfuscates the overwhelming systemic obstacles presented by histories of slavery and segregation, as well as those posed by ongoing discrimination and poverty. Most importantly, it disguises the inherent connection between the accumulation and dispossession of the earlier period and the resulting capital, cultural and economic, wielded by some today.

Kim (1999) shows that there is another element to this binary as well. The model minority myth does not merely cloak histories of inequity; it also undermines the contemporary political movements that would redress them. It does this by disseminating a conceptual association between Asian American success and apolitical behavior and juxtaposing these against the supposed failures of African Americans and their political movements. More than this, the model minority myth constructs the conditions for an outright conflict between Asian and African Americans that serves only to position whiteness as benefactor. The notion that African Americans, as bad minority, are bullying Asian Americans, the model minority, allows whites to intervene on the side of the ostensible victim. This transforms the narrative of race relations in the United States from a discussion of the structural racism of the nation's political economy into a tale of the petty squabbles of non-white groups. All told, the model minority myth persistently elides the hegemony of whiteness from national conversations around race and political economy.

Professional Athletes as Model Minority Subjects

It is perhaps not difficult to understand, then, why Kyung-Jin Lee has suggested that model minorities function "in effect to be the nation's spies" (2002, p. 253). There is certainly a temptation to hold the individual accountable for complicity with the model minority stereotype given the relative privileges afforded to those who embody it. This is especially true when we look at the ways in which the model minority stereotype has come to operate through the representation and objectification of the bodies of celebrated individual subjects. I have written elsewhere (Kalman-Lamb, 2013) about the ways in which the body of the athlete, specifically Jose Bautista of Major League Baseball's Toronto Blue Jays in the context of Canadian multiculturalism, comes to stand in as icon for an entire model minority. My argument there, as here, is that individual model minority subjects have tremendous power as representational figures. This is particularly true of professional athletes, who, as purveyors of the most consumed form of entertainment in North America, are constantly scrutinized and discussed in the popular media. Yet the fact that model minority subjects may receive a measure of privilege in exchange for their acquiescence to the role demanded of them does not mean that it is just to hold them accountable for the structural conditions that produce and require the model minority stereotype. All people deserve and desire a world in which they are capable of making choices around occupation and identity free from constraint. Model minority subjects are no different; that we do not live in such a world is not a responsibility that can be laid at their feet.

This is an injunction that must be kept in mind as we move into a discussion of Jeremy Lin. The discussion of the representation of any specific model minority figure is ultimately a discussion of structural racism and political economy. The model minority subject is merely the body assumed for representational purposes by model minority discourse. This is why I reject Lee's assertion that "[m]odel-minority discourse is therefore not a case of providing 'models' at all. Rather, it is a cultural gateway, a language of authority to filter and justify those who belong and can therefore flourish, and those who deserve to be left behind" (p. 251). It is true that model minority discourse serves to privilege and discriminate according to race. However, we cannot dismiss how it does so: primarily through representation—the model. In order to unpack the insidious workings of this discourse, we must remain attentive to the bodies it uses to broadcast its meanings. The question now at hand is whether Jeremy Lin is one of those bodies.

Linsanity and Representation

First, though, let us begin with the question of who Jeremy Lin is and why he is worthy of discussion. Lin is a professional basketball player currently playing for the NBA's Los Angeles Lakers. It is Lin's history prior to his arrival in Los Angeles that is worthy of particular note, however. Lin was born and raised in California in a devout Christian family of immigrants from Taiwan. He attended Harvard University, where he starred on the basketball team, ultimately earning a chance to play in the NBA in 2010 with the Golden State Warriors. In late 2011, Lin was acquired by the New York Knicks. At the time, he was a relative unknown to most North American sports fans. This fact radically changed in February of 2012, when Lin became a global celebrity by leading the Knicks to a series of improbable wins as the team's starting point guard. Overnight, "Linsanity" was born (Gregory, 2012, February 27). By the end of that season, Lin had earned a lucrative new contract with the Houston Rockets and become one of the most famous people in the world.

Lin's remarkable popularity is undoubtedly imbricated with his identity as an Asian American, for he is the only Asian American in the NBA and by far the most successful player of East Asian lineage since Yao Ming played for Houston. This fact makes Lin arguably the most visible and publicized Asian American in the United States today. As such, he is positioned as a crucial figure for model minority discourse. The questions at hand, then, are how Lin has been represented in the popular U.S. national news media and what that representation tells us about model minority discourse. These are pertinent questions in part because Lin's very identity as a high-performance athlete stands as an implicit rebuttal to the myth. Consequently, he wields the representational potential to pose a significant challenge to model minority discourse.

A word on representation is necessary here. Analysis of popular culture texts of all sorts is not haphazard or arbitrary. Rather, such analysis must be firmly anchored by intertextual context (Hall, 1997). The way we read works of representation is informed by our understandings of and assumptions about the world we live in. These assumptions and understandings influence the way we interpret what we are reading and watching. Although there are myriad ways in which particular words, phrases, or images can be read in a vacuum, this immense scope is circumscribed by the dominant codes of meaning that exist within a given cultural and historical context. The model minority myth is precisely the sort of dominant code I am describing here. This myth has become the normative lens through which Americans, including Asian Americans, define and understand Asian American identity. This identity and its concomitant attributes tend to be signalled through the use of particular words and concepts such as "discipline," "hard work," "intelligence," etc. Any time these words are used to characterize an Asian American person in American popular culture, they resonate with this broader cultural context and reproduce the myth of the model minority. In what follows, I have drawn on coverage of Lin in the popular national and New York print and electronic media to provide what I believe is a representative sampling of the way Lin has been most visibly represented.

Finally, before proceeding to a more nuanced discussion of the ways in which Lin has been represented, it is worth reminding ourselves that most non-white public figures (like most non-white people in general) continue to be subject to explicit forms of racial discrimination. Lin is no exception to this phenomenon. Twice on separate *ESPN* platforms, Lin's exploits were discussed under the banner of the headline "Chink In The Armor" (Carbone, 2012, February 19). These insidious punning uses of a racial slur are an important reminder that although there is significant value to discussions of more complex and veiled forms of structural racism, such discussions should not obfuscate the reality that blatant racism continues to be a fact of everyday life for most non-white people.

Jeremy Lin and the Trailblazer Narrative

Nevertheless, for the most part, coverage of Jeremy Lin's remarkable rise to celebrity is not marked by such overtly racist commentary. Rather, it largely takes on a celebratory tone, trumpeting Lin as a trailblazer for a new form of Asian American identity. I will refer to stories of this kind as "trailblazer narratives." Articles in this vein frame Lin as an antidote to traditional model minority stereotypes. Clemmons (2011) sets such a tone even prior to the "Linsanity" of 2012 in an article on *ESPN.com*. She speaks to Asian American men with an involvement in youth basketball about what Lin means to them:

> "He's the first Asian kid to make it," said Darren Yamashita, of the Northern California Nisei Athletic Union Basketball League. "It shows the Asian-American kids here that they can do it; they can compete at the highest level."

> "We have fans who love him," said Rich Twu, who founded the Dream League, an amateur basketball league for men and women in the Bay Area and New York. "But

you also have the Asian-Americans who want to blend in as an American and say, 'He's not playing well, so what's the big fuss.'" (2011, March 16)

Here we have the common-sense version of the Jeremy Lin story. As a basketball player, Lin challenges stereotypes about Asian Americans and functions as a trailblazer for other Asian Americans who wish to defy the norms that constrain them to academic and professional work. Indeed, Lin is so unconventional that his exploits are rejected by some members of the community who have internalized the imperatives of this discourse, for they view him to be a threat to their identity and their ability to be accepted in the United States, which this identity offers through its denial of structural racism. In the same vein, a year later, Beck of the *New York Times* talks to an Asian American about the meaning of Lin:

> "It's just a real point of pride, the success he is having," said Carl Park, a 35–year-old graduate student in Chicago and a first-generation Korean-American.
>
> Park grew up a Milwaukee Bucks fan, but he roots for Lin wherever he plays.
>
> "It represents a step for the Asian-American community as it becomes part of American culture more broadly," Park said. (2012, February 7)

The tone of these pieces is common to most of the discussion of Lin disseminated in popular print and electronic media. Indeed, most articles strike a similarly triumphalist note, proclaiming Lin the founder of a new brand of Asian American identity.

However, although the message of most articles seems to explicitly challenge the model minority stereotype, something else seems to be going on as well. In the *New York Times* article cited above, despite the prevailing theme that Lin is a trailblazer, we find the following statement from his mother: "'I think people are surprised, because people don't know him, or maybe he's a pioneer,' Shirley Lin said. 'There's not that many Harvard players, not that many Asian-Americans. He's just kind of like underdog. But he works hard'" (2012, February 7). Although Lin's mother positions her son as a "pioneer," in the next breath she sends a very different message by calling him an "underdog" who "works hard." These are classic tropes of the model minority stereotype. It seems that even as Lin appears to challenge the conventional social role allotted to Asian Americans, and thus transcend the model minority myth, he is simultaneously re-inscribed within the myth. He may play basketball, but he does so precisely the way a model minority subject should: with hard work and diffidence.

It should be acknowledged that it is tempting to look at the above example and argue that, as a direct quotation, it should not be held up as an example of model minority discourse. Indeed, the claim can be made that this is merely what one person thinks, and nothing more. The problem with this line of thinking is that it ignores both the agency of the journalist and the social context in which this statement is made. To the former point, it is easy to lose sight of the fact that journalists, photographers, editors, and those who generally fashion what it is the public consumes under the moniker of the media ultimately make choices about what they will portray. Although they may use the words of another (say Lin's mother), they have the ability to choose which words are selected and how those words are framed. In this way, their stories are in themselves a form of representation, not bare documentation of fact. Likewise, as I discussed earlier, stories like this one exist in a broader social context, which anchors meaning according to the logic of normative social codes. For these reasons, it is important and necessary to examine even the most seemingly documentary forms of representation.

Lin's mother is not alone in slipping from the trailblazer narrative to a more conventional model minority paradigm. In a different *New York Times* story, Luo (2012, February 11) writes of himself: "For me, as an Asian-American, the chants of 'M.V.P.!' raining down on Lin at the Garden embody a surreal, Jackie Robinson-like moment." Luo invokes the archetypal athletic trailblazer to underline Lin's significance as a challenge to the model minority stereotype. Yet, immediately after, he writes, "Just as meaningful to me as a Christian, however, is the way the broadcasters have hailed Lin as not just the 'Harvard hero' but the 'humble Harvard grad.' His teammates appear just as overjoyed at his success as he was. Both seem to be testaments to his character." There is a swift reversion here to the discourse of the model minority. Luo's chief satisfaction in Lin comes from his humility and character. These are the traits that ostensibly define Asian Americans. Thus, Lin's appeal is not so much that he transcends this norm as that he reaffirms it on a bigger stage. Luo continues, "Lin comes across as soft-spoken and winsome; he comes across as thoughtful. He comes across, actually, as a distinctly Asian-American Christian, or at least like so many that I know." The salient detail here is that Luo explicitly articulates Lin's personal attributes as essentially cultural traits. Lin becomes a metonym for Asian Americanness: the ultimate model minority subject.

A *Sports Illustrated* story by Torre (2012, February 20) makes a similar reversal. Like the others we have seen, it begins with a trailblazer narrative:

> Lin would brush off racist jeers from opposing fans ("Sweet and sour pork!") and Ivy League opponents (he was called "Ch---" on the court) to average 16.4 points, 4.5 assists and 2.4 steals as a senior. (In high school taunts directed him to orchestra practice, volleyball, the math team—anywhere but basketball.)... Today, of course, millions of Asian-Americans are hoping that Lin's arrival sparks the obliteration of so much cognitive dissonance. There have been other Asians in the NBA, most notably Yao Ming. "But we've never had any skill players," says David Chang, a Korean-American hoops junkie and the owner-chef of New York City's renowned Momofuku restaurants. "And being Asian in America, you grow up with the notion that you're not as athletically talented as everyone else. This is all about changing expectations, and all these ridiculous notions of what an Asian should be."

Ultimately, and perhaps inevitably, however, this article too turns to the model minority myth:

Lin, who's worked endlessly on his strength and his jump shot in the past year, is a normal-sized, Christian, first-generation Asian-American. He's excelled academically, faced racism on the court, been cut twice and sent to the D-league four times. Now he's an NBA sensation amid the cultural diversity of hoops-starved New York. Opponents aside, who wouldn't be a fan?

When Torre ultimately makes his case for why Lin deserves to be universally embraced, he reverts to a list of attributes that make Lin a model minority subject: his work ethic, his religion, his immigrant status, his academic success, and the fact that he has not let racism hold him back. He becomes merely another example for all immigrants and minorities to follow, an embodiment of the American Dream.

Jeremy Lin as Model Minority Subject

In many cases, the trailblazer narrative does not even appear in coverage of Lin. Instead, the model minority myth emerges right from the start. I quote at length from an *ESPN.com* piece by Keown (2012, February 14) that particularly exemplifies this approach:

You know how people from an athlete's past always say they saw it coming? They never, ever doubted, and now they can't believe it took the rest of the world this long to catch up? Well, Diepenbrock isn't one of those guys...

"I wasn't sitting there saying all these Division I coaches were knuckleheads," Diepenbrock says. "There were legitimate questions about Jeremy."

Diepenbrock starts to say something else, then stops. "I already got in trouble with Jeremy for saying this, so I probably shouldn't," he says. Then, a few seconds later, he says, "Oh, what the hell. I'll say it anyway and get in trouble twice: Jeremy was not a good practice player."

Really? The hard-working kid from Harvard, undrafted, cut by two NBA teams— *not a good practice player?* Go ahead: shatter our dreams.

But wait. Diepenbrock's not finished. After a year at Harvard, Lin returned to Palo Alto and asked his old coach, "Can you work me out?"

"Now?" Diepenbrock asked. "I was here every day for three years, and now you want me to work you out?"

Lin, ever the pragmatist, said, "Yes, because now I know I need it."

From that point on, a workout fiend was born. During the lockout, Lin's schedule read like a brochure for Navy SEAL BUD/S training:

10–11 a.m.: Agility training
11–noon: Weight training

1–2: Shooting work, with private coach
2–4: Individual work

Lin played whenever he could, which meant playing in Sunday morning pickup games with his two brothers and joining Diepenbrock's night-league team. "I'm a 48–year-old fat guy working on my jumper, and my night-league point guard is the talk of the NBA," Diepenbrock says. "If you knew who this guy is at his core—it's such a *real* story, so good it's unreal. When he was in high school, if there was alcohol at a party, he'd immediately turn the other way. He's such a good person."

What is noteworthy about this passage is the way in which Keown crafts a very particular narrative to account for Lin's experiences. The fact that Lin "was not a good practice player" is not presented as an essential part of his identity (as it likely would be for an African American player). Rather, Lin's essence is defined by the fact that he is "a hard-working kid from Harvard," "a workout fiend," someone who subjects himself to "Navy SEAL BUD/S training." There is an alternative story that could be written here: Lin was a typical young person, who, when confronted with the possibility of losing the chance to pursue his ideal occupation, pushed himself to work harder. Upon achieving the goal of playing professionally, he then took the job seriously and acted like the professional he was (five hours of basketball-related fitness and skill development during off-season days does not sound like an overly rigorous or obsessive regime). It is only within the discourse of the model minority that the quotidian experiences of a professional athlete are transformed into hallmarks of exceptionality. Ultimately, as an Asian American, Lin is "at his core...such a good person."

A little later in Keown's (2012, February 14) article we learn, "The only time Diepenbrock had a problem with the Lin family was when Shirley would approach him and say, 'Coach, Jeremy has an A-minus in math. I don't think he's going to be able to play this week.'" Here again we have a re-assertion of Asian hyper-intellectualism and hard work: this is the culture Lin comes from, so it is no wonder he has worked his way to NBA success. The Lin family is an example for all to emulate, for hard work truly does lead to prosperity in America. The narrative that Lin's success is a product of particularly hard work and self-discipline is a common one. Beck (2012, February 24) of the *New York Times* writes:

Jeremy Lin's rise did not begin, as the world perceived it, with a 25–point explosion at Madison Square Garden on Feb. 4. It began with lonely 9 a.m. workouts in downtown Oakland in the fall of 2010; with shooting drills last summer on a backyard court in Burlingame, Calif.; and with muscle-building sessions at a Menlo Park fitness center.

It began with a reworked jump shot, a thicker frame, stronger legs, a sharper view of the court—enhancements that came gradually, subtly, through study and practice and hundreds of hours spent with assistant coaches, trainers and shooting instructors over 18 months.

Quite simply, the Jeremy Lin who revived the Knicks, stunned the N.B.A. and charmed the world—the one who is averaging 22.4 points and 8.8 assists as a starter—is not the Jeremy Lin who went undrafted out of Harvard in June 2010. He is not even the same Jeremy Lin who was cut by the Golden State Warriors on Dec. 9.

Beyond the mystique and the mania lies a more basic story—of perseverance, hard work and self-belief.

Beck has penned perhaps the quintessential model minority narrative without actually marshalling the language of race. What he has provided is a recapitulation of the attributes of the model minority subject (he leaves it to the reader to associate these characteristics with Lin's Asian-ness). Lin's success, according to Beck, is a function of "lonely 9 a.m. workouts," "shooting drills. . . on a backyard court," and "muscle-building sessions." For Beck, this amounts to a story of "perseverance" and "hard work." Yet, again, what the author has described is simply the life of a professional basketball player. There is nothing exceptional about the amount of effort or work here (relative to that of his colleagues). What is exceptional is his *performance*. The fact that Beck dwells on "perseverance" and "hard work" is the signifier that the model minority discourse is at work. Lin is coded as a try-hard Asian American, and this simultaneously serves to render him comprehensible as an Asian American athlete and to position him representationally as a model to be followed.

Another Torre article for *Sports Illustrated* (2012, February 27) picks up on a different model minority theme. Writing of Lin's relationship with his teammates, he quotes the player: "'Tyson's so eager and such a humble guy, and Landry's the exact same way,' says Lin, unfailingly deferent. 'We're all out there together, buying in.'" This brief passage is notable for two reasons. The first of these is the adjective chosen by the author to describe Lin: "deferent." The common idiom of the professional athlete is the cliché, and Lin demonstrates his fluency here, emphasizing the collective effort of his team and the merits of his teammates. There is nothing noticeably unusual about Lin's quote, yet Torre chooses to characterize the player as *particularly* deferential. In doing so, the writer, perhaps unwittingly, betrays the assumption that Lin, as an Asian American, is a model minority subject. It is unlikely that the same language would have been used to describe an African American player, so often presumed in the sports media to be selfish and recalcitrant.

While one function of the model minority myth is literally to model permissible modes of Asian American identity, another is to reveal the consequences of failing to do so. A *New York Times* editorial (2012, February 16) provides a subtle reminder of how tenuous model minority status is:

Lin is getting paid $500,000, a fraction of the $18 million or so the Knicks have lavished on each of their two superstars, Carmelo Anthony and Amar'e Stoudemire. But it's Lin's team now. He is its emotional center and playmaker—spreading the ball around with deft passing, spotting the open man, making everyone around him better. The other night against Sacramento, Lin got only 10 points, well below his recent numbers, but he dished out 13 assists.

This is very different from the basketball that the Knicks and many other teams usually play, which is to get the ball to the superstar and watch the superstar make his move, leaving everyone else standing around and, in the Knicks' case, on the short end of the score.

It will be interesting to see how Lin meshes with the superstars. Stoudemire has recently returned after his brother's funeral; Anthony has been sidelined with an injury. The hope among Knicks fans, of course, is that they will continue to play team basketball. The Knicks would not be the only winners. So would all those young fans who now want to grow up to be Jeremy Lin.

Although this may appear to be a straightforward summation of the Jeremy Lin story, there is an insidious subtext here that is central to an understanding of how the model minority subject functions not only as a model to be followed, but also as a form of discipline. As we have seen, a crucial aspect of the myth is the binary it produces between the model and the abject. In this case, Asian Americans are broadly framed as exemplars, while African Americans are condemned as failures. We see this in the way that Lin is compared to Carmelo Anthony and Amar'e Stoudemire (and also to other unnamed "superstars" who can implicitly be read as African American given prevailing assumptions about the "racial" constitution of the NBA). Lin is "deft. . . making everyone around him better." He is a team player, and paid merely a pittance for that. Anthony and Stoudemire (and other professionals), on the other hand, are framed as selfish, overpaid, and, perhaps, implicitly even lazy. In a perverse twist, then, these wealthy and accomplished men are transformed into a version of the conventional dehumanizing stereotype: lazy, ostentatiously accessorized, welfare recipients. They live off the largesse that "the Knicks have lavished on" them even as Lin grinds away for his small, but sufficient, income.

This income must be sufficient because to ask for more is to disrupt the delicate tightrope the model minority subject must walk between grudging toleration and disavowal (Kalman-Lamb, 2013). This is a highly ambivalent position, for the person caught in this bind is simultaneously aware of what s/he has to lose as well as how much of a strain this precarious position inflicts upon her or him. Thus, the model minority subject is often caught in between, not quite reproducing the model minority myth, not quite contesting it. A *CNN.com* (Park, 2012, August 24) story captures this tension in Lin: "He also fielded questions about being Asian in the NBA and getting through stereotypes. 'I'm naturally stubborn and hard headed,' he told the audience. 'Don't let people tell you what you can't and can do. People try to say you can't do this, you can't do that. Continue to chase what you love doing, work hard at it.'" Here Lin engages directly with the question of myth, suggesting that he feels constrained by stereotypes about what he can and cannot accomplish. Yet, immediately after, he reproduces the myth, citing precisely the characteristics of the model minority as the tools he uses to succeed on the court.

Although Lin's relationship to the myth may be somewhat conflicted, his insight into the ways in which it operates is unquestionable. In a story for *CBSS-PORTS.com* (Golliver, 2012, February 24), he is quoted as saying, "But I think just being Asian-American, obviously when you look at me, I'm going to have to prove myself more so again and again and again, and some people may not believe it. . . . I know a lot of people say I'm deceptively athletic and deceptively quick, and I'm not sure what's 'deceptive.' But it could be the fact that I'm Asian-American. But I think that's fine. It's something that I embrace, and it gives me a chip on my shoulder." By foregrounding for readers exactly how language operates to construct the model minority myth, Lin makes a meaningful intervention against model minority discourse by refusing to be adorned with the mantle of model minority subject. This is a powerful representational move, albeit one that did not receive much in the way of media attention. Nevertheless, Lin provides a window here into the possibility that exists for a different minority persona, one that resists being appropriated by hegemonic discourses.

CONCLUSION

The phenomenon of "Linsanity" provides valuable insight into the mechanisms of the model minority myth. Asian Americans are not supposed to be basketball players, according to model minority discourse. Yet, the fact that one of the most visible Asian Americans in recent memory *is* a basketball player has done little if anything to disrupt the way that the myth has come to shape the narratives written about him. What this demonstrates is that the myth is anything but monolithic. Rather, it is capable of morphing into whatever form required to sustain the underlying material conditions that make it necessary. The model minority stereotype does not exist in a vacuum. It is an ideological mechanism for a political economy predicated on racialized labor. As such, it is capable of a nearly infinite number of permutations and accommodations. Given this reality, it would be illogical and unjust to hold a particular subject, such as Jeremy Lin, accountable for its effects; the myth existed long before him, and it will inevitably outlast him as well. Yet, Lin is not without agency.

As a celebrated public figure, he does have some capacity (albeit limited) to choose how he will be represented and, in doing so, to intervene in the dissemination of the model minority myth. Although the efficacy of such an intervention would assuredly be limited—structural issues such as a political economy reliant on the exploitation of racialized labor require structural remedies—it would not be meaningless. The model minority myth exists precisely because there is a fundamental two-way relationship between structural-material conditions and ideology. While the former is over-determined in this dynamic, the latter is not insignificant. Lin and other athletes thrust into the subject position of the model minority do have some ability to effect change. To attempt to do so is to risk facing the approbation and disavowal that is heaped upon the abject other. It is thus a courageous and somewhat Sisyphean task, one that may ultimately leave more than a "chip on [the] shoulder." For even entertaining the possibility of challenging the model minority myth, let alone actually taking steps in that direction, Lin deserves a significant measure of respect. The task of demystifying it completely belongs to all of us.

Questions for Reflection

1. What does it mean to say that there is a binary relationship between the "model minority subject" and the "bad immigrant" or "abject other"? How are these figures connected? What are possible implications of this connection?
2. What is the relationship between the model minority subject and the broader political economy? What representational purpose does the model minority subject serve?
3. Does sporting culture in the United States feed into the myth of the American Dream? How? Why? Where does race fit into this dynamic?
4. Can an Asian/Asian American athlete resist being represented as a model minority subject? If so, how?
5. What is Jeremy Lin's political responsibility? To what extent is he complicit in the model minority myth?

REFERENCES

Abdel-Shehid, G. (2004). *Who da man? Black masculinities and sporting cultures.* Toronto: Canadian Scholars Press.

Beck, H. (2012, February 7). From ivy halls to the garden, surprise star jolts the NBA. *New York Times.* Retrieved December 1, 2014, from http://www.nytimes.com/2012/02/08/sports/basketball/jeremy-lin-has-burst-from-nba-novelty-act-to-knicks-star.html

Beck, H. (2012, February 24). The evolution of a point guard. *New York Times.* Retrieved December 1, 2014, from http://www.nytimes.com/2012/02/25/sports/basketball/the-evolution-of-jeremy-lin-as-a-point-guard.html?pagewanted=all

Bolaria, B. S., & Li, P. S. (1985). *Racial oppression in Canada.* Toronto: Garamond Press.

Carbone, N. (2012, February 19). ESPN fires writer over racial slur in Jeremy Lin headline. *Time.* Retrieved December 1, 2014, from http://newsfeed.time.com/2012/02/19/espn-fires-writer-over-jeremy-lin-racial-slur-headline/

Clemmons, A. K. (2011, March 16). Jeremy Lin: NBA's Cinderella story. *ESPN.com.* Retrieved December 1, 2014, from http://sports.espn.go.com/dallas/news/story?id=6099342

Dhamoon, R. (2009). *Identity/Difference politics: How difference is produced and why it matters.* Toronto: University of British Columbia Press.

Dua, E., & Lawrence, B. (2005). Decolonizing antiracism. *Social Justice, 32*(4), 120–143.

Fanon, F. (2008). *Black skin, white masks.* (R. Philcox, Trans). New York: Grove Press.

Gao, F. (2010). A comparative analysis of the meaning of model minority among ethnic Koreans in China and the United States. *Comparative Education, 46*(2), 207–222.

Golliver, B. (2012, February 24). Jeremy Lin: Bias provides 'chip on shoulder.' *Cbssports. com*. Retrieved December 1, 2014, from http://www.cbssports.com/mcc/blogs/entry/22748484/34980303

Gregory, S. (2012, February 27). Linsanity! *Time*. Retrieved December 1, 2014, from http://content.time.com/time/magazine/article/0,9171,2107031,00.html

Hage, G. (2000). *White nation: Fantasies of white supremacy in a multicultural society*. New York: Routledge.

Hall, S. (1997). The spectacle of the 'other.' In S. Hall (Ed.), *Representation: Cultural representations and signifying practices* (pp. 223–290). London, UK: Open University.

Jeremy Lin's Team. (2012, February 16). *New York Times*. Retrieved December 1, 2014, fromhttp://www.nytimes.com/2012/02/17/opinion/jeremy-lins-team.html

Kalman-Lamb, N. (2013). The athlete as model minority subject: Jose Bautista and Canadian multiculturalism. *Social Identities 19* (2), 238–253.

Keown, T. (2012, February 14). Jeremy Lin's HS coach is surprised, too. Retrieved December 1, 2014, from *ESPN.com*. http://espn.go.com/espn/commentary/story/_/id/7574452/jeremy-lin-high-school-coach-surprised-too

Kibria, N. (2002). *Becoming Asian American: Second-generation Chinese and Korean American identities*. Baltimore, MD: The Johns Hopkins University Press.

Kim, C. J. (1999). The racial triangulation of Asian Americans. *Politics & Society, 27*(1), 105–138.

Lee, J. K.-J. (2002). Where the talented tenth meets the model minority: The price of privilege in Wideman's "Philadelphia Fire" and Lee's "Native Speaker." *NOVEL: A Forum on Fiction, 35*(2/3), 231–257.

Lee, S. J. (1996). *Unraveling the "model minority" stereotype: Listening to Asian American youth*. New York: Teachers College Press.

Luo, M. (2012, February 11). Lin's appeal: Faith, pride and points. *New York Times*. Retrieved December 1, 2014, from http://www.nytimes.com/2012/02/12/sports/basketball/the-knicks-jeremy-lin-faith-pride-and-points.html?pagewanted=all

Mackey, E. (2002). *The house of difference: Cultural politics and national identity in Canada*. Toronto: University of Toronto Press.

Palumbo-Liu, D. (1994). Los Angeles, Asians, and perverse ventriloquisms: On the functions of Asian America in the recent American imaginary. *Public Culture, 6*(2), 365–381.

Park, M. (2012, August 24). Asian fans cheer 'Linsanity.' *CNN.com*. Retrieved December 1, 2014, from http://www.cnn.com/2012/08/24/world/jeremy-lin-hong-kong

Puar, J. K., & Rai, A. (2004). The remaking of a model minority: Perverse projectiles under the specter of (counter)terrorism. *Social Text, 22*(3), 75–104.

Sharma, N. (2006). *Home economics: Nationalism and the making of 'migrant workers' in Canada*. Toronto: University of Toronto Press.

Torre, P. S. (2012, February 20). From couch to clutch. *Sports Illustrated*. Retrieved December 1, 2014, fromhttp://sportsillustrated.cnn.com/vault/article/magazine/MAG1194909/2/index.htm

Torre, P. S. (2012, February 27). A run like no other. *Sports Illustrated*. Retrieved December 1, 2014, from http://sportsillustrated.cnn.com/vault/article/magazine/MAG1195161/2/index.htm

CHAPTER 13

PLEASING THE "AUNTIES"

Navigating Community Expectations within the Model Minority both in the United States and in India

Amardeep K. Kahlon

In his memoir *In Hanuman's Hands*, best-selling Asian Indian American author Cheeni Rao (2009) writes of a time when he went to his mother after being expelled from college. His mother closed the door on him, saying, "I can do nothing more for you. You are now in Hanuman's Hands." Hanuman, who is part ape and part human, is a Hindu deity who symbolizes the eternal struggle of good against evil. Hanuman represents the good. In a collection of stories about South Asian students, Asha Gupta, an Asian Indian American student, candidly reflects how deeply she has struggled with familial expectations: "My obsession with making my family proud and honoring my culture is at the crux of my struggles with identity. This worry extends to almost every aspect of my life" (Garrod & Kilkenny, 2007, p. 134–135). Literature, and my own experiences, suggest that there is more behind the Asian Indian American success story than meets the eye. It is not a one-dimensional, flat book. In reality, it is a pop-up, four-dimensional book that has multiple layers existing beneath the plain pages on top.

Killing the Model Minority Stereotype: Asian American Counterstories and Complicity,
pages 219–232.

There is limited knowledge and understanding of the Asian Indian American population that is burdened by family expectations, community expectations, institutional expectations, and their own self-expectations of academic and professional excellence. The paucity of research on this population creates the invisible minority where students' needs may be ignored based on unfounded assumptions on the part of the community, the family, and the institution.

The present chapter is based on a study conducted in the Southern United States at an elite public university named Southern State University.[1] This hermeneutic, phenomenological study revealed the pressure some Asian Indian American students face when they deal with issues of family honor.

Asian Indian Americans appear to be the great American success story with successes in politics, business, and now even in the Miss America pageant. However, upon closer scrutiny, the Asian Indian American story (and Asian American story overall) is not at all simple, and it is becoming increasingly complex, far more varied and nuanced than most people believe. The model minority stereotype, rather than being helpful for the Asian American community, tends to silence and render invisible the complexity of the Asian American community. It also isolates the Asian American community from other communities of color because of the subtext of the stereotype—the notion of "model" minority presumes that something is wrong with other (non-model) minorities.

In order to fully understand why Asian Indian Americans are known as a model minority, it is worthy to mention some of the success stories of the visible members of this population. I provide this context not to advance the notion of model minority. On the contrary, I highlight these so-called success stories in order to provide a landscape for the perpetuation of the model minority myth (*cf.* Petersen, 1966). There are many Asian Indian Americans who have achieved great honors and have been exemplified in the national media. Although they have been largely overlooked in the literature (Mehta, 2011), Asian Indian Americans have been touted as the model minority both in media outlets and in population statistics. According to a 2007 U.S. Census Bureau report, roughly sixty-eight percent of Asian Indian Americans had a bachelor's degree compared to the national average of twenty-seven percent (Suro, Kocchar, Passel, & Escobar, 2007). The median income of Asian Indian Americans is $51,000, whereas the median income of the U.S. population as a whole is around $44,000 (Suro et al., 2007). It is estimated that sixty-one percent of Asian Indian Americans in the United States are in managerial, executive, and professional occupations, compared to forty-five percent for the total Asian-American population and thirty-four percent for the total U.S. population (Suro et al., 2007; Wadhwa, Saxenian, Rissing, & Gereffi, 2007).

As entrepreneurs, Asian Indian Americans have earned a reputation for themselves. Among engineering and technology startup firms in the United States, twenty-six percent listed an Asian Indian as a founder or co-founder. This number

---

[1] A pseudonym.

suggests that Indians have started more companies than immigrants from the UK, China, Japan, and Taiwan combined ("Indian Americans—A Story of Achievement", 2000; Wadhwa et al., 2007).

Asian Indian Americans have also made gains in political fields that had erstwhile been elusive to them. Indian-born Bobby Jindal, a Republican whose birth name was Piyush Jindal, is the current governor of Louisiana. A 2010 cover of *Newsweek* features Nikki Haley, the Republican governor from South Carolina, as the new face of the aging white Republican Party (The Face of the New South, 2011). Nikki Haley is a second generation Asian Indian American who was born to Sikh parents. She won the South Carolina governor's race by a wide margin and became the first female, non-white governor of the state (Davenport & Adcox, 2010). Last, but not least, is Kamala Harris, the new Attorney General of California, who has been touted by *The New York Times* as one of the seventeen women most likely to be the first female president of the United States (Zernike, 2008). In 2013, Nina Davuluri became the first Asian American to be crowned Miss America—she is of Asian Indian origin. Thus, not only have Asian Indian Americans, like the larger Asian American group, built a reputation for themselves for academic achievement, but they have also made forays into the world of public service, elected government, and social circuits. These statistics are remarkable considering the Asian Indian American immigrants' journey from 1965, when they were finally allowed to bring their families into the United States.

What is not evident is the other, less visible and important side of the Asian Indian American story—the fact that this community is not monolithic. In the U.S., the Asian Indian American community differs in all the ways that other ethnic and racial groups do: according to socioeconomic status, English fluency, immigrant experience, as well as the contexts in which various families have arrived to the U.S. In actuality, Asian Indian American students represent both ends of the achievement spectrum and everything in between. While they are depicted as high achievers, they are also average and most in need. The proliferation of the stereotype of the nerdy Asian is dangerously limited and only presents a skewed view of the real experiences of this diverse group. There is no single or unbending Asian Indian American narrative.

Cultural plurality can create a cultural conflict between children and parents. The birth culture, which the children see in the home, directly clashes with the dominant culture outside the home (Das & Kemp, 1997; Farver, Narang, & Bhadha, 2002). Conflict arises when the children attempt to either blend the two dichotomous cultures together or try to create an impermeable membrane between the two (Gupta, 1997). Not only does this lead to conflict, it may also lead to a confused state of identity: a commonly used term among youth of Asian Indian descent is *ABCD* or *American Born Confused Desi*[2] (Gupta, 1997), indicating that youth have a difficult time reconciling these two identities.

---

[2] Desi refers to an individual of South Asian origin living abroad.

Most Asian Indian American parents are very involved in the academic and social choices that their children make (Ang & Goh, 2006; Baptiste, 2005; Farver et al., 2002). In fact, some parents are willing to sacrifice the happiness of their child to ensure that they secure a prestigious major or career—the two most common among Asian Indians being the highly competitive fields of medicine and engineering (Dundes, Cho, & Kwak, 2009). When students are faced with such pressures, they may seek support from their peer groups, from institutional services such as counseling, or from their families (Atri & Sharma, 2006). Asian Indian American students face challenges when they visit college counseling centers, as many counselors may not recognize the cultural and ethnic components of student stress (Yoo, Burrola, &Steger, 2010). In addition, among Asian Indian Americans, family support can be a challenge as family honor is tied to the academic achievement of the student (Ly, 2008; Saran, 2007). Family honor, in a large way, involves pleasing the "aunties,"[3] or the community. It is for this reason that failure is shunned and that the aim is to achieve the highest academic success. Failure is perceived as dishonorable and not in keeping with Asian Indian beliefs and cultural norms (Tewari, 2002).

These stressors can manifest themselves in significant and tragic ways: the Centers for Disease Control (CDC) and the National Institute of Mental Health (NIMH) both list Asian Americans as a whole at a higher risk of suicide (McFadden, 2010), with the former reporting that the suicide rate among Asian American youth between the ages of 15 and 24 is much higher than other groups (Leong, Leach, Yeh, & Chou, 2007). The pressures of conforming to the model minority and lack of communication with parents are cited as leading factors in suicide among Asian Americans (Cohen, 2007). Further, there is an internalization of the pressures related to the aforementioned factors.

Thus, the combination of cultural value conflicts and high academic expectations sets the stage for mental stress and anxiety among members of the Asian American population, of which Asian Indian Americans are the second largest group.

The scholarship on Asian Indian American college students is sparse. This has frustrated scholars of higher education. In my consultation with Professor Rupam Saran of City University of New York, she confirmed the paucity of research on Asian Indian Americans and lamented how she was forced to use the broader Asian American group as the basis for her research on Asian Indian Americans (R. Saran, personal communication, October 17, 2011). She also stressed the urgent need for more and immediate research on this population. Saran (2007), in her research, examined how the complexities of the model minority phenomenon impacted the experiences of Asian Indian students. Saran investigated family influences on academic achievement by studying the downsides of positive stereotyp-

---

[3] In the Asian Indian American community, any woman who is older—whether a friend or a relative— is known as Aunty.

ing. Results of Saran's observations and interviews in three elite schools in New York City revealed that the model minority status had created identity issues for Asian Indian students. They were not white, but they were considered "honorary Whites." Students equated being Indian with hard work, high grades, and high teacher/parent expectations. Saran suggests that the students in the study came to school with rich cultural and social capital. However, Saran's study also revealed the dark side of the model minority label. Students were constantly reconstructing their identity while dealing with the stress of being labeled as high achievers. The students were forced to fit into an identity "given to them by a dominant culture" (Saran, 2007, p. 76).

Asian Indian students are caught in the crosshairs of family honor, parental expectations, community expectations, and also living up to the label of the model minority. This can create considerable stress for the students.

While there are positives to being the model minority, there also is a permeable membrane that can allow members of this population to cross over to the dark side of this label by inducing stress, anxiety, and sometimes even the worst: suicide. Family and community approval are both very important to Asian Indian American parents. An authoritarian parenting style, combined with a need to protect family honor, lead to intergenerational conflict. A difference in cultural value adoption between the first and second generation also leads to intergenerational conflict. These factors, together, become stressors that generate significant stress for the children. The children feel a need to live up to a certain label or standard. An actual or perceived inability to live up to the high expectations of both parents and community leads to further stress, thus perpetuating a cycle of high expectations and the resultant stress. Based on my research, I present the model that illustrates the interplay of influencing factors on the second-generation children of first generation Asian Indian immigrants. An illustration of this model is presented in Figure 13.1.

The aforementioned model affirms the one that was proposed by Mahalingam (2013) in the Idealized Cultural Identity Model. Mahalingam's model states that an interplay of factors leads to an idealized cultural identity, which leads to resilience, which further leads to depression, anxiety, and stress.

Chandrika, a sophomore at Southern State, perceived that, to her parents, success was in large part a measure of how other people thought of her. As will be evidenced further in this chapter, family honor and community perception are very important in the Asian Indian American population. Chandrika disagreed with this definition of success and further speculated that perhaps her parents looked for societal validation since she was an only child. Chandrika relayed that her parents "always refer back to what other people think." In other words, this translated to what the aunties would think. Chandrika's parents judged her as successful if she was "given as an example as one of the best people in whatever profession [she's pursuing]. I think that for them matters a lot—other people, again, other people's perception of [her success]."

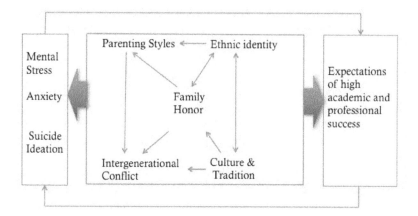

FIGURE 13.1. Model to Represent the Interplay of Factors Influencing the Second-Generation Model Minority. These Factors Lead to Stress and Anxiety on One End and Expectations of High Achievement on the Other.

Chandrika did not subscribe to her parents' definition of success, as she believed that a desire to live by other people's approval could be "taken to an extreme," adding further that she didn't "care about what other people think of [her] as long as [she is] happy and [her] parents are happy." Although her parents also wanted to see her happy, for them it was "about the society and what they think."

Of all the participants in the aforementioned study, Chandrika and Sundar gave perhaps the most impassioned accounts of being stereotyped as model minority. Sundar revealed his opinions about the model minority myth in the following dialogue about being the target of stereotyping:

Sundar: Yes and heavily enforced from both sides.

AK: From both sides? Describe [what you mean by] both sides.

Sundar: Both sides being those within the "Model Minority" and those who have from outside you have got all other groups who form either majority or other I guess "underrepresented minorities" and they look to us as the examples. . . I feel the term is both prescriptive and descriptive. . . in that when people describe me as the "Model Minority" it's not only an unsaid or unvoiced expectation that I am supposed to perform better, it's said, it's very explicitly said, oh but you are Indian of course you have gotten A on this test. Or oh but you are Indian of course you are an engineer or a doctor or related profession. And in that sense I am definitely against the use of that term, I mean it's very valid, very applicable, very useful term and it's required in order to discuss this issue, but hearing myself described as part of "Model Minority" it always creates this feeling of uneasiness in myself, because it feels like it's an unfair expectation, it's not that I am supposed to do better than other people because of my ethnicity or because of my background, but on the other hand it is very useful as a descriptor and I can definitely see why it is so prevalent and used today, because every time we talk about the "Model Minority" in this fashion, we are describing something that's very real and very clear and very easily backed up by statistical methods. . . it's a useful descriptor, I don't like it being applied to myself but I definitely see why it is.

Aishwarya, another sophomore at Southern State, cautioned against labeling a population in a certain manner since "every race, every culture, every group has its own stereotype and there are people who fit in and there are people who don't, but at the same time putting that label on there doesn't make it true." Chandrika also conveyed the pitfalls of being labeled a model minority. She spoke of the stress it caused for her and possibly for other Asian Indian American students. The kind of stress she described could have far-reaching repercussions for the student's physical, mental, and emotional health as well as towards their academic progress. She described her dilemma:

So at some instances, I feel embarrassed to ask for help for Math and Science because people perceive me as already knowing it, so I feel like if I ask for help then they will think I am stupid, but I don't do that anymore, but I definitely did that in high school and summer freshman year because when you are in your top programs and you are Indian or you are Asian then asking for help is kind of like oh wait, do I really belong here? That's the kind of the emotion that you feel.

In addition, Chandrika indicated that the stress of the model minority label was hardly one-dimensional; rather, it was all encompassing and multi-dimensional. She said why it was extremely stressful: "I am expected to perform not only what my parents want me to do and what I want to do myself and not only what my [own] community expects me to do, but what people outside of my Indian community expect me to do." Two participants, Kira and Paarth, felt that being labeled a model minority was an honor and an advantage. Chandrika did not feel that being labeled a model minority was an honor; rather she said it was "quite the reverse." She cautioned against becoming complacent about the label or embracing the label:

It gives you kind of a disadvantage because you are put on another level that you may not already be at. . . you maybe up the same level as the white kid applying or the Latino kid applying and if you [are] already put at that level before they have even had a chance like assess you as like an individual person, independent of color and race and ethnic standing. . . if you already expect it to perform at a higher level than the other people applying and you don't need it, it's not fair. . . I feel like society should definitely know that they should stop trying to put people in certain categories. . . look at American kids, there are so many different levels of intelligence and you can say that oh, well Jewish people tend to be smarter, it's like no, maybe that Jewish kid hung out with an impoverished neighborhood in New York or something and he didn't have the prep school education or anything then you are going to judge him against all of the other Jewish kids that went to prep school and that's not fair.

Among Asian Indian Americans, family honor is foundational as most parental decisions are deeply rooted in protecting and enhancing the honor and prestige of the family. Activities that dishonor the family are strongly discouraged. Children are taught from a young age to care about "what the aunties think." Of the eight participants in this study, six reported family honor to be at the forefront of nearly every action and decision regarding their future.

For Gia, one of the study participants, family honor played a more important role in her parents' expectation of good citizenship than academics. They expected her to represent the family in a manner that would uphold the family name in the community. Gia reported that her grandparents, who were two generations removed from her, were more subscribed to the concept. Since she grew up in a joint family, where her grandparents lived in the same house, for them "it's more of an academics equals family honor than it is for [her] parents."

Family honor permeated all aspects of the students' lives. Aishwarya spoke passionately about family honor throughout the interviews. Speaking of career choice, she reported that the "pressure is definitely there" to "be a doctor...or something," so that parents could tell people "that their kid is whatever, is studying to become whatever, or has a degree in whatever. It's more about that social pride there which kind of furthers a cycle [of conflict] in my opinion." Aishwarya found it hard to subscribe to the notion of family honor recalling that, at times, her mother, fearing what the "aunties" might think of her, even critiqued her appearance. Aishwarya related that while she attended a local Asian Indian wedding, her mother commented on Aishwarya's hair thusly: "You should do [your hair a certain way] because someone else did something...[it was all] about other people." Aishwarya found that this was "a very ridiculously way to live your life based on what other people might say or think or what they do." She said, "I really don't care what [other people] think." Such divergent thinking often created conflict in Aishwarya's household: "Perception is a lot more important to my parents as to what other people will think." Aishwarya perceived that, to her parents, it was very important to maintain a clean public image for fear of how friends and community members would judge the family.

Like Aishwarya, Chandrika was distressed that family honor played a big role in academic and non-academic activities. In the traditional family where she was raised, the opinion of other members of the Indian community was important. Chandrika perceived that her activities were judged through the matchmaking lens. Further, Chandrika reported that her parents worried about the time when they would search for a match for her and that, when that time came, what the "aunties" thought and knew about her could impact the marriage plan. Chandrika expressed, "I honestly don't care what the aunty down the street thinks," adding that she was not "going to marry someone according to [the aunties'] wishes." Instead, she said, "I am going to pick someone that [me and my parents] agree on." While Chandrika completely understood the underlying reasons behind her parents' beliefs, she labeled such thinking as "dumb," and she conveyed that her parents' "opinion mattered the most," not what "what aunties and uncles say at parties."

Chandrika relayed that her parents constantly watched how her actions and those of her friends could possibly impact Chandrika's standing in the community. When a friend hacked into Chandrika's Facebook account and playfully changed her status to something that her father deemed inappropriate, Chandrika's father called not just the friend who changed the status, but her other friends as well to chide them. Chandrika speculated that her father's reactions arose from his concern that community members could have seen this "inappropriate" status, and it would present an opportunity for community members to gossip about Chandrika. Although Chandrika understood the roots of her parents' traditional thinking as being based on their own upbringing in India, she still questioned the constant dependence on validation from the aunties.

Likewise, Sundar, an Engineering student, grappled with the importance of family honor in every aspect of life. He disclosed that most academic and personal decisions in his life were a "public relations campaign" to uphold the family honor. He explained:

> I think family honor is more or less the reason why any choice that's made or any large decision has to either be a) initiated by my parents or b) approved by my parents. So, I have, at least in that weird twilight zone between the Indian culture and this culture, I do have some sort of leeway and that I can initiate a lot more choices than they usually would make on my behalf. But at the same time, the issue of honor is still foremost and to them [and] I still need to get their approval.

Sundar lamented that, at times, he felt that honor became more important to his parents than his personal happiness. Although he "[accepted in] some fashion because it is a genuine statement to be made," he also felt that "[the emphasis on family honor] is blown out of proportion sometimes." Regardless, Sundar "[went] along with it just for [his] parents' sake."

Further, Sundar indicated that, when asked by the aunties how school was going, the response could not be a perfunctory "okay." A casual question produced "an undercurrent of actual expectation that you are going to provide a positive answer and that is going to be acceptable to them, because if it's not then they will carry the conversation further trying to figure out what's going wrong." The family honor notion among Asian Indian Americans tied closely with the model minority stereotype, where everyone within and outside the community expects the students to perform well. The pressures of family honor created stress for the students and impacted intergenerational communication. Parental communication towards students about grades, as in Aishwarya, Sundar, and Chandrika's cases, was, in part, motivated by the stress of proving to—or bragging to—people within the community about the child's academic choices and academic performance. The pressures to perform well constantly, to never reveal weaknesses to anyone including friends, to live within traditional boundaries while trying to succeed in a modern culture, to always watch over one's shoulder to see if one is living up to community expectations, all led to stress and intergenerational communication issues.

Sundar captured the Asian Indian American sentiment towards counseling and seeking relief from the stress created by intergenerational issues and cultural issues mentioned above thusly:

> [My parents] don't distinguish between personal stress and academic stress or any of those other things that may cause me to seek [counseling] services. So if there is anything wrong like that it should never be broadcast. And however the family or the community wants to deal with it is varied in the response, but the first step is that nobody else should know about it. . . There is definitely an expectation that students in the "Model Minority" or Asian Americans within that subset are not expected to have problems like this. And if we do that we are not ever supposed to advertise it or develop it or show it at all to anybody else, because admitting that would be a sign of weakness—that's just unacceptable.

The participants critiqued the model minority stereotype, describing it as "unrealistic" and "too much pressure." They blamed the stereotype for creating a "grade-grubbing mentality" and what Chandrika called "G.P.A. whores." Contrary to being an honor, the model minority myth generated stress as it created pressure on these students to perform better than others. It resulted in a misrepresentation of the entire Asian Indian American population and did not account for within-group differences. A nuanced finding was that two participants perceived the model minority stereotype to be an honor since it set them apart from their peers. The findings that the model minority stereotype generated stress for the majority of this sample aligned with prior research conducted by Baptiste (2005), Saran (2007), and Lee, Juon, Martinez, Bawa, and Ma (2009).

There was an expectation from the parents that the students would uphold the family honor, both through their public behaviors as well as through their academic and professional accomplishments. Pleasing the "aunties" was very important to the parents and less important to the participants, thus generating intergenerational issues.

There is a soul-searching needed within the community about how parental desires and wishes are communicated to the students. The participants in this study were resentful of constantly having to please the "aunties." They wanted to learn from their own mistakes and did not want their lives to be scripted: where in one stage of life they went to school, in another they got married, and in a third they had children—thereafter they were free to explore. They wanted to explore now.

It is my hope that the publication of these findings will generate a new dialogue between first generation parents and their second-generation children. I also wish to clarify that the purpose of this chapter is not to criticize Asian Indian parents, rather to bring forth the perspectives of the children and enable members of the Asian Indian American community and the non-Asian community to understand the feelings of these students.

RECOMMENDATIONS FOR FUTURE RESEARCH

While this study was a relatively small phenomenological, qualitative study conducted on eight undergraduate students at Southern State University, a tier-one research university in the Southern United States, it may serve as a springboard for future studies.

With the exception of one student, the sample in this study belonged to middle class and upper middle class socioeconomic status. An examination of an Asian Indian population from a low socioeconomic status (SES) would benefit the existing body of literature on Asian Indians, both for institutions and for the larger Asian Indian American community. Such research would provide valuable information on what role SES plays in the achievement orientation of this particular ethnic group in comparison with other minorities.

While conducting the current study, I was intrigued about the prospect of interviewing first generation Asian Indian American parents in order to get their perspectives on how they perceived their children's interactions with them and what community perceptions and family honor meant to the parents. Research focused on parents would validate the findings of the current study.

The sample in the current study indicated that the attitudes of parents has changed slightly from high school to college. A longitudinal study that follows a selected sample of Asian Indian American students from early high school through early career would provide valuable data on how perceptions about parents change over time. As well, such a study would provide valuable information on how the perceptions of success change for Asian Indian American students and how they negotiate the model minority stereotype at different stages in their academic development.

The values of the second generation Asian Indian American participants in this study were shaped by first-generation parents who immigrated to this country, struggled to settle down, and then made a successful life for themselves. As the students in the current study perceived, first-generation parents wanted success for their children to prevent them from struggling the way the parents did to establish themselves. However, the second-generation children grew up in comfort without the upheaval of migratory distress of the first generation. Research on the third- or even fourth-generation Asian Indian Americans would provide valuable data on whether immigrant experiences drive the pressure to be perfect or if this drive for excellence can be attributed to a race or class of people.

Yet another area of potential in the study of Asian Indian Americans is a second-generation Asian Indian American sample at the community college level along with the parents. A sample of students who found themselves at the community college by choice, by circumstance, or as a mandate from their family could help provide valuable information on how community pressure and the demands of family honor cause these parents to describe their children's academic journey.

Finally, there is a paucity of scholarship about Asian Indian American students who have chosen to completely drop out of college or not pursue a college education, contrary to their parents' expectations. During the interviews, one participant informed me that children who dropped out or failed are used as warning examples by parents to forewarn children what could happen to them if they did not aim for high academic achievement. Far from receiving any sympathy or empathy, struggling Asian Indian American students appeared to be ridiculed or silenced. While there has been scholarship about the accolades that Asian Indian American students earn, there appears to be a lack of scholarship about those Asian Indian American students who prove that the model minority is but a myth.

Questions for Reflection

1. In the model, the author seems to suggest that family honor is at the heart of the model minority dilemma. Based on your readings and research, along with the conclusions of this study, do you agree or disagree with this conclusion? Explain your answer with supporting citations.
2. In this chapter the author suggests that the model minority is not an honor, rather it is the contrary. How does the model minority myth drive a wedge between different ethnicities?
3. This chapter was based on a study conducted at an elite public university in the Southern United states. Is that representative of the Asian American population? Why or why not?
4. One of the study participant states that "every race, every culture, every group has its own stereotype and there are people who fit in and there are people who don't, but at the same time putting that label on there doesn't make it true." Comment on this in the broader context of all ethnic minorities and the stereotyping thereof.
5. What are the conclusions you draw from this chapter about the model minority myth?

REFERENCES

Ang, R., & Goh, D. (2006). Authoritarian parenting style in Asian societies: A cluster- analytic investigation. *Contemporary Family Therapy, 28*(1), 131–151. doi: 10.1007/s10591–006–9699–y

Atri, A., & Sharma, M. (2006). Designing a mental health education program for South Asian international students in United States. *Californian Journal of Health Promotion, 4*(2), 144–154.

Baptiste, D. A. (2005). Family therapy with East Indian immigrant parents rearing children in the United States: Parental concerns, therapeutic issues, and recommendations. *Contemporary Family Therapy, 27*(3), 345–366. doi: 10.1007/s10591–005–6214–9

Cohen, E. (2007). Push to achieve tied to suicide in Asian-American women. *CNN News.* Retrieved December 1, 2014, from http://edition.cnn.com/2007/HEALTH/05/16/asian.suicides/.

Das, A. K., & Kemp, S. F. (1997). Between two worlds: Counseling South Asian Americans. *Journal of Multicultural Counseling & Development, 25*(1), 23–33.

Davenport, J., & Adcox, S. (2010, November 3). Tea Party-backed Haley SC's 1st woman governor. *ABC News.* Retrieved December 1, 2014, from http://abcnews.go.com/Politics/wireStory?id=12039726

Dundes, L., Cho, E., & Kwak, S. (2009). The duty to succeed: Honor versus happiness in college and career choices of East Asian students in the United States. *Pastoral Care in Education, 27*(2), 135–156. doi: 10.1080/02643940902898960

The Face of the New South. (2011). In *Nikki Haley for Governor* retrieved December 1, 2014, from http://www.nikkihaley.com/newsweek-coverstory-on-nikki-haley-woman-on-the-verge

Farver, J. A. M., Narang, S. K., & Bhadha, B. R. (2002). East meets West: Ethnic identity, acculturation, and conflict in Asian Indian families. *Journal of Family Psychology, 16*(3), 338–350. doi: 10.1037/0893–3200.16.3.338

Garrod, A., & Kilkenny, R. (Eds.). (2007). *Balancing two worlds: Asian American college students tell their life Stories* (1st ed.). Ithaca, NY: Cornell University Press.

Gupta, M. D. (1997). "What is Indian about You?": A gendered, transnational approach to ethnicity. *Gender and Society, 11*(5), 572–596. doi: 10.1177/089124397011005004

Indian Americans—A story of achievement. (2000, September). Retrieved December 1, 2014, from http://www.indianembassy.org/indusrel/clinton_india/india_americans.html

Lee, S., Juon, H.-S., Martinez, G., Bawa, J., & Ma, G. (2009). Model minority at risk: Expressed needs of mental health by Asian American young adults. *Journal of Community Health, 34*(2), 144–152. doi: 10.1007/s10900–008–9137–1

Leong, F. T. L., Leach, M. M., Yeh, C., & Chou, E. (2007). Suicide among Asian Americans: What do we know? What do we need to know? *Death Studies, 31*(5), 417–434. doi: 10.1080/07481180701244561

Ly, P. (2008). Caught between two cultures. *Diverse Issues in Higher Education, 25*(14), 24–25. doi: 1562229201

Mahalingam, R. (2013). Model minority myth: Engendering cultural psychology of Asian immigrants. In E. L. Grigorenko (Ed.), *Handbook of U.S. immigration and education* (pp. 119–136). New York: Springer.

McFadden, C. (2010, January 6). The growing rate of depression, suicide among Asian American students, *Pacific Citizen.* Retrieved December 1, 2014, from http://www.pacificcitizen.org/site/details/tabid/55/selectmoduleid/373/ArticleID/490/reftab/0/Default.aspx?title=The_Growing_Rate_of_Depression_Suicide_Among_Asian_American_Students_

Mehta, S. (2011). *Achievement motivation, acculturation, and gender as predictors of psychological well-being in Asian Indian students in the U.S.* Unpublished dissertation. Alliant Interntional University, San Francisco, CA.

Petersen, W. (1966, January 6). Success story, Japanese-American style. *New York Times Magazine.* Retrieved December 1, 2014, from http://inside.sfuhs.org/dept/history/US_History_reader/Chapter14/modelminority.pdf

Rao, C. (2009). *In Hanuman's hands: A memoir.* New York: HarperOne.

Saran, R. (2007). Model minority imaging in New York: The situation with second generation Asian Indian learners in middle and secondary schools. *Anthropologist, 2,* 67–79. Retrieved December 1, 2014, from http://krepublishers.com/06–Special%20Volume-Journal/T-Anth-00–Special%20Volumes/Anth-SI-02–Indian%20Diaspora-Web/T-Anth-SI-02–06–067–079-Saran-R/T-Anth-SI-02–06–067–079–Saran-R-Tt.pdf

Suro, R., Kocchar, R., Passel, J., & Escobar, G. (2007, February). The American community—Asians: 2004. *Asian Community Survey Reports.* Washington, DC: U.S. Census Bureau. Retrieved December 1, 2014, from http://www.census.gov/prod/2007pubs/acs-05.pdf

Tewari, N. (2002). *Asian Indian American clients presenting at a university counseling center: An exploration of their concerns and a comparison to other groups.* Unpublished dissertation. Southern Illinois University at Carbondale, Carbondale, IL.

Wadhwa, V., Saxenian, A., Rissing, B., & Gereffi, G. (2007). America's new immigrant enterpreneurs. Retrieved December 1, 2014, from http://people.ischool.berkeley.edu/~anno/Papers/Americas_new_immigrant_entrepreneurs_I.pdf

Yoo, H. C., Burrola, K. S., & Steger, M. F. (2010). A preliminary report on a new measure: Internalization of the Model Minority Myth Measure (IM-4) and its psychological correlates among Asian American college students. *Journal of Counseling Psychology, 57*(1), 114–127. doi: 10.1037/a0017871

Zernike, K. (2008, May 18). She just might be president someday. *New York Times,* p. 1.

CHAPTER 14

PERPETUATING THE MODEL MINORITY STEREOTYPE IN THE FACE OF HIGHLY VISIBLE, AND HIGHLY NEGATIVE, EXTERNAL EVENTS

Daisy Ball

INTRODUCTION

On April 16, 2007, the deadliest school shooting in U.S. history occurred. Seung-Hui Cho, an undergraduate student at Virginia Tech, killed 32 people, shot and wounded 17 others, and then took his own life (Virginia Tech Review Panel, 2007). A little over one year later, Chinese graduate student Haiyang Zhu stabbed and decapitated his acquaintance, Xin Yang, as they chatted over coffee in the Au Bon Pain Café in the Graduate Life Center at Virginia Tech (Virginia Tech Review Panel, 2007). In this chapter, I consider the possibility that since these horrific events, the status of Asian Americans on campus may have transformed.

Killing the Model Minority Stereotype: Asian American Counterstories and Complicity,
pages 233–262.
Copyright © 2015 by Information Age Publishing
233

TAKING A GLANCE BACK: CAMPUS
CLIMATE AT VIRGINIA TECH

The events of April 16th brought to mind earlier research I conducted, with William E. Snizek, on campus climate at Virginia Tech (see Ball & Snizek, 2006). The purpose of our project was to examine the values and concerns of college students as expressed through desktop graffiti. According to Abel and Buckley (1977), graffiti can be a revelatory form of communication:

> Graffiti is a form of communication that is both personal and free of the everyday social restraints that normally prevent people from giving uninhibited reign to their thoughts. As such, these sometimes crude inscriptions offer some intriguing insights into the people who author them and into the society in which these people belong (Abel & Buckley, 1977, p. 3).[1]

Therefore, we took desktop graffiti as our centerpiece of study: we assessed the nature and extent to which college students at Virginia Tech engaged in desktop graffiti, arguing that the graffiti found on student desktops is an excellent unobtrusive (Webb, Campbell, Schwartz, & Sechrest., 2000), or indirect, measure of student values, attitudes, fantasies and/or behavioral dispositions.

The academic study of graffiti goes back decades, to the publication of the first scholarly study of graffiti in 1935. Read (1935) was first inspired to study graffiti after a trip out West in which he observed a great deal of graffiti on the stalls of many a public restroom. As Read puts it, "It was borne upon me that these inscriptions are a form of folk-lore that should be made the subject of a scholarly study" (1935, p. 17). And, as Reisner (1974) notes in his *Encyclopedia of Graffiti*, graffiti is an especially valuable social artifact because it is "[t]he voice of the common man...topics too sensitive, too bigoted, too outrageous for the official version are the natural province" (Reisner,1974, p. 6). Graffiti allows for self-expression; moreover, graffiti affords one the ability to weigh on topics that may be too delicate for public discourse. Graffiti may also reveal valuable information about social deviance: "The analysis of graffiti could provide vital information for investigations of the breakdown of discipline and order, or into the workings of the moronic or ego-starved or bored mind" (Reisner, 1974, p. 8).

Components of "Indoor" Graffiti

Graffiti as an artifact is generally categorized as either "indoor" or "outdoor;" our analysis of desktop graffiti is necessarily classified as indoor. Previous analyses of indoor graffiti have focused on graffiti found in bathroom stalls; sex is the most common theme of lavatory graffiti. Our study analyzed a novel surface: that

---

[1] According to the *American Heritage Dictionary* (2000), "The word *graffiti* is a plural noun in Italian. In English, *graffiti* is far more common than the singular form *graffito* and is mainly used as a singular noun in much the same way data is" (p. 570). Therefore, in this chapter I use the term graffiti.

of the student desktop. While not identical, desktop and lavatory graffiti are both classified as "indoor," and therefore share similarities.

Gonos, Mulkren, and Poushinsky (1976) argue that graffiti provides writers an outlet through which they are able to express sentiments no longer acceptable in public discourse; viewpoints unpopular in the public sphere may be covertly expressed via the underground, or informal, method of graffiti writing. The stuff of graffiti, then, is most often a reflection of otherwise repressed values, attitudes, and beliefs, to which stigma has been attached (Goffman, 1963; Gonos et al., 1976).

Scholars of graffiti distinguish between the graffiti writing of males compared to females. Male graffiti tends to be more negative, including racially prejudiced graffiti (e.g., Bruner & Kelso, 1981; Otta, 1993; Schreer & Strichartz, 1997; Stocker et al., 1972), more homophobic graffiti (e.g., Schreer & Strichartz, 1997; Stocker et al., 1972), and more insults (e.g., Bruner & Kelso, 1981; Otta, 1993). Females are more likely to ask questions (Fitzpatrick, Mulac, & Dindia, 1995; Tannen, 1994), disclose personal information (Dindia & Allen, 1992), and refer to emotion (Fitzpatrick et al., 1995; Goldsmith & Dun, 1997; Mulac, Studley, & Blau, 1990). Males are more likely to give opinions (Mulac et al., 1990), use expletives (Bayard & Krishnayya, 2001; Limbrick, 1991), and use longer sentences (Mulac, 1989; Mulac et al., 1990; as cited in Green 2003).

Our Study of Graffiti

Campus climate is a hot topic across a range of disciplines. Through our novel study of student-authored desktop graffiti, we sought to add to the literature on campus climate. We collected graffiti from a random sample of nine classrooms in two buildings on campus. The graffiti from each room was analyzed according to amount and content.

Following Gonos et al. (1976), we expected to find graffiti that reflected sentiments that might best be described as "non-P.C.": we expected to find graffiti referencing sex and race, generally considered to be two topics that are in many ways "off limits" in contemporary American culture.

Our study did encounter a basic ecological fallacy—one does not know who is truly responsible for the graffiti being analyzed—is every student participating, or just a handful? Such fallacies as the ecological fallacy stem from the incorrect pairing of theory and methods. Figure 14.1 below depicts the various fallacies possible when conclusions are incorrectly drawn in this manner.

According to Robinson (1950), an ecological fallacy is "[s]imply drawing inferences about an individual's behavior on the bases of coincidence of two grouped properties" (Robinson, 1950, p. 351). A related fallacy—the nosnibor fallacy—is simply the reverse of the ecological fallacy: the researcher tries to draw group-level inferences based on individual-level data (Snizek, Fuhrman, & Miller, 1979). Keeping both fallacies in mind, it would be misleading to claim that the results of our study were representative of the student body as a whole: our

Theoretical	Methodological Approach		
Orientation	Low Empirical	Moderately Empirical	Highly Empirical
Realist	**Consistent**	Nosnibor Fallacy	Nosnibor Fallacy
Quasi realist Quasi nominalist	Errors of dummy-variable analysis	**Consistent**	Errors of collapsing data
Nominalist	Ecological Fallacy	Ecological Fallacy	**Consistent**

FIGURE 14.1. Potential Fallacies and Pitfalls Stemming from the Errant Fit Between Theory and Methods. Source: Snizek et al. (1979, p. 206)

data was simply suggestive of aggregate trends and cannot be specifically identified with any student or group of students. However, the data do stand to serve as an *indicator* of the concerns of today's college student.

Moving along, nine classrooms were randomly selected in two buildings of interest on campus—one which typically holds liberal arts classes, and the other which typically holds engineering classes. From these classrooms (six in the liberal arts building, and three in the engineering), every desk was analyzed for the presence of graffiti. Data were collected during the winter break of 2003. A total of 419 desks comprised the sample. The content of every instance of graffiti found on each desk was recorded. In all, 5,285 individual pieces of graffiti were recorded. After discarding 3,527 examples of graffiti that were unintelligible, the remaining 1,758 specimens of graffiti were categorized in order to reveal the most common themes.

Summary of Findings

The most common themes found in our sample of graffiti were, in order of occurrence: Virginia Tech; sex; Greek organizations; and drugs, with Greek organizations and drugs ranking as the third most common theme. For the purposes of this chapter, I will briefly discuss two themes: that of sexual graffiti—*the second most popular category*; and, that of racist graffiti, *one of the least popular categories uncovered*.

The sexual graffiti was primarily concerned with one of two topics: oral sex or anti-homosexual sentiments. Of the 287 pieces of graffiti of a sexual nature analyzed, 109 (37.9%) refer to oral sex and 71 (24.7%) are of an anti-homosexual nature. This finding supports Gonos et al. (1976), who suggest that topics forbidden from public discourse may manifest in the form of indoor graffiti. Public discussions of oral sex, and public expressions of an anti-homosexual nature are both taboo in the present day.

On the other end of the spectrum is racist graffiti, of which a dearth was found: *only seven pieces of the 1,758 pieces of categorized graffiti are of a racist nature*. Each of the seven pieces targets Asians: namely, the graffiti refer to either Vietnamese or Koreans. Some representative examples: "Koreans eat dog," "Go home and fuck yourself, Vietnamese." Relevant to this discussion is that Asian Americans are the largest racial minority group at Virginia Tech. Our findings may suggest that racism tends toward the largest minority group on campus, whomever that may be, rather than the typical black-white dichotomy. Still, we are presented with a puzzle: following Gonos et al. (1976), does the lack of racist graffiti suggest that racism is still alive and well in public discourse? And, what to make of the anti-Asian focus of the graffiti?

ISSUES OF THE PRESENT DAY

The findings from our study of desktop graffiti sparked my interest in assessing campus climate at Virginia Tech following the aforementioned horrific events, this time via in-depth interview. The current chapter was informed by several theoretical paradigms, including the racial threat thesis, the model minority stereotype, and stereotype threat, each of which I will briefly review.

The Racial Threat Thesis

As the relative size of the minority group increases, the racial threat thesis holds, members of the majority group perceive an increased threat to their power. Members of the majority group will respond by taking steps to maintain power in what is seen as a race-based competition for scarce resources (Blalock, 1967; Blauner, 1972; Blumer, 1958). Within the racial threat thesis, there are three central hypotheses: competition over political power; competition over economic resources (Blalock, 1967); and the threat of black-on-white crime (Liska & Chamlin, 1984).

Like all theories, there are limitations to the racial threat thesis. According to D'Alessio, Stolzenberg, and Eitle (2002), while research on racial threat has informed the discipline, it has methodological, conceptual, and theoretical shortfalls. A central problem stems from the multitude of ways the concept of "racial threat" has been measured (D'Alessio et al., 2002). Racial threat has been conceived of as group threat (Blumer, 1958), realistic conflict theory (Bobo, 1988), power threat (Blalock, 1967), threat hypothesis (Liska & Chamlin, 1984), minority group threat (Jacobs & Wood, 1999), social threat (Liska, 1992), and power theory (Giles & Evans, 1986). The definitions have left little conceptual clarity regarding the term "racial threat" (D'Alessio et al., 2002).

Additionally, while there are the three hypotheses within racial threat literature, most studies simply state that racial threat is a result of a change in the size of the black population; as it increases, threat increases (D'Alessio et al., 2002). A handful of studies attempt to distinguish between the various dimensions of racial threat; those that have made this distinction typically include a measure of economic threat. Even fewer specifically measure political threat (see Beck, Massey & Tolnay, 1989; Brown & Warner, 1992; Jacobs & Helms, 1999; Myers, 1990).

D'Alessio et al. (2002) attempt to fill the void by suggesting in their research that political threat, economic threat, and black-on-white crime threat *together* influence social control of blacks.

And this points to an additional shortcoming in racial threat literature: it rarely addresses racial groups outside the black-white dichotomy. This void in the literature directly relates to the present research. As Parker, Stults, and Rice (2005) note, research on additional minority groups should be given increased attention. Considering the significant growth of both the Asian and Hispanic populations in recent decades, considering racial threat only as it relates to blacks and whites presents a limited portrait of reality in the United States (Parker et al., 2005).

Thus, while the phenomenon of racial threat can be illuminating, we can shed more light on the topic. We see that when black-on-white crime goes up, blacks are perceived as an increased threat to whites. Similarly, after 9/11, having a darker complexion and being associated with the Middle East and/or Islam often garnered one negative attention (Collins, 2006). As it stands, Asian Americans are less often considered a threat. There is little fear that they will commit criminal or violent acts; when they have been perceived as a threat, that threat comes in the form of competition, due to their "model minority status" (Chou & Feagin, 2008, pp. 13–14). The present study seeks to understand what happens when Asian Americans come to be seen as a political, economic, and criminal threat.

The Myth of the Model Minority

Stacey Lee (2009), in *Unraveling the Myth of the Model Minority: Listening to Asian American Youth*, presents a concise definition of a complex and problematic stereotype, the myth of the model minority:

> The model minority stereotype depicts Asian Americans as academic superstars. Images of Asian American math geniuses, computer science experts, and high school valedictorians are ingrained in the minds of Americans. According to the stereotype, Asian Americans are successful in school because they work hard and come from cultures that believe in the value of education (Lee, 2009, p. 61).

Both the popular media and scholarly literature have contributed to the perpetuation of this stereotype (Lee, 2009). Popular media accounts of Asian Americans focus on their achievements in school and the workplace (Chou & Feagin, 2008), as have scholarly accounts. There is little attention to intragroup variability among Asian Americans.

While earlier stereotypes concerning Asian Americans cast them as "others," as "outsiders"—consider historian Ronald Takaki's (1993) characterization of early Asian immigrants to the States as "strangers from a different shore," stereotyped as "heathen exotic, and unassimilable" (p. 8)—stereotypes emerging in the U.S. in the 1960s cast a noticeably more positive light on this group. Zia (2000) notes in *Asian American Dreams: The Emergence of an American People*, when turmoil amongst other immigrant groups began to brew, Asian Americans were suddenly recast as the "American Success Story":

> As urban ghettos from Newark, NJ to Watts in Los Angeles erupted into riots and civil unrest, Asian Americans suddenly became the object of 'flattering' media stories. After more than a century of invisibility alternating with virulent headlines and radio broadcasts that advocated eliminating or imprisoning America's Asians, a rash of stories began to extol [their] virtues (p. 46).

This stereotype shift is most commonly attributed to the publication of two influential articles: sociologist William Petersen's 1966 essay "Success Story, Japanese American Style," published in *The New York Times*, and *U.S. News and World Report's* 1966 feature article "Success Story of One Minority Group in U.S." Petersen's essay argued that Japanese Americans were better off, economically and educationally, than all other groups, including Caucasians, while the article from *U.S. News* stated that through "hard work," Asians had become "economically successful" in the U.S. The positive headlines did not stop there—in each decade since, there has been a deluge of success stories featuring Asian Americans. And, political leaders have readily adopted the sentiments of the media, and repeated them in influential discourse. Consider just a few lines from then-President Reagan's "Remarks at a Meeting With Asian and Pacific-American Leaders" (February 23, 1984):

> Asian and Pacific Americans have helped preserve [the American dream] by living up to the bedrock values that make us a good and a worthy people.... It's no wonder that the median income of Asian and Pacific American families is much higher than the total American average. After all, it is values, not programs and policies that serve as our nation's compass. They hold us on course. They point the way to a promising future....

For modern sociologists, however, the "model minority" is a myth. While typically presented as a positive label, social scientists have shown this label to be untrue and in many cases, detrimental.

The statistics offered by journalists and politicians have failed to identify geographic pockets that Asian Americans inhabit—places that have high salaries, but also significantly higher costs of living than other spots in the United States. Thus, alongside all other income-earners, Asian Americans may appear to surpass, but when considered alongside cost of living, a different picture emerges. Consider this from Takaki's (1989) *Strangers From a Different Shore: A History of Asian Americans*:

> ... In their celebration of this "model minority," the pundits and the politicians have exaggerated Asian-American "success" and have created a new myth. Their comparisons of incomes between Asians and whites fail to recognize the regional location of the Asian-American population. Concentrated in California, Hawaii, and New York, Asian Americans reside largely in states with higher incomes but also

higher costs of living than the national average: 59 percent of all Asian Americans lived in these three states in 1980, compared to only 19 percent of the general population (p. 8).

Adherence to the model minority myth has detrimental effects on Asian Americans: they tend to be lumped together as a single group, and a successful one at that; those segments of "Asian American" who are not succeeding, much less thriving, are overlooked or seen as spectacular failures (they've failed even when their culture is so successful!). This has real consequences, including not receiving needed and deserved social services. As Takaki (1989) writes "[For] groups that are not doing well, such as the unemployed Hmong, the Downtown Chinese, the elderly Japanese, the old Filipino farm laborers… to be out of sight is… to be without social services. Thinking Asian Americans have succeeded, government officials have sometimes denied funding for social service programs designed to help Asian Americans learn English and find employment" (p. 8). Moreover, being lumped into a single group denies each sub-group's unique characteristics, and may cause individuals to feel as though they must conform to the expectations of the model minority stereotype (Chou & Feagin, 2008; Takaki, 1989).

Stereotype Threat

Identity contingencies are introduced by Claude M. Steele (2010): These are the circumstances with which you must "deal" in a given situation if you have a given social identity. Identity contingencies influence us from two angles—some constrain our actual behavior. Others, as powerful if not more so due to their subtlety, influence us by adding an "edge" to our experience—something Steele (2010) terms "stereotype threat." Normally socialized members of society have a basic understanding of the general consensus surrounding, say, racial groups, gender roles, socioeconomic standing, etc. Thus, hearkening back to Charles Horton Cooley's (1902, 1909) conception of the "looking-glass self," normally socialized individuals possess a basic understanding of social desirability, and this knowledge impacts our identity. We measure ourselves against the consensus and may even come to identify closely with how the consensus takes stock of us (or how we believe it does).

Social psychologist Gordon Allport (1954) noted that members of a stigmatized group often become "obsessively concerned" when a stereotype related to them is made salient. Reactions range from anger and aggression to anxiety, social withdrawal, and even "self-hating" (Stone, Lynch, Daley, & Smojeling, 1999). Stereotype threat draws our attention to the identity that is being threatened— i.e., women in math classes are more aware of their gender than women buying groceries. Being a member of a negatively stereotyped group poses a substantial threat to self-regard (Crocker, Major, & Steele, 1998). So the woman in a math class, knowing that there is a stereotype that women are not as good as men at mathematics, may identify herself as "bad at math," even with no evidence to back up that claim. Labels in the form of stereotypes have real consequences for those so-labeled in a range of settings.

THE PRESENT STUDY

While my earlier study did not reveal a significant amount of racist graffiti on student desktops at Virginia Tech, that which was revealed stigmatized Asian Americans. I wondered, "Does Virginia Tech house a hostile campus climate for Asian Americans?" How has campus climate for Asian Americans been impacted by the events of April 16th and the GLC incident? At the center of this chapter is my work on race relations following two violent and criminal episodes at Virginia Tech, in which both cases the perpetrators were Asian.

My considerations of the racial threat thesis, the model minority stereotype, and stereotype threat have all been pursuant to my focal research: How have Korean and Chinese American undergraduates at Virginia Tech constructed their identities, and has this identity construction process been affected by the sensational crimes committed by Asians on their campus?

According to the racial threat thesis, African Americans are increasingly viewed as a threat by whites as the size of the African American population increases; they are perceived to pose a growing threat in terms of crime as well as economic and/or political resources (Blalock, 1967; Liska & Chamlin, 1984). Yet the racial threat thesis has not been applied rigorously to other minority groups. Asian Americans are commonly thought of as the model minority (Chou & Feagin, 2008; Lee, 2009), and considered a threat only because of unfair competition—that is, they are thought to be smart and hard-working, thus an economic and possible future political threat. As a group, Asian Americans are not regarded as a criminal threat.

After the mass shooting and public beheading that took place on the campus of Virginia Tech, however, I wondered whether Asian Americans' stereotype threat might be increased. What happens when sensational crimes play against dominant stereotypes? How would members of a minority group perceive their reputation in the community? And how have Asian American students worked to control or modify perceptions of their group following such horrific events?

In order to ascertain the experiences of Asian American undergraduates at Virginia Tech, and in light of the recent horrific events, I conducted in-depth interviews with 18 Korean and Chinese American students from May 2010 through May 2011. I hoped to learn about their experiences at Virginia Tech, and how (or if) those experiences had been impacted by April 16th and/or the GLC incident. I hypothesized that, based on my earlier study on campus climate, Asian Americans may experience a hostile climate at Virginia Tech. I hypothesized that the events of April 16th and the GLC incident may have served to fuel that hostility. I was interested in learning if my Asian American interviewees experienced race-based prejudice and/or discrimination; and, if they perpetuated the model minority stereotype, or worked actively to fight it.

Pseudonym* and Gender**	Race	Place of Birth	Came to the US, if applicable	Class Standing	Major
Annie Chon (F)	Korean American	Virginia	N/A	Junior	Hospitality & Tourism Management
Duncan Lau (M)	Chinese American	China	Age 1.5 yrs	Senior	Biochemistry
Felicia Kang (F)	Chinese American	Virginia	N/A	Junior	Psychology
Fiona Pi (F)	Korean American	Korea	Age 6yrs	Sophomore	Industrial & Systems Engineering
Finn Chio (M)	Chinese American	Virginia	N/A	Freshman	TBD [planning on Electrical Engineering & Computer Science]
Genji Meng (M)	Chinese American	China	Age 14yrs	Senior	Electrical Engineering
Hen Ye (M)	Chinese American	Virginia	N/A	Senior (5th yr)	Accounting; Finance; Management
Josie Chin (F)	Chinese American	China	Age 4yrs	Senior	Industrial & Systems Engineering
Jackson Sa (M)	Korean American	Korea	Age 15yrs	Sophomore	Architecture
Kathy Song (F)	Chinese American	China	Age 13yrs	Junior	Management & Marketing
Kaiser Tang (M)	Chinese American	China	Age 4yrs	Senior	Biology & English
Mason Wu (M)	Chinese American	Massachusetts	N/A	Junior	Psychology
Mitch Niu (M)	Chinese American	Virginia	N/A	Sophomore	Computer Science
Mark Bok (M)	Korean American***	Virginia	N/A	Senior	Math
Orion So (M)	Korean American	Pennsylvania	N/A	Sophomore	Architecture
Ronald Im (M)	Korean American	Virginia	N/A	Senior	Hospitality & Tourism Management
Sam Xu (M)	Chinese American	Taiwan	Age 8yrs	Senior	Industrial & Systems Engineering
Trudy Chua (F)	Chinese American	Virginia	N/A	Sophomore	Math

*Alphabetized by first name

**M=Male; F=Female

***Mark initially identified as Korean American; however, his family comes from Vietnam

FIGURE 14.2. Demographic Information of Study Participants

Having reviewed social scientific literature and theory, I formulated three divergent theses:

1. Korean and Chinese American undergraduates at Virginia Tech actively work to combat stereotypes linked to the model minority label.
2. Korean and Chinese American undergraduates at Virginia Tech actively work to distance themselves and their ethnic group from the events of April 16th and the GLC incident, embracing the model minority label in the wake of the crimes.
3. Korean and Chinese American undergraduates at Virginia Tech actively work to distance themselves from both the model minority label and the events of April 16th and the GLC incident.

In the following section, the findings from my interviews will be discussed and analyzed, and the degree to which my theses were supported will be revealed.

Participants

Interviews were conducted with 18 Asian Americans: Korean ($n = 6$) and Chinese ($n = 12$) American undergraduate males and females from 2010–2011. Because in-depth interviews are at the center of this study, my sample remained small. Asian Americans are understudied in terms of their lived experience within the university community. Korean and Chinese Americans are a significant minority on college campuses throughout the U.S.; they are members of the largest minority group at Virginia Tech, Asian American. Please see Figure 14.2, above, for background information about study participants.

FINDINGS

Through the course of my interviews, a number of themes emerged. In this chapter, I focus on the following three themes: (1) two criminal events at Virginia Tech, (2) racial experiences at Virginia Tech, and (3) support for the model minority stereotype. Although each of these themes cannot be dealt with exclusively, as often the conversation incorporates two or more themes, I organize the discussion along thematic lines. I begin with a discussion of the horrific events; I then focus on racial experiences at Virginia Tech; and finally, I discuss my respondents and the model minority stereotype.

After April: The Mass Shooting

One strategy I used during the interviews to gauge the importance of April 16th may seem counterintuitive, but turned out to be quite telling: I did not bring the events of April 16th up. I wanted to see if, in conversations about their experiences at Virginia Tech, and in particular, their experiences with race/ethnicity at Virginia Tech, April 16th was something that respondents brought up independently.

In all but three cases, respondents did mention April 16th at some point in the course of the interview; when they did so, it was raised in a casual manner, sometimes as almost an afterthought. Several respondents did mention being worried, initially, that there would be backlash aimed at the Asian American community. However, those worries, according to my respondents, and the possibility of backlash, quickly passed. Take for example these statements from Duncan Lau [male; Chinese American; senior], whose words are representative of my respondents:

> **Duncan:** I mean, we'll mention it [racist jokes], but it's not like a huge deal, you know? And, another thing, is like, you know, the events of, like, the April 16th thing did cause some issues for a few of my friends, one was, he got his apartment egged or something and things like that.
>
> **Daisy:** And why did he think he was the target of that?
>
> **Duncan:** Cause he was Asian, or Chinese, you know?
>
> **Daisy:** Do you recall his reaction after that?
>
> **Duncan:** He just told us about it and we were like oh, that's so fucked up, I mean he wasn't like terribly distraught we, everyone, just thought it was messed up, but it's like you know we're not going to go light a bunch of torches and get mad or something.
>
> **Daisy:** So, since April 16th, have you noticed a change in the way you perceive yourself or are perceived by the student body or community, or [similar changes] in your friends?
>
> **Duncan:** Um...not terribly, you know, there is more concern about like people are going to start like judging us or like, yeah, we might be afraid more ignorant people might just like think about things like that, but I haven't noticed anything, I haven't experienced anything terribly bad myself.

Duncan acknowledges the events of April 16th, and the initial concerns that he and his friends shared. However, he rejects the idea that misguided backlash toward the Asian American community is something to be very concerned about: "... he wasn't like terribly distraught..." He also implies that his group should not, or is not interested in, drawing attention to the incident via public protest: "... it's not like you know we're going to go light a bunch of torches and get mad or something." So, according to Duncan, misplaced race-related backlash, when aimed at his racial group, is not something to protest.

In the following selection, Kaiser Tang [male; Chinese American; senior] brings up April 16th when I ask him how Asians are perceived by the community—both the campus community and town/county residents. He characterizes April 16th as a test—one which Virginia Tech and the surrounding community passed with flying colors. Keep in mind that, as was Duncan, Kaiser was a student at Virginia Tech before and after the events of April 16th:

Daisy:	What do you think the community's perception of Asian Americans is, is it positive, negative, and do you think it's changed over the last four years?
Kaiser:	Um, well. I think a big test of that, um, was the shooting, and um, when I found out about that, that the shooter was Asian—at first, there was a rumor that the shooter was Chinese, and I just let out a huge sigh, like—not of relief. I thought, oh my goodness, now everyone's going to be like [switches into a Southern accent], "Ohh, Chineeese people are weird... " But, the thing is like, most people here, the surrounding area is all Southern, and with that comes all that typical prejudice, you know, of white America, so, I was afraid that things were going to be different—and they HAVEN'T. So, I would say in the past four years, nothing's changed that much in terms of general opinion. And I think that people, you know, Tech students, in general, are very warm, and I think they're very welcoming....I'm never around people that would discriminate, so maybe asking me is not a good, you know, resource, because I've never met the kind of people that would make those kinds of jokes—I mean, everyone knows the typical Asian stereotypes: "Oh, help me fix my printer!" and all those kinds of things, but they're all said in fun it's not like, they're very P.C., I've never really experienced discrimination—
Daisy:	At Tech?
Kaiser:	Anywhere.

Kaiser acknowledges he found the initial news that the shooter was Asian American daunting, but goes on to turn this memory into a "water into wine" tale. He argues that the community's lack of backlash toward the Asian American community is testament to the fact that racial prejudices may be a thing of the past.

In this segment, Kaiser makes two additional statements that are noteworthy: "I'm never around people that would discriminate, so maybe asking me is not a good, you know, resource, because I've never met the kind of people that would make those kinds of jokes." Kaiser claims that he is never around people who hold prejudicial views—as though he has been able to cleanse his life of that sort of character. He goes further when he states that he has "never met the kind of people that would make those kinds of jokes." Kaiser at first suggests he is able to navigate the social world and avoid people who hold race-based prejudicial views. He then takes it further by suggesting he has, in fact, never even met people who fall into that category.

Kaiser closes the segment by normalizing race-based jokes: those of which he has heard, he treats as though they are benign; he even goes so far as to say that of the race-based jokes he has heard, they are "very P.C." This statement from Kaiser seems like a contradiction. Kaiser's final statement in this segment reminds the reader that he has, apparently, lived a life devoid of race-based prejudice and discrimination: "I've never really experienced discrimination... Anywhere."

Genji Meng [male; Chinese American; senior] also spoke independently about April 16th: his sentiments are representative of both Duncan's and Kaiser's, and my respondents' overall. In the following selection, Genji reminisces about April 16th and the community's reaction to the events of that day. Similar to Duncan and Kaiser, Genji acknowledges that he was slightly nervous because the perpetrator was Asian, but then goes on to describe Virginia Tech as a place where "we're all Hokies, we're like family, one family":

Genji: Oh, yeah—and, like 4/16....I was here for that.

Daisy: Did you notice—before that and after that—a change in people's attitudes?

Genji: Ohhhh, uh, actually, I was little scared when that thing happened because, I'm afraid that people are going to like stereotype Asians—like "Asian, oh you bad, you crazy" and so but, in this community, we, like, I think there's nothing like that. So, but my friend, who's Korean, and they have the, the Korean high school in NOVA, he got beat up because the shooter was Korean, so in other places, but in here I feel like nothing serious, we grew [grown] up, college kids. The other thing, though, you know, it's one people who caused this, it's not like the whole race, the group—nothing like that. I feel like we're all Hokies, we're like family, one family. I never felt like "Oh, Genji, you Asian, you crazy." No. I mean, I was a little scared, like, right after that happened, but, I mean, in the end, nothing, no, no, no—no, no, I never got any negative, like, feedback.

A few elements of Genji's statement stand out. As I noted above, Genji suggests that there is something unique about the community at Virginia Tech—that people are regarded as "Hokies" [the school mascot] above all else, to be a Hokie is to be a member of one great big family. He also suggests that members of the community are too mature to lash out at Asian Americans in response to April 16th— "... we grew up [we're grown up], college kids." It may be something that people in other areas do, or people of less maturity, but not college students, and certainly not Hokies.

Another element from Genji's statement that is noteworthy: "....I never felt like 'Oh, Genji, you Asian, you crazy'...." In making this statement, Genji suggests the possibility that his identity is in part a reflection of the community's perception of him—his very own "looking-glass self" (Cooley, 1902, 1909). Because he did not feel an attitude shift on the part of his community, he did not find the events of April 16th had an impact on his sense of self or identity.

The Graduate Life Center Incident

While the Graduate Life Center (GLC) incident occurred almost two years after April 16th, the events of April 16th were still fresh on the minds of many at Virginia Tech at the time. However, these two events were handled by the University in starkly different ways, and were consequently given differing amounts of media coverage. While the University used April 16th to essentially launch a rebranding campaign of Virginia Tech, minimal attention was given to the GLC incident.

When my respondents spoke of April 16th, they often followed this with a few words about the incident in the GLC. If and when respondents did not raise the issue of the GLC incident, I first asked if they were aware of it [due to very light media coverage, one would occasionally come across students, faculty, and staff who had somehow missed news of this event]. All respondents knew of it, but they had significantly less to say about the incident than they did about April 16th. Once I had established that they knew of the GLC incident, I asked them to tell me what they knew of it, and if anything race-related had stemmed from the incident. Consider these representative words from Duncan:

Daisy:	What about after the GLC incident? Do you recall that?
Duncan:	Aw, yeah, the GLC incident.
Daisy:	Do you recall any [racial] backlash after that?
Duncan:	Um, no, not terribly, but it's just like, again, within ourselves, we're like a little concerned, it's like uh-oh, this might look bad or something, and like, uhhh, yeah.

Similar to his discussion of April 16th, Duncan acknowledges initial concern about the incident, but according to him, these concerns quickly passed. A recurring trend that emerged when respondents discussed the GLC incident was that it was an isolated incident, and stemmed from personal problems, perhaps linked to mental illness. This sentiment was voiced repeatedly, and mirrors the (very thin) coverage of the GLC incident by the media, in which it was framed as an isolated incident, unrelated to the University, and almost surely the work of a mad man.

According to my respondents, very little was discussed concerning the GLC incident within the Asian American community at Virginia Tech. The topic did not seem to be of great interest or concern to this community. In the following segment, I ask Orion So [male; Korean American; sophomore] about the event at the GLC:

Daisy:	Okay, and then, this thing happened in the GLC, you were here for that?
Orion:	GLC? The Chinese?
Daisy:	Yes.

Orion:	I heard of it, that was the year before me.
Daisy:	That was the year before you? Okay, so, what did you, what conversations did you hear about it?
Orion:	I've heard, that Chinese guy pulled out like Chinese cooking knife and chopped off a Chinese girl's head... Yeah, and in AVP, I mean ABP [Au Bon Pain], and this lady who was working there was so traumatized no one saw her again after that day. She never came back to work. Stuff like that... I don't know that much about that one.
Daisy:	Okay, okay, but that [incident] didn't have any impact on you?
Orion:	Uh uh. No.

Orion's discussion of the GLC incident was representative of my respondents': he knew a little about it, "stuff like that," he was not particularly concerned or knowledgeable about it, and he had not been impacted by it in any way. None of my respondents reported extended discussions about the incident; while all respondents knew of the incident, their knowledge was very limited, and they did not express care or concern for or about the incident.

Race in the Classroom and on Campus

Through the course of the in-depth interviews, I aimed to learn more about respondents' experiences at Virginia Tech, especially those that were in some way related to their race/ethnicity. In interview after interview, race played an insignificant role in the discussion. Based on my respondents' accounts, race did not present a challenge to this sample of Asian Americans at Virginia Tech.

When negative racial experiences were brought up, they were done so in a light-hearted fashion, and respondents assured me that race really was nothing to worry about. In some instances, respondents went so far as to suggest that race no longer existed, or did not matter. In some cases, if race was presented as an issue, it was an intragroup issue—that is, race was used as a source of humor or taunting by insiders, not outsiders.

I asked respondents about race as a dynamic with both professors and fellow students. As Sam Xu [male; Chinese American; senior] states, 90% of professors at Virginia Tech are "really great" when it comes to this issue:

Daisy:	Let's talk a little about your experience as a student as it relates to your professors. Did you feel because of your race, any positive or negative experiences from like faculty or in classes, so maybe the way that other students treated you or faculty members treated you or was that not an issue?
Sam:	That was, no I don't think that was ever an issue. Professors here are for the most part, really great, like, like, personal-

ity wise and person wise, like I would say like 90% is really great…

Genji takes it one step further: he is one of several respondents who claim to have never experienced "anything that is racial, negative-wise":

Daisy:	Do you recall any negative experiences with professors or students, related to your race/ethnicity?
Genji:	Uhhhhhh……
Daisy:	Or positive experiences related to your race/ethnicity?
Genji:	Uhhh…racist issues, let's see…
	[long pause]
Daisy:	Okay, let's see, what were we talking about…
Genji:	Uhhh…the racist—
Daisy:	Yeah, experiences—sometimes they can be positive, sometimes negative—what have you experienced?
Genji:	Hmmm… let's see—negative wise, I don't think I've really experienced *anything* that is racial…

One sees from the above that getting my respondents to discuss their racial experiences at Virginia Tech was difficult: I had to nudge them repeatedly to address the topic. This was not due to discomfort concerning the topic, but rather nonchalance. Along the same lines as Genji, respondent Mason Wu [male; Chinese American; junior] recounts his experiences related to race at Virginia Tech, a discussion during which he, too, proclaims he has not faced racism:

Daisy:	Okay, so we hear positive stereotypes of Asian Americans, and negative stereotypes of Asian Americans—positive tend to be more prevalent when it comes to Asian Americans. Have you experienced positive stereotyping while at Tech?
Mason:	Not really, maybe I'm just like one of those rare cases where like, I've never experienced like racism, toward myself, just for being Asian anywhere—I mean, a lot of that could just be I grew up in Massachusetts, where no one says anything bad about anybody, but even like down here, I definitely like, I saw it happen many times, but it never happened to me.
Daisy:	What did you see?
Mason:	Oh, just like um, like in middle school and high school like um someone was just like making jokes about like Asians, you know, if he's not studying right now, he must be sleeping, something like that. Silly things like that. But, I don't know, maybe, it coulda just been because I was friends with a lot of different people there you know, no one ever felt the need to

	just like throw barbs at you, you know, for me, I've never… But I've never experienced any racism just for being Asian. Just, just like the harmless, I'd call it like playful, racism—that's just like, I mean it is racism, but it's not like hurtful in any way.
Daisy:	Such as?
Mason:	Well, it's a lot of the same stuff, it's just like, even among Asians, this is something—I'm just gonna bring this up real quick, the whole concept of "Asian time"….
…	
Daisy:	Well, so far, every one for the interviews has been on time! But maybe that's because they assume I don't know about Asian time.

Mason first says he has not experienced racism; he then goes on to say he has only experienced "playful racism." He states that it is not harmful; he follows this with an explanation of the concept of "Asian time," a stereotype that says Asian Americans are notoriously late. So, in the course of our interview about race-based prejudice and discrimination, Mason himself negatively stereotypes members of his own racial group.

Related to this are statements about racial experiences at Virginia Tech from Finn Chio [male; Chinese American; freshman]: he mentions racially-based humor among his friendship groups, and the role that he plays in perpetuating racially-based stereotypes:

Daisy:	… So let's see, have you had any negative experiences based on your race at Virginia Tech while you've been here?
Finn:	Not really. There has never been a chance where I've been, like, "Oh… I really wish I weren't Asian right now."… Nothing, really.
Daisy:	Okay, that's interesting. And, do you and your friends talk about race as it relates to your experiences on campus, or anything like that?
Finn:	We make Asian jokes a lot—like, about people in computer science.
Daisy:	…Does it ever bother you, or do you play along with it?
Finn:	Sure [I play along with it]—if they knew it offended me, they wouldn't do it.
Daisy:	Okay. I mean, sometimes things get playful, and then you do become uncomfortable. But that doesn't happen? No.
Finn:	I mean, it's a positive stereotype, so I don't see why you would—
Daisy:	Okay, what types of positive stereotypes?

Finn:	Like, how Asians need to be smart and get "A"s and be good at math… or computer science… that we have to do a lot of homework and study all the time.

So, Finn claims to have had no negative race-related experiences—and when it comes to race-related jokes, he is often the instigator! In our conversation, he does not grasp how a positive stereotype—especially not one featuring his racial group—could be in any way detrimental to members of that group. To Finn, this is counterintuitive.

And, Hen Ye's [male; Chinese American; 5th year senior] racial experiences at Virginia Tech appear to be overwhelmingly positive. When he does speak of race-related issues at Virginia Tech, his comment is positive in nature, and is in reference to a diversity initiative on campus with which he is involved:

Daisy:	In terms of when you're considering race as you've experienced it at Tech, what experiences, positive or negative, have you had, as it relates specifically to your race?
Hen:	To my race, I can't really think of anything specific…
Daisy:	Have you experienced any forms of racial discrimination or stereotyping, anything like that at Tech?
Hen:	Not really, everyone is really nice. Virginia Tech has been trying to take an initiative on diversity with the Pamplin multicultural diversity counsel. I think this is its fifth year so it's relatively new. It's really accepting I feel on campus.

Hen is one of a number of respondents who say they feel welcome on campus, that the Virginia Tech community—from professors to students to townsfolk—have welcomed them with open arms. The recent crimes do not seem to have changed this; in fact, they may have increased community solidarity. Hen is also one of a number of respondents who mention their involvement with organizations devoted to issues of diversity. Only one of my respondents stated that they wished there was more diversity at Virginia Tech; still, this respondent reported having had an overall positive experience while at Tech.

From the above discussion, the horrific crimes—crimes I was concerned would expand Asian Americans' stereotype threat—seem to be of little interest to my male respondents. The very subject of racial experiences at Virginia Tech, similarly, are of little interest to my male respondents. A number of them seem-hard pressed for things to say when I ask about race at Virginia Tech.

My female respondents told a remarkably similar story—they were unconcerned with the horrific crimes, and their racial experiences were slim to none. For example, when I ask Kathy Song [female; Chinese American; junior] about her racial experiences at Virginia Tech, she claims that being Asian American is not significant:

Daisy:	In terms of your experiences as an Asian American [at Virginia Tech], do positive things stand out —or negative things stand out—and let's start with the positive—think of experiences directly related to your race and ethnicity that are positive in nature, and have happened on campus or in your classes?
Kathy:	Um… you know I'm not really sensitive about my race at all, so I don't think being Asian American is any different… um, I don't know—if that answers it?
Daisy:	… Do you feel that you were treated differently by professors or classmates simply because of your race or no?
Kathy:	Mm nmm, no.
Daisy:	Okay, and in terms of negative experiences have you had any— tied to that?
Kathy:	No, no.

Kathy says that being Asian American, for her, is no different—her race does not cause her differential treatment typically associated with stigma (Goffman 1963), even in the light of recent and high-profile crimes. My interviews with both males and females, Korean American and Chinese American undergraduates at various stages in their academic careers at Virginia Tech, resulted in a startling similar story, a story about positive experiences, about acceptance, an almost story-book-like version of what we hope college will be! Thus, my concern that Asian Americans' stereotype threat would expand—in what I saw to be an already heated environment—following the crimes, was quelled. Even when I nudged respondents to expand on their knowledge of, or feelings about, the crimes, the conversation did not progress. Similarly, my respondents were not particularly interested in discussing their racial experiences at Virginia Tech. Repeatedly, I sensed that respondents were thinking to themselves, "Why is a sociologist concerned with Asian Americans' status at Virginia Tech? It's all good. We're Hokies."

So, if my respondents were not interested in talking about race or crime [typically heated discussion topics], what *was* on their minds? What *did* spark their interests? What consumed their thoughts, and perhaps distracted them from topics such as race and crime? Moving along, we see that the answer may lie in the maintenance of their model minority status.

The Model Minority Stereotype

During the course of each interview, I asked respondents about the presence of the "model minority" stereotype at Virginia Tech. An overwhelming majority of my respondents protested that they received differential treatment; when they did note being treated differently, the importance of such treatment was downplayed—they spoke of race-based stereotyping as "usual" or "normal." Genji indicates that racial commentary has not been prominent in college—it was something he witnessed as a youngster, but it did not appear on his radar so much in college—after all, he says, *everyone* in college is smart:

Daisy:	What about positive experiences?
Genji:	Positive, you mean like "Ah, you Asian, you smart" something like that?
Daisy:	Yeahhhh, do you hear a lot of that kind of thing?
Genji:	Not, not like a whole lot, because in college like everyone, they all smart, you know like. In high school maybe a little more like "Ah, wow."

Ronald Im [male; Korean American; senior] at first acknowledges the model minority stereotype, but then quickly downplays its significance. Several respondents handled the topic in this manner—they briefly acknowledged it, and then shifted the conversation to a discussion of how insignificant the stereotype is to them.

Daisy:	Do you hear things, like, model minority types of things—like, you're good at math, that sorta thing?
Ronald:	Yeah… but, these are all things that don't matter to me.
…	
Daisy:	Um, okay… so, we talked about some of the stereotypes… in terms of the model minority… is this something that—is this a conversation you have even to this day with your friends? Is it something that preoccupies you, or is it something that, once again, you just laugh it off and it's not a big deal to you?
Ronald:	Yeah, not a big deal…

Ronald says the model minority stereotype does not matter to him, and is not a topic of concern, or even discussion, amongst his friends. While the stereotype may be out there, it is not having an impact on Ronald, nor, apparently, members of his social circle.

Several respondents were unfamiliar with the stereotype—I had to preface questions about it with an explanation of what it was. For example, Felicia Kang [female; Chinese American; junior] had not heard of this stereotype. When I explain it to her, she claims that she has not been cast as a model minority in the classroom:

Daisy:	One final thing that I want to ask about is stereotypes—we've been talking mostly about negative stereotypes—what about positive stereotypes? Have you been positively stereotyped?

	And by that we mean—have you heard the term "model minority"?
Felicia:	I haven't actually.
Daisy:	... Have you been singled out specifically by your professors as a model minority—not that they use that specific term?
Felicia:	Not here, definitely not here...

Along the same lines, in my conversation with Annie Chon [female; Korean American; junior], I asked if she had experienced stereotypes—positive or negative—associated with her race/ethnicity. She replied, "Uh...I can't think of anything that like stands out as positive or negative, really." When I followed this by asking if she was familiar with the concept of the "model minority," her answer was simple: "No."

Respondents' Complicity in Perpetuating the Model Minority Stereotype

Beyond my interest in respondents' experiences with the model minority stereotype, I was also interested in identifying the portions of their narratives that worked to support this stereotype—and, I found overwhelming support for this stereotype. The following is a discussion of "evidence" of the model minority in my sample. *All respondents* support the idea of the model minority in their discussions of themselves as students; many do so repeatedly—for the sake of brevity, I offer a sample of statements that demonstrate my respondents' complicity in perpetuating this stereotype. We hear again from Finn, whose support of the model minority stereotype is abundant. I have collapsed his statements so as to highlight instances in which he supports the stereotype:

Finn:	My dad has always been an "academiac;" he has a PhD. Ever since I was a little kid, I always told myself I was going to get a PhD just 'cause my dad did it... He's an economist.... So, yeah, he's quite the "academiac." He went to college at the age of sixteen I believe... He always bragged about that. Yeah.... Graduate level study has always been in the background for me; it was always assumed I would do it... I just always thought that that was how it was supposed to be, so I guess when I was seven maybe [I knew I'd go to graduate school]... TJ: That's the magnet high school in our area.... Number one... [My sister is] at Stanford....did a five-year master's program in biology... She recently applied to med schools, and she got into all of her top choices.... I would say that my major extra-curricular activity was policy debate... I got really into it. I went to summer camp twice for policy debate; it was like a month-long

> sleep-away camp where you just debated all day long...My
> sister actually founded this organization called "Debate Mas-
> ters" where she—well, she and one friend would teach middle
> school students high school policy and debate. Then, when she
> went off to college, I started taking over everything, and then I
> registered us with the IRS. We're now a 501c(3) organization,
> 'cause it's a non-profit. We're registered with all the people,
> and it's really cool....I just want to have at least one contribu-
> tion to the field [to his field of study]. You know, like the "Chio
> Amplifier" or the "Chio Effect." I don't know, an invention or
> research. I don't know yet... I just want something there. I also
> plan on saving the world....Right now I'm thinking through en-
> ergy security. I think one reason why there is so much instabil-
> ity in the world is because people can't secure energy as easily
> as they would like to. Gas prices fluctuate; suppose maybe we
> go to war for energy—I don't know what your political views
> would be—but some people think we go to war for energy in
> the Middle East.... You know, if we had energy security, I don't
> think there would be a legitimate need for war.... I'm thinking
> either efficiency—or a different source. One of those two direc-
> tions. I don't—I haven't done enough in my field of study yet
> [keep in mind Finn is a freshman]... I'm pretty sure I want to
> go somewhere with a bigger name for grad school.

Almost everything Finn shares about himself, including information about himself as a student, and as a participant in extracurricular activities, demonstrates his
complicity in perpetuating the model minority stereotype. During our conversation, there were a few instances in which he denigrated himself as a student when
compared to his sister; yet, through his discussion of his sister's accomplishments
at Stanford and getting into medical school, as well as mention of his father's
"academiac" status, he continues to offer support for this stereotype. This was
a common pattern: if and when respondents did say something negative about
themselves as students, they would still offer support of the stereotype in one of
several ways. Above, we see Finn extending support of the stereotype via his family members' accomplishments. In the case of others, such as Trudy Chua [female;
Chinese American; sophomore], while they acknowledge not always living up to
this stereotype, their expectations of themselves remain high:

Trudy: I think I pulled my first all-nighter in third grade and my teacher was so sweet and I guess especially being young, I really
looked up to her. She was a wonderful teacher. I remember her
being disappointed. This is in regards to a different assignment

but I missed the first deadline and I just didn't turn it in and for a long time she was disappointed. I was sad too because I looked up to her. For a lot of my academic career I was a really big procrastinator and it caused me a lot of guilt.

Several pieces of Trudy's statement are noteworthy: one, that she pulled her first "all-nighter" in third grade. Second, that when she perceived her teachers were disappointed in her, this "caused her a lot of guilt." A number of respondents expressed having very high expectations of themselves, and experiencing guilt when they fell short of these expectations.

Respondents' high expectations for themselves were fueled by teachers, as Trudy indicates, as well as by parents. A majority of respondents noted that their family—in most cases, their parents—placed a high value on education. Many of them spoke about their parents' desire for them to attend an Ivy League institution—needless to say, all respondents were students at Virginia Tech, which is decidedly not "Ivy League." This did not stop respondents such as Duncan from addressing both high parental expectations, and their attempts to, eventually, fulfill them:

Duncan:	… There's a lot of pressure to go to a good school, you know, like the stereotype goes, and um, my parents really wanted me to go to UVA, and like I didn't get into to UVA because like I wasn't very diligent for my first two years of high school and then became more diligent, and then got to where I am now eventually, but uh—
Daisy:	What do you mean, stereotype?
Duncan:	Oh, like uh, [Asian] parents are just always like, uh, Harvard, MIT, UVA and this and that, what is VT? You know, like, forget *that*….

Duncan then attempts to add to his school's prestige, noting that "Tech is like, Tech's like where UVA was at when I was applying, you know? It's like 3.9 to get in or something like that, in fact, I know UVA was like 3.9 and Tech was like 3.5…" And, even though Virginia Tech's prestige has apparently increased, parents, have no fear: near the end of the interview, Duncan reveals his parents' dreams will come true, after all: "… I think I've done quite well, I'm going to UVA med school next year…"

In sum, all of my Korean and Chinese American respondents were complicit in perpetuating the model minority stereotype. Many did so overtly, such as Finn, whose monologue we considered, above. Even when respondents spoke critically of themselves or their academic performance, they did so in such a way to offer support for this stereotype: they either diminished their accomplishments, but in comparison to another Asian American, such as a family member; or, they admitted their "former selves" had slipped up here and there, but their biography always ended on a positive note. Not a single respondent stated that academics and/or success were unimportant; none worked to actively combat the myth of the model minority, even in the rare instances when they were critical of themselves or the stereotype. Self-criticism was not the norm, and was fleeting. The overwhelming message from each interview was that the respondent was a high achiever to whom success mattered a great deal.

CONCLUSION

Earlier, I set forth several propositions. After an analysis of the in-depth interviews, it becomes clear that propositions A) [Korean and Chinese American undergraduates at Virginia Tech actively work to combat stereotypes linked to the model minority label] and C) [Korean and Chinese American undergraduates at Virginia Tech actively work to distance themselves from both the model minority label and the events of 4/16 and the GLC incident] are not supported by the data. Responses indicate moderate support for proposition B) [Korean and Chinese American undergraduates at Virginia Tech actively work to distance themselves and their ethnic group from the events of April 16th and the GLC incident, embracing the model minority label in the wake of the crimes].

Interview respondents were surprisingly unconcerned with the recent horrific events that occurred at Virginia Tech. A number of respondents did acknowledge initial concern when news of these events broke; however, this concern was quickly put to rest by the caring and inclusive community at Virginia Tech. "Distancing" involved a number of strategies, including the following assertions: "we're all Hokies," "this is a warm, caring environment, so naturally we didn't face backlash," and "while the events were horrific, they were not a product of group, circumstance, or environment, but rather of individual mental instability." Any concern my respondents had about being Asian American at Virginia Tech did not appear to have real-world consequences for them: if a concern did exist, it was not enough to keep my respondents from continuing attending Virginia Tech, or making significant decisions for their future (such as a change in where to attend graduate school or a commitment to dissuade others like themselves from attending).

Respondents also distanced themselves from recent horrific events by simply not showing that much knowledge about or interest in these crimes. To my surprise, neither April 16th nor the GLC incident became the focal point of any of my interviews. In some instances, respondents were not even aware of very basic details about these events. Thus, my respondents did not perceive that their stereotype threat had been expanded to include "criminal threat." Rather, these crimes were explained away as isolated incidences.

Each respondent conformed to the model minority stereotype repeatedly in the course of the interview—many respondents did so throughout. While it is not abundantly clear that respondents offered support for the model minority stereotype as a way to distance themselves and group members from the horrific events, it is an important possibility to consider. Only one respondent seemed aware of the detriments of the "model minority" label, and was tangentially aware of the body of scholarship that's been collected on this topic. To the contrary, most respondents were still in the stage of fully-accepting, and even proudly exhibiting, their model minority status, and were therefore clearly complicit in perpetuation of this stereotype. By downplaying their race, race relations, and the horrific events, respondents were able to direct attention to what they perceive to be the positive features of their group: those features encompassed in the model minority stereotype.

Questions for Reflection

1. How did the author's earlier research on desktop graffiti inspire, in part, the current study?
2. How can desktop graffiti serve as an unobtrusive measure of campus climate? From a methodological standpoint, why is "unobtrusive" a key word here?
3. This chapter was informed by three theoretical paradigms: racial threat thesis, model minority stereotype, and stereotype threat. Briefly explain these three schools of thought.
4. The author set forth three divergent propositions at the start of this project. Which, if any, of these propositions were supported by the data? Please explain.
5. Finally, the research discussed in this article was in response to current, albeit tragic, events. What current events of the present day do you believe should be the centerpiece of social science research? Explain your reasoning.

REFERENCES

Allport, G. W. (1954). *The nature of prejudice*. Palo Alto, CA: Addison Wesley.

American Heritage Dictionary. (2000). London, UK: Houghton Mifflin.

Abel, E. L., & Buckley, B. E. (1977). *The handwriting on the wall: Toward a sociology and psychology of graffiti*. London, UK: Greenwood Press.

Ball, D. B., & Snizek, W. E. (2006). Desktop graffiti: An unobtrusive measure of student culture and campus climate. *National Social Sciences Perspectives Journal, 32*(1), 5–13.

Bayard, D., & Krishnayya, S. (2001). Gender, expletive use, and context: Male and female expletive use in structured and unstructured conversation among New Zealand university students. *Women and Language 24*, 1–15.

Beck, E. M., Massey, J. L., & Tolnay, S. E. (1989). The gallows, the mob, the vote: Lethal sanctioning of Blacks in North Carolina and Georgia, 1882 to 1930. *Law & Society Review, 23*, 317–331.

Blalock, H. M. (1967). *Toward a theory of minority-group relations.* New York: Wiley.

Blauner, R. (1972). *Racial oppression in America.* New York: Harper & Row.

Blumer, H. (1958). Race prejudice as a sense of group position. *The Pacific Sociological Review,1*, 3–7.

Bobo, L. (1988). Group conflict, prejudice, and the paradox of contemporary racial attitudes. In P. A. Katz & D. A. Taylor (Eds.), *Eliminating racism: Profiles in controversy: Perspectives in social psychology* (pp. 85–114). New York: Plenum Press.

Brown, M. C., & Warner, B. D. (1992). Immigrants, urban politics, and policing in 1900. *American Sociological Review, 57*(3), 293–305.

Bruner, E. M., & Kelso, J. (1981). Gender differences in graffiti: A semiotic perspective. In S. Montague & W. Arens (Eds.), *The American dimension* (pp. 239–252). Sherman Oaks, CA: Alfred.

Chou, R., & Feagin, J. (2008). *The myth of the model minority.* Boulder, CO: Paradigm.

Collins, P. H. (2006). *From black power to hip hop: Racism, nationalism, and feminism.* Philadelphia, PA: Temple University Press.

Cooley, C. H. (1902). *Human nature and the social order.* New York: Scribner & Sons.

Cooley, C. H. (1909). *Social organization: A study of the larger mind.* New York: Scribner & Sons.

Crocker, J., Major, B., & Steele, C. (1998). Social stigma. In D. T. Gilbert, S. T. Fiske, & G. Lindzey (Eds.), *The handbook of social psychology, volume 2* (pp. 504–553). Boston, MA: McGraw-Hill.

D'Alessio, S., Stolzenberg, L., & Eitle, D. (2002). The effect of racial threat on interracial and intraracial crimes. *Social Science Research, 31*(3), 392–408.

Dindia, K., & Allen, M. (1992). Sex differences in self-disclosure: A meta-analysis. *Psychological Bulletin, 112*(1), 106–124.

Fitzpatrick, M. A., Mulac, A., & Dindia, K. (1995). Gender professional language use in spouse and stranger interaction. *Journal of Language and Social Psychology, 14*, 18–39.

Giles, M. W., & Evans, A. S. (1986). The power approach to intergroup hostility. *Journal of Conflict Resolution 30*, 469–486.

Goffman, E. (1963). *Stigma: Notes on the management of spoiled identity.* New York: Simon & Schuster.

Goldsmith, D. J., & Dun, S. A. (1997). Sex differences and similarities in the communication of social support. *Journal of Social and Personal Relationships, 14*, 317–337.

Gonos, G., Mulkren, V., & Poushinsky, N. (1976). Anonymous expression: A structural view of graffiti. *The Journal of American Folklore, 89*, 40–48.

Green, J. (2003). The writing on the stall: Gender and graffiti. *Journal of Language and Social Psychology, 22*, 282–296.

Jacobs, D., & Helms, R. (1999). Collective outbursts, politics, and punitive resources: Toward a political sociology of spending on social control. *Social Forces, 77*(4), 1497–1523.

Jacobs, D., & Wood, K. (1999). Interracial conflict and interracial homicide: Do political and economic rivalries explain white killings of blacks or black killings of whites? *American Journal of Sociology, 105*(1), 157–190.

Lee, S. J. (2009). *Unraveling the "model minority" stereotype: Listening to Asian American youth* (2nd ed.). New York: Teachers College Press.

Limbrick, P. (1991). A study of male and female expletive use in single and mixed-sex settings. *Te Reo, 34*, 71–89.

Liska, A. (1992). *Social threat and social control*. Albany, NY: SUNY Press.

Liska, A. E., & Chamlin, M. B. (1984). Social structure and crime control among macrosocial units. *American Journal of Sociology, 90*(2), 383–395.

Mulac, A. (1989). Men's and women's talk in same sex and mixed-sex dyads: Power or polemic? *Journal of Language and Social Psychology, 8*, 249–270.

Mulac, A. & Lundell, T.L. (1986). Linguistic contributors to the gender-linked language effect. *Journal of Language and Social Psychology 5*, 81–101.

Mulac, A., Studley, L. B., & Blau, S. (1990). The gender-linked language effect in primary and secondary students' impromptu essays. *Sex Roles, 23*, 439–469.

Myers, M. A. (1990). Black threat and incarceration in postbellum Georgia. *Social Forces 69*, 373–93.

Otta, E. (1993). Graffiti in the 1990s: A study of inscriptions on restroom walls. *Journal of Social Psychology, 133*, 589–590.

Parker, K. F., Stults, B. J., & Rice, S. K. (2005). Racial threat, concentrated disadvantage, and social control: Considering the macro-level sources of variation in arrests. *Criminology, 43*(4), 1111–1134.

Petersen, W. (1966, January 6). Success story: Japanese American style. *The New York Times Magazine*, 20–21, 33, 36, 38, 40.

Read, A. W. (1935). *Lexical evidence from folk epigraphy in Western North America: A glossarial study of the low element in the English vocabulary*. Paris: Privately published.

Reagan, R. (1984, February 23). *Remarks at a meeting with Asian and Pacific Americans leaders.* Retrieved December 1, 2014, from: http://www.reagan.utexas.edu/archives/speeches/1984/22384a.htm

Reisner, R. (1974). *Encyclopedia of graffiti*. New York, NY: Macmillan Publishing.

Robinson, W. S. (1950). Ecological correlations and the behavior of individuals. *American Sociological Review, 1*, 341–357.

Schreer, G. E., & Strichatz, J. M. (1997). Private restroom graffiti: An analysis of controversial social issues on two college campuses. *Psychological Reports, 81*, 1067–1074.

Snizek, W. E., Fuhrman, E., & Miller, M. K. (Eds.) (1979). *Contemporary issues in theory and research: A metasociological perspective*. Westport, CT: Greenwood Press.

Steele, C. M. (2010). *Whistling Vivaldi: And other clues to how stereotypes affect us*. New York: W. W. Norton.

Stocker, T. L., Dutcher, L. W., Hargrove, S. M., & Cook, E. A. (1972). Social analysis of graffiti. *Journal of American Folklore, 85*, 356–366.

Stone, J., Lynch, C., Daley, J., & Smojeling, M. (1999). Stereotype threat effects on Black and white athletic performance. *Journal of Personality and Social Psychology, 77*, 1213–1227.

Tannen, D. (1994). *Talking from 9–5*. London, UK: Virago.

Takaki, R. (1989). *Strangers from a different shore: A history of Asian Americans*. Boston, MA: Back Bay.

Takaki, R. (1993). *A different mirror: A history of multicultural America*. Boston, MA: Little, Brown.

Webb, E., Campbell, D., Schwartz, R., & Sechrest, L. (2000). *Unobtrusive measures.* London, UK: Sage.

Virginia Tech Review Panel. (2007, August). *Mass shootings at Virginia Tech.* April 16, 2007. Report of the Virginia Tech Review Panel presented to Timothy M. Kaine, Governor, Commonwealth of Virginia. Retrieved December 1, 2014, from https://governor.virginia.gov/tempcontent/techpanelreportcfm

Zia, H. (2000). *Asian American dreams: The emergence of an American people.* New York: Farrar, Straus, & Giroux.

CHAPTER 15

A FEW GOOD ASIANS

Unpacking Cultural Dimensions of the Model Minority Myth and Deconstructing Pathways to Complicity

Tien Ung, Shalini Tendulkar, and Jocelyn Chu

The study of rhetoric does not free us from rhetoric. It teaches, rather that we cannot be freed from it, that it represents half of man. If truly free of rhetoric, we would be pure essence. We would retain no social dimension. We would divest ourselves of what alone makes social life tolerable, of the very mechanism of forgiveness. For what is forgiveness but the acknowledgement that the sinner sinning is not truly himself, plays but a misguided role? If always truly ourselves, which of us shall scape hanging?
—*Richard A. Lanham (1976, p. 8)*

INTRODUCTION

It is widely documented that Asian Americans[1] in the United States (U.S.) have achieved great success. According to a study by the Pew Research Center (2014),

---

[1] In this chapter we use the terms Asians, Asian Americans, and Asian American and Pacific Islanders (AAPIs) interchangeably to denote persons living in the United States with Asian ancestry or lineage irrespective of their immigration and/or citizenship status.

Killing the Model Minority Stereotype: Asian American Counterstories and Complicity,
pages 263–290.

Asian Americans are the highest-income, best-educated, and fastest-growing racial group in the United States. However, this perception can be misleading. Analyses of racially disaggregated data show that Asian American and Pacific Islanders (AAPI) face high rates of chronic and communicable diseases, poor mental health, exposure to violence, and insufficient access to health and mental health care. In 2008, Asian Americans/Pacific Islanders (AAPIs) aged 19–24 years had an acute hepatitis B incidence that was 1.6 times greater than non-Hispanic whites of the same age. In 2010, Asian American women (ages 18+) were least likely to have had a Pap test (68.0%) compared with non-Hispanic white (72.8%), non-Hispanic black (77.4%), Hispanic/Latino (73.6%), and American Indian/Alaska Native (73.4%) women (Centers for Disease Control, 2013). Research conducted by Barringer, Takeuchi, and Xenos (1990) suggests that while Asians may have higher levels of educational attainment, their economic returns are in fact lower than their White counterparts.

Data from the National Latino and Asian American Study (NLAAS) show that Asian Americans as a group have lower rates of mental illness than other groups. However, disaggregated results reveal differences in the prevalence of mental illness by immigration status and English speaking capacity (Takeuchi et. al., 2007). Other researchers have singled out specific life circumstances that moderate varying rates of mental illness among AAPIs. For example, community studies show that 41–60% of Asian women report experiencing physical or sexual violence perpetrated by an intimate partner in their lifetime.

Asian American and Pacific Islanders (AAPIs) on the whole are less likely to report mental health symptoms to friends and family, and seek treatment less often, which contributes to underreporting (Abe-Kim et al., 2007; Africa & Carrasco, 2011) and exacerbates significant risk. For example, U.S.-born Asian-American women have a higher lifetime rate of suicidal thoughts (15.9 percent) than that of the general U.S. population (13.5 percent). Among leading causes of death in the U.S., suicide was the 8th leading cause of death for Asian Americans even though it was the 11th leading cause of death among all racial groups combined. Suicide was the second leading cause of death for Asian Americans between 15 and 34 years of age. Additionally, Asian Americans have the highest suicide rate among females from all racial backgrounds between the ages of 65 and 84 (Duldulao, Takeuchi, & Hong, 2009; Heron, 2011; Xu, Kochanek, Murphy, & Tejada-Vera, 2010).

Such disparities persist across other health indicators and age groups in the AAPI population, yet the problems faced by individuals in these ethnic cohorts receive scant attention. Health scholars explain that disparities within the AAPI communities are obscured by the persistence of the model minority myth (MMM), a belief that AAPIs among all U.S. minority communities are most like Western Europeans and, therefore, their upward mobility is largely driven by shared values such as a strong work ethic, reverence for education, and meritocratic beliefs (Chou & Feagin, 2008; Lee, 1996, 2001; Lin, 2005; Tendulkar, et al., 2012;

Trinh-Shevrin, Islam, & Rey, 2009). Consequently, these beliefs suggest that the AAPI community is problem free, highly educated, compliant, and independently resourceful. Recent literature and rhetoric is directed toward Asian American and Pacific Islanders' complicity in perpetuating the model minority myth (Iyer, 2014; Pyke, 2010; Ty & Verduyn, 2008; Yamamoto, 1997).

In this chapter, we argue that the existing discourse about complicity requires a deeper understanding of the rhetoric associated with the model minority myth, and a deeper analysis of the meaning of complicity, especially as it pertains to identity and the politics of representation. Using in-depth interviews with four Asians living in the Northeast of the United States, we present findings from a phenomenological study of the experiences of Asians in order to explore cultural dimensions of the MMM, which are often left unchallenged in popular rhetoric surrounding the stereotype. In so doing, we reveal the paradoxical nature of complicity and posit that complicit behavior is complex, neither straightforward nor uni-dimensional—a chaotic intersection of twists and turns, both intentional and unintentional, and driven by larger systemic processes. We illustrate that bifurcation of the model minority myth and complicity into mutually exclusive views— i.e., Asians are model citizens or not, and are complicit in promoting this or not— fails to fully capture the particular experiences and identities of the Asians we interviewed. Our analytic and epistemological lens stems from a combination of multiple perspectives to include critical race theories; theories of rhetoric, coherence, and reconciliation advanced by communication scholars; as well as legal philosophy delineated within anti-discrimination laws and jurisprudence.[2]

MODEL MINORITY MYTH

Since the middle of twentieth-century post-war America, Asian Americans as a group have been stereotyped as a "model minority."[3] Coined in the mid 1960s following the publication of two articles—one written by sociologist William Petersen (1966) in the *New York Times Magazine* and the other published by *U.S. News & World Report*—the term has since served as a benchmark by which all Asians are judged. Simply put, the "model minority" label is a stereotype that characterizes Asian Americans as ambitious, hard working, intelligent, obedient, self-disciplined, and serious (Ho & Jackson, 2001). It is a myth because these characteristics are commonly operationalized by measures of high economic and goal attainment, a drive for educational prestige, and an acceptance of racial is-

---

[2] We will not address the issue of complicity and the politics of identity from these bodies of scholarship, but for the interested reader, the works of Patricia Hill Collins, Kimberleé Crenshaw, Darren Hutchinson, Eric Kwan, Lawrence McPhail, Chandra Mohanty, Karen Pyke, Shireen Roshanravan, and Eric Yamamoto offer a substantive grounding.

[3] A full review of literature associated with the model minority myth and its effects on Asians is beyond the scope of this book chapter. Interested readers are directed to the following works to highlight just a few: Chen and Hawks (1995); Leong, Chao, and Hardin (2000); Li, G. (2005); Takaki (1994). and Wong, Faith Lai, Nagasawa, and Lin (1998).

sues and problems faced by Asians in the United States (Chou & Feagin, 2008), effectively masking diverse counter-stories reflective of Asians as a population group. The salience of the model minority myth has been attributed to its deliberate and perpetual use as a mechanism to reinforce a racial hierarchy with Whites at the top in order to maintain structural oppression and injustices (Chou & Feagin, 2008; Lee, 1996; Pyke, 2010; Suzuki, 1989).

Within this context, Asian Americans live a duality that is difficult to reconcile and that in many ways, argues Louie (2004), compels them to excel. Trytten and colleagues (2012) studied the degree to which the MMM was supported among Asian American engineering students, for example. They conducted 227 interviews with 159 students to examine which dimensions of the MMM were most often reported among Asian Americans, how they viewed other Asian Americans, and how the MMM impacted their lived experiences. Of note in their findings was that Asian Americans were not always aware of the ways in which they endorsed different dimensions of the model minority myth; interestingly, while many of the participants denied the stereotype applied to them, they continued to project the stereotype onto other Asian students. Studies such as this one promote the idea and call into question whether Asians are complicit in their own oppression (Iyer, 2014; Jung, 2012), while other studies accentuate how Asians are simultaneously perceived by Whites and other racial groups as a threat and targeted (Hartlep & Lowinger, 2014; Li, 2005; Lin, 2005; Maddux, Galinsky, Cuddy, & Polifroni, 2008; McGowan & Lindgren, 2006). Consequently, it should logically follow that the complicity of Asians in perpetuating and promoting the model minority stereotype cannot be extricated from rhetoric and discourse about race and race relations in the United States.

The question of whether Asians are complicit in perpetuating the model minority myth has become as politicized as the myth itself, evidenced by the national attention and fierce debates following the *Ho v. San Francisco Unified School District* lawsuit (Liu, 1998; Wu, 2003). The current discourse surrounding complicity of Asian Americans perpetuating their own oppression narrows the scope of rhetorical argumentation, specifically as it relates to the phenomenon of race and racial relations in America. Claims, for example, that Asians are complicit in perpetuating a stereotype that bears oppressive consequences for them may not reflect intentionality but rather internalized oppression (Pyke, 2010). As noted by communication scholar Lawrence McPhail in an address about his experience as an expert witness in the International Criminal Tribunal for Rwanda (McPhail, 2010, p. 4):

> Rhetoric … has both a productive and a critical function: as a productive practice it is concerned with how writers and speakers construct messages used to persuade audiences; as a critical practice it focuses on the modes of proofs used in such arguments to describe, interpret, and evaluate them. … Since such uses of language are not always logical, ethical, or emotionally neutral, rhetoric has often been seen in a negative light and the term has taken on a largely pejorative meaning such as when

a speaker's argument is dismissed as mere rhetoric. ... I found that rhetoric also had a much more noble lineage. That it is concerned with the ability of individuals to integrate diverse conceptions of reality, and thus *to make better choices*. As such I realized that an alternative reading of rhetoric could offer a powerful heuristic for understanding the ethical, political and epistemological assumptions of race and racism.

A closer examination of the rhetoric underlying the model minority myth, and specifically the nature of this alleged complicity in perpetuating the belief, can benefit the design of prevention and intervention efforts on behalf of Asians and promote—as McPhail suggests—better choices across the board. Two important questions therefore underlie this exploratory study:

1. How do Asian Americans navigate an authentic and legitimate life course under the pervasive and ubiquitous presence of the model minority myth?
2. What is the nature of complicity among Asian Americans with respect to the model minority myth?

STUDY OVERVIEW

Study Design

In this chapter we explore the complexity of living under the model minority discourse, drawing on a phenomenological design to examine the nature of complicity in the experiences of Asians. Phenomenology is the in-depth study of a specific circumstance with the expressed goal of describing as much of its associated experiences as possible, to fully understand the essence of the phenomenon. Dahlberg, Dahlberg, and Nyström (2008) describe phenomenology as "lifeworld research," the purpose of which is "to describe and elucidate the lived world in a way that expands our understanding of human being and human experience" (p. 37). Given that the focus in phenomenological research is on deeper analysis and full and nuanced understanding, rather than theme saturation in service of theory building or generalization, a small and purposive sample was appropriate for this work (Brocki & Wearden, 2006; Smith & Osborn, 2009).

Participants

In documentary filmmaking and photo essays/collections, which have long been used to deepen rhetoric and perspectives about complex social issues (Thabault, 2013), photographers and filmmakers must know when to zoom in as well as when to zoom out to accurately and fully capture specificity, depth, and scope of their subject. A similar stance is taken in our phenomenological approach to this study. Four Asians between 25 and 45 years of age living in the Northeast region of the United States were interviewed over the course of three months (February–April, 2014). Of the four participants, two are female, and two are male. Two are first generation Asians who migrated to the United States later in their lives, while the remaining two were born and raised in the United States. One participant is an adopted person raised in a White family with another adopted sibling of the same gender but of a different Asian ethnicity. The four participants self identify with four different Asian ethnic groups: Chinese, Taiwanese, Nepalese, and of Korean heritage. One of the four participants is married, one is in a long-term relationship, and the remaining two are single. Each of the participants was selected to provide this study with a wider lens, allowing for an in-depth look at their diverse and broad backgrounds with context as an accompaniment to explore the meaning of being Asian in the U.S.

REFLEXIVITY—THE LENS THROUGH WHICH WE INTERPRET AND BRING MEANING

The importance of reflexivity—"attending systematically to the context of knowledge construction, especially to the effect of the researcher, at every step of the research process" (Cohen & Crabtree, 2006, para 1)—is commonly accepted in social sciences as critical to the integrity of research. Transparency about the epistemological, theoretical, ontological, personal, and interpersonal roots and influences of scholars designing, conducting, analyzing, and disseminating research is not new. In fact, Kant observed in a letter to Jacob Sigismund Beck in July of 1794:

> We can only understand and communicate to others what we ourselves can produce.
> … The composition itself is not given; on the contrary, we produce it ourselves: we
> must compose if we are to represent anything as composed (even space and time).
> We are able to communicate with one another because of this composition. (as cited
> in Zweig, 1999, p. 482)

To this end, reflexive methods employed in this study included having multiple researchers (Cohen & Crabtree, 2006) who conducted self interviews with one another to delineate our own experiences as Asian women—exploring our childhood experiences, upbringing, professional choices, current ways of living, as well as any influences derived from our respective disciplines (Mauthner & Doucet, 2003). We also employed a voice-centered relational method of data analysis (Brown, Tappan, Gilligan, Miller, & Argyris, 1989; Brown & Gilligan, 1992; Mauthner & Doucet, 1998). Here we offer a brief overview of reflexive discoveries from these efforts.

The first author is a 42–year-old, Vietnamese female. Her work as a social work practitioner-scholar in the field of child protection and trauma has fueled questions about the intersection of human, social, and cultural capital in the development of identity, and its influence on the promotion of healing, recovery, and wellness. In her words:

> My parents fled with me and my sisters from Vietnam in 1975. … We fled literally
> as Saigon fell in April; I was nearly 4. I have spent most of my life here and am a

U.S. citizen. ... Living as a Viet in the U.S. has meant that I am never able to separate my racial identity from the politics of race and particularly the Vietnam War. Anti-Vietnamese sentiment was very strong when we came. My mom told me when we first arrived in America, we sat on the tarmac in California for several hours because they were afraid for our safety and did not want to de-plane us with growing protests on the other side of the gates. They ended up re-routing us to Ft. Chaffee, Arkansas where we were processed. I watched my parents labor painfully to prove their worth here. That's how they always talked about our living here—we have to prove our worth. My mom came to work one day to find an American flag draped over her desk with the message go home—we had just become naturalized U.S. citizens. Becoming a model minority was never a question. Last summer, I went back to Vietnam, the first time in 38 years. There is so much I am still processing, but one thing that became apparent for me was how my narrative, my family's narrative has been so infiltrated by American discourse—American analysis of the war, of the people...yet still, even today we live in the margins and on the periphery of the national dialogue, almost invisible. When I was finally able to literally see the people of my country of birth, it finally dawned on me, the war was a *civil* war—Viet against Viet, and in some sense, me against them. But the irony and craziness was in the sense making—my cognitive sense-making was driven by my loss and longing for Vietnamese connections, but my affective experience was punctuated by my understanding of the U.S. Civil War, and the ways in which I identified with the plight of African Americans, not fellow South Vietnamese. I thought when I went to Vietnam I was going to finally be able to turn myself right side up after a lifetime of living upside down in the U.S., but I left not really knowing which side is up or right.

The second author is a 40–year-old South Asian female who works as a community-based researcher; she immigrated to this country at the age of 11. In her words:

I am a mother, wife, daughter, and sister. The process of conceiving this project, interviewing our participants and deconstructing their narratives was an introspective journey for me. It forced me to think about my own upbringing, my relationships with my family and friends, and how my life has been affected by the model minority myth. I came to this country at the age of 11, after spending many years moving to different countries in the Middle East with my family. My parents settled in New York when I was 11. My first educational experience in the U.S. was in a private girls school in New York City where I was one of the few Asians and surrounded by girls from affluent NYC families. I had a difficult time making friends but remember being appreciated by my peers for my academic accomplishments. I once memorized the entire poem "The Walrus and the Carpenter" from *Alice in Wonderland* and proudly presented it in front my class, a sea of expectant faces of my peers following along in their poetry books. My parents moved soon after to the suburbs of New York where I was, again, one of few Asians in the school system. The process of assimilating to my new environment was neither an immensely challenging, nor an immensely smooth process. My parents worked hard to share our culture and values with us, and I remember lapping these up eagerly, awed by the songs, dances, colors, faith, and community that my parents integrated into our lives. Throughout this time, I worked on myself, finding my way to college, graduate school, and finally to a doctoral degree, prompted all the while by own desire to do well and do good and by the pride that my parents demonstrated in my achievements.

The third author is a 45–year-old Chinese female whose interest in immigration and minority status comes from experiences of growing up in Australia and then moving to the U.S. to pursue graduate studies. In her own words:

My family moved to Sydney from Hong Kong, where I was born, when I was 7 years old. I had never known what it was like to be perceived as different until I landed in white suburban Sydney in the late 1970s. Australia had proudly instituted immigration policies at the turn of the 20th century to limit the influx of newcomers from other lands that did not preserve its reputation as one of the "last British outposts in the South Seas." It was not until 1973 that the final vestiges of the "White Australia Policy" were finally dismantled. Growing up in a country with this legacy meant there was always an undertone of feeling unwelcomed for me. It was not unusual to see "Asians Go Home" graffiti on the walls of my college campus. The interesting thing is that geographically speaking, Australia sits within the confines of Asia, and with the influx of Asian migration, especially post-Vietnam war, an Asian presence in Australia was inevitable. Asians in Australia, like the U.S., have excelled, many of them under adverse circumstances. Finding myself as a naturalized citizen of the U.S. now, I continue to be interested in exploring immigrants and barriers that keep them on the "outside." The label of the model minority and the yoke it has placed on new generations of Asians in the U.S. represents the "insider/outsider" tension that newcomers like immigrants continue to face.

Methods[4]

Using the method of in-depth interviewing for phenomenological inquiry described by Siedman (2012), we relied primarily on open-ended questions about the participants' childhood, family backgrounds, education, and work life, along with their experiences living in the United States as a racial minority. The interview guide developed by the authors was informed by a literature review using multiple databases and relevant terms, including but not limited to *model minority, model minority myth, Asian health stereotypes*, and *complicity*. The investigators first developed a large interview guide consisting of over 25 interview questions. We then discussed the relevance of each question to our research and reduced the number of interview items to 15, including relevant sub-questions and probes.

The questions were organized into three major categories: life history including family background, childhood and upbringing, influential people and career/educational choices; exploration of the model minority and associated experiences; and lastly, reflection on choices made and inspirations.

We included explicit questions about participants' lived experiences with dimensions of the model minority stereotype predominantly discussed in the literature, such as their definitions of success to include an evaluation of their own

---

[4] The Simmons College School of Social Work Institutional Review Board approved this research, and consent forms were reviewed with and signed by all participants.

success, their perspectives about education, and their thoughts about race and racism to include their awareness and understanding of the model minority myth stereotype (*cf.* Chou & Feagin, 2008). In addition, we asked each participant about driving values, significant life influences, and significant life events. The in-depth interviews were audiotaped with the permission of the participants and subsequently transcribed for analysis. Direct quotations below were altered only if this facilitated interpretation.

MODEL MINORITY MYTH DEFINED

Our sample was not intimately familiar with the model minority stereotype overall. The variance in the depth of participants' understanding of and familiarity with the label was not associated with their nativity status, nor did it seem to be associated with age, occupation, or gender. For example, one of the foreign born participants was able to describe the implications of the model minority myth only in relation to health disparities which was learned in the context of his work.

> Because of my work..., last year I dealt a lot with healthcare issues and I have been reading up [on] research papers—government data that they publish on Asian Americans and—in general we are okay, because they do generalize us in one big pot. Once I dig a little bit deeper, Chinese have issues with hepatitis B, Indian with diabetes, and Vietnamese women with cervical cancer. And by generalizing, labeling all of us as a model minority, that is detrimental. [Participant 4, male, foreign born]

Another participant, also working in the area of health, was not familiar with the term at all; however, the ubiquitousness of its sentiment was something that he recognized, as evidenced in his reference to the recent controversy surrounding Amy Chua's book, *Battle Hymn of the Tiger Mom*. In response to the questions about his familiarity with the term, he shared:

> No. Actually, I did not know that, so thank you. So the concern is we are going to miss certain things. ... Interesting, I did not think of that. Wow. Actually very good point, thanks for explaining that. I was not clear on the definition behind it. That's really interesting. ... On that note, maybe it is a slightly different thing, but where does the Tiger mom supposedly fit in? [Participant 1, male, foreign born]

Similarly, a U.S. born Asian participant was not at all familiar with the term either:

> I'm not sure. I'm really not sure. From just the term itself, [it] does sound like, what does an Asian female typically experience being in the majority but I...I mean I'm not really sure how I define that. [Participant 3, female, U.S. born]

The participant adopted and raised in a White family was the only one who could define the concept with confidence, clarity, and without seeking direction or receiving any prompting from us as interviewers. This participant described the MMM as:

... a construct...that APAs don't face any kinds of disparity—they don't experience any kinds of problems—and we know that is not true. I think it implies that the APA American experience is uniform. I think it implies that other minorities are not model or somehow undesirable or that for some reason we are, you know, quote unquote deserving of success. Then I was also thinking on the other side of that is a status to live up to, you know in some way, you know, you are not Asian if you are not embracing the model minority myth. And I think, I tie [that] to deserving of success, a back handed ethics system at work because the simplification of what is perceived as Eastern values which has to do with hard work, paternalism in some senses, so I think that's what comes up. [Participant 1, female, U.S. born]

The model minority rhetoric, in a sense, is a story about Asians told by White sociologists and journalists in their language (*cf.* Ladner, 1998; Petersen, 1966). As such, it represents the use of rhetoric as a social practice that enables the "ruling class to gain *ownership of speech*" (Barthes, 1994, pp. 13–14, italics in original). Analyzed through this lens, perhaps it was not such a surprise that some of our participants were not as aware of the label and stereotype as we had initially expected. Since the myth originated in the news media, one could argue it was taken as fact irrespective of the absence of evidence behind the writers' conclusions and the absence of cultural authenticity that would have required inclusion of the voices of those who owned and lived the experiences being interpreted—namely, Asian people themselves.

EXPOSING THE MODEL MINORITY MYTH: MODEL ACQUIRED VS. MODEL IMPOSED

Cultural authentication from Asian participants in this study suggests the rhetoric or language of the model minority myth is spoken from two different dialects. The White dialect reflects the popular discourse characterizing Asians as being hardworking, directed by success, educationally driven, non-confrontational, conforming and compliant or uncomplaining. In contrast, the Asian dialect reflects cultural and ethnic ways of living, passed down through generations, shaped and molded by migration. The responses to our interview questions made clear the dichotomy between these two dialects. Scratching below the surface of the lived experiences of the Asians we interviewed, and exploring the context of the lives of our participants, revealed a much richer interpretation of the meaning and values associated with being a model Asian than what has been superficially imposed on Asians by the model minority stereotype.

One major theme and three underlying cultural drivers surfaced in our analysis of the participant's narratives about what makes a model Asian person. The main overarching theme was that our Asian participants were action oriented. They lived their life with purpose exemplified by actions rather than rhetoric. The familiar Western adage of putting one's money where one's mouth is often came to mind, along with the popular saying that actions speak louder than words. To this end, what was observed about Asians and compiled into the label of model minority could be reflective of the orientation of doing over saying and practice over rhetoric.

This action-oriented worldview was especially pronounced when our participants were confronted with hardship. Putting down one's head and working even harder seemed to be the way of coping and building stamina, sometimes in an effort to refuel in lieu of giving up, but mostly for family honor and ancestral homage. One participant talked about this in relation to his own family's culture and ways of knowing while sharing where his inspiration and motivation stemmed from. In his words:

> I would say it would be—certainly my parents and my family—I would say in general, my parents, my grandparents. It's not necessarily that they sat me down told me their great life story that influence me, it is more of a fact that I guess I look at where they are today. They own a home, cars, having me, they generated all of this while immigrating here with nothing. So it's not like they came here with any level of cash. Not at all, they were here, they started washing dishes, cooking at restaurants—sent me back to Taiwan, even still with—paying back then, they don't have internet, so paying $300.00 a month making international calls to make sure everyone in Taiwan is okay. They never had to tell me that, it's more looking back and seeing them, their actions, which led me to what I have today in that I am incredibly grateful for. [Participant 4, male, foreign born]

Being action driven meant prioritizing opportunity over hardships, emphasizing optimistic perspectives over pessimistic ones, even in the face of racism as this same participant notes:

> So regardless, I did tell them, I think they understood, but I think in their—in my parents—it was actually one, uh—a few years back I talked to them, do they believe in racism—they actually don't. I think because they do see America as the land of opportunity—freedom, and that they I guess maybe lucky for them in their prospect when they talk to their bosses, colleagues, perhaps they were never discriminated against, or maybe I am just thinking they don't, they don't quite sense it.

> But I think the number one thing with them is that they tend to see the good in things. That in America you can have your problems but there's gonna be more opportunities than problems.

In looking more closely at the emerging themes associated with participants' actions, we find that our participants were driven by values and beliefs that were reflective of different dimensions of Asian philosophy, social norms, or political climate. In this next section we identify some of these cultural drivers and associate them with their explicit or manifest specific actions, contrasting this against the rhetoric of the model minority label perpetuated by the White dialect. In so doing, we hope to deepen the rhetoric about the model minority stereotype in order to more fully begin to explore the nature and implications of complicity that follows.

Cultural Driver 1: Karmic Predetermination

When asked about the dimension of the model minority stereotype that Asians are driven by the pursuit for achievement or success as manifested by an unrelenting educational drive and/or economic ambitions, many of the participants explained that achievement and success were not the motivating forces behind the ostensible drive for education, money conscientiousness, or even being hard working. Rather, the participants reinforced the importance of being debt free, of learning from life, of taking care of one's family, and of contributing back to society and others.

In the words of Participant 4:

> Success in life—is to have a family that cares about you, friends that care about you. To have money, to have a good standard of living, to be disease free, but most importantly, to be able to create an equilibrium.

> You're having all this great stuff, it's because you're benefitting from all of these resources that's available out there. So part of the success is to make sure that your input is the same as your output, so that you commit just as much to society, to the environment so that it can—it balances what you take in as well. Because on a long enough timeline, Earth will not be able to sustain everyone to live a successful life." [Male, foreign born]

In a different yet similar vein about learning and giving back, Participant 1 observed:

> I am very privileged and I try to keep that in mind. And along with that is positive thinking. I starting thinking if they can make it, I certainly can because I started from—from a better place, I had more advantages. Then I think of the ability to be successful in unconventional ways, so for me I am not necessarily tied to the idea of financial success. That's pretty liberating. [Female, U.S. born]

In the words of Participant 2:

> Earlier I was saying I did not get different or better treatment as an Asian or minority and that is fine. Personally I am not a big fan of quota system. So we need to explore, we need to learn, we need to grow our ideas and be constructive. For example, I have a student loan, so prior to getting my education, making sure I make my payments on time. To me that is constructive. If I promise something I need to make sure I take care of this. So I don't carry somebody's loan over my grave. So that needs to be taken care of. If I was loan free I will feel pretty good. That is major success. [Male, foreign born]

Many Asians believe in reincarnation and in one's spiritual connections to one's ancestral heritage. Combined, these two beliefs inform a deep conviction about the interdependency of destiny or fate on one hand, and impermanence (e.g., that nothing lasts forever) on the other. Consequently, it is common for Asians to be driven by both the idea of interconnectedness—the belief that all things, especially people, are connected and therefore responsible to one another—and by a sense of karmic predetermination, the belief essentially that we are born (again and again) for the sole purpose of learning from our past mistakes. Participant 4 described it this way:

> I do feel like what I have now is all because of—my ancestors—my family, the hardships they've gone through to give me what I have now, so I guess that's why I like to spend my year giving back in appreciation." [Male, foreign born]

He added:

> I would—I think I have special thanks to a lot of the people, negative people in my life too, because it is really through them that I see how I can be better. [Male, foreign born]

Therefore, actions are in part driven by one's intention towards others, both past and present. In this context, relationships, particularly familial relationships, are at the center of social living, whereby honoring social ties, particularly family ones, is often prioritized. Additionally, living in balance and harmony without excess and taking a committed stance favoring continuous learning are core principles that guide action. As a result, it was typical for Asians in our interviews to be debt conscious, and pragmatic, as well as to promote intergenerational caretaking and civic duty and engagement. As illustrated by Participant 4:

> I am doing a lot of community based work in the betterment of people while all of my friends they are all in the for profit world doing finance and accounting and all that. But the thing is a lot of my friends they all tell me that I seem to be the happier of the two compared to them or people that they know. Because I do honestly care and like my job." [Male, foreign born]

Participant 2 reflected:

> I don't know if it is a cultural phenomenon, sometimes it just doesn't make sense to me. But if I am eating a tangerine if I am peeling it off, I like to offer it even though people don't want it, that is fine, I am still like do you want a piece? My success is for everyone. Shared responsibility, shared everything. [Male, foreign born]

The same participant elaborated:

> For me, I think, I mean it is cultural stuff. But for me it is a bit different approach, the inspiration would be I have a good job, I am standing on my feet, and I am able to help out my extended family either monetarily or even helping them with something that they are confused about. I would like to be available all the time, it wouldn't be like they have to call me a month in advance and then can we talk about this issue at the end of May. If something comes up I like to be available for them tonight. The other thing is helping back home, we do help back home. If somebody says, hey can you...I am stuck, can you send me $300.00, if I have it, sure. So to me, that can be a little different. In a sense that makes me get up in the morning and then get going, do what I need to do, my part and then if that helps to benefit somebody on the other end, then that inspires me on a day to day business. I am happy and proud to say I help my extended family.

Cultural Driver 2: Honor Driven

In discussions about model minority labels pertaining to being rule driven and therefore obedient and conforming, participants in our study promoted the principle that Asians are relational, not necessarily rule driven. Therefore, the notion of one's self does not exist in isolation. Rather, one can only exist as a result of others, organized systemically in growing contexts. This was evident in participant references to the self in relation to and as an extension of ancestors, family, community, and the world. The idea of a self independent of these social relations was not possible to conceive. Honoring social relations across contexts is critical to the experiences and ways of being of Asian participants in our study. Significant efforts are made to show loyalty, respect for authority, and to save face, or the practice of socially engaging in ways that promote dignity and reduce shame in the other person. For the participants, obedience and conformity were not demonstrated for obedience and conformity's sake, but rather as a signal of respect for the other person—an effort to reduce shame, promote dignity, show gratitude, and even in some circumstances to meet external expectations. In the following excerpt, we hear how participant 2 directly addressed racial hostility in the workplace:

> Certain settings I hear people talking about different races. Generally if I know the group or the crowd, if I feel okay, I say, "What was the concern? You know, let's talk about it." But let's say if it's a coffee shop and I don't know anyone, then I hear someone making fun of different culture or different races, then I can't do much because I don't know and I don't feel comfortable to intervene. But let's say, in the work setting if I know different groups are talking about different races, I would say, "Let's talk about it, what's bothering you? Which part are we concerned about?" I try to do that to learn more, understand more, and then be part of the group that sometimes we may not know about other things instead of guessing and then talking in the back room, it's a good idea to kind of discuss. That's what I try to do." [Male, foreign born]

For Participant 4, professional and financial achievement were motivated by a drive for honor and well-being, not necessarily a drive for success. Honor for this participant, like the other three participants, was multi-dimensional and included homage to parents' struggles as immigrants as well as to extended family. Making family proud and ensuring that their sacrifices were not for naught inspired many of our participants' choices.

> I—this doesn't quite explain the whole story, but I do have a phrase that I say to people that there is no honor in being poor. Because you're really hustling everyday, working hard, feed your family, helping your friends, but at the same time, if you're not helping yourself, I guess your health will deteriorate one day, and there will be—there is a time-clock on you. So wealth is very important. [Male, foreign born]

Cultural Driver 3: Balance and Harmony

Associated with the model minority myth is the thinking that Asians are risk averse, weak, and non-confrontational. These beliefs underscore the idea that Asians are passive. Participants in our study were quite the opposite. They talked extensively about actively navigating and negotiating their social environment. In addition, participants gave multiple examples of the ways in which they were constantly evolving and adapting to the world around them while still trying to make meaning of who they were along with the cultural beliefs and values that were important to them. These behaviors seemed to be rooted in the belief that management of conflict and difference is best acquired through balance and harmony, consistent with the ideas of interdependency, impermanence, karmic pre-determination, and honoring social relations.

Participant 4 shared specifically how his criteria for evaluating his own success must involve a balance between his needs and passions and honoring his parents. Since he has not achieved this balance, he does not see himself as successful even as a high level administrator in a non-profit organization:

I would say no because my parents have no [idea] what it is that I do and it is kind of hard to explain the concept of working in my position as director to a state agency benefitting Asian Americans and such—that is really hard to explain to them. Have I tried, sort of, have they fully absorbed what I have said, no—but how does that make me feel? Uhhhh, I am okay with it. [nervous laughter] I am okay with it because part of it I know that really it is to gain some experience, knowledge, you know I feel good helping folks, and in this type of role and this type of experience you can't get anywhere else, so, but I did comfort them so this this is a short term thing, it's not going to be my career path, later on do you want to make money of course but currently I just value experience more than monetary value. [Male, foreign born]

In similar fashion but in a different context, Participant 3 shared with us how she strove to achieve balance between herself and others. In these reflections she explained how she shaped herself to bring happiness to her teachers in school. Later in the interview, she explained how she designed the disclosure of her plans to move out of state to attend college:

My parents were like school and education and college is important. And so I strived for that. ... They didn't really push the perfectionisms. I think I did that to myself. I don't know if that had anything to do with the minority myth. I think it was my own personality. I was trying to do the best I could for my teacher. I was doing my best to please others. And so I think I pushed myself. I think part of that was my own internal thing. And I was going back to always trying to please others.

I knew [my parents] would be supportive of me school wise. I knew moving to a different state, city, I knew they would be more overprotective. So I did everything that I had to—including the interview, [I reminded myself] my cousin is already here so I could just come—prepare them financially; all they have to do is sign the dotted line. I don't even need their permission, but I still feel like I wanted their blessing. [Female, U.S. born]

Negotiation and navigating conflict in a balanced and harmonious way did not preclude participants in our study from setting boundaries if they felt such was needed. To this end, it is important to note that boundary setting was not engaged as a mechanism of confrontation, but rather as an opportunity to maintain balance and harmony.

Quite possibly because my biggest asset, my biggest skill set is community building, I work well with people, talk with folk, but I think the way I carry myself—it's— diplomatic. I do see every story having two sides to it. Someone tells me something bad about a person, I try to think about the other person's take on it. I try to balance the world … [Participant 4, male, foreign born]

Up to this point, we have illustrated that for our participants, being a model Asian is about putting action before speech or sentiment and that actions speak louder than words. We have also identified underlying drivers associated with this organizing principle and highlighted associated behaviors. Finally, we have compared these manifest behaviors (model minority myth acquired) with the elements of the model minority label that has been imposed (model minority myth imposed) on Asians by Whites in the U.S. (See Table 15.1 below).

One could argue that complicit behavior is also an extension of this algorithm, another way of acting to one's integrity, particularly in response to a need for coherence, dignity, and belonging against the context of ambiguity, shame, and marginalization. We discuss this possibility next.

TO BE, OR NOT TO BE—A MODEL MINORITY

A popular koan[5] in Asian rhetoric called Discussions in the Sand illustrates the participants' experience of living as an Asian person in the U.S. The koan il-

---

[5] Koans, in many Asian traditions are stories and/or propositions that carry multiple meanings, told and re-told to promote deep contemplation and therefore a fuller understanding about the philosophy of life and living. Discussions in the sand: A learned foreign scientist came to Aksehir and said he wanted to challenge the wits of the most knowledgeable person in the city. The townsfolk called for Nasreddin Hoca. When the Hoca arrived, the foreigner drew a circle in the sand with a stick. The Hoca frowned, took the stick, and divided the circle in two. The foreigner then drew another line through the circle that divided it into four equal parts. The Hoca pretended to gather three parts toward himself and to push the remaining part toward the foreigner. The foreigner then raised his arm above his head, and, wiggling his extended fingers, he slowly lowered his hand to the ground. The Hoca did exactly the same thing but in the opposite direction, moving his hand from the ground to a height above his head. And that completed the foreigner's tests, which he explained privately to the city council. "Your Hoca is very clever man," he began, "I showed him that the world is round and he confirmed it but indicated that 'it also has an equator.' And when I divided the world into four parts, he indicated that it is 'three parts water and one part land,' which I can't deny. Finally, I asked what is the origin of rain? He answered quite rightly that 'water rises as steam to the sky, makes cloud, and later returns to earth as rain.'" When they got him alone, the ordinary townsfolk asked the Hoca what the challenge was all about? The Hoca said, "Well, that other fellow first asked, 'Suppose we

TABLE 15.1.   Model Minority Myth Exposed

Model Minority Myth Acquired	Model Minority Myth Imposed
Karmic Predetermination: • Noble thinking (e.g., Honoring family, balanced and non-excessive living, valuing continuous learning) • Noble action (e.g., debt conscious, intergenerational caretaking, civic engagement, pragmatic)	Achievement Oriented: • Educationally driven • Hard working • Economically ambitious • Shrewd/frugal
Honor Directed: • Face saving • Loyal • Respect for authority	Rule Driven: • Obedient • Conforming
Belief in Balance and Harmony: • Active negotiator • Persistently adaptive • Strategically flexible	Passive: • Risk aversive • Weak • Non confrontational

luminates a fundamental fallacy of the model minority discourse, which has not been a focal point of discussions, yet must be in order to fully consider the nature of complicity. While both the learned foreign scientist and Hoca, the native wise man, walked away from their debate convinced of their respective victories, neither was aware that their dialectic match was taking place in two completely different domains of deliberation. They were essentially engaged in a simultaneous but asynchronous debate. In our interviews with participants, we found that participant behaviors that could be considered complicit were more reflective of the complex multi-dimensionality of identity that results from living in between two cultures than of the linear pathways implied within a bifurcated continuum.

If we stay within this metaphor of language and its varying dialects, then complicity would be, in its simplest form, a case of something lost in translation at best and a case of intentional maneuvering for one's own advantage without regard for the "other" at worst. In its most complex but perhaps its clearest form, however, complicity reflects everything in between the two ends of this continuum. As previously noted, Asians are action oriented. The deep values and beliefs that underlie their ways of doing are not seen—but known to them and manifest in their ways of being (e.g., how they respond in the social environment, raise their families,

---

have this round tray of baklava?' So, I said, 'You can't eat it all by yourself, you know. So, I'll take half.' Then he got a little rude, saying, 'What will you do if I cut it into four parts?' That upset me, so I said, 'In that case, I'll take three of the parts and only leave you one!' That softened him up, I think, because then, with the motion of his hand, he said, 'Well, I suppose I could add some walnuts and pistachio nuts on top of the baklava.' I cooled down too and said, 'That's fine with me, but you'll need to cook it under full flame, because an ash fire just won't be hot enough.' When I said that, he knew I was right, and gave up the game." Retrieved April 28, 2014, from http://www.nozen.com/silent4.htm

approach their work, etc.). Complicity is an action that cannot be divorced from these values, nor can it be separated from the current and very dominant politically and culturally bound rhetoric of racialization in the U.S., and particularly from the politics of identity representation. To be complicit, in other words, is to knowingly contribute to wrongdoing or to another person's malevolent agenda.

Although the participants in our study did reflect some of the more popular elements of the stereotype, all but one of them were unfamiliar with the model minority myth and of its implications. Navigating their life course under the ubiquitous pervasiveness of the model minority myth was illustrated more by a constant struggle for acceptance and coherence amidst loneliness and isolation than by knowing collusion to promote the advancement of one race over others. To this end, we concluded that complicit behavior among our participants could not be extricated from their experiences as a racialized other—both foreign and domestic or local. In this context, two themes emerged from participant interviews about complicit behaviors. Firstly, all the participants in our study spoke repeatedly of the drive for coherence in their ways of living and being in the United States. Coherence for them was reflected both by a blending of different cultural norms and beliefs—or active resistance in order to maintain ethnic ties—and by ways of knowing and doing. Secondly, our participants underscored the need for dignity and belonging to reflect on whether they have been complicit in perpetuating the model minority myth.

Coherence through Blending

In reflecting on their lives and their choices, the participants' narratives repeatedly surfaced themes pertaining to finding meaning and making sense of ambiguities and differences between their ways of knowing and being, influenced by their countries of origin and their families. Complicit behaviors derived from discoveries rooted in these reflections about day-to-day living as an "Other," and sometimes as a marginalized and foreign other.

> ... but I think my parents also kind of realized that it was important for us to get assimilated into the Caucasian culture, especially being born here. I think in some ways they also, look back now, they tried to push us into that. So we could feel more easily, adapt to this. So I do feel that I have some of the American upbringing more, especially to the fact that had very, pretty much, almost everybody in my community was Caucasian. [Participant 3, female, U.S. born]

The same participant stated:

> I didn't feel as much pressure in that sense. It may have been more learning from their own upbringings too. I had the piano and had activities. My brother had taekwondo. Some of the mix that is typical of an Asian family. But parts were also, we want you to push for extra curricular activities not for that because we want you to get into a good college, but, and we know for that to happen you need to have somewhat of a versatile background in addition to the grades. They were also thinking in terms of the American culture as well in terms of that perspective.

Coherence through Resistance

In addition, participants also spoke often of resistance as a strategy to make sense and make meaning of competing values that stemmed from varying cultural demands or expectations. To this end, they shared stories punctuated by themes of persevering through difficult challenges, actively navigating social situations to avoid difficulties, or actively waiting out conflict and/or tensions.

> I don't want to give minority myth the power to shape how I behave. So if I am quiet, you know this is just me; it is not because I am Asian. So I try to fight/confront it [*inaudible*] that way, and then when I do speak out I want to make sure I am speaking out for [the right] reasons, not because I am thinking about they are making assumptions about me. [Participant 1, female, U.S. born]

The same participant reflected:

> As far as I can tell, Asians are perceived as being the closest to Whites and so they're the most privileged class—as you can get but, I guess what I have thought about a lot is—there's a—there is a color barrier in addition to you know gender or whatever barriers, and I don't think we will ever be perceived as White and have that equal privilege or live in a color blind society. When you … success I touched upon this before, you're confirming the model minority benefits White people. It allows us/them to create this class of workers who don't create problems, who have a great [work] ethic, you know but who don't rise. You know it's privilege but I think it's very limited privilege.

Dignity and Belonging

The participants in our study emphasized repeatedly the importance of dignity and belonging when we asked them about stereotypical model Asian behaviors. Fitting in to their communities for those who were U.S. born or learning how to master their host societies for those who were foreign born punctuated their experiences and served as strong motivators. The appeal and allure of the American dream was also something they all frequently referenced. This suggests the stereotypical characteristic—overachievement, attributed to Asians as a racial group, is rooted more in participants' attempts to be more American and to live the American lifestyle than in their Asian worldviews. Pushing beyond these externally imposed expectations and pressures and finding an authentic and culturally relevant sense of coherence, dignity, and belonging seemed to be their definition of success rather than achievement. Surviving was the driving factor, not success, and certainly not intentional complicity in perpetuating model minority or Asian stereotypes.

In the words of Participant 1:

> Some regrets, but overall, not so much. But if there [has] been only one path that I have thought of, what if I had remained at Bentley College, utilized the benefit of four year scholarship, also the internship I had that summer because it was a guaran-

teed four year internship with Price Waterhouse Cooper and a guaranteed job placement afterwards as well? If I had continued down that route, I would have graduated 2006, so right now I would have worked eight years, I would have generated a good substantial amount of wealth right now, but instead, I am living, I am doing okay, so there is that what if. There is that one path I could have gone on. … But if I had continued that path I would not be the person I am today, which is to always think of others as well. Success by definition, which is to balance input-output as opposed to if I have gone down that path, my success would be to just make as much money as I could have. That would be the biggest difference—in which of the two would I rather be, I would rather be where I am right now. [Male, foreign born]

For Participant 2 mastery and belonging were important goals, reflected in surviving culture shock and finding community:

In the beginning it was very exciting. And then the couple of things was very hard upon arrival—not knowing the culture, not knowing healthcare stuff ... Cultural shock, the language, difficulties, and then not knowing the system, how to navigate, not having proper assistance. I mean I should not say proper assistance, I mean there were, there are, but not knowing how to get there was a big shock. I would say it took my between one and two years to navigate some basic stuff. … So I kind of tried to, luckily I had a few friends who I knew back in Nepal, they were Americans, they were peace course volunteers. I would kind of check in with them, and you know this is what is going on, what is next, what should be done? And they were very helpful, because they knew Nepali culture and they were from America; they kind of had both. That was a big help. Later on we connected with more Nepali friends who have moved to the States either a couple of years before me or they were in the process of coming, and so we formed this community and I wouldn't say tight knit community but I, we have some friends we share the day to day business, what's going on, how we are doing, any problems, this kind of thing. But I don't think on the family part is still very happy that I am this far and then they are worrying, but now I can share with them—it was hard in the beginning but things are good. Things are improving. It's good to know that you can navigate the system and be part of it. Of course, I miss them and they miss me, but it is much easier than ten years ago. [Male, foreign born]

Another participant explained complicit behaviors in the context of finding dignity and self worth over conforming to external norms and pressures:

But also having a sense of like inner self worth. I can explain that a little bit more. This is also mostly my own internal thing. Maybe it was influenced by upbringing, I don't know. For me I was always looking at like…what do I need…to get the best grade. To get the A. To study hard. But I was always kind of looking to that, how do I please others, how do I obey authority? And sometimes that's good, but I looked to it so much that, that's what made me happy. But that was the only thing that made my happy. And so in some ways, it was only about pleasing others or obeying others. As long as I do what I'm told. As long as I follow this I'll be okay. But I was never really learning to be happy just within myself. That was something I really had to learn. [Participant 3, female, U.S. born]

CONCLUSION—IT'S ALL IN THE FRAMING

Much of the literature about the model minority myth is focused on determining its accuracy, its effect on Asians, or its function as a mechanism for sustaining racial hierarchy and thus structural oppression and injustices. Consequently, much of the scholarship rhetoric surrounding the model minority myth is entangled in the politics of identity representation and has evolved into fierce debates about the degree to which AAPIs are complicit in perpetuating the stereotype. In this phenomenological study, we were not focused on (although we do remain concerned about) the effect of the model minority stereotype on Asians, but were instead rather curious about the current discourse regarding complicity. To this end, we felt it important to explore, not whether the MMM accurately represents Asians, but rather, Asian views of stereotypically model characteristics. We also felt it pertinent to investigate Asian perspectives about what is model. Our query enabled us to differentiate White interpretations of Asian ways of being in the world and Asian-specific views of the construct "model."

Through these phenomenological interviews about the model minority myth, along with our own reflexive inquiries, we have come to understand that unpacking complicity and delineating it from the whole of culture is critical. Otherwise we risk promoting essentialism in complicity rhetoric, and miss the opportunity to fully embrace possibilities that stem from organizing our ways of knowing and being around complexity and intersectionality. In other words, the rhetoric associated with complicity currently does not take enough into account epistemological drivers of culture and thus of behavior, identity, and psychology. In our phenomenological study social (spiritual, philosophical, and cultural), political, and economical influences shed light on the drivers and intersectionalities that underlie complicity. Given the magnitude and pervasiveness of the model minority myth, it is impossible to consider complicity among AAPIs without considering the social, political, and economical epistemologies that underlie the experiences of AAPIs. To this end, complicit behavior among AAPIs is inextricable from the issue of migration and its influence on identity, values, and behavior. A critical examination of complicity among AAPIs, therefore, has to involve peering through the lenses of migration, politics, economics, and values together and not solely through the rhetoric of race and racial relations in the U.S.

In closing, we offer three suggestions for consideration in future studies and scholarship in relation to complicity and the model minority myth.

SUGGESTION 1: REFRAME THE WORK AND THEREFORE THE SALIENT QUESTIONS

The framing of Asian experience in the United States as a myth complicates the discourse and confounds efforts to engage in actionable dialogue about what is possible and what must change. *Myth* suggests that something is false, unreal, or imagined. It suggests that somehow the AAPI experience is not real rather than underscoring that the AAPI experience is highly complex and requires deeper analysis. Marriage of the construct *model minority* with *myth* puts the AAPI in a no-win situation—to be model means that one is either acting in a way that is not authentically Asian, or that one is complicit in promoting oppression of Asians. While it is clear from the literature that the addition of myth to the construct of model minority was intended to capture "an unproved or false collective belief that is used to justify a social institution" (Random House, 2014), its use in this manner seems isolated to highly educated (i.e., academics) or politically informed individuals. Recall that only one of our participants—who incidentally was adopted and raised by White parents—could offer an unprompted definition of the term, even though all of our participants were highly educated.

Discovering that nearly all of the participants we chose to interview did not recognize the term really put the question of complexity into perspective and promoted for each of us, as authors and as Asian scholars, a sense of doubt about whether complexity and the current discourse associated with the model minority myth is useful or has culturally authentic relevance. For those who are involved in daily decision-making at the local level (e.g., administrators, human resource people, practitioners across all disciplines) and to the general public, we argue the use of myth makes things complicated. Furthermore, efforts over the years by Asians and other scholars to dismantle the myth have resulted in the unintended consequence of within-group blame, which arguably underlies the complicity debate. Consequently, these dynamics converge to work against the manifest intention of the complicity debate—raising awareness to inspire collective action against social injustices.

We suggest a shift to more explicit dialogue and study about the needs and experiences of Asians living in the United States. As mentioned in brief at the beginning of this chapter, the Asian community living in the United States is highly diverse, complex, and in varying states of need physically, emotionally, and socially. As such, we aim to inspire rhetoric driven by action leading to design and development of solutions to these pressing health and social issues faced by our community, rather than rhetoric driven by reaction to systemic and institutional oppression and discrimination. The recent work of Fong (2007) and Trinh-Shevrin, Shilpi, and Rey (2009) offers excellent models for the future direction and possibilities embedded in this work through a reframing of the focus of the issues.

SUGGESTION 2: RELOCATE THE EMPHASIS AND SHIFT TO PROMOTION OF RACIAL AND ETHNIC PRIDE

Related to our point above, we suggest a shift in emphasis to the idea of *model* and away from an emphasis on *minority*. Shifting the emphasis to model reflects the very real challenge of transforming not only our rhetoric and race and race relations, but also our thinking and action. A discourse analysis of the history of the term model minority myth (Lee, 1996) demonstrates why the idea of a model *minority* took such firm root in the racial history of the U.S. As has been illustrated in the model minority myth scholarship, the promotion of the concept provided a strong counter argument to the exposure of racism in America by identifying a minority group that seemed to rise above oppression and hardship, thereby diluting critical analysis about the presence and impact of institutionalized discrimination.

In our study, social and cultural influences surfaced as drivers of stereotypical Asian behavior. This validated our understandings that there is much to be proud of about Asian worldviews and ways of being. By extricating these behaviors from stereotypical interpretations by the dominant White class as perpetuated by the model minority rhetoric, we were able to re-claim philosophical and epistemological roots of Asian psychology and the ways in which these roots informed the adaptation of our Asian participants to diverse and often challenging social contexts. We also realized that resilience and triumph over oppression and hardships is the story of all minorities, each with their own model ways of being that are deeply rooted in their historical, cultural, and spiritual narratives. Therefore, shifting to an emphasis on what is model among the experiences of minorities in a racialized social system is our suggested stance. Such a stance yields endless possibilities for innovation and solutions, which can be designed around the resilience and strengths of minority groups rather than their needs and deficits. As suggested by Lawrence McPhail—rhetoric focusing on negative difference ultimately leads to circular and confounded thinking and in some ways impedes the intention in all important debates of moving through things and essentially of moving forward in a meaningful and, we would add, *just* manner. To this end, we hope the direct outcome will be more culturally authentic and responsive strategies for addressing disparities in health and mental health faced by minorities living in the U.S., instead of more charitable giving and deficit driven models of care. Finally, we suggest that such a paradigm shift could promote an emphasis on prevention in addressing these issues.

SUGGESTION 3: UNDERSCORE COHERENCE OVER COMPLICITY IN ADDRESSING RACE RELATIONS

It should naturally flow from our previous two suggestions that our final suggestion would be an appeal to explore and integrate more of McPhail's work in the area of coherence over complicity in addressing race relations in the United States as it pertains to the case of Asian and Pacific Islanders. As was evident in our interviews, nearly all of our participants were unaware of the term model minority and its meaning. It is difficult therefore to frame their behaviors as complicit in perpetuating oppressive worldviews and actions. Moreover, given the multiple ways in which our participants repeatedly talked about how the intersection of their social and cultural lives informed their identities, their motivations, their ways of living, and their ways of managing the complex contexts of their lives in a racialized America, the original question about complicity did not seem appropriate or accurate. What seemed more valid to us in capturing their lives and describing their experiences was a narrative of coherence. This was supported by our own considerations about our lives and experiences as Asian women living in America. In describing the possibilities of a rhetoric of coherence in African American communities, McPhail noted (1998, p. 127):

> Coherence facilitates the goals of Afrocentricity by emphasizing methodological and epistemic flexibility, and by focusing on similarities and well as differences: It privileges no one position at the expense of others *because it begins with the assumption that all positions are interrelated and interdependent.*

In this fashion the focus on coherence would manifest "reconciliation [and] would entail 'discovering, managing, and synthesizing' the diverse social realities" constructed and experienced, imposed, and suffered by racial groups in relation to one another (Hatch, 2003, p. 738).

In closing, we offer reflections about the limitations of our study as a final word. Our findings and conclusions are based on interviews with four individuals, all residing in the North East region of the U.S. While our sample size is valid and falls within the parameters and purpose of phenomenological inquiry (Lester, 1999), the perspectives of our participants may be called into question as not necessarily representative of the AAPI experience. In an effort to address this valid critique, and given the plethora of literature on the diversity of Asian American identity, we intentionally selected and recruited participants with very diverse backgrounds and from varying Asian ethnic groups. Consequently, we determined that participant profiles reflected a diverse experience and understanding of being Asian American. Our participants are both male and female, and were foreign born and U.S. born, and hailed from four different ethnic groups. In addition, we were particularly interested in recruiting an Asian person who was adopted and raised in a White family. This allowed us to note the limitation (or even relevance) of the "model minority" reference, and therefore any complicit motives to promote its reputation.

We recognize that regional differences exist related to the history of Asian immigration, the presence of or connection to an Asian enclave, and the degree to which Asians have assimilated into the dominant culture (i.e., contextual factors) exist. Again, to this end, the design, guided by a phenomenological approach, was appropriate given the nature of the questions under exploration. We underscore that the findings here are preliminary and warrant a further analysis, which includes both returning to our four participants to delve deeper into the interpretation of their responses, which we have laid out, and engagement with a wider selection of new participants to continue this exploration. Lastly, in future work, it would be important to explore the influence of class as part of the intersectionality matrix, and to explore whether alternative motives underlie ostensibly complicit behavior when exploring class differences. This is not something that explicitly emerged in the data we reviewed, though it would be something to intentionally consider in designing future studies.

Questions for Discussion

1. In what ways is the model minority myth oppressive? To whom is it oppressive? Are there other groups that have been oppressed besides Asians? In what ways have other groups benefited/not benefited from this?

2. What impact does culture have on identity? How does context impact the relationship between culture and identity?

3. What are some examples of resistance against the model minority myth? What are some barriers to this resistance?

4. Are Asians complicit in perpetuating the model minority myth? Why or Why not?

5. Do the authors' arguments have relevance for other marginalized communities? Explain.

REFERENCES

Abe-Kim, J., Takeuchi, D. T., Hong, S., Zane, N., Sue, S., Spencer, M. S., ... & Alegría, M. (2007). Use of mental health–related services among immigrant and US-born Asian Americans: Results from the National Latino and Asian American Study. *American Journal of Public Health, 97*(1), 91.

Africa, J., & Carrasco, M. (2011, February). *Asian-American and Pacific Islander mental health.* Retrieved December 1, 2014, from http://www.namisf.org/files/news/AA-PIListeningSession.pdf

Asian and Pacific Islander Institute on Domestic Violence. (2014). *Statistics on violence against API women.* Retrieved December 1, 2014, from http://www.apiidv.org/resources/violence-against-api-women.php

Barringer, H. R., Takeuchi, D. T., & Xenos, P. C. (1990). Education, occupational prestige, and income among Asian Americans. *Sociology of Education, 63*(4), 27–43.

Barthes, R. (1994). *The semiotic challenge.* Los Angeles, CA: University of California Press.

Brocki, J. M., & Wearden, A. J. (2006). A critical evaluation of the use of interpretative phenomenological analysis (IPA) in health psychology. *Psychology and Health, 21*(1), 87–108.

Brown, L. M., & Gilligan, C. (1992). *Meeting at the crossroads: Women's psychology and girls' development.* Cambridge, MA: Harvard University Press.

Brown, L. M., Tappan, M. B., Gilligan, C., Miller, B. A., & Argyris, D. E. (1989). Reading for self and moral voice: A method for interpreting narratives of real-life moral conflict and choice. In M. J. Packer & R. B. Addison (Eds.), *Entering the circle: Hermeneutic investigation in psychology* (pp. 141–164). Albany, NY: State University of New York Press.

Centers for Disease Control. (2013). Asian American Populations, July 2, 2013. Retrieved December 1, 2014, from http://www.cdc.gov/minorityhealth/populations/REMP/asian.html#10

Chen Jr., M. S., & Hawks, B. L. (1995). A debunking of the myth of healthy Asian Americans and Pacific Islanders. *American Journal of Health Promotion, 9*(4), 261–268

Chou, R. S., & Feagin, J. R. (2008). *The myth of the model minority: Asian Americans facing racism*. Boulder, CO: Paradigm.

Cohen, D., & Crabtree, B. (2006). *Reflexivity. Qualitative research guidelines project: A comprehensive guide for designing, writing, reviewing and reporting qualitative research*. Princeton, NJ: The Robert Wood Johnson Foundation. Retrieved December 1, 2014 from http://www.qualres.org/HomeRefl-3703.html

Dahlberg, K., Dahlberg, H., & Nyström, M. (Eds.). (2008). *Reflective lifeworld research* (2nd ed.). Lund, Sweden: Studentlitteratur.

Duldulao, A. A., Takeuchi, D. T., & Hong, S. (2009). Correlates of suicidal behaviors among Asian Americans. *Archives of Suicide Research, 13*(3), 277–290.

Fong, T. (2007). *The contemporary Asian American experience: Beyond the model minority* (3rd ed.). Englewood Cliffs, NJ: Prentice Hall.

Hartlep, N. D., & Lowinger, R. J. (2014). An exploratory study of undergraduates' attitudes toward affirmative action policies for Asian Americans in college. *Equity & Excellence in Education, 47*(3), 370–384. Retrieved December 1, 2014, from http://www.tandfonline.com/doi/pdf/10.1080/10665684.2014.933694

Hatch, J. B. (2003). Reconciliation: Building a bridge from complicity to coherence in the rhetoric of race relations. *Rhetoric & Public Affairs, 6*(4), 737–764.

Heron, M. (2011). Deaths: Leading causes for 2007. *National Vital Statistic Reports, 59*(8), 1–95.

Ho, C., & Jackson, J. W. (2001). Attitude toward Asian Americans: Theory and measurement. *Journal of Applied Social Psychology, 31*(8), 1553–1581.

Iyer, V. (2014). *Our complicity with excess*. Retrieved December 1, 2014, from http://aaww.org/complicity-with-excess-vijay-iyer/

Jung, S. (2012). *Left or right of the color line? Asian Americans and the racial justice movement*, Retrieved December 1, 2014, from http://www.changelabinfo.com/reports/ChangeLab_Left-or-Right-of-the-Color-Line.pdf

Ladner, J. A. (Ed.). (1998). *The death of White sociology: Essays on race and culture*. Baltimore, MD: Black Classic Press.

Lanham, R. A. (1976). *The motives of eloquence: Literary rhetoric in the renaissance*. New Haven, CT: Yale University Press.

Lee, S. J. (1996). *Unraveling the "model minority stereotype": Listening to Asian American youth*. New York: Teachers College Press.

Lee, S. J. (2001). More than "model minorities" or "delinquents": A look at Hmong American high school students. *Harvard Educational Review, 71*(3), 505–529.

Leong, F. T., Chao, R. K., & Hardin, E. E. (2000). Asian American adolescents: A research review to dispel the model minority myth. *Advances in Adolescent Development, 9*, 179–207.

Lester, S. (1999). An introduction to phenomenological research. *Stan Lester Developments*, 1–4. Retrieved December 1, 2014, from http://www.sld.demon.co.uk/resmethy.pdf

Li, G. (2005). Other people's success: Impact of the "model minority" myth on underachieving Asian students in North America. *KEDI Journal of Educational Policy, 2*(1), 69–86.

Lin, M. W. (2005). When being good is good… and bad: The dilemma of Asian Americans as the model minority in the United States. Retrieved December 1, 2014, from https://kb.osu.edu/dspace/bitstream/handle/1811/424/Marissa_Lin_Honors_Thesis. pdf?sequence=1

Liu, C. M. (1998). Beyond black and white: Chinese Americans challenge San Francisco's desegregation plan. *Asian American Law Journal, 5*(1), 341–351.

Louie, V. S. (2004). *Compelled to excel: Immigration, education, and opportunity among Chinese Americans.* Redwood City, CA: Stanford University Press.

Maddux, W. W., Galinsky, A. D., Cuddy, A. J., & Polifroni, M. (2008). When being a model minority is good... and bad: Realistic threat explains negativity toward Asian Americans. *Personality and Social Psychology Bulletin, 34*(1), 74–89.

Mauthner, N. S., & Doucet, A. (1998). Reflections of a voice centered relational method of data analysis: Analysing maternal and domestic voices. In Ribbens, J. & Edwards, R. (Eds.), *Feminist dilemmas in qualitative research: Private lives and public texts* (pp. 119–144). London, UK: Sage.

Mauthner, N. S., & Doucet, A. (2003). Reflexive accounts and accounts of reflexivity in qualitative data analysis. *Sociology, 37*(3), 413–431.

McGowan, M. O., & Lindgren, J. (2006). Testing the model minority myth. *Nw. UL Rev., 100*, 331–377.

McPhail, M. L. (1998). From complicity to coherence: Rereading the rhetoric of Afrocentricity. *Western Journal of Communication, 62*(2), 114–140.

McPhail, M. L. (2010). *Confessions of an expert witness: Rhetoric, politics and ethics at the international criminal tribunal for Rwanda.* Retrieved December 1, 2014, from http://www.smu.edu/~/media/Site/Provost/Ethics/pdfs/mcphail.ashx

Petersen, W. (1966, January 6). Success story, Japanese-American style, *New York Times Magazine.* Retrieved December 1, 2014, from http://inside.sfuhs.org/dept/history/ US_History_reader/Chapter14/modelminority.pdf

Pew Research Center. (2014). The Rise of Asian Americans, Pew Research Center, April 13, 2014. Retrieved December 1, 2014, from http://www.pewsocialtrends. org/2012/06/19/the-rise-of-asian-americans/

Pyke, K. (2010). An intersectional approach to resistance and complicity: The case of racialized desire among Asian American women. *Journal of Intercultural Studies, 31*(1), 81–94.

Random House Dictionary. (2014). Myth. (Defn. 5)*.* Retrieved June 13, 2014, from http:// dictionary.reference.com/browse/myth

Roshanravan, S. M. (2009). Passing-as-if: Model-minority subjectivity and women of color identification. *Meridians: Feminism, Race, Transnationalism, 10*(1), 1–31.

Siedman, I. (2012). *Interviewing as qualitative research: A guide for researchers in education and the social sciences.* New York: Teachers College Press.

Smith, J. A., & Osborn, M. (2009). Interpretative phenomenological analysis. In J. A. Smith, P. Flowers, & M. Larkin (Eds.), *Interpretative phenomenological analysis: Theory, method and research* (pp. 53–80). Thousand Oaks, CA: Sage.

Suzuki, B. H. (1989). Asian American as the "model minority": Outdoing whites? Or media hype? *Change,* 13–19.

Takaki, R. (1994). Asian Americans: The myth of the model minority. *Crisis in American Institutions,* 181.

Takeuchi, D. T., Zane, N., Hong, S., Chae, D. H., Gong, F., Gee, G. C., ... & Alegría, M. (2007). Immigration-related factors and mental disorders among Asian Americans. *American Journal of Public Health, 97*(1), 84–90.

Tendulkar, S. A., Hamilton, R. C., Chu, C., Arsenault, L., Duffy, K., Huynh, V., ... & Friedman, E. (2012). Investigating the myth of the "model minority": A participatory community health assessment of Chinese and Vietnamese adults. *Journal of Immigrant and Minority Health, 14*(5), 850–857.

Thabault, B. (2013, April 4). CJ Carter interview. *Theory Magazine.* Retrieved December 1, 2014, from http://theory-magazine.com/cj-carter-interview

Trinh-Shevrin, C., Islam, N., & Rey, M. (2009). *Asian American communities and health: Context, research, policy, and action.* San Francisco, CA: Jossey-Bass.

Trytten, D. A., Lowe, A. W., & Walden, S. E. (2012). "Asians are good at math. What an awful stereotype:" The model minority stereotype's impact on Asian American engineering students. *Journal of Engineering Education, 101*(3), 439–468.

Ty, E., & Verduyn, C. (Eds.). (2008). *Asian Canadian writing beyond autoethnography.* Waterloo, Canada: Wilfrid Laurier University Press.

Wong, P., Faith Lai, C., Nagasawa, R., & Lin, T. (1998). Asian Americans as a model minority: Self-perceptions and perceptions by other racial groups. *Sociological Perspectives, 41*(1), 95–118.

Wu, F. H. (2003). Arrival of Asian Americans: An agenda for legal scholarship. *The Asian Law Journal, 10*(1), 1–12. Retrieved December 1, 2014, from http://scholarship.law. berkeley.edu/cgi/viewcontent.cgi?article=1082&context=aalj

Xu, J., Kochanek, K. D., Murphy, S., & Tejada-Vera, B. (2010). Deaths: Final data for 2007. *National Vital Statistics Reports, 58*(19). Hyattsville, MD: National Center for Health Statistics; 2010. Retrieved December 1, 2014, from http://www.kansasinfantmortality.org/files/nvsr58_19–2007_final_data.pdf

Yamamoto, E. K. (1997). Critical race praxis: Race theory and political lawyering practice in post-civil rights America. *Michigan Law Review, 95*(4), 821–900.

Zweig, A. (Ed.). (1999). *Correspondence: The Cambridge edition of the works of Immanuel Kant.* Cambridge, UK: Cambridge University Press.

PART IV

CONSIDERATIONS WHEN CONDUCTING RESEARCH
ON THE MODEL MINORITY STEREOTYPE

CHAPTER 16

A PRIMER ON RESEARCH VALIDITY FOR CONDUCTING QUANTITATIVE STUDIES OF THE MODEL MINORITY STEREOTYPE

Grant B. Morgan and Kari J. Hodge

You can't fix by analysis what you bungled by design.
—*Light, Singer, and Willett (1990, p. viii)*

Imagine planning a trip to an academic conference, a vacation, or a business trip with no information on where you were going, how you were going to get there, or when you would arrive or return. How would you prepare for such a trip? How would you know if you were in the correct place at the correct time, or if the trip was successful? Chances are that you would not know the answers to these questions without a plan with specific purpose in mind. In fact, if one did happen to find oneself at the correct place at the correct time, it would be purely by chance alone.

Killing the Model Minority Stereotype: Asian American Counterstories and Complicity,
pages 293–310.

When conducting research within the social sciences, researchers wisely do not allow randomness to govern their research endeavors. Rather, social science researchers use a guiding theory to develop one or more research questions that they seek to answer with a carefully planned investigation.

The research design provides the road map and specifies all of the travel details for a research study. That is, the design outlines how all of the pieces of the research study fit together to allow for conclusions to be reached *about the specific research question(s) of interest*. Without a well-crafted plan in place, the conclusions that are possible at the end of a study are unlikely to relate to the original research question(s). To this end, many decisions must be made about the research design or plan at the outset of the study to maximize the likelihood that *possible* conclusions are the *desired* conclusions. This chapter will discuss many of the decisions (and consequences) that must be made when planning a research study because the researcher who leaves these decisions to chance will likely find himself or herself with data that do not allow the conclusions about the research questions of interest. In other words, if the data collected are based on flawed processes, there is no type of statistical analysis that can fully compensate for the problems.

In this chapter we first define research validity and the four types of research validity. Second, we discuss two types of research fallacies. Third, we expand upon internal validity. Fourth, we expand upon external validity. Fifth, we discuss sampling strategies and population inference. Last, we introduce a few methodological and analytic considerations for several designs before providing our concluding remarks.

DEFINITION AND ROLE OF VALIDITY IN THE RESEARCH PROCESS

Within the context of social sciences, the research process broadly refers to the systematic investigation of specific, theoretically guided questions and hypotheses regarding the relationship(s) between phenomena of interest within the population of interest. In many contexts, including those outside of research, validity is a term that refers to "accuracy" or "correctness" in some sense. In research, the term validity may be thought of as the degree to which the conclusions drawn based on the evidence provided by the study are correct with respect to the research questions posed at the beginning of the study. For example, if one sought to answer a research question about the assimilation of Asian Americans, then s/he would design a study that would provide the most compelling evidence on which s/he could draw her conclusion. That is, s/he would study a group of Asian Americans that represent the larger group of Asian Americans about whom her/his conclusions will describe, and s/he would collect reliable data on the experiences and attitudes of the Asian American participants that are strong indicators of assimilation. The validity in her/his case would be the degree of correctness in her/his conclusion.

There is a subtle nuance to this wording that should be made clear. Validity is not an entity to be obtained; rather, it is a quality inherent to decisions, conclusions, or inferences. Thus, researchers must carefully and thoughtfully develop studies that are likely to yield trustworthy information about the population of interest, construct(s) of interest, relationship(s) of interest, or, in other words, research question of interest. Clearly, there are many aspects of the research design to be considered. Below we elaborate on the four types of research validity: (1) conclusion, (2) construct, (3) internal, and (4) external. These four types of validity are related to each other but have different focal points within the research study.

TYPES OF RESEARCH VALIDITY

Conclusion Validity. Conclusion validity—which is sometimes referred to statistical conclusion validity—is a frequently overlooked and infrequently understood aspect of research studies. This type of validity refers to the degree to which statistical conclusions about the relationships in the data are correct. Many readers will be familiar with the process of null hypothesis significance testing (NHST) in which researchers make a decision about whether or not to retain the statistical null hypothesis as being potentially true based on a conditional probability (i.e., p value). The authors prefer the construction of confidence intervals as opposed to NHST, but we discuss NHST in this section due to its prevalence in graduate research methods courses. The null hypothesis is a statistical hypothesis about the value of a parameter that characterizes the population of interest. Researchers can then test the tenability of the null hypothesis by examining the probability of getting the data collected in the study if the null hypothesis were true. A small probability (p value) could mean that one has collected extreme data due to a fluke, or it could mean that the null hypothesis is false. In most cases, researchers will find the latter more reasonable and conclude that the null hypothesis is false.

An example may help clarify this idea. Suppose a researcher is interested in whether or not Vietnamese or Filipino students tend to have higher standardized reading scores on average. He designs a study to collect the standardized reading scores from 40 10th grade Vietnamese students and 40 10th grade Filipino students. He randomly selects these 80 students from a well-defined population of these students. The traditional statistical procedure for examining two independent groups is the t test. This test assumes that the scores of the participants are normally distributed and that the variability of scores is the same for both groups of participants. The test also assumes that all participants are not related in any way nor share meaningful relationships. Next, the researcher constructs a confidence interval about the difference between Vietnamese and Filipino students, and this confidence interval is -5 to -2. Using a Type I error rate (α) of 5%, which is typical for social science, the researcher could then conclude with 95% ($1 - \alpha\%$) confidence that the true difference in standardized reading scores in the Vietnamese and Filipino 10th grade populations is between 2 and 5 points in favor of Filipino students. This range of values is based on the tenability of the model assumptions stated above. If these assumptions are not tenable then the confidence interval is incorrect, and unfortunately it is not possible to know in what way it is incorrect. It may be too narrow, or it may be too wide. In either case, the statistical conclusion that the researcher reached would be incorrect, and this would represent a problem with the study's conclusion validity.

Type I Errors. The researcher cannot know with certainty if the null hypothesis is true. Yet, the null hypothesis is treated as being either true or false. If the null hypothesis is true, the researcher should retain it, and if it is false, then the researcher should reject it. A false rejection of a true null hypothesis is referred to as a *Type I error*. To protect oneself against this type of error, the researcher can establish the highest risk (i.e., probability) that s/he is comfortable assuming. This probability is called the maximum allowable Type I error rate and is typically denoted as α. In the social sciences, α is usually set to .05 or 5%. Clearly, if one makes a Type I error, then his or her decisions about the research question will be incorrect.

Type II Errors. As stated above, if the null hypothesis is true, the researcher should retain it, and if it is false, then the researcher should reject it. The failure to reject a false null hypothesis is referred to as a Type II error. Though not generally viewed as problematic as Type I errors, Type II errors result in researchers, say, concluding there is no relationship between variables of interest when there really is a relationship. The probability of making a Type II error is typically denoted as β, and values at or below .2 are considered acceptable. Perhaps more common is to consider the inverse of the Type II error rate—statistical power, which can be computed as $1 - \beta$. That is, statistical power is the probability of correctly rejecting a false null hypothesis. Ways of increasing statistical power are increasing the sample size, increasing α, increasing the sensitivity of cognitive or psychological instruments, or increasing the degree of falsehood that one hopes to detect. If the null hypothesis is false, increasing statistical power gives the researcher a higher probability of rejecting it and making the correct decision about the statistical hypothesis of interest in the study. A summary of the possible decisions and associated errors is provided in Table 16.1.

Confidence Intervals and Effect Sizes. The above discussion focused on the use of NHST. The use and misuse of NHST has been debated for

TABLE 16.1. Summary of Decisions About the Null Hypothesis in Statistical Significance Testing

		Null Hypothesis (H$_0$)	
		True	**False**
Decision	**Retain H$_0$**	Correct Decision	Type II error (β)
	Reject H$_0$	Type I error (α)	Correct Decision (*Power = 1– β*)

decades, and many educational and psychological academic journals now prefer the reporting of confidence intervals and effect size estimates. Mathematically, all point null hypotheses are false, which casts some doubts on the utility of NHST, which tests only a single null hypothesis. Constructing confidence intervals, on the other hand, provides a simultaneous test of all possible null hypotheses. That is, confidence intervals contain all plausible values of the population parameter of interest associated with the Type I error rate (α) set by the researcher. Not only do confidence intervals provide the plausible values of the population parameter, but they also provide information about the precision afforded by the study. A very wide confidence interval (i.e., wide range of plausible values) shows less precision, whereas a very narrow confidence interval (i.e., small range of plausible values) shows more precision. Clearly, this provides researchers with much more information than the NHST, which results in a rejection or retention of the null hypothesis.

Confidence intervals should also be accompanied by effect size estimates. It is well known that statistical significance testing is heavily influenced by the size of the sample used in the study. In fact, with a large enough sample, any hypothesis will be "statistically significant" even if the difference is minuscule and of no practical importance. An effect size measure is a standardized measure of "practical" significance that is less heavily influenced by the sample size. Due to its standardization, it allows for comparisons to be made across studies in some cases. Which estimate of effect size to report differs by statistical procedures. Interested readers should consult Cohen (1988) for information on specific effect size measures for different designs.

Additional Considerations. There has been some discussion here on the topic of *p* values. It should be noted that the trustworthiness of *p* values is in part based on the tenability of model assumptions associated with various statistical procedures. For many researchers, the common assumptions for multigroup analysis (e.g., *t* tests, analysis of variance) are independently and normally distributed errors as well as homogeneous error variances. If these assumptions are not tenable, then the *p* value provided by the statistical software is not to be trusted. It is advised that analysts check the tenability of all model assumptions before conducting and interpreting the results of the inferential analysis.

Construct Validity. Construct validity refers to the degree to which the variables used in a study are representative of the theoretical constructs of interest. In many areas of educational and psychological research, scholars recognize that they are dealing with the actual constructs that exist in their guiding theory. These constructs are often referred to as latent variables, which are theoretical and not directly observable. Instead, researchers must create variables that allow for the manifestations of the latent variables to be observed. Thus, construct validity is a measurement issue. Construct validity can be thought of as the accuracy of decisions made about the construct based on the information provided by a cognitive or psychological instrument.

Construct validity comes with its own subtypes of validity (i.e., content- and criterion-related) that must be addressed by the researcher. Content-related validity refers to how well a set of items on a cognitive or psychological instrument represents the construct of interest. Evidence for an instrument's content-related validity is usually provided in the form of detailed descriptions of expert involvement in item writing and the percentage of items that adhere to the instrument specifications as informed by the researcher's guiding theory. Criterion-related validity refers to the degree of association between the instrument and another criterion, which is typically an alternative operationalization of the same or related constructs. In some cases, the criterion used is a future event or behavior. For example, a researcher seeking to determine the relationship between college admission scores with first year college grade point average among Asian American students will use the first year GPA as the future event. Thus, the college admission test score would be examined in a predictive manner of college GPA. This sort of investigation provides evidence for a measure's "predictive validity." If the criterion is available at the same time as the instrument under investigation, then the investigation provides evidence for the instrument's "concurrent validity." Criterion-related validity can also be provided by the direction of the relationship between focal instrument and the criterion. If the researcher hypothesizes that the relationship will be a moderate to strong positive one, this provides evidence for "convergent validity." If the researcher hypothesizes that the relationship will be a weak or negative one, this provides evidence for "discriminant validity."

Interested readers should see Crocker and Algina (1986) for more detail. Any researcher wishing to provide evidence for a measurement's construct validity must consider its reliability. Reliability can be thought of as the consistency with which information is produced. Within the context of research, reliability is a necessary condition for construct validity. That is, information produced by a cognitive or psychological instrument that is inconsistent across time, judges, samples, or administrations will necessarily negate the possibility of making correct decisions about the construct of interest. For the most part, construct validity affects the variables used in the study. If the theoretical constructs of interest in the study are measured poorly or improperly, then it is very unlikely that the researcher will reach the correct and appropriate conclusions regarding the guiding research question(s).

External Validity. External validity refers to the degree to which the findings of a study generalize to and across populations, in other settings, in different places, and at different times. Populations refer to the types of people that are of research interest. Places refer to the geographic locations. One might be interested in determining if research findings hold in the United States as well as Southeast Asia. Setting refers to environments of research interest. One might be interested in determining if research findings hold for public as well as private schools. Time refers to the period of time of research interest. One might be interested in determining if findings from 10 years ago still hold in the modern day. Clearly, no study can span all populations, all settings, all places, and all times. The challenge for researchers is to design a study that will be most relevant for a target population in a target setting in a target place at a pertinent point in time. No researcher should conduct a study under the delusion that his or her study will answer a research question for good. Replication of studies is crucial so that the field of interest has more information about how phenomena relate within the different combinations of people, settings, places, and time. We expand on the topic of external validity below.

Internal Validity. Internal validity refers to accuracy of causal inferences drawn between the variables in the study. The ability to explain phenomena in terms of cause and effect is desirable for many researchers. If one knows the source and relationship of the cause to the effect, then manipulation of the cause may be possible in order to obtain the desired effect. The gold standard for studies that seek to make causal inferences is the experimental design. One very common experimental design consists of multiple conditions to which participants are randomly assigned. In many cases, random assignment is not possible in which case researchers may opt for a quasi-experimental design, such as a regression discontinuity design, time series design, or a design that involves propensity score matching. These designs are beyond the scope of this chapter, but interested readers should see Algina and Olejnik (1982); Box, Jenkins, and Reinsel (2008); Rosenbaum and Rubin (1983); Shadish, Cook, and Campbell (2002); Stuart and Rubin (2007); Thistlethwaite and Campbell (1960); and Thorndike (1942). There are three conditions that need to be met in order to infer a causal relationship, each of which can be addressed in an experimental design. The first condition is temporal precedence, which requires that the cause happen before the effect. The second condition is covariation. That is, the effect is present if and only if the cause occurred, and the effect must be absent if the cause did not occur. In an experiment, there should be at least a treatment group and a control group. This configuration allows the researcher to assess what happens when the cause (i.e., treatment) is present versus absent. The third condition is that alternative explanations of the effect have been ruled out. Randomly assigning participants into the conditions, or groups, will remove systematic error in the long run. We expand on the topic of internal validity below.

RESEARCH FALLACIES

Ecological Fallacy. A fallacy is an error in reasoning based on unsound logic. Of the two most common research fallacies, we begin with the ecological fallacy. The ecology of a study includes the element(s) that the study participants interact with and operate within. The ecological fallacy occurs when researchers base conclusions about individuals on the analysis of grouped or aggregated data. The "model minority" stereotype is partially based on the ecological fallacy. For example, suppose a researcher finds that Koreans outperform their White counterparts on the SAT in a local school district. Based on these findings, he concludes that any incoming Korean high school students should not receive SAT preparatory instruction. That aggregated analysis suggests that Korean students score higher on the SAT than White students clearly does not mean that every Korean student will score higher than every White student. Such a conclusion would be a fallacious decision.

Exception Fallacy. The exception fallacy occurs when a researcher observes a phenomenon in a single person but falsely concludes that the observation applies to all members of the group to which the person belongs. The model minority can be viewed as an example of this type of fallacious reasoning. For example, suppose a researcher conducted a study that included a participant who self-identified as Vietnamese. Over the course of the study, the researcher finds that this single participant consistently reported higher levels of family stability. From this information, the researcher concludes that members of Vietnamese families experience less family instability than members of White families. Such a conclusion will most certainly not hold in all cases. It would be equally problematic for the researcher to conclude that members of families from Southeast Asia or even families from Asia experience less family instability than members of White families, even though the model minority stereotype supports such claims. When presented this way, such conclusions seem absurd. Yet, there are many examples in the "model minority" history that illustrate the exception fallacy. For example, there may be views that all Asian are good at sports based on the success of Jeremy Lin in the National Basketball Association and Hideo Nomo or Hideki Matsui in Major League Baseball (Hartlep, 2012; Kalman-Lamb, 2013; Mayeda, 1999). Another example of the exception fallacy may be the view that Asians are concentrated in elite four-year colleges and universities when there are many Asians attending two-year colleges (CARE, 2008, 2010).

INTERNAL VALIDITY EXPANDED

Above we introduced the concept of internal validity as the accuracy of cause-and-effect inferences made within a research study. In this section we would like to expand upon the topic to include discussion of some of the potential phenomena that could threaten the internal validity of the study. As many of us well know, social science research does not take place in a vacuum where participants are protected from the countless influences and events that exist outside of the study. Below are several of the common threats that may weaken or negate causal inference drawn from a study.

Threats to Internal Validity. The single-group threats discussed in this section follow the discussion put forward by Trochim and Donnelly (2006), who have an excellent introductory text on the subject of research methods. We strongly recommend their text to interested readers.

Mortality Threat. The mortality threat occurs when participants drop out of the study for any reason. If the mortality occurs due to some random process, then the threat to internal validity should be minimal. The mortality threat becomes problematic when attrition is due to a nonrandom process. For example, suppose a researcher was studying the effectiveness of a reading intervention among first generation Chinese students in second grade. Midway through the study, several parents of students who have lower reading skills withdraw their students from the study. At the conclusion of the study, the reading program's effectiveness may be artificially inflated or deflated. In either case, the conclusion reached about the program's impact on student reading skills would be biased.

History Threat. The history threat occurs when an event beyond the researcher's control occurs during the study that affects all participants in some manner. Suppose a researcher developed an intervention to assist Asian immigrant students cope with bullying from American students during the fall semester of 2001. After the terrorist attack in New York on September 11, many of the study participants may have experienced an elevation in typical bullying by American students out of hatred/fear towards those not born in the United States. In addition to being an exception fallacy on the part of the American students, these circumstances may have resulted in the program being found ineffective when in fact its effectiveness or lack thereof was tied more strongly to the impact of the terror attack on 9/11 than to the program itself.

Testing Threat. The testing threat occurs in pre-/post-test designs when participants have been clued in to the pertinent aspects of an intervention by way of the pre-test. In a study, for example, of a statistics advancement program of high school students, participants may have an inclination about what specifically to pay attention to based on the particular questions asked on the pre-test. In such a case, the post-test scores may be slightly artificially inflated, which would lead to an inaccurate decision about the relationship between the statistics program and statistics ability as indicated by the post-test scores.

Instrumentation Threat. The instrumentation threat occurs in pre-/post-test designs when there are differences between the actual tests that are given as the pre- and post-test. Consider the same example from the previous section. Suppose the post-test given to the students at the end of the statistics advancement program was much more difficult than the pre-test. The result of this difference in test difficulties might suggest that the statistics program was less effective than it was in actuality. This again would lead to an inaccurate decision about the effectiveness of the statistics program among high school students.

Maturation Threat. The maturation threat occurs in studies that last long enough for the study participants to change in some meaningful way over the course of the study outside of the variable of interest. Hopefully, people mature and develop over time naturally, which may confound the results of a study. Concluding that a program was responsible for a change in the study participants when natural development is the cause would be an inaccurate conclusion. One way to address this threat is to include a group of participants who do not take part in the treatment (i.e., control group), which allows the researcher to evaluate the natural development of people similar to those taking part in the treatment.

Regression Threat. The regression threat is actually a statistical phenomenon that may occur when extreme measures are observed. Extreme observations are less common than observations near the mean (i.e., arithmetic average). Chances are that the observation following an extreme one will be closer to the mean. This is the regression threat. Suppose that students are given a pre-test before a lesson that covers the scientific method, and everyone scores terribly for one reason or another. Chances are that the students would score higher on a parallel form of the pre-test with no science instruction at all! Thus, when the post-test is given scores may increase to a larger extent because the scores were near the bottom to begin with. Concluding that the science instruction accounted for all of the increase in scores would be inappropriate.

Additional Considerations. The threats discussed above are applicable to single group and multiple group studies, but additional threats exist that apply specifically to designs with social interaction. These threats are compensatory rivalry, diffusion of treatment, resentful demoralization, and compensatory equalization of treatment. The first three of these threats involves one group's reaction to knowing that they are in the comparison group, so they alter their behaviors. The final threat is particularly common in educational settings due to the emphasis on equality. From an internal validity perspective, it is essential that one group not take part in the treatment or program for comparison purposes. Yet, in education, administrators may offer compensatory services to the comparison group because they are not receiving the intervention under investigation. As a result, the post-test scores may end up being similar, which prevents the researchers from being able to draw appropriate causal inferences.

This section has bombarded the reader with potential problems with research studies. It is common for instructors of research methods courses to be asked by students if it is possible to design a *good* research study. The answer to this question should be multi-faceted. Obviously, there are many elements and phenomena that the researcher much consider when designing his or her study. Some of these elements are outside of the researcher's control, so the challenge is to design the best study possible given the available resources while being as transparent as possible. We stated earlier that no single study is going to definitively answer a research question. We, as researchers, must continue to build on the knowledge base by designing the best studies we can, replicating others' studies, and being transparent when presenting our methodologies and results so others can do the same.

EXTERNAL VALIDITY EXPANDED

The major concern of external validity (ecological validity) is the degree to which findings can be generalized across populations, settings, and time (Maxwell & Delaney, 2004). Sample selection is a key factor in external validity. The specific technique used to select the sample in relation to the research question and the characteristics of the population with which the researcher wishes to generalize are discussed further. Threats to external validity include sample bias, lack of representation, failure to respond, response bias, invalid observations of construct, wording effects, and specificity of variables.

Populations. Populations are a defined collection of persons, objects, or events. When designing a study from which a researcher wants to generalize, s/he must obviously first identify the population to which generalizations are desired. Based on the phenomenon under investigation, the population should be identified based on one's guiding theory. As such, the population defined at the outset of a study is the ***target population***. This term is used because this is the population that researchers wish to target with their generalizations. The researcher must define the population in terms of people, setting(s), place(s), and time(s) based on theoretical

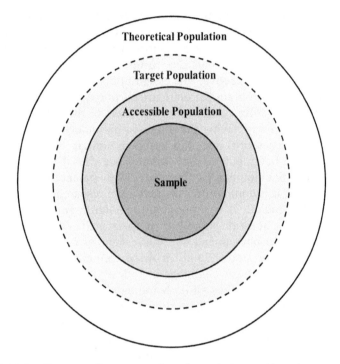

FIGURE 16.1. Conceptual representation of population and its subsets.

specification. Therefore, the target population may also be referred to as the **_theoretical population,_** though the theoretical population also extends beyond the target population (see Figure 16.1). The researcher will rarely, if ever, be able to draw study participants from the entire target population. More likely, the researcher will only have access to a subset of the target population due to resource constraints. This subset of the target population is typically referred to as the **_accessible population_**. That is, the accessible population is the group of people who possess characteristics of interest from which the researcher can realistically select participants (Gay, Mills, & Airasian, 2006).

In most studies, researchers will not likely have the time, money, or energy to collect data from the entire accessible population. Therefore, samples are drawn from the accessible population. In order to increase the generalizability of the study findings, the sample should be representative of the target population. There are many sampling strategies available to researchers, some of which we discuss below. The _best_ sample is the one that represents the population in terms of people, context, place, and time, regardless of how the sample was drawn; however, those sampling strate-

Where is the study in comparison to the population?

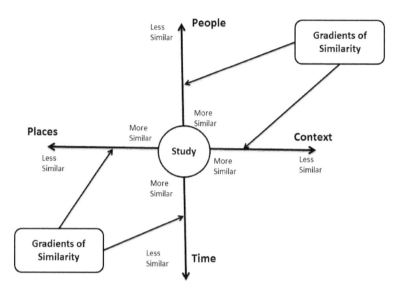

FIGURE 16.2. Ideal Location of a Study's Sample Within the Four Dimensions that Represent the Population. Note that it is possible for a sample to be representative on one or more of the dimensions without necessarily being representative of all dimensions. Each arrow in the diagram represents gradients of similarity. Ideally, the study's sample is similar to all dimensions of the target population.

gies that involve a random process are *most likely* to yield a representative sample. When the sample is not representative of the population, then one cannot be sure if the findings will generalize to the target population. That is not to say that the findings will not generalize to *some* population, but not necessarily *the target population* that was defined at the beginning of the story. Therefore, the actual population to which findings generalize when the sample is not representative of the target population may be referred to as the ***unknown population***. Brady and O'Regan (2009) argue that a non-random sample is an issue of external validity in that participants are less likely to be a true representation of the target population. Employing a non-random sampling procedure more likely recruits participants from an unknown population, therefore limiting generalizability to the population of interest. Figure 16.2 shows the ideal location of a study's sample within the four dimensions that represent the population. Note that it is possible for a sample to be representative on one or more of the dimensions without necessarily being representative of all dimensions. We discuss sampling procedures that involve a random process below.

Sampling. Samples are subsets of a population, and researchers may select participants through a variety of methods. In quantitative research, random sampling procedures are one way to increase the likelihood that the sample will be representative of the population of interest. We discuss the most commonly used methods below.

Simple Random Sampling. Under simple random sampling every member of the accessible population has an equal chance of being selected. Therefore, selecting one person has absolutely no bearing on the selection of any other member. A sample must be selected through a random process. One way to select a sample from a known population is to assign each person an identification number and then randomly select identification numbers from a table of random numbers or with a random number generator on the computer. Systematic sampling is similar but is derived from a known list of the population where the investigator selects every k^{th} person, based on the size of the population and the size of the sample needed (Hinkle, Wiersma, & Jurs, 2003).

Stratified Random Sampling. Some populations may be heterogeneous and thus comprised of multiple subgroups, such as gender, political affiliation, or any other demographic characteristic. Although extremely unlikely, it is *possible* for simple random sampling to identify a sample that is unbalanced on one or more of these characteristics. For example, it is possible that a simple random sample of 100 Asian students returns 90 Chinese students, 10 Korean students and no students from any other ethnicity. If the researcher wants to guarantee himself or herself that a sample has some specified composition of demographics, then stratified random sampling might be considered. Under this strategy, the members of the accessible population are divided into groups called strata. Then, a simple random sample is selected from each strata through a proportional allocation procedure. That is, if the researcher wants a sample of 100 students of which 25 are Chinese, 25 are Korean, 25 are Filipino, and 25 are Vietnamese, then s/he could randomly select the appropriate number of students from each strata.

Cluster Random Sampling. Cluster sampling is a random sample of intact groups, such as classrooms or schools, called clusters, from the accessible population. Cluster sampling may be used when it is not feasible to split up members of a cluster. To conduct a cluster random sample, each member must only belong to one cluster, but clusters may have different numbers of members. Rather than randomly selecting individual participants, clusters are randomly selected from the population, and all members of the selected cluster are included in the sample. This sample strategy is very common in social science research. For example, suppose a researcher is interested in studying a statewide curriculum implantation; school districts would be randomly selected and then classrooms within those districts would be randomly selected (Hinkle et al., 2003). Despite the frequency of its use, cluster random sampling is not consistent with experimental design. Regardless, there are statistical procedures (i.e., multilevel modeling) that permit its use in social science research. Multilevel modeling is introduced in chapter 17 of this volume.

THREATS TO EXTERNAL VALIDITY

Sampling Bias. A sample is said to be biased if there is a lack of representation of the characteristics of the population of interest. Sampling bias occurs when there is unequal probability of being selected across members of the accessible population. One example of sampling bias is the caveman effect. Early humans are frequently thought of as having lived in caves because many artifacts have been discovered in caves. What may be overlooked is that early humans lived other places besides caves, but artifacts in caves were better preserved than, say, those of early humans who lived on the coast. In our investigations of early humans there is unequal probability of including artifacts of cave dwellers than coast dwellers.

Nonresponse and Response Bias. Nonresponse bias occurs when those people who do not respond or choose not to participate in a study differ in some way from those who do respond or choose to participate. This form of bias is most common in survey research. The impact of nonresponse bias may be difficult to assess, but the likelihood of nonresponse bias increases as the number of respondents/participants decreases.

Response bias is caused by invalid observations of constructs due to some phenomenon such as wording effects or social desirability. The validity of observations of constructs refers to inferences made about observations or measurement tools that actually represent the construct being investigated. Wording effects are subtle changes in the words or order of words that may impact a participant's responses. Wording questions in a way that illuminates the researcher's opinion may unduly influence participants to answer the question in a way that they believe favors the researcher. Similarly, social desirability occurs when participants report what is socially desirable on a survey instead of what s/he might actually believe.

Specificity of Variables. The research must provide an operational definition of each variable of interest in order for readers to ascertain the degree to which the study is generalizable to other contexts. Inadequately operationalized variables make it problematic to identify the setting and procedures to which the variables can be generalized. Furthermore, it is imperative to fully and adequately operationally define the independent and dependent variables. In the absence of these definitions, the possible generalizations are unclear at best and incorrect at worst.

ANALYTIC CONSIDERATIONS

We wish to point out here that we have not yet discussed specific statistical analyses. This was purposefully done to support the opening quotation that statistical analysis cannot compensate for questionable research designs. In fact, analyzing data collected from a very solidly designed study is generally much simpler than from poorly designed studies. In the section on conclusion validity, we discussed the importance of assessing the tenability of model assumptions when conducting statistical analysis. Undoubtedly, in some cases researchers will determine that statistical model assumptions are untenable, in which case they may turn to a nonparametric statistical procedure or bootstrapping. Each of these topics is beyond the scope of this chapter, but interested readers should see Chernick (1999), Marascuilo and McSweeney (1977), and Mooney and Duval (1993). In other cases, the researchers may determine that it is not theoretically consistent to assume that only one population underlies a set of data. Fortunately, there are statistical procedures that can accommodate such theoretical expectation. Generally, these procedures are subsumed by mixture models (see chapter 17 of this volume). Finally, there are also statistical procedures that can help researchers minimize the probability of committing an ecological fallacy by using only aggregated data. When data have a hierarchical structure, it is not necessary to aggregate up or disaggregate down to a certain level of analysis. Models that accommodate hierarchically structured data are commonly referred to as multilevel models (see chapter 17 of this volume). The point we wish to make is that statistical analysis should be determined by the research design, which is the guiding framework for the study. The research design is what ensures that researchers most efficiently and effectively answer the specific research question(s) of interest. After all, Fisher (1938) appropriately stated that "[t]o consult the statistician after an experiment is finished is often merely to ask him to conduct a *post mortem* examination. He can perhaps say what the experiment died of" (p. 17)

CONCLUSIONS

The purpose of this chapter has been to introduce two common research fallacies as well as the four types of research validity that, if properly addressed, may help researchers avoid incorrect decisions and, in turn, may lessen the likelihood that consumers of research make ecological and/or exception fallacies. We also provided expanded discussions of internal and external validity. By expanding these sections we do not intend to relegate the importance of construct and conclusion validity, because these also play an important part in research validity. In fact, construct validity is a major consideration for minimizing threats to external validity. We elaborated on internal and external validity because these types of validity are strongly related to ecological and exception fallacies that are unfortunately found in social sciences, particularly in areas such as the "model minority" stereotype (Hartlep, 2013). We assert that researchers who attend to the four types of research validity will design studies from which appropriate conclusions can be drawn that generalize to the group(s) of people under investigation.

Questions for Reflection

1. What is the relationship between the research question(s), research design, and statistical analysis?
2. What are the relationships between conclusion validity and external validity?
3. Is it possible to have external validity without internal validity and vice versa? If so, how?
4. Is it possible to have external validity without construct validity?
5. Which type(s) of validity is/are most strongly related to exception and ecological fallacies?

REFERENCES

Algina, J., & Olejnik, S. F. (1982). Multiple group time-series design: An analysis of data. *Evaluation Review*, *6*(2), 203–232.

Box, G. E. P., Jenkins, G. M., & Reinsel, G. C. (2008). *Time series analysis: Forecasting and control* (4th ed.). Hoboken, NJ: John Wiley & Sons.

Brady, B., & O'Regan, C. (2009). Meeting the challenge of doing an RCT evaluation of youth mentoring in Ireland a journey in mixed methods. *Journal of Mixed Methods Research*, *3*(3), 265–280.

CARE (The Commission on Asian American and Pacific Islander Research in Education). (2008). *Asian Americans and Pacific Islanders. Facts, not fiction: Setting the record straight.* Retrieved December 1, 2014, from http://professionals.collegeboard.com/profdownload/08–0608–AAPI.pdf

CARE (The National Commission on Asian American and Pacific Islander Research in Education). (2010). *Federal higher education policy priorities and the Asian American and Pacific Islander community.* Retrieved December 1, 2014, from http://apiasf.org/CARErepor+t/2010_CARE_report.pdf

Chernick, M. R. (1999). *Bootstrap methods: A practitioner's guide.* New York: John Wiley & Sons.

Cohen, J. (1988). *Statistical power analysis for the behavioral sciences* (2nd ed.). Hillsdale, NJ: Lawrence Erlbaum.

Crocker, L., & Algina, J. (1986). *Introduction to classical and modern test theory.* Pacific Grove, CA: Wadsworth.

Fisher, R. A. (1938). Presidential address. *Sankhya: The Indian Journal of Statistics*, *4*(1), 14–17.

Gay, L. R., Mills, G. E., & Airasian, P. W. (2006). *Educational research: Competencies for analysis and applications* (8th ed.). Upper Saddle River, NJ: Pearson Merrill Prentice Hall.

Hartlep, N. D. (2012). Harvard to the NBA: Deconstructing Jeremy Lin as a "model minority." *Korean Quarterly, 15*(3), 18.

Hartlep, N. D. (2013). *The model minority stereotype: Demystifying Asian American success.* Charlotte, NC: Information Age.

Hinkle, D. E., Wiersma, W., & Jurs, S. G. (2003). *Applied statistics for the behavioral sciences.* Boston, MA: Houghton Mifflin.

Kalman-Lamb, N. (2013). The athlete as model minority subject: Jose Bautista and Canadian multiculturalism. *Social Identities, 19*(2), 238–253.

Light, X., Singer, X., & Willett, X. (1990). *By design: Planning research on higher education.* Cambridge, MA: Harvard University Press.

Marascuilo, L. A., & McSweeney, M. (1977). *Nonparametric and distribution-free methods for the social sciences.* Monterey, CA: Brooks/Cole Publishing.

Mayeda, D. T. (1999). From model minority to economic threat: Media portrayals of major league baseball pitchers Hideo Nomo and Hideki Irabu. *Journal of Sport and Social Issues, 23*(2), 203–217.

Maxwell, S. E., & Delaney, H. D. (2004). *Designing experiments and analyzing data: A model comparison perspective* (2nd ed.). Mahwah, NJ: Lawrence Erlbaum Associates.

Mooney, C. Z., & Duval, R. D. (1993). *Bootstrapping: A nonparametric approach to statistical inference.* Thousand Oaks, CA: Sage.

Rosenbaum, P. R., & Rubin, D. B. (1983). The central role of the propensity score in observational studies for casual effects. *Biometrika, 70*(1), 41–55.

Shadish, W. R., Cook, T. D., & Campbell, D. T. (2002). *Experimental and quasi-experimental designs for generalized causal inference.* Boston, MA: Houghton Mifflin.

Stuart, E., & Rubin, D. B. (2007). Best practices in quasi-experimental designs: Matching methods for causal inference. In J. Osborne (Ed.), *Best practices in quantitative methods* (pp. 155–176). Thousand Oaks, CA: Sage.

Thistlethwaite, D. L., & Campbell, D. T. (1960). Regression-discontinuity analysis: An alternative to the ex post facto experiment. *Journal of Educational psychology, 51*(6), 309–317.

Thorndike, R. L. (1942). Regression fallacies in the matched groups experiment. *Psychometrika, 7*(2), 85–102.

Trochim, W. M., & Donnelly, J. P. (2006). *Research methods knowledge base.* Mason, OH: Atomic Dog.

CHAPTER 17

STATISTICAL PROCEDURES FOR ADDRESSING RESEARCH FALLACIES SUCH AS THE MODEL MINORITY STEREOTYPE

Grant B. Morgan and Kari J. Hodge

Let us begin by stating that the importance of the design in any research endeavor cannot be overstated. The design serves as the guiding plan for all decisions and activities throughout a research study and ensures that the study appropriately answers the research question(s) of interest. Furthermore, the statistical analysis should be determined by the research question(s) and guiding theoretical expectation.

Generally, it is advisable for researchers to employ a statistical procedure with the appropriate level of complexity. That is, it is ill advised to use a highly complex set of analyses if the research question(s) does/do not justify their use, just as it is ill advised to use an overly simple set of analyses for a research question that warrants more complex procedures. We acknowledge that conducting quantitative/empirical educational and psychological research can be very challenging given an infinite number of potential influences and confounding variables. That said, we do not

Killing the Model Minority Stereotype: Asian American Counterstories and Complicity,
pages 311–333.

believe that quantitative researchers should unnecessarily limit themselves analytically when more advanced procedures are available that can accommodate the complex data structures that are present in social science research. In fact, use of traditional analyses (e.g., analysis of variance, regression) may contribute to researchers making one of two research fallacies, or making an incorrect decision regarding potential relationships among variables in a study. In this chapter, we will discuss two research fallacies, followed by traditional statistical procedures for examining group differences. Next, we will discuss two statistical modeling procedures that may allow researchers studying phenomena like the "model minority" stereotype to more efficiently and effectively align their analysis with guiding research questions and/or theoretical expectation.

RESEARCH FALLACIES

Ecological Fallacy. A fallacy is an error in reasoning based on unsound logic. Of the two most common research fallacies, we begin with the ecological fallacy. The ecology of a study includes the element(s) that the study participants interact with and operate within. The ecological fallacy occurs when researchers base conclusions about individuals on the analysis of grouped or aggregated data. The model minority stereotype is partially based on the ecological fallacy. We should note first that fallacies are made by misinterpretations of data provided through statistical analysis, not the analysis itself. That said, let us consider how ecological fallacies may be more likely among inexperienced analysts using, say, analysis of variance (ANOVA). The one-way ANOVA model is a method for testing the equality of two or more group means. The two-group comparison is typically conducted using a t test, but a two-sided hypothesis test can also be done using the one-way ANOVA. The null hypothesis (H_0) and alternative hypothesis (H_1) for the one-way ANOVA is typically written as:

$$H_0 : \mu_1 = \mu_2 = \ldots = \mu_k$$

$$H_1 : \mu_k \neq \mu_{k'}, \text{ for some } k \neq k'$$

Suppose for the purposes of this discussion that the null hypothesis is rejected with $1 - \alpha\%$ confidence. What does this mean? It means that there is sufficient evidence to conclude that at least one of the *group means* is different from at least one of the other *group means*. Some hypothetical context may help. Suppose a researcher concludes that Korean students had higher scores on average than Chinese students. Notice that we did not say that every Korean student had a higher score than every Chinese student. In fact, there very likely were Chinese students who outperformed

Korean students. The difference that was discovered by the researcher was between the Korean and Chinese students, *on average*. If the same researcher randomly selected one additional Korean student and one additional Chinese student, then she might predict based on ethnicity that the Korean student might score higher than the Chinese student. Such a prediction would be justified by the findings. To conclude that the Korean student is smarter than the Chinese student would be fallacious. A probabilistic positioning of the two students would be justified by the study findings. A deterministic positioning of the students on the basis of ethnicity would be an example of an ecological fallacy. Thus, the results provided by ANOVA must be interpreted with care, and researchers *should not* overstep what the analyses suggest.

Exception Fallacy. The exception fallacy occurs when researchers draw conclusions about groups based on the characteristics of one member of the groups. The flawed judgment that is inherent to the exception fallacy is the root of many sexist and racist views. In the same vein, the "model minority" stereotype is, again, partially based on this sort of fallacious reasoning. In the section above, we illustrated a hypothetical instance of an ecological fallacy made with ANOVA. We will illustrate a hypothetical instance of an exception fallacy using regression.

Regression analysis is most commonly used to examine the relationships between a continuous outcome variable and one or more continuous or categorical predictor variables. In regression, all variables are measured at the individual level, so outcomes can be predicted for an individual based on his or her values on a set of variables. The results of individual variables' predictive relationship are expressed with a regression coefficient that shows how much one might expect the outcome variable to change based on an increase in the predictor variable. Consider the hypothetical linear regression model below where math score (Y) is being predicted by reading score (X):

$$Y_i = .5X_i + e_i$$

The regression coefficient in this case is .5. This means that we would expect the math score to increase by .5 points for a one-unit increase in reading score. Additionally, if we knew that a randomly sampled student had a reading score of, say, 26, then we could predict that his math score would be 13 (13 = .5 * 26). The e_i in the model represents the difference between the student's predicted score and actual score, or error. The mean of the errors in the population is assumed to be zero.

With this simple model in place, suppose that a researcher was able to identify the individual students in the study and determined that a Japanese student in School Z had performed particularly well. From this information the researcher concluded that Japanese students in School X must be outperforming the non-Japanese students in the school. Although this conclusion is a positive one that favors both Japanese students and School Z, it is still an exception fallacy. In fact, there are several problems with this scenario. First, the analyses conducted do not support this conclusion, and the research has fallen into the exception fallacy. Second, the researcher treated the cases differentially due to inside knowledge of the participants. It is advised to use numeric identifiers in the data to prevent this type of unethical behavior on the part of the analyst. It may also help protect against fallacious conclusions.

TRADITIONAL STATISTICAL PROCEDURES FOR EXAMINING GROUP DIFFERENCES

In this section, we present the basic concepts and model assumptions associated with regression analysis and ANOVA. We also discuss the potential consequences of violated model assumptions and inappropriate application of the procedures.

Regression. As stated above, regression analysis is a statistical procedure that can be used to examine relationships between a continuous outcome, or criterion, variable and one or more predictor variables. The general regression model for one or more predictors can be expressed as:

$$Y_i = B_0 + \sum_{j=1}^{J} B_j X_{ij} + e_i$$

Therefore, if there were only one predictor, the model would be written:

$$Y_i = B_0 + B_1 X_1 + e_i$$

If there were three predictors, the model would be written:

$$Y_i = B_0 + B_1 X_1 + B_2 X_2 + B_3 X_3 + e_i$$

There are actually several more regression model assumptions than are typically discussed in many statistics textbooks. Pedhazur (1982) states the regression assumptions as follows:

1. The predictors are fixed. This means that if the study were repeated the same values of the predictors would be used.
2. The predictors are measured without error. This means that each predictor is perfectly measured.

3. There is a linear relationship between the actual and predicted values.

4. The errors are homoscedastic. This means that the variance of the errors is the same for all levels of the predictors.

5. The errors are normally distributed. This means that the differences between the participants' observed and predicted scores follow a normal distribution.

6. The errors are independent. This means that all of the people in the study do not share any meaningful relationships.

7. The errors are not related to the predictors. This means that correlation between the differences between the participants' observed and predicted scores and the participants' values on the predictors is zero.

Of these seven model assumptions, only certain ones are testable, but the assumption that we wish to highlight in this section is the independent error assumption (#6). In educational data, this assumption is particularly problematic because students do share a meaningful relationship. That is, groups of students are taught by the same teacher. As a result, students who share a teacher or are in the same school are not considered statistically independent. If students are not independent, then regression analysis will produce results that are not trustworthy.

An additional consideration with regression analysis in educational research is that many researchers desire to include variables that reflect student-level information as well as teacher- or school-level information. Suppose that a researcher incorrectly used a traditional regression analysis with school-level variable in a model that predicts a student-level outcome variable. Conclusions about individuals based on aggregated (i.e., group) data are subject to aggregation bias. The mistake of making decisions about individuals based on group data should remind the reader of another topic (you guessed it, the ecological fallacy). The problem with using aggregated data for individual-level outcomes is well documented via Simpson's paradox. Simpson's paradox, also known as the Yule-Simpson effect, can be observed when disaggregated group analysis reveals, say, a positive trend in the data, but aggregated analysis reveals a negative trend. That is, the trend is reversed when groups are aggregated into a single analysis. Furthermore, Robinson (1950) showed that individual-level relationships can be reversed through aggregation. In fact, the seminal paper by Robinson (1950) was one of the first that examined ecological inference in a systematic manner. We recommend that all social science researchers read his paper, especially model minority researchers who utilize quantitative analyses.

Another caveat is that caution must be taken when entering variables into a model that is submitted to regression analysis. Fortunately, there are models that can accommodate data with a hierarchical structure (e.g., students within the same classroom), which allow researchers to model variables that apply to different levels of analysis. The section on multilevel modeling below provides a brief introduction to such models.

Analysis of Variance. One-way ANOVA is used to test whether or not group means differ from one another. Thought of differently, ANOVA is used to predict a continuous outcome variable with a categorical predictor variable. The assumptions of ANOVA are similar to those of regression, but we wish to highlight the three commonly stated assumptions. They are as follows:

1. The errors are independent. This means that the differences between the participants' actual and predicted values are uncorrelated.
2. The errors are normally distributed. This means that the differences between the participants' observed and predicted scores follow a normal distribution.
3. The variances of the errors are equal for each of the k groups in the study. This means that the variance of the errors is the same for each of the k groups.

We have already discussed the importance of the independence assumption in the section on regression. Therefore, in this section we will illustrate problems that may arise with untenable assumptions. In many studies that involve Asian American students, group comparisons are commonly made by aggregating the students together. This practice should be called into question when considering the differences between Asian American subgroups. This topic is relevant to our discussion of ANOVA because each of the groups in ANOVA is believed to represent a single population. The subgroup differences that may exist within the Asian American student body are inconsistent with the single underlying population idea that is inherent in ANOVA.

To clearly demonstrate this data structure, we simulated data for two Asian subgroups and presented the frequency distribution in Figure 17.1. It is clear to see that there are two distinct distributions by Asian subgroup. Next, we produced a frequency distribution ignoring the subgroups and treating all Asian students in one group (see Figure 17.2).

In Figure 17.2, not only are the subgroups indistinguishable, but also the distribution in Figure 17.2 would likely pass statistical inspection of model assumptions for ANOVA. The question then becomes how a researcher would make such a determination if statistical inspection would not clue him or her in to the possibility of multiple underlying groups. The

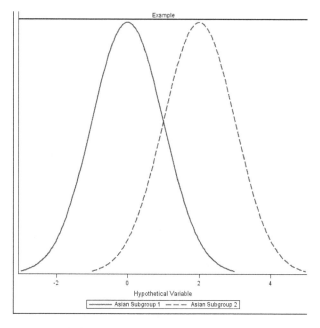

FIGURE 17.1. Two Underlying Distributions Comprised of Asian Students with Distinct Sets of Characteristics

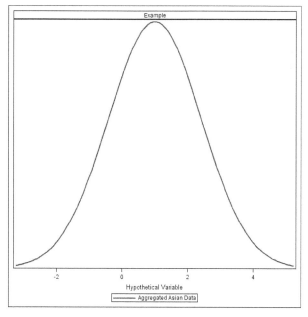

FIGURE 17.2. Example of Overlapping Distributions of Asian Students

answer is one's guiding theory. If meaningful underlying subgroups are theorized, then there are models that can accommodate this. The section on mixture modeling below provides a brief introduction to such models.

MULTILEVEL MODELING

Multilevel modeling refers to an analytic framework that models data collected at multiple levels. Other names that readers may encounter for multilevel models are hierarchical linear models, random coefficient models, or mixed models. In the sections below we provide an introduction to some of the details of multilevel modeling.

Rationale. In traditional statistical analysis, interpretation is simpler when all of the variables are measured at the same level. That is, if the student is the unit of analysis, then all of the variables reflect some characteristic of the student. When an aggregated variable, such as a school-level variable, is included when multiple students attend each of the multiple schools, then there may be a statistical dependency. As stated previously, regression analysis with an aggregated variable is not advised. Multilevel modeling provides the researcher with a tool that can show how much of the variability is attributed to the school as well as return a set of model parameters that best describe the entire sample rather than a different set of parameters for each school.

Data Structure. To this point, we have discussed "levels" of analysis. The different levels of analysis are the basis for the hierarchical structure of the data. Suppose a researcher conducted a study in 25 middle schools. In each of those middle schools, she sampled 30 Asian American students. Her data would be considered structured. She would have 30 students within each of the 25 middle schools. The overall sample size would be 750 (25 schools x 30 students = 750), but the students are nested within schools. This so-called "nesting" is precisely the data structure that multilevel models take advantage of. Students can be nested within classrooms, classrooms can be nested within schools, schools can be nested within districts, and so on. The lowest level in the analysis is always considered level-1, and the level number increases for each level of nesting. For example, in the case of students nested within classrooms, students would be considered level-1 and classrooms would be considered level-2.

Some Models. There are several models that are commonly used in educational research. Before discussing the models, let us first introduce the concept of a random effect. In order to illustrate the concept, we first consider a fixed effect. In traditional one-way ANOVA, for example, the grouping variable is commonly considered fixed because the study includes all of the groups of interest. That is, the groups are fixed. In a study where schools make up the grouping variable, on the other hand, the study likely does not include all schools of interest. Chances are, the schools in such a study are considered a random sample from a larger population of schools. Schools would be considered a random effect. Rather than estimating the mean for each school in the study, it is possible to capture this information in a different way—with the variance of the school means. The variance is a measure of variability that is greater than or equal to zero. If there is no variability in the school means, then one could conclude that all of the school means are equal. If the variance of the school means is greater than zero, then one could conclude that there are differences between school means. Below we explain three common multilevel models.

Random Effects ANOVA Model. The first multilevel model is the random effects ANOVA:

$$Y_{ij} = \mu + e_{ij} + u_{0j}$$

The estimated parameters in this model are the grand mean (μ), the variance (σ^2) of the level-1 random effect (e_{ij}), and the variance (τ_{00}) of the level-2 random effect (u_{0j}). The level-1 and level-2 random effects are assumed to be normally distributed with a mean of zero. This model is occasionally referred to as the unconditional means model and can be used to determine how much of the variability can be explained by the level-2 units. The estimate of variance explained by level-2 is called the intraclass correlation coefficient (ICC). The ICC is computed as:

$$ICC = \frac{\tau_{00}}{\tau_{00} + \sigma^2}$$

If the ICC is equal to zero, then the independence assumption from regression analysis is tenable, and multilevel modeling is unnecessary. Traditional regression analysis may be used because only level-1 is needed. If the ICC is equal to one, then all of the variability in the outcome is explained by the level-2 units, and multilevel modeling is also unnecessary because only level-2 is needed.

Means-as-Outcomes Model. The second model is the means-as-outcomes model. It can be expressed:

$$\text{Level 1:} \quad Y_{ij} = B_{0j} + e_{ij}$$

$$\text{Level 2:} \quad B_{0j} = \gamma_{00} + u_{0j}$$

When the level-1 and 2 models are combined, it can be expressed:

$$\text{Mixed Model:} \quad Y_{ij} = \gamma_{00} + e_{ij} + u_{0j}$$

Although the model in the example above does not have level-1 predictors, it is possible to include level-1 predictors into the model.

Random Coefficients Model. The second model is the random coefficients model, which can be expressed:

$$\text{Level 1:} \quad Y_{ij} = B_{0j} + B_{1j} X_{1ij} + e_{ij}$$

$$\text{Level 2:} \quad B_{0j} = \gamma_{00} + u_{0j}$$

$$B_{1j} = \gamma_{10} + u_{1j}$$

When the level-1 and 2 models are combined, it can be expressed:

$$\text{Mixed Model:} \quad Y_{ij} = \gamma_{00} + \gamma_{10} X_{1ij} + u_{1j} X_{1ij} + u_{0j} + e_{ij}$$

The model shown here does not include a level-2 predictor, but it is possible to model one or more level-2 predictors. What is unique about this model is that the slopes (i.e., relationship between the predictor and outcome variable) are allowed to vary by school. Though each slope is not individually estimated, the variance of the slopes (τ_{11}) is estimated to capture the variability in the slopes.

Intercept- and Slopes-as-Outcomes. The last model is the intercept- and slopes-as-outcomes model. With one predictor at level-1 and level-2, the model can be written:

$$\text{Level 1:} \quad Y_{ij} = B_{0j} + B_{1j} X_{1ij} + e_{ij}$$

$$\text{Level 2:} \quad B_{0j} = \gamma_{00} + \gamma_{01} W_j + u_{0j}$$

$$B_{1j} = \gamma_{10} + \gamma_{11} W_j + u_{1j}$$

When the level-1 and 2 models are combined, the mixed model can be expressed:

$$\text{Mixed Model:} \quad Y_{ij} = \gamma_{00} + \gamma_{01} W_j + \gamma_{10} X_{1ij} + \gamma_{11} W_j X_{1ij} + u_{1j} X_{1ij} + u_{0j} + e_{ij}$$

In this model, the intercept and slopes are allowed to vary across schools.

Graphical Display of Fixed and Random Effects. We acknowledge that the formulaic expression of these models may be difficult for readers with limited previous exposure to multilevel models. Figures 17.3 through 17.5 below show the difference between fixed and random slopes and intercepts.

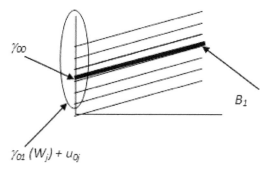

FIGURE 17.3. Example of Graph with Random Intercepts and Fixed Slopes. Here the thick line represents the average intercept and average slope for all schools. The smaller lines represent schools. All lines are parallel, which reflects the fixed slope. The space between the lines at the y-axis reflects the differences in school intercepts.

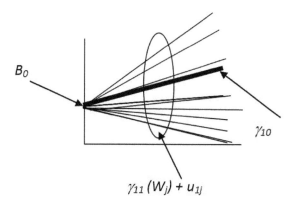

FIGURE 17.4. Example of Graph with Fixed Intercepts and Random Slopes. Here the thick line represents the average intercept and average slope for all schools. The smaller lines represent schools. All lines have the same value on the y-axis, which reflects the fixed intercepts. None of the lines are parallel to another line, which reflects the differences in slope (i.e., random slopes).

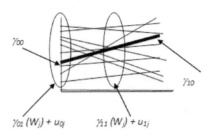

FIGURE 17.5. Example of Graph with Random Intercepts and Random Slopes. Here the thick line represents the average intercept and average slope for all schools. The smaller lines represent schools. All lines have different values on the y-axis, which reflects the different intercepts (i.e., random intercepts). None of the lines are parallel to another line, which reflects the differences in slope (i.e., random slopes).

EXAMPLE

In this section, a relatively simple example will be used to show how multilevel modeling can be applied to a multivariate dataset. The data used in this example were simulated to demonstrate the type of information that is available in multilevel analysis. The dataset includes 600 Chinese and Filipino students in public or private schools. The standardized mathematics test score will be used as the dependent variable.

Model 1. Given that multilevel modeling allows researchers to empirically examine the tenability of the independence assumption, we first computed the ICC, which again can be thought of as the correlation between students within each school. For these data, the ICC was computed using the following information.

```
## Linear mixed model fit by REML
## Formula: math_score ~ 1 + (1 | school)
##     Data: hlm.data
##    AIC  BIC logLik deviance REMLdev
##   4057 4070  -2026     4052    4051
## Random effects:
##  Groups   Name        Variance Std.Dev.
##  school   (Intercept) 10.9     3.31
##  Residual             45.3     6.73
## Number of obs: 600, groups: school, 45
##
## Fixed effects:
##             Estimate Std. Error t value
## (Intercept)   17.487      0.573    30.5
```

The ICC for these data was:

$$ICC = \frac{\tau_{00}}{\tau_{00} + \sigma^2} = \frac{10.9}{10.9 + 45.3} = .194$$

The ICC indicates that 19.4% of the variability in student math scores is attributable to one or more school-level variables. Said another way, the correlation between students within schools is .194, which is clearly a violation of statistical independence. This ICC justifies the use of multilevel modeling instead of ordinary least squares (OLS) regression. Fitting an OLS regression model would produce results that are biased and may lead to incorrect conclusions.

One may also use the model output to predict the mathematics score of a randomly selected student. The prediction equation is:

$$MATH = \gamma_{00} + u_{0j} + e_{ij}$$

Both random effects, u_{0j} and e_{ij} are expected to have a mean of 0. We now can use the prediction equation to get a predicted value of:

$$M\hat{A}TH = 17.487 + 0 + 0 = 17.487$$

Therefore, if one did not know anything about the students or schools in this study, one could predict the mathematics score of a randomly selected student to be 17.487.

The output above shows how the variance in the outcome variable is partitioned into the student- and school-level variables. The total variability in the math scores is $10.9 + 45.3 = 56.2$, and the ICC tells the researcher that 19.4% of the variability is due to school-level information. This also tells the researcher that 81.6% of the variability in math scores is due to student-level information. We can introduce new variables that contain information about students and/or schools in order to explain some of the variability at each level.

Model 2. Next, we added a school-level predictor variable that indicates whether the school was public or private. The output is shown below.

```
## Linear mixed model fit by REML
## Formula: math_score - private + (1 | school)
##     Data: hlm.data
##    AIC  BIC logLik deviance REMLdev
## 4051 4068  -2021     4045    4043
```

```
## Random effects:

##  Groups    Name          Variance Std.Dev.

##  school    (Intercept)   9.31     3.05

##  Residual                45.23    6.73

## Number of obs: 600, groups: school, 45

##
## Fixed effects:

##              Estimate Std. Error t value
## (Intercept)   16.309     0.705    23.13

## private        2.840     1.098     2.59

##

## Correlation of Fixed Effects:

##           (Intr)

## private -0.642
```

From this output, one can see that the estimates have changed. In Model 1, the intercept estimate of the school was 10.9, and in Model 2, the residual variance estimate of the school, taking the sector into account, is 9.3. Therefore, we were able to reduce the intercept variance from 10.9 to 9.3. This indicates that 14.7% of the school-level variability is due to whether the school was public or private. This estimate of variance reduction comes from:

$$\frac{\tau_{00(1)} - \tau_{00(2)}}{\tau_{00(1)}} = \frac{10.93 - 9.3}{10.9} = .147$$

We can also use the model output to predict the mathematics scores of students based on which type of school they are in. The prediction equation is:

$$MATH = \gamma_{00} + \gamma_{01} PRIVATE_j + u_{0j} + e_{ij}$$

Both random effects, u_{0j} and e_{ij}, are expected to have a mean of 0. Private schools were coded as "1," and public schools were coded as "0." We now can use the prediction equation to get a predicted value for private schools of

$$\hat{MATH} = 16.30 + 2.84(1) + 0 + 0 = 19.14$$

and a predicted value for public schools of

$$\hat{MATH} = 16.30 + 2.84(0) + 0 + 0 = 16.30$$

Therefore, if one only knew that a randomly selected student attended a private school, one could predict that his or her mathematics score would be 2.84 points higher.

Model 3. Next, we added a student-level predictor variable that indicates whether the student was Chinese or Filipino. The output is shown below.

From the output above, one can see that the estimates have changed.

```
## Linear mixed model fit by REML
## Formula: math_score ~ chinese + (1 | school)
##    Data: hlm.data
##    AIC  BIC  logLik deviance REMLdev
## 4048 4066  -2020    4042    4040
## Random effects:
## Groups   Name        Variance Std.Dev.
## school   (Intercept) 10.3     3.20
## Residual             44.7     6.69
## Number of obs: 600, groups: school, 45
##
## Fixed effects:
##              Estimate Std. Error t value
## (Intercept)  18.578    0.657     28.29
## chinese      -2.080    0.655     -3.18
##
## Correlation of Fixed Effects:
##          (Intr)
## chinese -0.524
```

In Model 1, the residual variance estimate of the student was 45.3, and in Model 3, the residual variance estimate of the student, taking the ethnicity into account, is 44.7. Therefore, we were able to reduce the residual variance from 45.3 to 44.7. This indicates that 1.3% of the student-level variability is due to whether the student was Chinese or Filipino. This estimate of variance reduction comes from:

$$\frac{\sigma^2_{(1)} - \sigma^2_{(2)}}{\sigma^2_{(1)}} = \frac{45.3 - 44.7}{45.3} = .013$$

We can also use the model output to predict the mathematics scores of students based on their ethnicity. The prediction equation is:

$$MATH = \gamma_{00} + \gamma_{10} CHINESE_i + u_{0j} + e_{ij}$$

Both random effects, u_{0j} and e_{ij}, are expected to have a mean of 0. Chinese students were coded as "1," and Filipino students were coded as "0." We now can use the prediction equation to get a predicted value for Chinese students of

$$M\hat{A}TH = 18.58 - 2.08(1) + 0 + 0 = 16.50$$

and a predicted value for Filipino students of

$$M\hat{A}TH = 18.58 - 2.08(0) + 0 + 0 = 18.58$$

Therefore, if one only knew that a randomly selected student was Chinese, one could predict that his or her mathematics score would be 2.08 points lower than a student who is Filipino.

Model 4. To demonstrate the full utility of multilevel models, we added one school-level predictor variable that indicates whether the school was public or private and one student-level predictor that indicates whether the student is Chinese or Filipino. The output is shown below.

```
## Linear mixed model fit by REML
## Formula: math_score ~ private + chinese + private * chinese + (1 | school)
##    Data: hlm.data
##    AIC  BIC logLik deviance REMLdev
## 4041 4067  -2015     4035    4029
## Random effects:
## Groups   Name        Variance Std.Dev.
## school   (Intercept)  8.71    2.95
## Residual             44.75    6.69
## Number of obs: 600, groups: school, 45
##
## Fixed effects:
##                  Estimate Std. Error t value
## (Intercept)       17.345     0.803   21.61
## private            3.027     1.305    2.32
## chinese           -1.933     0.771   -2.51
## private:chinese   -0.467     1.436   -0.32
##
## Correlation of Fixed Effects:
##               (Intr) private chines
## private       -0.615
## chinese       -0.515  0.317
## privat:chns    0.277 -0.572 -0.537
```

Like the other models, we can use the model output to predict the mathematics scores of students based on their ethnicity and which type of school they attend. The prediction equation is:

$$MATH = \gamma_{00} + \gamma_{10} PRIVATE_j + \gamma_{20} CHINESE_i +$$

$$\gamma_{11} PRIVATE_j * CHINESE_i + u_{0j} + e_{ij}$$

Both random effects, u_{0j} and e_{ij}, are expected to have a mean of 0. Chinese students were coded as "1," and Filipino students were coded as "0"; private schools were coded as "1," and public schools were coded as "0." Based on the model output above, we could predict the mathematics score of a Chinese student in a private school as:

$$\hat{MATH} = 17.34 + 3.03(1) - 1.93(1) - .47(1 * 1) = 17.97$$

We could predict the mathematics score of a Chinese student in a public school as:

$$\hat{MATH} = 17.34 + 3.03(0) - 1.93(1) - .47(0 * 1) = 15.44$$

We could predict the mathematics score of a Filipino student in a private school as:

$$\hat{MATH} = 17.34 + 3.03(1) - 1.93(0) - .47(1 * 0) = 20.37$$

We could predict the mathematics score of a Filipino student in a public school as:

$$\hat{MATH} = 17.34 + 3.03(0) - 1.93(0) - .47(0 * 0) = 17.34$$

This model included an interaction between school type and student ethnicity. The interaction indicates that although students in private schools generally score higher than students in public schools, Chinese students do not score quite as highly in private schools as Filipino students do. Given that OLS regression cannot accommodate hierarchically structured data, multilevel modeling is uniquely able to estimate relationships, such as the ones examined here. Specifically, multilevel models may allow an interested researcher to study the differential effect of certain school-level variables across Asian subgroups. We should note again that the data presented here were generated by the authors and do not necessarily reflect true relationships. We used the data to demonstrate the types of relationships that one may examine with multilevel modeling.

ADDITIONAL APPLICATIONS AND CONSIDERATIONS

Multilevel modeling has many potential applications. The models presented here were presented within the context of examining organizational effects, but they can be and are often used to examine growth of students. If data were collected from a set of students across several years, those measures would be correlated within each student. Therefore, the measurements (i.e., time) can also be conceptualized as being nested within each student. This allows for student growth to be monitored across time.

The models presented here are linear models. As such there are a number of model assumptions that must be made. Assessment of the model assumptions necessary for linear modeling is complex, but Bell, Schoeneberger, Morgan, Kromrey, and Ferron (2010) developed a computer program that aids researchers with this task. Readers should see Raudenbush and Bryk (2002) for an excellent discussion of the necessary model assumptions. We should also note that multilevel modeling and the model building process take considerable expertise. We recommend that researchers consult a statistician when conducting multilevel modeling.

MIXTURE MODELING

Mixture modeling is a general term that refers to a set of analyses for data that have two or more underlying populations. That is, the data under investigation are theorized to be comprised of a mixture of multiple populations. Mixture modeling can be applied to longitudinal or cross-sectional data, but the discussion in this chapter focuses on cross-sectional data. Cross-sectional mixture analysis is sometimes referred to as finite mixture modeling because the data are presumed to be a mixture of multiple populations of which there are a finite number.

Rationale. Finite mixture modeling (FMM) is used to identify groups of cases underlying a multivariate dataset (Lazarsfeld & Henry, 1968). These procedures have been referred to in the literature under many different names, such as mixture likelihood approach to clustering (Everitt, 1993; McLachlan & Basford, 1988) and model-based clustering (Banfield & Raftery, 1993). The goal (and challenge) of FMM is the classification of similar objects into one of K groups, or classes, of unknown form and frequency. If a researcher does not hypothesize that there are multiple classes underlying a dataset, then obviously FMM is not justified. The form of the group refers to parameters that distinguish the groups, such as cluster-specific means, variances, and covariances (Vermunt & Magidson, 2002), and the frequency refers to the number of underlying groups.

Using Figures 17.1 and 17.2, we discussed the problems of treating data under which multiple groups lie as if there were only one group. FMM is a statistical procedure that can be used to explore whether or not there is statistical evidence that supports the existence of multiple underlying groups. If multiple groups are discovered, then the groups can be treated separately as opposed to mistakenly treating all of the cases the same.

Data Structure. Unlike data used in multilevel models, data for mixture modeling should all reflect the same level of information. For most educational and psychological purposes, the data reflect individual-level characteristics. This makes sense given that the purpose of the procedure is to classify individuals into groups based on the individuals' characteristics. Grouping is done such that members of the same group are more similar to each other than members of two different groups.

SOME MODELS

Latent Class Models. Under FMM, the classification variable is conceptualized as a latent, categorical variable. Observed, or manifest, variables are used as indicators of the latent group membership. Models that used all categorical indicators are referred to as latent class models. The general latent class model can be expressed

$$f(y_i|\Phi) = \sum_{k=1}^{K} \pi_k f_k(y_i|\rho_k, \Sigma_k)$$

where the distribution of the indicators (y_i) is based on the probability that a certain response pattern is observed for case i. From the equation, the estimated parameters are π_k, the group mixing weight, and ρ_k, which represents the probability of a particular observed response on a particular observed variable conditioned on the class membership (Collins & Lanza, 2010), and values in the class variance-covariance matrix, Σ_k. Values for the ρ_k estimates may range between 0 and 1. In order to determine if a single observed variable is an important indicator of the latent variable, one must examine the pattern of response probabilities across all response alternatives and across all classes. The mean vector of probabilities for all items used in the classification may be identified for each class.

Latent Profile Models. Models that used all continuous indicators are referred to as latent profile models. The general profile class model can be expressed

$$f(y_i|\Phi) = \sum_{k=1}^{K} \pi_k f_k(y_i|\mu_k, \Sigma_k)$$

where the distribution of the indicators (y_i) is based on the probability that a certain response pattern is observed for case i. This model illustrates that the distribution for each of the K groups can be defined by the class mean vector, $\boldsymbol{\mu}_k$, and variance-covariance matrix, $\boldsymbol{\Sigma}_k$. When no distributional restrictions are imposed on the set of observed variables other than multivariate normality, the mixing weights, class centroids, and class-specific covariance matrix must be estimated. A primary goal in latent profile analysis is to identify classes that differ with respect to these parameters.

Mixed Mode Models. When conducting research in education, researchers often collect data on various metric levels. Whereas latent class and latent profile models are based on only categorical or continuous indicators, respectively, cluster models may also be specified based on sets of indicators of different scale types. For example, one may collect data from a sample of students that includes scores on a battery of educational assessment instruments, parents' annual income, and age in addition to information that reflects the students' demographic information, such as race/ethnicity, sex, and special education classification.

In mixed mode FMM all indicators are not required to be measured at the same metric level. Thus, from Vermunt and Magidson (2002), the general FMM can be re-written for mixed mode FMMs as

$$f(\mathbf{y}_i|\boldsymbol{\Phi}) = \sum_{k=1}^{K} \pi_k \prod_{j=1}^{J} f_k(\mathbf{y}_i|\boldsymbol{\theta}_{jk})$$

where $\mathbf{y}_i$ denotes the profile of scores for case i across the set of variables, K is the number of underlying classes, J is total number of indicators, π_k denotes the probability of belonging to class k (i.e., class prevalence), and $\boldsymbol{\theta}_{jk}$ is the set of model parameters.

With each of the models presented above, there is a host of fit indices that aid researchers with selecting the correct model. Morgan (in press) showed that the performance of the fit indices is not compromised when using FMM with mixed mode data.

EXAMPLE

Hartlep, Morgan, and Hodge (*cf.* chapter nineteen in this volume) provided an application of FMM for the identification of Asian subgroups using those identified as Asian in the ELS:2002 dataset. They selected the three-class model as the best approximating model of those examined. They discovered classes were of similar sizes. The first class was composed of 29.4% of the students, the second class made up 32.6% of the sample, and the third class was the largest, representing 38.0% of the sample.

The third class was characterized by students whose parents had more varied but slightly higher education levels on average and whose parents had slightly higher educational aspirations. Mothers and fathers tended to have educational levels between high school and four-year degrees but had slightly fewer four-year degrees or higher and fewer high school degrees or lower. This class had students of slightly above below SES index (M = 0.04, SD = 0.34) and standardized test scores (M = 52.7, SD = 8.8).

The second class was characterized by students whose home language was predominantly English (45.4%) and West/South Asian (37.1%), and whose parents were much more educated. Among mothers and fathers, about 90% had graduated from college or higher, and 60% had graduate degrees (e.g., Masters, Ph.D., M.D., J.D.). This class had above average SES (M = 1.00, SD = 0.33) and standardized test score composites (M = 59.5, SD = 8.9).

The first class was the smallest of the three. The most commonly spoken home language among students in this class was West/South Asian (68.0%). Well over half (67.4%) of the mothers and 45.6% of the fathers of students in this class did not finish high school, and about half of these parents reported educational aspirations for their child of four-year degree completion. The SES (M = -1.01, SD = 0.36) and test score (M = 48.1, SD = 9.0) composites for students in this class were well below average and were clearly the lowest of the three classes.

The third, and largest, class consisted of 24.0% Southeast Asian, 20.1% Korean, and 20.6% Chinese students. The second latent class was 26.0% South Asian, 22.6% Korean, and 21.4% Chinese. The first class was predominantly Southeast Asian (59.3%) and 20.9% Chinese students.

There appear to be different characteristics for each class, which the study authors contend problematizes the model minority stereotype. One class tended to have very highly educated parents and tended to speak English at home, and another class had very poorly educated parents and tended to speak an Asian language at home. Given that the analysis is based only on the Asian students in ELS:2002, they found compelling evidence that refutes the model minority stereotype.

ADDITIONAL APPLICATIONS

Gibson (1959) and Lazarsfeld and Henry (1968) are considered the first to make use of LCC with empirical situations, but Pearson (1894) was the first to fit mixture models consisting of two normal distributions. Clearly, these models have been available for many years, but the methods are becoming increasingly popular due to advances in technology and computing power. Prior to these technological advances, the procedural complexity involved in running FMM models was prohibitive to most applied researchers. There are countless applications of mixture modeling in education. Researchers have begun to use more advanced models to examine student growth across time and then classify students into groups on the basis of their growth trajectories. Such models are referred to as growth mixture models.

Another application of mixture models may involve the estimation of transition probabilities between latent growth trajectories. In the FMM discussed in this chapter, individuals are assigned to groups based on the probability they have of belonging to each group given the model. That is, based on the characteristics of each group as well as the characteristics of each individual, he or she receives a probability of belonging to each group based on the alignment between the group- and individual-level characteristics. The individual is then placed into the group to which he or she has the highest probability of belonging. Still other mixture models allow each individual to have partial membership in each group.

A final note of caution is warranted. Like multilevel modeling, mixture modeling is a rather technical statistical procedure that must be conducted with care. Also like multilevel modeling, there are many modeling decisions throughout the analysis that must be made based on statistics and guiding theory. We always recommend consulting a mixture-modeling expert when conducting these analyses

Questions for Reflection

1. How can research fallacies be avoided when using analysis of variance and regression?
2. How does mixture modeling help researchers avoid research fallacies?
3. How does multilevel modeling help researchers avoid research fallacies?
4. Can any statistical procedure prevent a researcher from reaching fallacious conclusions? Why or why not?
5. What other aspects of the model minority stereotype could be investigated using multilevel or mixture modeling?

REFERENCES

Banfield, J. D., & Raftery, A. E. (1993). Model-based Gaussian and non-Gaussian clustering. *Biometrics, 49,* 803–821.

Bell, B. A., Schoeneberger, J. A., Morgan, G. B., Kromrey, J. D., & Ferron, J. M. (2010). Fundamental diagnostics for two-level mixed models: The SAS[®] macro MIXED_DX. In *Proceedings of the SAS[®] Global Forum 2010 conference.* Cary, NC: SAS Institute Inc.

Collins, L. M., & Lanza, S. T. (2010). *Latent class and latent transition analysis: With applications in the social, behavioral, and health sciences.* Hoboken, NJ: John Wiley & Sons.

Everitt, B. (1993). *Cluster analysis.* London, UK: Edward Arnold and Halsted Press.

Gibson, W. A. (1959). Three multivariate models: Factor analysis, latent structure analysis, and latent profile analysis. *Psychometrika, 24*(3), 229–252.

Lazarsfeld, P., & Henry, N. (1968). *Latent structure analysis.* New York: Houghton-Mifflin.

McLachlan, G., & Basford, K. (1988). *Mixture models: Inference and applications to clustering.* New York: Marcel Dekker.

Morgan, G. B. (in press). Mixed mode latent class analysis: An examination of fit index performance for classification. *Structural Equation Modeling.*

Pearson, K. (1894). Contributions to the mathematical theory of evolution. *Phil. Trans. Roy. Soc. London, 185,* 71–110. Retrieved December 1, 2014, from http://rsta.royalsocietypublishing.org/content/185/71.full.pdf+html

Pedhazur, E. J. (1982). *Multiple regression in behavioral research* (2nd ed.). New York: Holt, Rinehart, & Winston.

Raudenbush, S. W., & Bryk, A. S. (2002). *Hierarchical linear models: Applications and data analysis methods* (2nd ed.). Thousand Oaks, CA: Sage.

Robinson, W. S. (1950). Ecological correlations and the behavior of individuals. *American Sociological Review, 15,* 351–357.

Vermunt, J. K., & Magidson, J. (2002). Latent class cluster analysis. In J. A. Hagenaars & A. L. McCutcheon (Eds.), *Applied latent class analysis* (pp. 89–106). Cambridge, UK: Cambridge University Press.

CHAPTER 18

THE "MODEL MINORITY" MYTH

A Critical Race Theoretical Analysis of Asian Americans in America's Most Segregated City

Nicholas D. Hartlep and Antonio L. Ellis

Milwaukee Asians are twice as likely as whites to receive a subprime refi-
nance loan—the highest Asian-white disparity in the nation.
—*Metropolitan Milwaukee Fair Housing Council (2005)*

INTRODUCTION

Unless it is "model-minority" related (Lee, 2001, 2003, 2005, 2007, 2009; Lee,
Wong, & Alvarez, 2009; Lou, 1989), it seems as though Asian Americans[1] neither demand, nor receive much attention. Indeed, over time they have been labeled by scholars as the "forgotten" minority (United States Commission on Civil
Rights, 1977), the "reticent" minority (Chew, 1994), the "not-so-silent" minority
(Paek & Shah, 2003), and the "super" minority (Teranishi, 2002). Nevertheless,
in the majority of the cases Asian Americans are deemed model minorities by society. Unfortunately, though, the *model minority* moniker is a *myth* and has been
found to have negative consequences for Asian Americans (Palmer, 1999; Tay-

Killing the Model Minority Stereotype: Asian American Counterstories and Complicity,
pages 335–355.

ag, 2011; Zhou & Gatewood, 2000). This supposedly positive stereotype labels Asian Americans[2] as highly successful and worthy of praise for working hard and achieving at high levels (Lee, 2005). But what the model minority does is divide and conquer minorities, preventing them from forming coalitions. Moreover, the myth is used as evidence that society is colorblind and meritocratic. The model minority myth's emphasis on meritocracy serves to erase the diversity and heterogeneity found within Asian American subgroups as a result of "ethnic gloss" (Trimble & Dickson, 2005). Trimble and Dickson (2005) state that "ethnic gloss presents the illusion of *homogeneity* where none exists" and warn scholars that the "ethnic gloss can violate . . . external validity" (p. 413, italics added).

Therefore, Asian Americans, through the lenses of *model minority* and "ethnic gloss," appear *homogeneous* from the outside, when in fact they are *heterogeneous* within (Hartlep, 2012a; Lee, 2007). The model minority myth implies Asian Americans experience the world in a singular way, and that this experience is relatively problem-free. The issues of homogenization and erasure are therefore focal issues for the Asian American community, and deservedly should receive attention. We chose to base our study where Asian Americans live in Milwaukee, Wisconsin, the most segregated city in America (Denvir, 2011), because we wanted to confirm whether or not they truly were integrated with mainstream Whites.

Although our chapter analyzes the residential loci of six Asian American subgroups in Milwaukee and the suburbs that surround the city—Chinese, except Taiwanese; Japanese; Korean; Vietnamese; Hmong; and Other Asians—our chapter focuses particular attention on the Hmong in Wisconsin due to their unique racialized experiences, which we will explain in further detail.

PURPOSE OF THE STUDY

The Black-White binary so often present in social scientific research is self-limiting insofar as it does not adequately consider the experiences of Asian Americans. Thus, we contend, as have others before us, that research must move beyond the Black-White binary and include the experiences of Asian Americans (e.g., see Wing, 2007; Wu, 2002). By focusing upon the experiences of Asian Americans in Milwaukee, we intend to decenter Whiteness by valuing the experiences of marginalized and subordinated people. Given that Critical Race Theory (CRT) counter-narrates majoritarian stock-stories through exposing contradictions of colorblindness and meritocracy (e.g., see Ladson-Billings, 1998, 1999, 2005; Ladson-Billings & Tate, 1995; Lynn, 1999, 2002; Lynn & Jennings, 2009; Lynn & Parker, 2006; Lynn, Yosso, Solórzano, & Parker, 2002; Yosso, 2005), our study aimed to expose the "dirty laundry"—for lack of a better term—of racism and racial residential segregation (Su, 1998). Specifically, our intent was to counter the stock story that Asian Americans are a *model minority* and integrated into the White mainstream.

Model Minority Stereotype

Due to space limitations, this chapter does not go into incredible depth on the model minority myth. For a good review of the model minority stereotype, consult the following works: Alvarez, Juang, and Liang (2006); Bell, Harrison, and McLaughlin (1997); Bhatt (2003); Chae (2004); Chang and Villazor (2007); Chen (2004); Chen and Yorgason (1999); Chu (1997); Coalition for Asian American Children and Families (2011); Daseler (2000); Education Trust (2010); Farole (2011); Freedman (2005); Guillermo (2011); Gupta, Szymanski, and Leong (2011); Hall (2001, 2002); Hartlep (2012a, 2012b); Lee (2001, 2003, 2005, 2007); Lee and Ying (2001); Lew (2004, 2006); Li and Wang (2008); Palmer (1999); Tayag (2011); Tran and Birman (2010); Van Ziegart (2006); Victoria (2007); Wallitt (2008); Weaver (2009); Winnick (1990); Wong (1976); and Wong and Wong (2006). The model minority holds that Asian Americans are well adjusted and accepted into the bosom of mainstream American society. If this is true—that Asian Americans are welcomed into the mainstream—then it is safe to assume that they should not be found to be residentially segregated.

Our chapter begins by citing two incidences in Wisconsin that serve as "counterstories" (Solórzano & Yosso, 2002; Yosso, 2006) to dispel the notion that Asian Americans do not experience racism and/or inequity. We hope these lesser-known incidents will illustrate that the Asian American population is overlooked and ignored (Lew, Chang, & Wang, 2005), as well as racially victimized. Our chapter is further subdivided into three sections: First, we share the setting and the context of our case study. Second, we describe numerous nefarious ways that Asian Americans are purposefully neglected by mainstream society. We rely on critical historiography and the tenets of CRT for many of our assertions. We then transition to a discussion on the implications of being perceived as a model minority (Tayag, 2011; Weaver, 2009) and why we believe that the image of the model minority is not factual and should be rejected by Crits. Third, in the penultimate sections of our chapter, we review the study's methodology and findings. Our findings seem to indicate that Asian Americans are segregated in Milwaukee, Wisconsin, and should not be considered a model minority.

Asian American Racism in Wisconsin

Lee's (1997, 2005; 2009) qualitative studies on Hmong high school students in Wisconsin point to the different ways in which Hmong students are viewed by their schoolteachers in racist contexts. For instances, traces of yellow-peril prejudice persist in contemporary times in the state of Wisconsin. A salient example occurred in Meteor, Wisconsin, during Thanksgiving weekend in 2004. Chai Soua Vang, a 36–year-old Hmong man, was accused of shooting eight hunters, six of whom died, and all of whom were white men (Moua, 2007). Vang was sentenced to six life sentences (Moua, 2007). In what could only be labeled racist, after the hunting incident, according to Baldillo, Mendy, and Eng (2005), "Custom Now, a store in Mankato, Wisconsin, carried bumper stickers that read 'Save a Hunter. Shoot a Mung'"(p. 5).[3] Others have written about this and other Hmong hunting incidents in Wisconsin (e.g., see Fredrix, 2007; Haga, 2007; Imrie, 2008; Schein & Thoj, 2007).

Three years later, on January 6, 2007, Cha Vang, 30, of Green Bay, was found dead, one night after he was reported missing in the Peshtigo Harbor Wildlife Area in northeastern Wisconsin (Fredrix, 2007). In the court case, *State of Wisconsin v. James Allen Nichols* (State of Wisconsin, 2007), James Nichols, 28, of Peshtigo, Wisconsin, was convicted of second-degree intentional homicide and sentenced to 69 years in prison (Siegle, 2007). In the court case documents, Nichols was said to have despised the Hmong, openly sharing his racist sentiments toward Asian Americans.

These two examples of anti-Hmong violence in Wisconsin are counterstories to the model minority majoritarian stock story that affirms Asian Americans as model citizens. The model minority metanarrative is antithetical to the anti-Asian animosity and violence that Asian Americans experience on a day-to-day basis.

METHOD

Setting and Context

Data used in this study were procured from the National Center for Education Statistics' (NCES) School District Demographic System (SDDS). In addition to 1990, 2000, and 2010 SDDS data, this case-study (Stake, 1995) designed investigation also called upon GIS mapping technology (Clemmer, 2010) as an analytical tool. The authors of this study also relied on simple statistical analyses (tests of mean differences) to support their overall findings. This case study investigates the residential loci of Asian American students in Milwaukee. The case is the city of Milwaukee and the suburban school districts that border it (Stake, 1995). The GIS maps in this study use racial populations that represent the number of people—all people—within each school district.

IGNORED = INVISIBLE: THE HMONG

Hmong Quilts

A salient example of how Asian Americans are rendered invisible by White supremacy is the belief that Amish make "local quilts," which overlooks the Hmong quilt-makers that actually manufacture and make these supposedly cultural artifacts (e.g., see Gibson, 2006). Gibson (2006) shows that during the 1960s local Hmong women of Lancaster, Pennsylvania created handmade quilts as a way to help generate income for their families. Readers of Gibson's (2006) article "Familiar Patterns: Hmong and Mennonite Quilt makers in Lancaster County" (2006) learn that the quilts gained popularity during this era because of their designs, patterns, color schemes, and fabrics. Marriage and childbirth were among the many occasions where quilts were given as gifts, symbolizing love and care. More importantly, though, quilt making served as a way to preserve the Amish's society and as a way of detaching themselves from the outside world (Gibson, 2006).

The mainstream's (and the Amish's) commodification of these cherished cultural artifacts, along with the act of not giving recognition to the Hmong who make them, is more insidious than lying; it intentionally *ignores* and thereby renders the Hmong quilt-makers and their history *invisible*. For the Hmong, the quilts were in fact "story cloths" that Hmong women created in refugee camps to tell their stories of struggle and tragedy through their needlework (Lackey, Stefaniak, Centenno, & Urban Anthropology Inc., 2004). Intentionally ignoring the contributions of Asian Americans is prevalent, pervasive, well-documented, and serves to make the Hmong (and other Asian Americans) invisible.[4] Moreover, adding to a historical narration and historical amnesia, colorblindness serves as an agent and mechanism that discounts Asian American contributions (such as the Hmong's contribution to the Central Intelligence Agency in the Vietnam War effort).

Hmong Poverty

Lani Guinier and Gerald Torres (2002) write how colorblindness "permits policy analysts to ignore the high poverty rate among Asian Americans because *it is not supposed to be there*" (p. 57, italics in original). Colorblindness in this case, embodied in the model minority stereotype, serves to ignore the poverty of Asian Americans while revering their putative paragon successes. This false sense of "success" can be traced back to how Asian American students are viewed in schools as model minorities whose diverse and complex experiences remain hidden (Lee, 1994, 2007). This "pariah-turned-paragon" rhetoric maintains White supremacy and encourages further marginalization of Asian American people as "satyrs-turned-saints." The most current data indicate that the Hmong have some of the highest rates of poverty in Wisconsin (UW-Extension, 2000).

Problem Statement

Scholars have studied the Hmong in Wisconsin (e.g., see Dearborn, 2008a, 2008b; Koltyk, 1998; Lee, 1994, 2005, 2007, 2009). However, there has not been a case study conducted on the Asian American population in Milwaukee, Wisconsin—the most segregated city in America—using GIS Mapping technology and a critical race theoretical framework. Despite the dramatic growth of the Asian American population in Milwaukee, this population, especially the Hmong, remains a largely invisible minority group. Ball and Tyson (2011) state that for educational researchers *non satis scire*, or "to know is not enough." The present critical race theoretical case study attempts to understand and explain why Asian Americans' stories and experiences are overlooked or ignored in Milwaukee, despite the population's immense growth (Lackey, Stefaniak, Centenno, & Urban Anthropology Inc., 2004). Its chief argument is that *to know* about Asian invisibility *is not enough*; scholars must draw attention to Asian American invisibility, illustrating why it is insidious and must end, helping to advance the civil and social rights of Asian Americans (Wei, 2010).

THEORETICAL FRAMEWORK

The researchers utilized a critical race theoretical (CRT) lens to examine issues of race at the institutional levels in segregated suburban schools that touch the city of Milwaukee (Chapman, 2011; Hartlep, 2010; Horsford, 2011). Schools are often spaces where race and racism go un-discussed and are not clearly understood by many students (Stovall, 2006a). CRT assumes that issues of race and racism are central to the experiences of U.S. citizens and are indelibly woven into the social hierarchies, institutional practices, and psychological mindsets of people in the United States (Hartlep, 2010; Horsford, 2011; Ladson-Billings & Tate, 1995).

When the authors of this case study speak of *racism*, they reflect upon Wellman's (1977, p. xviii) definition: "Culturally sanctioned beliefs which, regardless of the intentions involved, defend the advantages Whites have because of the subordinated positions of racial minorities." CRT is intentionally deployed to depict the historical and current contexts of schooling in the suburban cities that touch Milwaukee, Wisconsin. Milwaukee is an especially useful city for a CRT (Buenavista, Jayakumar, & Misa-Escalante, 2009; Chang, 1999; Teranishi, Behringer, Grey, & Parker, 2009) case study since there is a Hmong Charter school in the city, as well as the fact that Milwaukee has a fairly large Hmong population. Hmong American Peace Academy (HAPA) is the first Hmong Charter School in Wisconsin (HAPA, 2012). Lee (2007) wrote that "[t]here are two Hmong Charter Schools in the U.S., one in Milwaukee and one in Minneapolis" (p. 175). However, eight years later, Lee's (2007) chapter statement is no longer accurate. The authors estimate that there are now at least nine Hmong Charter schools in the United States.[5]

Critical Race Theory Tenets

Scholars have identified specific principles while using CRT to examine social and racial inequality (Crenshaw, 1995; Delgado & Stefancic, 1993, 2000, 2001; Dixson & Rousseau, 2005; Lynn & Adams, 2002; Gillborn, 2009; Parker, Deyhle, & Villenas, 1999; Parker & Lynn, 2002). CRT (1) critiques the U.S. legal system, (2) recognizes racism as an institutional phenomena in U.S. society, (3) interrogates claims of race neutrality and universal treatment of all citizens, (4) relies on counter narratives as a means to highlight the knowledge of people of color, and (5) is intersectional in its analysis in critiquing sexism and classism (e.g., see Dixon & Rousseau, 2006; Stovall, 2006b, 2006c; Taylor, Gillborn, & Ladson-Billings, 2009).

Concepts of CRT such as "interest convergence," "counterstories," "ahistoricism," and "whiteness as property" (Chang, 1999; Harris, 1995) are used in this chapter in order to analyze how macro-structural and macro-social patterns of segregation lead to the invisibility of Asian Americans in Milwaukee. The historical development of suburban towns, and the government's role in denying people of color (including Asian Americans) access to fair housing, are *prima facie* examples of how Whiteness developed as an identity and was maintained through the geographic barriers of housing segregation in Milwaukee. Consequently, Whiteness has now come to mean property and power (Harris, 1995). White "interest convergence" (Bell, 1980) in Milwaukee has occurred through the creation of desegregation programs, such as Chapter 220, to initially allow students into suburban schools. In Milwaukee, Chapter 220 is the name for a Voluntary Student Transfer Program. This program is designed to racially integrate schools by giving minority students the opportunity to attend schools in suburban areas that are predominantly White. This case study identifies the dramatic growth of Asian Americans in Southeastern Wisconsin while also problematizing Asian Americans' invisibility, discrimination, and segregation (Dearborn, 2008a; Weisberg, 2003).

RESEARCH STUDY

Data Collection and Setting

The setting of this case study was purposeful. Milwaukee is the most segregated city in America (Denvir, 2011), and its public school district is the largest in Wisconsin. Furthermore, Wisconsin is home to the third largest National Hmong American community: Lee (2007) notes that "[t]he largest Hmong American communities are in California (65,095), Minnesota (41,800) and Wisconsin (33,791)" (p. 174). Problematically, despite Asian Americans' incredible growth and presence in the state and city, whenever Milwaukee's segregation problem is talked about, it is often framed as a Black-White phenomenon. This racial binary gives no credence to the struggles of Asian American students or their political and educational invisibility.

In fact, nine years after the *Brown vs. Board of Education* of 1954, which struck down "separate but equal" schooling in the United States, the Milwaukee Public Schools (MPS) District was still faced with segregated schools (NAACP, 1963); however, Asian Americans were not a part of this desegregation/integration discourse. This is not surprising to critical scholars, and it is one reason why the authors undertook this case study of Asian Americans in Milwaukee.

As a result of the self-limiting Black-White binary, Kim (1999) has written how Asians are racially triangulated with Blacks and Whites. According to her analysis, the model minority stereotype is created by White supremacist opinion-makers. The willful exaggeration of the educational excellence of Asian Americans serves to demonize mainly Blacks and Latinos. Kim (1999) writes, "The valorization of Asian Americans as a *model minority* who have made it on their own cultural steam only to be victimized by the 'reverse discrimination' of race-conscious programs allows White opinion makers to lambast such programs without appearing racist—or to reassert their racial privileges while abiding by the norms of colorblindness" (p. 117, italics added). By focusing on Black villains and Asian victims, affirmative action becomes a rhetorical device that the conservative use not only to triangulate Asians, but also to divide them from Blacks by making them "honorary" Whites. Thus, affirmative action is perceived not to be necessary for Asian Americans because they are held to be well integrated into the mainstream.

Milwaukee, Wisconsin

Asian Americans have been studied in Wisconsin. For instance, Hein's (2006) study compared the Hmong in Eau Claire, Wisconsin with those in Milwaukee, Wisconsin, while Dearborn's (2008b) study examined two segregated Hmong enclaves—the Northwest Hmong enclave and the Vliet Street Hmong enclave—in Milwaukee. The authors of this study were interested in studying the Hmong American population in Milwaukee, given that the authors were aware that Asian Americans have been known to experience discrimination when purchasing and renting homes (e.g., see Weisberg, 2003).

If we are to fast forward to present day Milwaukee, sixty-one years post-*Brown*, not much has changed or improved for non-White minorities (including Asian Americans). The city of Milwaukee had a population of 594,883 in 2010 (U.S. Census, 2010), of which (60.6 %) were White, (26.8%) were Black, (13.3%) were Hispanic, and (3.4%) were Asian American. The 2010–11 Milwaukee Public Schools' student population was 82,444. Of this total, (56.6%) were African American, (22.6%) were Hispanic, (11.9%) White, (4.8%) Asian American, (3.2%) other, and (.8%) Native American (MPS, 2011). Milwaukee is an appropriate case study given that the percentage of Asian American students in its Public Schools (4.8%) exceeds the city's (3.4%) overall percentage of Asian Americans. Equally important to note, Milwaukee is now the fourth poorest city in the United States (MacIver News Service, 2010) as poverty continues to pulverize pupils in the Milwaukee Public Schools. Most insidious, though, is that according to Richards and Poston's (2011, para 3) analyses of 2010 U.S. Census data, "the percentage of Wisconsin children age 5 to 17 living in poverty rose from 12.9% to 17%" from 2007 to 2010. Ten years earlier, in 2000, the rate of poverty among all Asians in Wisconsin (19.8%) was more than double the poverty rate in the total state population (8.7%) (Minority Health Program, 2008).

DATA ANALYSIS

Data analysis was conducted using critical historical analyses, GIS mapping, and simple statistical analyses. In the sections that follow, the authors illustrate how Asian American students are rendered invisible, despite the fact that they are a significant part of the growing population in the greater Milwaukee Metropolitan area as well as the state of Wisconsin.

Historical Analysis

In the 2002 report *Racial and Ethnic Residential Segregation in the United States: 1980–2000* (Iceland, Weinberg, & Steinmetz, 2002) it was found that Asian and Pacific Islanders and Hispanics experienced increases in segregation, but those increases were generally *larger* for Asians and Pacific Islanders than for Hispanics. In fact, Asians have historically been segregated, and Charles (2003) writes that "Asian segregation from whites is on the rise" (p. 169). A critical historical analysis indicates that relatively few documents or reports have contained national data on Asian American segregation (e.g., see Brooks, 2009; Chun & Zalokar, 1992; Frankenberg, Lee, & Orfield, 2003).

One notable exception is Turner, Richardson, and Ross (2007), whose data from the Housing Discrimination Study (HDS2000), sponsored by the Department of Housing and Urban Development (HUD) and conducted by the Urban Institute, provides "the first national estimates of discrimination against Asians and Pacific Islanders" (p. 47). Indeed, according to Turner, Richardson, and Ross (2007) the HDS2000 data seem to indicate "that Asian home buyers face levels of discrimination as *high or higher* than African Americans and Hispanics" (p. 55, italics added). This should not be surprising given that real estate agents may assume that Asian Americans have large families (i.e., intergenerational Hmong families), which may influence existing neighborhood dynamics. Takaki (1998) writes that historically Asians were segregated through discriminatory residential actions, which led to the eventual formation of urban ethnic enclave neighborhoods (i.e., Chinatowns, Koreatown, Manilatown, Thaitown, Little Phnom Penh, Little Tokyo). Chun and Zalokar (1992) write about Asian American housing-related incidents in which racist fliers were distributed in hopes of intimidating Asian American homeowners to move and also to deter other Asian Americans from moving into the neighborhood. Similar incidents have been documented as having happened in the states of California, Maine, and New York. These racially motivated hate crimes and acts of residential discrimination have impacted Cambodian, Chinese, and Korean Americans. The most heinous example perhaps could be "a fire set by arsonists which left 31 Cambodians homeless in Lynn, Massachusetts, in December *1988*" (Chun & Zalokar, 1992, p. 31, italics added).

Historically a Pariah: Yellow Peril

Politics of race have been used historically to prevent Asian Americans from challenging residential segregation. Brooks (2009) informs her readers in *Alien Neighbors, Foreign Friends: Asian Americans, Housing, and the Transformation of Urban California* that, historically-speaking, white homeowners would "create private agreements, known as racial restrictive covenants, that barred residents of certain areas from selling to anyone not wholly 'of the Caucasian race'" (p. 26). Historically, Asian Americans were deemed disposable and viewed as a "yellow peril" that should be prevented from integrating fully into dominant society. However, this slowly changed as Hmong began immigrating to the United States (Anderson, Miskevich, Jacobs, & KOCE-TV, 2008). Most of the original Hmong refugees that came to the United States and now reside in Milwaukee were sponsored by Lutheran and Catholic Social Services (Lackey, Stefaniak, Centenno, & Urban Anthropology Inc., 2004).

Contemporarily a Paragon: Model Minority

Undoubtedly, the idea that Asian Americans have reached educational, occupational, and social success of meteoric proportions has contributed to their invisibility. Their needs and social concerns go unnoticed because society homogenizes the Asian American population and perceives them as not needing social support. The assumption of success is a "double-edged" sword. According to Teranishi (2004), "The assumptions about the educational achievement of Asian Americans has excluded them from the debate over school desegregation even though Asian Americans have faced a history of residential isolation in the U.S." (p. 255). But the research tells us that Asian Americans in Milwaukee are not all successful in acquiring housing or employment. According to the Metropolitan Milwaukee Fair Housing Council (2005), "Unemployment rates for blacks, Latinos, *Asians*, and American Indians are significantly higher than those of whites in the City of Milwaukee" (p. i, italics added). Asian American residential segregation remains an understudied phenomenon, which is problematic since the schools that children attend are primarily predicated on the neighborhoods in which they live.

FINDINGS

We have provided a CRT and critical historical analysis of how macro-structural and macro-social patterns of segregation lead to the invisibility of Asian Americans, as well as how these structural and social patterns led to the increase number of Asian Americans residing in Milwaukee and the adjacent suburbs. Strong patterns that emerged from our GIS mapping illustrate that the Asian American student population in Milwaukee continues to grow at greater rates than other racial groups. According to the 2010 Census, the "Asian population grew faster than any other major race group between 2000 and 2010" (Humes, Jones, & Ramirez, 2011, p. 4). In light of this immense regional and national growth, Asian Americans are not "forgotten," but instead "ignored." Salient findings include the following:

1. Between 1990 and 2000, there was a 25% (24.8) increase of minorities in the Milwaukee Public Schools District (See Figure 18.1), most of whom were Hmong (See Figure 18.2).

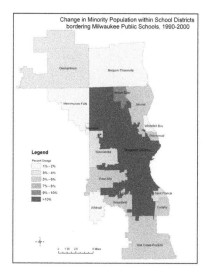

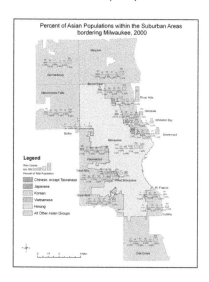

FIGURE 18.1.   Change in Minority
Population, 1990–2000

FIGURE 18.2.   Percent of Asian
Populations, 2000

2.   Comparing the 2000 population totals of all the suburban cities that touch Milwaukee to those of 2010, Asian Americans were the only statistically significantly different racial student population ($t = -2.13$, $p <$ .001, $df = 15$). The Asian American population mushroomed by a factor of 1.5 over these ten years.

3.   Brown Deer, historically a White, Milwaukee suburb, underwent a complete racial reversal in just 20 years—from 1990–2010 there was a 31.4% change in minority population—and the community now is a majority minority city (See Figure 18.3). Interestingly, this is a result of large numbers of Chinese moving into Brown Deer.

4.   A "White-belt" exists in certain areas of the greater-Milwaukee area, but it has been "yellowing" due to the decompressed housing market—such as owners versus renters—and also per capita income (See Figures 18.4 and 18.5).

While some scholars have conducted important research on Asian American segregation in higher education—as in the case of Korean American segregation in Illinois (Abelmann, 2009)—not enough work has been produced on the persistent problem that this study undertook: residential segregation of Asian Americans. Residential segregation is important to study given that where one lives directly impacts the schools one attends, which has cascading life consequences.

In order to place our local findings in a national context, we turned to residential and wealth reports (Applied Research Center, 2009), in particular the Pew Re-

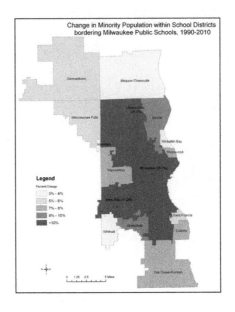

FIGURE 18.3. Change in Minority Population 1990–2010

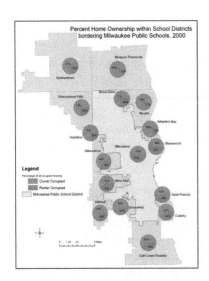

FIGURE 18.4. Percent Home Ownership, 2000

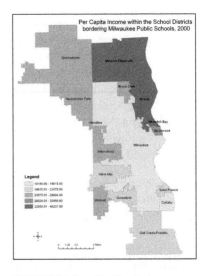

FIGURE 18.5. Per Capita Income, 2000

search Center (2011) report that found that Asians' wealth has dwindled dramatically during the great recession. According to this report, Asian Americans' "net worth fell from $168,103 in 2005 to $78,066 in 2009, a drop of 54%" (p. 5). Also, as the demographics of the community (Milwaukee) continue to shift from what was once a White majority, to what is now a minority White city. This CRT case study has reviewed critical historical and contemporary examples of the most vicious and pernicious examples of Asian residential segregation in Milwaukee, Wisconsin, and elsewhere in the United States. Asian Americans have a history of being excluded and segregated (e.g., see Spring, 2001).

The separation of Whites and Asian Americans—residential segregation—is an issue of importance due to the fact that the realities of the two groups are drastically different. As a result, Lee, Wong, and Alvarez (2009) write that "*Asian Americans* are more likely to live in poverty than *non-Hispanic Whites*" (p. 71, italics added). In Milwaukee, the unemployment rate for "Asians is more than double that of whites" (MMFHC, 2005, p. 16) and "Asians and African Americans are over 2 times as likely as whites *not to have a high school diploma*" (MMFHC, 2005, p. 20, italics added). Lastly, Asian Americans' position within the housing market during the "Great Recession" is a problematic one: not only in Wisconsin, but also in other states. Consequently, Vega (2009) notes the following: "Asians, many of them living in foreclosure-ravaged California, suffered the sharpest drop in homeownership [in 2008], eclipsing declines felt by whites, blacks and Hispanics" (para 1).

Questions for Reflection

1. What is the purpose of the model minority myth?
2. How can teachers and administrators mitigate the model minority belief within educational environments?
3. In what ways does colorblindness serve as a mechanism that discounts Asian Americans' contributions to American history?
4. How do macro-structural and macro-social patterns of segregation lead to the invisibility of Asian Americans in Milwaukee?
5. In what ways did the *Brown vs. Board of Education of 1954* ruling impact the Milwaukee Public Schools between 1954–1964?

NOTES

1. The authors of this chapter use the term Asian American referring to Chinese, Japanese, Korean, Indian, Filipino, Vietnamese, and other Southeast Asian groups. We intentionally and purposefully do not use the term Asian Pacific American, since Pacific Islanders' unique histories are usually conflated with Asian Americans (see Diaz, 2004 for further

explanation). This chapter uses the following six subgroups of Asian Americans: (1) Chinese, except Taiwanese, (2) Japanese, (3) Korean, (4) Vietnamese, (5) Hmong, and (6) Other Asians. Attention is given to Hmong students due to the fact that they are a major Asian American group in Milwaukee.

2. Note that while we capitalize Asian American, Black, White, and White-ness throughout this chapter to emphasize race, we preserve outside quotes (which often use lowercase black and white, and hyphenate Asian-American) in their original form.

3. Despite the change in spelling, Mung is clearly referring to Hmong.

4. Two other examples are as follows: (1) The Korean American War is often referred to as the "Forgotten War" (e.g., see Blair, 1987; Clement, 1998); and (2) regarding the heroism of the Hmong in the Vietnam War, the conflict was called the "Secret War" (see Moua, 2007).

5. (1) Hmong College Prep Academy (St. Paul, MN), (2) Phalen Lake Elementary Hmong Studies and Core Knowledge Magnet, (3) HOPE (Hmong Open Partnerships in Education) Academy (St. Paul, MN), (4) Noble Academy (Minneapolis, MN), (5) Hmong International Academy (Minneapolis, MN), (6) Hmong American Peace Academy (Milwaukee, WI), (7) Community of Excellence (St. Paul, MN), (8) Praire Seeds Academy (Brooklyn Park, MN), and (9) Yav Pem Suab Academy (Sacramento, CA).

REFERENCES

Abelmann, N. (2009). *The intimate university: Korean American students and the problems of segregation.* Durham, NC: Duke University Press.

Alvarez, A. N., Juang, L., & Liang, C. T. (2006). Asian Americans and racism: When bad things happen to "model minorities." *Cultural Diversity and Ethnic Minority Psychology, 12*(3), 477–492.

Anderson, M., Miskevich, E., Jacobs, D., & KOCE-TV (Television Station: Huntington Beach, CA.). (2008). From Laos to Santa Ana: The story of the Hmong. Huntington Beach, CA: KOCE-TV.

Applied Research Center (ARC). (2009). *Race and recession: How inequity rigged the economy and how to change the rules.* Oakland, CA: Applied Research Center. Retrieved June 6, 2014, from http://arc.org/downloads/2009_race_recession_0909.pdf

Baldillo, A. J., Mendy, J., & Eng, V. (2005). Save a hunter, shoot a Hmong: A community held responsible—the assignment of blame by the media. *The Modern American, 1*(1), 3–7.

Ball, A., & Tyson, C. (2011). AERA annual meeting theme. Retrieved July 8, 2014, from http://aera.net/uploadedFiles/2012_Annual_Meeting_Theme.pdf

Bell, D. A. (1980). *Brown v. Board of Education* and the interest-convergence dilemma. *Harvard Law Review, 93*(3), 518–533.

Bell, M. P., Harrison, D. A., & McLaughlin, M. E. (1997). Asian American attitudes toward affirmative action in employment: Implications for the model minority myth. *Journal of Applied Behavioral Science, 33*(3), 356–377.

Bhatt, A. J. (2003). Asian Indians and the model minority narrative: A neocolonial system. In E. M. Kramer (Ed.), *The emerging monoculture: Assimilation and the "model minority"* (pp. 203–220). Westport, CT: Praeger.

Blair, C. (1987). *The forgotten war: America in Korea, 1950–1953.* New York: Times Books.

Brooks, C. (2009). *Alien neighbors, foreign friends: Asian Americans, housing, and the transformation of urban California.* Chicago, IL: University of Chicago Press.

Buenavista, T. L., Jayakumar, U. M., & Misa-Escalante, K. (2009). Contextualizing Asian American education through critical race theory: An example of U.S. Pilipino college student experiences. *New Directions for Institutional Research, 142,* 69–81.

Chae, H. S. (2004). Talking back to the Asian model minority discourse: Korean-origin youth experiences in high school. *Journal of Intercultural Studies, 25*(1), 59–73.

Chang, R. S. (1999). *Disoriented: Asian Americans, law, and the nation-state.* New York: New York University Press.

Chang, R. S., & Villazor, R. C. (2007). Testing the 'model minority myth': A case of weak empiricism. *Northwestern University Law Review Colloquy, 101,* 101–107.

Chapman, T. K. (2011). Critical race theory. In S. Tozer (Ed.), *Handbook of research in the social foundations of education* (pp. 220–232). New York: Routledge.

Charles, C. Z. (2003). The dynamics of racial residential segregation. *Annual Review of Sociology, 29,* 167–207.

Chen, C. H. (2004). "Outwhiting the Whites": An examination of the persistence of Asian American model minority discourse. In R. A. Lind (Ed.), *Race, gender, media: Considering diversity across audiences, content, and producers* (pp. 146–153). Boston, MA: Allyn and Bacon.

Chen, C. H., & Yorgason, E. (1999). "Those amazing Mormons": The media's construction of Latter-Day Saints as a model minority. *Dialogue: A Journal of Mormon Thought, 32*(2), 107–128.

Chew, P. K. (1994). Asian Americans: The "reticent" minority and their paradoxes. *William and Mary Law Review, 36*(1), 1–94. Retrieved June 6, 2014, from http://scholarship.law.wm.edu/cgi/viewcontent.cgi?article=1739&context=wmlr

Chu, N. V. (1997). Re-examining the model minority myth: A look at Southeast Asian youth. *The Berkeley McNair Journal, 5,* 167–176.

Chun, K., & Zalokar, N. (1992). *Civil Rights issues facing Asian Americans in the 1990s.* Washington, DC: Commission on Civil Rights. Retrieved December 21, 2014, from http://www.eric.ed.gov/PDFS/ED343979.pdf

Clement, T. P. (1998). *The unforgotten war (Dust of the Streets).* Bloomfield, IN: Truepeny.

Clemmer, G. (2010). *The GIS 20: Essential skills.* New York: ESRI.

Coalition for Asian American Children and Families (CACF). (2011). "We're not even allowed to ask for help": Debunking the myth of the model minority. New York: Pumphouse Projects. Retrieved December 21, 2014, http://cacf.org/

Crenshaw, K. (1995). *Critical race theory: The key writings that formed the movement.* New York: The New Press.

Daseler, R. (2000). Asian Americans battle "model minority" Stereotype. In A. Minas (Ed.), *Gender basics: Feminist perspectives on women and men* (2nd ed.) (pp. 45–49). Belmont, CA: Wadsworth.

Dearborn, L. M. (2008a). Reconstituting Hmong culture and traditions in Milwaukee, Wisconsin. *Traditional Dwellings and Settlements Review, 19*(2), 37–49.

Dearborn, L. M. (2008b). Socio-spatial patterns of acculturation: Examining Hmong habitation in Milwaukee's north-side neighborhoods. *Buildings and Landscapes, 15,* 58–77.

Delgado, R., & Stefancic, J. (1993). *Critical race theory: An annotated bibliography.* Charlottesville, VA: Virginia Law Review Association.

Delgado, R., & Stefancic, J. (2000). *Critical race theory: The cutting edge.* Philadelphia, PA: Temple University Press.

Delgado, R., & Stefancic, J. (2001). *Critical race theory: An introduction.* New York: New York University Press.

Denvir, D. (2011, March 29). The 10 most segregated urban areas in America. Retrieved June 24, 2014, from http://www.salon.com/news/politics/war_room/2011/03/29/most_ segregated_cities/slideshow.html

Diaz, V. M. (2004). "To 'P' or not to 'P'?": Marking the territory between Pacific Islander and Asian American studies. *Journal of Asian American Studies, 7*(3), 183–208.

Dixson, A. D., & Rousseau, C. K. (2005). And we are still not saved: Critical race theory in education ten years later. *Race, Ethnicity and Education, 8*(1), 7–27.

Dixson, A. D, & Rousseau, C. K. (Eds.). (2006). *Critical race theory in education: All god's children got a Song.* New York: Routledge.

Education Trust. (2010). *Overlooked and underserved: Debunking the Asian "model minority" myth in California Schools* [Policy Brief]. Oakland, CA: Education Trust West. Retrieved June 6, 2014, from http://www.edtrust.org/sites/edtrust.org/files/ETW %20Policy%20Brief%20August%202010--Overlooked%20and%20Underserved.pdf

Farole, S. (2011). Social justice implications of the model minority. *McNair Scholars Journal, 10,* 69–78.

Frankenberg, E., Lee, C., & Orfield, G. (2003). *A multiracial society with segregated schools: Are we losing the dream?* Cambridge, MA: Harvard Civil Rights Project. Retrieved December 19, 2014, from http://pages.pomona.edu/~vis04747/h21/readings/AreWe LosingtheDream.pdf

Fredrix, E. (2007, January 8). Hmong hunter revives memories of 2004. *Charleston Gazette,* 5A.

Freedman, J. (2005). Transgressions of a model minority. *Shofar: An Interdisciplinary Journal of Jewish Studies, 23*(4), 69–97.

Gibson, H. (2006). Familiar patterns: Hmong and Mennonite Quiltmakers in Lancaster County. *Journal of Mennonite Studies, 24,* 197–210.

Gillborn, D. (2009). Who's afraid of critical race theory in education? A reply to Mike Cole's 'The color-line and the class struggle.' *Power and Education, 1*(1), 125–131.

Guillermo, E. (2011). Advancing the race conversation: Chinese man vs. model minority. *Diverse: Issues in Higher Education, 28*(10), 20.

Guinier, L., & Torres, G. (Eds.). (2002). *The miner's canary: Enlisting race, resisting power, transforming democracy.* Cambridge, MA: Harvard University Press.

Gupta, A., Szymanski, D., & Leong, F. (2011). The "model minority myth": Internalized racialism of positive stereotypes as correlates of psychological distress, and attitudes toward help-seeking. *Asian American Journal of Psychology, 22*(2), 101–114.

Haga, C. (2007, January 14). In the woods, mistrust lingers among hunters. *Star Tribune,* 1A.

Hall, R. E. (2001). "Model minority" as eurocentric stereotype: Southeast Asian gangs. *Loyola Journal of Social Sciences, 15*(2), 135–146.

Hall, R. E. (2002). Myth of the "model minority": Stereotype and the reality of Asian-American gangs. *Asian Profile, 30*(6), 541–548.

HAPA. (2012). Hmong American Peace Academy. Retrieved April 2, 2014, from http://www.myhapa.org/

Harris, C. I. (1995). Whiteness as property. In K. Crenshaw, N. Gotanda, G. Peller, & K. Thomas (Eds.), *Critical race theory: The key writings that formed the movement* (pp. 276–291). New York: The New Press.

Hartlep, N. D. (2010). *Going public: Critical race theory and issues of social justice.* Mustang, OK: Tate.

Hartlep, N. D. (2012a). A segmented assimilation theoretical study of the 2002 Asian American student Population. Unpublished Dissertation. University of Wisconsin, Milwaukee. Milwaukee, WI.

Hartlep, N. D. (2012b). Harvard to the NBA: Deconstructing Jeremy Lin as a "model minority." *Korean Quarterly, 15*(3), 18.

Hein, J. (2006). Ethnic succession in the urban pecking order. In J. Hein (Ed.), *Ethnic origins: The adaptation of Cambodian and Hmong refugees in four American cities* (pp. 101–124). New York: Russell Sage Foundation

Horsford, S. D. (2011). *Learning in a burning house: Educational inequality, ideology, and (dis)integration.* New York: Teachers College Press.

Humes, K. R., Jones, N. A., & Ramirez, R. R. (2011). Overview of race and Hispanic origin: 2010 (Census Brief No. C2010BR-02). U.S. Census Bureau. Retrieved June 24, 2014, from http://www.census.gov/prod/cen2010/briefs/c2010br-02.pdf

Iceland, J., Weiberg, D. H., & Steinmetz, E. (2002). *Racial and ethnic residential segregation in the United States: 1980–2000* (Report No. CENSR-3). Washington, DC: U.S. Government Printing Office. Retrieved December 5, 2014, from http://www.census.gov/hhes/www/housing/housing_patterns/pdf/censr-3.pdf

Imrie, R. (2008, April 25). Hmong sportsmen's club is state's first: Goal is to ease racial tensions up north. *Capital Times,* C2. Retrieved February 8, 2014, from http://host.madison.com/news/local/hmong-hunting-club-sets-its-goals/article_f611c61e-c0e3-5487-ae75-1df41d65ce71.html?mode=story

Kim, C. J. (1999). The racial triangulation of Asian Americans. *Politics Society, 27*(1), 105–138.

Koltyk, J. A. (1998). *New pioneers in the heartland: Hmong life in Wisconsin.* Boston, MA: Allyn and Bacon.

Lackey, J. F., Stefaniak, R., Centenno, A., & Urban Anthropology, Inc. (2004). The amazing adaptation of the urban Hmong [DVD]. Milwaukee, WI: Urban Anthropology.

Ladson-Billings, G. (1998). Just what is critical race theory and what's it doing in a nice field like education? *Qualitative Studies in Education, 11*(1), 7–24.

Ladson-Billings, G. (1999). Preparing teachers for diverse student populations: A critical race theory perspective. *Review of Research in Education, 24*(1), 211–247.

Ladson-Billings, G. (2005). The evolving role of critical race theory in educational scholarship. *Race, Ethnicity and Education, 8*(1), 115–119.

Ladson-Billings, G., & Tate, W. F. (1995). Toward a critical race theory of education. *Teachers College Record, 97*(1), 47–68.

Lee, P. A, & Ying, Y. (2001). Asian American adolescents' academic Achievement: A look behind the model minority image. *Journal of Human Behavior in the Social Environment, 3*(3/4), 35–48.

Lee, S. J. (1994). Behind the model-minority stereotype: Voices of high- and low-achieving Asian American students. *Anthropology & Education Quarterly, 25*(4) 413–429.

Lee, S. J. (1997). The road to college: Hmong American women's pursuit of higher education. *Harvard Educational Review, 67*(4), 803–827

Lee, S. J. (2001). More than "model minorities" or "delinquents": A look at Hmong Americans high school students. *Harvard Educational Review, 71*(3), 505–528.

Lee, S. J. (2003). Model minorities and perpetual foreigners: The impact of stereotyping on Asian American students. In M. Sadowski (Ed.), *Adolescents at school: Perspectives on youth, identity, and education* (pp. 41–49). Cambridge, MA: Harvard Education Press.

Lee, S. J. (2005). *Up against whiteness: Race, school, and immigrant youth.* New York: Teachers College Press.

Lee, S. J. (2007). The truth and myth of the model minority: The case of Hmong Americans. In S. J. Paik & H. J. Walberg (Eds.), *Narrowing the achievement gap: Strategies for educating Latino, Black, and Asian Students* (pp. 171–184). New York: Springer.

Lee, S. J. (2009). *Unraveling the "model minority" stereotype: Listening to Asian American youth.* New York: Teachers College Press.

Lee, S. J., Wong, N. A., & Alvarez, A. N. (2009). The model minority and the perpetual foreigner: Stereotypes of Asian Americans. In N. Tewari & A. N. Alvarez (Eds.), *Asian American psychology: Current perspectives* (pp. 69–85). New York: Psychology Press.

Lew, J. (2006). *Asian Americans in class: Charting the achievement gap among Korean American youth.* New York: Teachers College Press.

Lew, J. (2004). The "other" story of the model minorities: Korean American high school dropouts in an urban context. *Anthropology of Education Quarterly, 35*(3), 297–311.

Lew, J. W., Chang, J. C., & Wang, W. W. (2005). UCLA community college review: The overlooked minority: Asian Pacific American students at community colleges. *Community College Review, 33*(2), 64–84.

Li, G., & Wang, L. (2008). *Model minority myth revisited: An interdisciplinary approach to demystifying Asian American educational experiences.* Charlotte, NC: Information Age.

Lou, R. (1989). Model minority? Getting behind the veil. *Change, 21*(6), 16–17.

Lynn, M. (1999). Toward a critical race pedagogy: A research note. *Urban Education, 33*(5), 606–26.

Lynn, M. (2002). Critical race theory and the perspectives of Black men teachers in the Los Angeles Public Schools. *Equity & Excellence in Education, 35*(2), 119–30.

Lynn, M., & Adams, M. (2002). Introductory overview to the special issue. Critical race theory and education: Recent developments in the field. *Equity & Excellence in Education, 35*(2), 87–92.

Lynn, M., & Jennings, M. E. (2009). Power, politics, and critical race pedagogy: A critical race analysis of Black male teachers' pedagogy. *Race, Ethnicity, and Education, 12*(2), 173–196.

Lynn, M., & Parker, L. (2006). Critical race studies in education: Examining a decade of research on U.S. schools. *The Urban Review, 38*(4), 257–290.

Lynn, M., Yosso, T. J., Solórzano, D. G., & Parker, L. (2002). Critical race theory and education: Qualitative research in the new millennium. *Qualitative Inquiry, 8*(1), 3–6.

MacIver News Service. (2010, September 29). Milwaukee's rank as 4th poorest city in nation comes amidst concerns over city's schools public safety. Retrieved November 27, 2014, from http://maciverinstitute.com/2010/09/milwaukees-rank-as-4th-poorest-city-in-nation-comes-amidst-concerns-over-citys-schools-public-safety/ Milwaukee Public Schools (MPS) (2011). Milwaukee Public Schools at a glance. Retrieved June 23, 2014, from http://mpsportal.milwaukee.k12.wi.us/portal/server. pt?open=512&ob jID=367&mode=2&in_hi_userid=2&cached=true

Metropolitan Milwaukee Fair Housing Council (MMFHC). (2005). City of Milwaukee analysis of impediments to fair housing. Retrieved December 18, 2014, from http:// www.ci. mil.wi.us/ImageLibrary/User/jsteve/MilwaukeeAI.pdf

Minority Health Program. (2008). *Wisconsin minority health report 2001–2005*. Madison, WI: Wisconsin Dept. of Health and Family Services, Division of Public Health, Bureau of Health Information and Policy, Minority Health Program.

Moua, S. (2007, April). Tension in the woods: Hmong hunters fall victim to hate crimes. *Hardboiled: The Asian American Newsmagazine, 10*(5), 4. Retrieved March 16, 2014, from http://hardboiled.berkeley.edu/issues/105/105.pdf

National Association for the Advancement of Colored People (NAACP). (1963). *De facto school segregation in Milwaukee*. Milwaukee, WI: NAACP.

Paek, H. J., & Shah, H. (2003). Racial ideology, model minorities, and the "not-so-silent partner:" Stereotyping of Asian Americans in U.S. magazine Advertising. *Howard Journal of Communications, 14*(4), 225–243.

Palmer, J. D. (1999). From the "yellow peril" to the "model minority": Asian American stereotypes from the 19th century to today. *Midwest History of Education Journal, 26*(1), 33–42.

Parker, L., Deyhle, D., & Villenas, S. A. (1999). *Race is—race isn't: Critical race theory and qualitative studies in education*. Boulder, CO: Westview Press.

Parker, L., & Lynn, M. (2002). What's race got to do with it? Critical race theory's conflicts with and connections to qualitative research methodology and epistemology. *Qualitative Inquiry, 8*(1), 7–22.

Pew Research Center. (2011, July 26). *Wealth gaps rise to record highs between Whites, Blacks and Hispanics* (Report No. 21). Retrieved December 23, 2014, from http:// www.pewsocialtrends.org/files/2011/07/SDT-Wealth-Report_7–26–11_FINAL.pdf

Richards, E., & Poston, B. (2011, November 30). Wisconsin schools see more children in poverty: Problem reaches from city to suburbs. *Milwaukee Journal Sentinel.* Retrieved on December 5, 2011 from http://www.jsonline.com/news/education/wisconsin-schools-including-suburbs-see-increase-in-poverty-bs38ffq-134731408. html

Schein, L., & Thoj, V. (2007). Occult racism: The masking of race in the Hmong hunter incident a dialogue between anthropologist Louisa Schein and filmmaker/Activist Va-Megn Thoj. *American Quarterly, 59*(4), 1051–1095.

Siegle, E. (2007, November 28). Wisconsin hunter gets 69 years in slaying. *USA Today*. Retrieved February 8, 2014, from http://www.usatoday.com/news/nation/2007–11–28–wisconsin-hunter-sentenced_N.htm

Solórzano, D. G., & Yosso, T. J. (2002). Critical race methodology: Counter-storytelling as an analytical framework for education research. *Qualitative Inquiry, 8*(1), 23–44.

Spring, J. (2001). Asian Americans: Exclusion and segregation. In J. Spring, *Deculturalization and the struggle for equality: A brief history of the education of dominated cultures in the United States* (3rd ed.) (pp. 55–67). New York: McGraw Hill.

Stake, R. E. (1995). *The art of case study research.* Thousand Oaks, CA: Sage.

State of Wisconsin. (2007). *State of Wisconsin v. James Allen Nichols*. Retrieved February 8, 2014, from http://www.doj.state.wi.us/news/files/Nichols_complaint.pdf

Stovall, D. (2006a). Where the rubber hits the road: CRT goes to high school. In A. Dixson & C. Rousseau (Eds.), *Critical race theory in education: All God's children got a song* (pp. 231–240). New York: Routledge.

Stovall, D. (2006b). Forgoing community in race and class: Critical race theory and the quest for social justice in education. *Race Ethnicity and Education, 9*(3), 243–259.

Stovall, D. (2006c). We can relate hip hop culture, critical pedagogy, and the secondary Classroom. *Urban Education, 41*(6), 585–602.

Su, J. A. (1998). Making the invisible visible: The garment industry's dirty laundry. *Journal of Gender, Race and Justice, 405*(1), 405–417.

Takaki, R. (1998). *Strangers from a different shore: A history of Asian Americans* (updated and revised). Boston, MA: Little, Brown.

Tayag, M. (2011, Spring). Great expectations: The negative consequences and policy implications of the Asian American "model minority" stereotype. *Stanford Journal of Asian American Studies, 4*, 23–31.

Taylor, E., Gillborn, D., & Ladson-Billings, G. (Eds.). (2009). *Foundations of critical race theory in education.* New York: Routledge.

Teranishi, R. T. (2002). The myth of the super minority: Misconceptions about Asian Americans. *The College Board Review, 195*, 17–21.

Teranishi, R. T., (2004). Yellow and *Brown*: Emerging Asian American immigrant populations and residential segregation. *Equity & Excellence in Education, 37*(3), 255–263.

Teranishi, R. T., Behringer, L. B., Grey, E. A., & Parker, T. L. (2009). Critical race theory and research on Asian Americans and Pacific Islanders in higher education. *New Directions for Institutional Research, 142*, 57–68.

Tran, N., & Birman, D. (2010). Questioning the model minority: Studies of Asian American academic performance. *Asian American Journal of Psychology, 1*(2), 106–118.

Trimble, J. E., & Dickson, R. (2005). Ethnic gloss. In C. B. Fisher, & R. M. Lerner (Eds.), *Encyclopedia of applied developmental science* (Vol. 1) (pp. 412–415). Thousand Oaks, CA: Sage.

Turner, M. A., Richardson, T. M., & Ross, S. (2007). Housing discrimination in metropolitan America: Unequal treatment of African Americans, Hispanics, Asians, and Native Americans. In J. Goering. (Ed.), *Fragile rights within cities* (pp. 39–60). Lanham, MD: Rowman & Littlefield.

United States Commission on Civil Rights. (1977). *The forgotten minority: Asian Americans in New York City: A report*. Washington, DC: The Commission.

U.S. Census. (2010). Retrieved July 20, 2014, from http://2010.census.gov/news/releases/oper ations/cb11–cn80.html

UW-Extension. (2000). Wisconsin's Hmong population: Census 2000 population and other demographic trends. Retrieved June 6, 2014, from http://www.apl.wisc.edu/publicat ions/HmongChartbook.pdf

Van Ziegart, S. (2006). Re-Appropriating the model minority stereotype: Reflections on the 2000 Organization of Chinese Americans convention. In S. Van Ziegart, *Global Spaces of Chinese Culture: Diasporic Chinese Communities in the United States and Germany* (pp. 21–58). New York: Routledge.

Vega, A. (2009). Homeownership fell in '08; Asians hit worst. Retrieved March 14, 2014, from http://seattletimes.nwsource.com/html/nationworld/2009914381_apusminori-tyhomeowners.html

Victoria, N. A. (2007). A+ does not mean all Asians: The model minority myth and implications for higher education. *The Vermont Connection, 28*, 80–88.

Wallitt, R. (2008). Cambodian invisibility: Students lost between the "achievement gap" and the "model minority." *Multicultural Perspectives, 10*(1), 3–9.

Weaver, S. (2009). Perfect in America: Implications of the model minority myth on the classroom. *Colleagues, 4*(2), 8–11.

Wei, W. (2010). *The Asian American movement*. Philadelphia, PA: Temple University Press.

Weisberg, L. (2003, July 2). Study finds housing bias against Asian-Americans. *The San Diego Union-Tribune,* B1, B4.

Wellman, D. T. (1977). *Portraits of White racism.* Cambridge, UK: Cambridge University Press.

Wing, J. (2007). Beyond Black and White: The model minority myth and the invisibility of Asian American students. *The Urban Review, 39*(4), 455–487.

Winnick, L. (1990). America's "model minority." *Commentary, 90*(2), 22–29.

Wong, L. (1976). The chinese experience: From yellow peril to model minority. *Civil Rights Digest, 9*(1), 33–35.

Wong, L. L., & Wong, C. (2006). Chinese engineers in Canada: A 'model minority'? and experiences and perceptions of the glass ceiling. *Journal of Women and Minorities in Science and Engineering, 12*(4), 253–273.

Wu, F. H. (2002). *Yellow: Race in America beyond Black and White*. New York: Basic Books.

Yosso, T. J. (2005). Whose culture has capital? A critical race theory discussion of community cultural wealth. *Race, Ethnicity and Education, 8*(1), 69–91.

Yosso, T. J. (2006). *Critical race counterstories along the Chicana/Chicano educational pipeline*. New York: Routledge.

Zhou, M., & Gatewood, J. V. (Eds.). (2000). *Contemporary Asian America: A multidisciplinary reader.* New York: New York University Press.

CHAPTER 19

AN ASIAN AMERICAN SUBGROUP ANALYSIS OF THE RESTRICTED-USE ELS 2002 DATASET

Mixture Modeling as a Way to Problematize the Asian American "Model Minority" Stereotype

Nicholas D. Hartlep, Grant B. Morgan, and Kari J. Hodge

INTRODUCTION

According to the model minority stereotype, Asian Americans in the United States are remarkably studious and successful (Hartlep, 2013, 2014; Kitano & Sue, 1973; Lee, 1994, 2001, 2005). Critics of this myth urge proponents to reconsider their assumptions and to acknowledge that this seemingly "positive" stereotype has many negative unintended consequences for the Asian American population. For instance, Asian American females are at increased risk for committing suicide due to intense pressure to live up to the myth (Leong, Leach, & Yeh, 2007; Noh,

Killing the Model Minority Stereotype: Asian American Counterstories and Complicity,
pages 357–380.

2007). Yet another unintended consequence is that Asian Americans are bullied due to the stereotype (Delucchi & Do, 1996; Koo, Peguero, & Shekarkhar, 2012).

The first author has written extensively about the negative consequences of the model minority myth (e.g., see Hartlep, 2013, 2014; Hartlep & Morgan, 2013), while the first and second authors have carried out significant work on demystifying the Asian American model minority stereotype. A limitation of this latter work is that the researchers did not differentiate between Asian American subgroups when examining the model minority stereotype (Hartlep & Morgan, 2013). The purpose of the present study, then, is to extend the first and second author's initial work by using finite mixture modeling (FMM) as an innovative methodological strategy to problematize the Asian American model minority stereotype (Kagawa-Singer & Hune, 2011).

This article begins by reviewing the history of the model minority stereotype in the United States.[1] Next, relevant literature is reviewed that specifically addresses why disaggregation is an effective research strategy to destabilize the myth. Next, FMM is introduced and described, followed by the authors' analysis of a nationally representative longitudinal dataset of Asian American high school students. The remainder of the article presents the argument for FMM as an innovative methodological contribution to dispelling the model minority stereotype of Asian Americans, explaining how and why it effectively calls into question the accuracy of this pervasive myth.

REVIEW OF LITERATURE

The contemporary model minority stereotype of Asian Americans belies deep roots in United States history, its legacy situated within a complex set of circumstances caused by social, political, educational[2], and immigration forces (Miyamoto, 1984; Sue & Wagner, 1973). The historical remnants of American xenophobia and political paranoia, evidenced both in the exclusion of the Chinese in the 1880s and in the lawful internment of Japanese in the United States in the 1940s, point to the theme that Asians in the United States have often been seen as a threat to national and economic security.[3] Indeed, many scholars believe such stereotypes have led to exploitation of Asians in the United States (e.g., see Hartlep, 2013, 2014; Chae, 2008; Ng, Lee, & Pak, 2007; Pak, 2001; Wong, 1985; Yamanaka & McClelland, 1994). So while the model minority stereotype is suggestive of *success*, it conceals a racist, xenophobic, colonialist, and anti-Asian American historical legacy.

The literature on the model minority stereotype is extensive (e.g., see Chao et al., 2013; Chang, 2011; Davé, 2013; Ip & Pang, 2005; Kalman-Lamb, 2013; Kim & Lee, 2013; Lee, 1994, 2001, 2003; Lee & Kumashiro, 2005; Leung, 2013; Lew, 2002, 2004, 2011; Li, 2005; Museus & Kiang, 2009; Ngo & Lee, 2007; Noh, 2013; Park & Park, 2005; Poon & Hune, 2009; Suzuki, 1980, 1989, 2002; Teranishi, 2002, 2010; Whaley & Noel, 2013; Ying, Lee, Tsai, Hung, Lin, & Wan, 2001). The "Model Minority Stereotype Project" website, which catalogs over

460 writings, is, to the best of our knowledge, the most extensive/comprehensive review of the model minority stereotype literature to date.[4]

While political and economic motivations historically have been behind the exclusion of the Chinese in the United States, with politicians using the fear of a "yellow peril" to maintain the economic and power status quos (Kitano, 1997, p. 193), Chae (2008) notes that Asians have been exploited via the model minority stereotype ever since they were used as strikebreakers in attempts to dissolve U.S. unions. Meanwhile, capitalists have often used Asians as a racial "wedge" to divide and conquer other non-White and non-Asian minorities, keeping them from gaining economic and political footholds in mainstream American life.

The contemporary model minority stereotype originates in William Petersen's (1966) article "Success Story: Japanese American Style" in *The New York Times Magazine*. In his story, Petersen contrasted the successes of Japanese Americans with the failures of African Americans. Petersen emphasized supposed cultural differences between Blacks and Japanese, focusing on Japanese industry and effort. The following is taken verbatim from this seminal article:

> But a Negro who knows no other homeland, who is as thoroughly American as any Daughter of the American Revolution, has no refuge when the United States rejects him. Placed at the bottom of this country's scale, he finds it difficult to salvage his ego by measuring his worth in another currency. The Japanese, on the contrary, could climb over the highest barriers our racists were able to fashion in part because of their meaningful links with an alien culture. (p. 40).

In order to appreciate the particular timing of Petersen's article, the historical context must be considered. Significantly, *The New York Times Magazine* published the story in the wake of Assistant Secretary of Labor Daniel Patrick Moynihan's (1965) *The Negro Family: The Case For National Action* (commonly referred to as the Moynihan Report), which blamed African-American ghetto culture for the difficulty this population was having (Hartlep, 2013, 2014). It is relevant to note that this criticism of African Americans was issued at the height of the civil rights movement, just as Jim Crow laws were being struck down and African-American-led revolts were calling attention to the systemic abuses of white supremacy. Chae (2008) rightfully points out that the positive image of Asians as a model minority has done more than just help European American society justify its structural inequality; the image has been used to reaffirm the underlying structure by shifting the minority problem to individuals and communities, thereby avoiding an examination of the unequal power structure of the society.

In light of these past manipulations of the stereotype, the contemporary claim that somehow Asian Americans are extra successful in school when compared to other ethnic and minority groups must be regarded with suspicion. Proponents of the narrative are selective in their use of data, presenting anecdotes that support the case without properly contextualizing Asian American success (Kao & Tienda, 1998). If history is any guide, a likely motivation for the current stereotype may be provided by Kim's (1999) theory of racial triangulation, which indicates that the model minority stereotype is a racist device that juxtaposes a supposedly successful minority group (Asian Americans) with deficient minority groups (African and Latino Americans), thereby maintaining white supremacy (Osajima, 2005).

Who Are Asian Americans?

According to the U.S. Census (2010), the U.S. Asian population grew faster than any other race group between 2000 and 2010. Somewhat obscured by this aggregated growth rate is the fact that the Asian American population is incredibly diverse and heterogeneous. Teranishi (2010) points out that the Asian American population is composed of 48 different ethnicities and that 300 different languages are spoken within this population. Several reports indicate why failure to disaggregate the Asian American population is highly problematic: (1) *A Dream Denied: Educational Experiences of Southeast Asian American Youth* (Um, 2003), (2) *Asian Americans in Washington State: Closing Their Hidden Achievement Gaps* (Hune & Takeuchi, 2008), and (3) *"We're Not Even Allowed to Ask for Help": Debunking the Myth of the Model Minority* (Coalition for Asian American Children and Families, CACF, 2011).

Previous Asian American model minority critiques have focused on different Asian American subgroups, such as Chinese (Qin, Way, & Mukherjee, 2008; Qin, Way, & Rana, 2008; Wong, 1976), Filipino (Cunanan, Guerrero, & Minamoto, 2006; Nadal, Pituc, Johnston, & Esparrago, 2010), Japanese (Hawkins, 2009; Martinelli & Nagasawa, 1987; Petersen, 1966; Yoshihama, 2001), Korean (Kang, 2010; Kim & Hurh, 1983), Southeast (Hall, 2001; Yang, 2004), and South Asian Americans (Mahmud, 2001). Asian American diversity and heterogeneity have caused researchers to recognize the necessity of disaggregating subgroups of Asians in studies (Maramba, 2011).

For instance, research has been conducted on the many different methodologies or approaches to demystifying the model minority stereotype (Li & Wang, 2008), although most support the notion that there is a critical need to disaggregate Asian American subgroups (e.g., see Baker, Keller-Wolff, & Wolf-Wendel, 2000; Maramba, 2011; Srinivasan, 2000).

Disaggregation of Asian American Data

Scholars point to the importance of examining the subgroups of Asian Americans in order to destabilize the model minority stereotype (e.g., see Chu, 1991; Kao, 1995; Li & Wang, 2008; Yamanaka & McClelland, 1994) and prevent cultural homogenization. Baker, Keller-Wolff, and Wolf-Wendel (2000) underscore the necessity of disaggregating subgroups when examining the academic achievement of Asian Americans. The three authors analyzed National Educational Longitudinal Study of 1988 (NELS: 88) data in order to test the differences between using aggregated racial/ethnic variables and disaggregated racial/ethnic variables. They found that problems arise when researchers use aggregated data when disaggregation is possible. Since heterogeneity is lost when data is not disaggregated, Baker, Keller-Wolff, and Wolf-Wendel conclude that aggregation causes findings to be inadequate and often inconclusive.

Galindo and Pong (2011) also used data from the National Educational Longitudinal Study (NELS:88), except they paired it with data from the Educational Longitudinal Study (ELS:02). The two researchers tested whether or not Asian American tenth grade students in 2002 performed as well as they did in 1990. They found that Asian American students were more likely to attend higher SES schools in 1990 than in 2002 and that there was a decline in Asian American parents' expectations for their children's education, relative to White parents' expectations. Galindo and Pong also found that Asian American student academic achievement decreased between 1990 and 2002. Galindo and Pong's cohort analysis was effective methodologically since it disaggregated Asian American students by different subgroups.

Similarly, Xiong and Joubert's (2012) report supports disaggregation of Asian American data. Xiong and Joubert indicate that data disaggregated by Asian subgroups is critical for obtaining an accurate picture of the needs and disparities that are typically hidden in aggregated data. CARE's (2013) report affirms this position, indicating that disaggregated data is highly useful since it reveals much about the Asian American population. CARE (2013) says that "the use of disaggregated data is an essential tool for advocacy and social justice, shedding light on ways to mitigate disparities in educational outcomes and improve support for the most marginalized and vulnerable [Asian American] populations" (p. 1).

Importantly, then, disaggregated data reveals that conclusions drawn from aggregate data analysis are not representative of individual Asian American subgroups. As currently conceived, however, disaggregation is not enough because the statistical procedures carried out with disaggregated data have underlying assumptions.

Mixture Models and Disaggregation

Many statistical procedures (e.g., multiple regression, analysis of variance), such as those carried out by Baker, Keller-Wolff, and Wolf-Wendel (2000) or Galindo and Pong (2011), often have an unstated or unrecognized assumption that the data reflect only one underlying population. This is problematic because it may result in oversimplification of the dataset and ignore the unique characteristics of specific underlying subgroups. Furthermore, if multiple populations underlie a dataset, then decisions based on statistical procedures that assume only one population may be incorrect. Fortunately, innovative statistical analytic procedures are available that do not require this assumption.

Analytic approaches such as mixture modeling treat a dataset as though the data were collected from a combination (i.e., mixture) of underlying populations, each of which has its own distinct characteristics (McLachlan & Peel, 2000). Mixture analysis offers researchers a unique set of analytic options for studying phenomena such as the model minority stereotype. To our knowledge, no such statistical examinations of the model minority stereotype have been conducted to date.

Purpose of this Study

The purpose of this study was to examine nationally representative longitudinal data of Asian American high school students through subgroup analysis. Specifically, this study examines the Chinese, Filipino, Japanese, Korean, Southeast Asian, and South Asian student and parent populations contained in the Educational Longitudinal Study of 2002 restricted dataset.

Through subgroup analysis and disaggregation, the model minority stereotype will either be supported or problematized via intergroup variation or intergroup consistency. The researchers employed a form of disaggregated analysis insofar as they used finite mixture modeling (FMM), which is a model-based approach that can be used to identify underlying subgroups of people who tend to have more similar values on the measured variables than with people in other subgroups. As was mentioned earlier, no such statistical examinations of the model minority stereotype have been conducted to date, making this study the first of its kind and extremely valuable for future research.

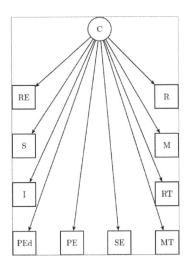

FIGURE 19. 1. Conceptual Model

Conceptual Model

Figure 19.1 below is a conceptual model. C represents the latent classification variable: RE represents race/ethnicity of student; S represents sex of student; I represents income of parent; PEd represents parent education; PE represents parent expectation; SE represents student expectation; MT represents math teacher expectation; RT represents reading teacher expectation; M represents math score; and R represents reading score. The conceptual model represents what the authors hypothesize: that there is a latent variable with different groups of students with similar characteristics (i.e., means, proportions) on these variables. The arrows point from the latent variable to the observed variables (squares) because an Asian American student's membership in one of the underlying groups is what accounts for differences in the observed variables. The authors of this study have to use the observed variables as indicators of group membership so that they can determine how many unique Asian American groups there are.

METHODS

Participants

The sample used in this study came from the Educational Longitudinal Study of 2002 (ELS:2002) dataset, which was "designed to monitor the transition of a national sample of young people as they progress from tenth grade through high school and on to postsecondary education and/or the world of work" (U.S. Department of Education, 2004). Interested readers can visit the ELS:2002 section of the Institute of Educational Sciences website for more information on the design of the ELS:2002.[5]

Permission to use the "restricted-use" ELS:2002 data was granted to the authors by IES, and was housed on a secured computer in accordance with the IES security requirements. The sample consisted of the 1,070 10th grade students who had complete data on the variables used in the study and who also self-identified as Asian.

The sample was composed of 52.0% females. The most commonly reported Asian subgroup backgrounds were Southeast Asian ($n = 310$, 28.4%) and Chinese ($n = 230$, 20.9%). The authors of this study acknowledge that there may be variability within the Southeast Asian classification; however, the data collected in the ELS:2002 did not disaggregate backgrounds within this ethnicity category. The authors' analysis disaggregates to the most specific level possible given the available data. Nearly half of the students ($n = 490$, 45.8%) reported living in the West region of the U.S., and about half ($n = 560$, 52.0%) reported living in suburban areas. Just over half of the students ($n =560$, 51.8%) identified a West/South Asian language (Arabic, Farsi, Urdu, Hindi/Tamil/Indian subcontinent language) as being their home language. English was the second most commonly report home language ($n =330$, 30.6%). With regard to home language, more specific

TABLE 19.1. Student Demographic Composition

Variable	Frequency (*n*)	Percentage (%)
Sex		
Female	560	52.0
Male	520	48.0
Home language		
English	330	30.6
Spanish		
Other European language	120	10.8
West / South Asian language[a]	560	51.8
Pacific Asian / Southeast Asian language[b]	70	6.6
Other language		
Test Accommodations		
No accommodations	1070	99.3
Extra time or other	10	0.7
First friend's race		
American Indian / Alaska native	10	0.5
non-Hispanic Asian	550	51.0
non-Hispanic Black or African American	50	4.4
Hispanic, no race specified	70	6.1
Hispanic, race specified	30	2.9
non-Hispanic more than one race	40	3.9
Native Hawaiian / Pacific islander	20	1.5
non-Hispanic White	320	29.8
Worked in high school		
Yes	240	22.7
No	830	77.3
Urbanicity		
Urban	450	42.3
Suburban	560	52.0
Rural	60	5.8
Region		
Northeast	200	19.0
Midwest	160	15.2
South	220	20.0
West	490	45.8

Notes. [a]Refers to Arabic, Farsi, Urdu, Hindi/Tamil/Indian subcontinent language
[b]Refers to a Chinese language, Japanese, Korean, a Filipino language, Vietnamese, Cambodian, or Other Southeast Asian language

TABLE 19.2.   Students' Parents' Demographic Composition

Variable	Frequency (*n*)	Percentage (%)
Mother's education level		
Did not finish high school	240	22.5
Graduated from high school or GED	230	21.2
Attended 2-year school, no degree	70	6.1
Graduated from 2-year school	70	6.8
Attended college, no 4-year degree	70	6.3
Graduated from college	280	26.0
Completed Master's degree or equivalent	80	7.7
Completed PhD, MD, other advanced degree	40	3.3
Father's education level		
Did not finish high school	170	16.1
Graduated from high school or GED	210	19.1
Attended 2-year school, no degree	70	6.8
Graduated from 2-year school	70	6.6
Attended college, no 4-year degree	80	7.3
Graduated from college	250	23.6
Completed Master's degree or equivalent	120	11.2
Completed PhD, MD, other advanced degree	100	9.3
Parents' educational aspirations for child		
Less than high school graduation	0	0.2
High school graduation of GED only	20	1.8
Attend or complete 2-year college / school	30	3.0
Attend college, 4-year degree incomplete	10	1.0
Graduate from college	430	39.7
Obtain Master's degree or equivalent	250	23.0
Obtain PhD, MD, or other advanced degree	340	31.4

information was unavailable. The authors treated these variables in the analysis to the greatest specificity the ELS:2002 data allowed. The most commonly reported mother's education level was high school diploma, GED, or less (*n* = 470, 43.8%), but 37% (*n* = 400) reported having graduated from college or higher. The father's most commonly reported education level was BA/BS or 4–year college degree (*n* = 470, 44.1%), while 35.2% (*n* = 380) reported completing high school, GED, or less. The most frequently reported educational aspiration for students by parents was a four-year degree (*n* = 430, 39.7%). The majority of students in the sample did not use testing accommodations (*n* = 1,070, 99.3%) and did not work (*n* =

830, 77.3%). The reported race/ethnic background of student's first friend was non-Hispanic Asian for 51.0% of the students and non-Hispanic White for 29.8% of the students. The complete demographic summary for students is presented in Table 19.1 and for parents is presented in Table 19.2.

Analysis

The authors used finite mixture modeling (FMM) to examine whether there were underlying subgroups of students who shared similar demographic characteristics. As noted earlier, FMM is a model-based approach that can be used for classification purposes to identify underlying subgroups of people who tend to have more similar values on the measured variables than with people in other subgroups. The procedure gets its name from the assumption that an observed dataset is comprised of a mixture of data collected from a finite number of mutually exclusive classes, each of which has its own characteristics. The goal of FMM-based classification procedures is to correctly classify similar cases into one of K subgroups whose characteristics are unknown *a priori* (McLachlan & Peel, 2000). FMM treats the underlying class variable as a categorical latent variable. As such, class membership must be measured indirectly using two or more observed, or indicator, variables, which are subject to measurement error. Although FMM often uses only categorical or quantitative indicators, Morgan (2015) showed that FMM can be productive with a combination of categorical and quantitative variables without decreasing model fit.

To employ FMM, researchers fit a series of competing models to the data and considered several pieces of information when selecting the best approximating model of those tested. The information considered in model selection is as follows: (1) parsimony, (2) interpretability, and (3) statistical fit indices. In the current research, the authors fit models that contained two through five underlying subgroups, or classes, and recorded the fit indices and class characteristics. The models were estimated using robust maximum likelihood in Mplus (v. 6.12, Muthén & Muthén, 2012) software. Mplus includes a variety of fit measures that can aid in model selection. We examined the Akaike information criterion (AIC), Bayesian information criterion (BIC), sample sized-adjusted Bayesian information criterion (aBIC), entropy, and the Lo-Mendell-Rubin likelihood ratio test (LMR).

Previous research has demonstrated that BIC-based estimates and LMR tend to be better performing indicators of model-data fit under a variety of research design conditions. We considered all of the fit indices but gave BIC-based estimates and LMR results more weight in the model selection process. For the AIC, BIC, and aBIC, relatively smaller values indicate better model fit. Entropy is a measure that provides the degree of certainty in classification procedures with one index. Thus, models that have higher values of entropy are considered better fitting models than models with lower entropy estimates. The LMR compares the improvement in fit between the $k - 1$ and k class models and provides a p-value that can be used to evaluate whether the improvement in fit for the inclusion of one additional class is statistically significant with $1 - \alpha\%$ confidence (Nylund, Asparouhov, & Muthén, 2007). The variables used as class indicators were sex, home language, mother's education, father's education, parent educational aspirations for student, work history, race of first friend, region, urbanicity, test accommodations, composite SES index, and composite standardized test score.[6] The SES index is a composite of mother's education and occupation, father's education and occupation, and family income that has a mean of 0 and standard deviation of 1. The composite standardized test score is the mean of the reading and math standardized scores that has been re-standardized to a T distribution (M = 50, SD = 10). After fitting the series of competing models and selecting one as the best fitting, contingency tables were constructed to examine the race/ethnicity composition of students in each of the identified classes.

RESULTS

As noted above, the authors fit a series of competing models beginning with the two-class model. The AIC, BIC, and aBIC are all unitless estimates that must be used comparatively in competing models. The estimated entropy for the two-class model was .87, which suggested that the classes were fairly well delineated. The LMR p-value supports a rejection of the null hypothesis that there are k – 1 underlying class. In other words, the LMR test results indicate that the two-class model fits better than a one-class model. When a third class was added, the model improved for all of the information criteria. Entropy decreased to .82, indicating that the two-class solution is a better fit. The LMR test results indicate that the three-class model fits better than a two-class model. When a fourth class was added, we observed improved model fit (i.e., smaller values) for AIC, BIC, and aBIC but to a lesser extent than previous model comparisons. The entropy value remained the same at .82, and the LMR results showed that the fit was not improved by adding a fourth class. While jointly considering the model-data fit information, model parsimony, and interpretability, the authors selected the three-class model as the best approximating model of those examined. A summary of the fit information for the models examined is presented in Table 19.3.

The discovered classes were of similar sizes. The first class was composed of 29.4% of the students; the second class made up 32.6% of the sample; the third class was the largest, representing 38.0% of the sample. The characteristics of

TABLE 19.3   Fit Summaries for Competing Models

Classes	AIC	BIC	aBIC	Entropy	LMR p-value
2	32665	33088	32818	.865	<.000
3	32083	32715	32312	.818	<.000
4	31864	32705	32168	.819	.81

TABLE 19.4. Class-Specific Student Demographics

Variable	Class 1 (%)	Class 2 (%)	Class 3 (%)
Sex			
Female	49.4	51.7	53.4
Male	50.6	48.3	46.6
Home language			
English	11.4	45.4	32.8
Spanish			
Other European language	5.7	16.3	10.0
West / South Asian language	68.0	37.1	51.7
Pacific Asian / Southeast Asian language	14.9	.9	5.1
Other language			
Test Accommodations			
No accommodations	99.4	99.7	99.0
Extra time or other	0.6	.03	1.0
First friend's race			
American Indian / Alaska native		0.9	0.5
Asian, non-Hispanic	68.7	40.9	46.1
Black or African American, non-Hispanic	3.2	4.6	5.1
Hispanic, no race specified	5.4	4.6	7.8
Hispanic, race specified	4.1	3.4	1.5
More than one race, non-Hispanic	2.5	5.7	3.4
Native Hawaiian / Pacific islander	1.3	0.9	2.2
White, non-Hispanic	14.9	39.1	33.3
Worked in high school			
Yes	21.5	20.3	25.7
No	78.5	79.7	74.3
Urbanicity			
Urban	57.0	32.0	39.7
Suburban	38.3	62.0	53.9
Rural	4.7	6.0	6.4
Region			
Northeast	13.3	19.7	22.8
Midwest	22.8	12.9	11.3
South	16.1	21.7	21.6
West	47.8	45.7	44.4

TABLE 19.5. Class-Specific Students' Parent Demographics

Variable	Class 1 (%)	Class 2 (%)	Class 3 (%)
Mother's education level			
Did not finish high school	67.4		7.1
Graduated from high school or GED	26.6	1.4	34.1
Attended 2-year school, no degree	3.2	1.4	12.5
Graduated from 2-year school	0.6	4.9	13.2
Attended college, no 4-year degree	1.6	4.0	12.0
Graduated from college	0.6	59.1	17.2
Completed Master's degree or equivalent	0.03	20.3	2.9
Completed PhD, MD, other advanced degree	0.0	8.9	1.0
Father's education level			
Did not finish high school	45.6		7.1
Graduated from high school or GED	36.1		22.3
Attended 2-year school, no degree	7.6	1.4	10.8
Graduated from 2-year school	3.8	1.7	13.0
Attended college, no 4-year degree	3.2	3.4	13.7
Graduated from college	1.9	38.3	27.9
Completed Master's degree or equivalent	1.3	28.3	4.2
Completed PhD, MD, other advanced degree		26.9	1.0
Parents' educational aspirations for child			
Less than high school graduation	0.6		
High school graduation of GED only	3.5	0.3	1.7
Attend or complete 2-year college / school	4.1	0.9	3.9
Attend college, 4-year degree incomplete	2.2	0.3	.7
Graduate from college	46.5	32.6	40.4
Obtain Master's degree or equivalent	20.3	22.9	25.2
Obtain PhD, MD, or other advanced degree	22.8	43.1	27.9

each will be discussed in the order of class size, and the class-specific summaries are provided in Tables 19.4 and 19.5.

The third class in the three-class solution, which represented the largest portion of the students, was characterized by students whose parents had more varied but slightly higher education levels on average and whose parents had slightly higher educational aspirations. Mothers tended to have educational levels between high school and four-year degrees but had slightly fewer four-year degrees or higher and fewer high school degrees or lower. This pattern was observed for fathers as well. Parents' aspirations for the students tended to be slightly lower than for the overall sample. The majority of parents reported that they hoped their children obtain four-year degrees or higher. There was also a slightly higher percentage of students who worked while in high school (25.7%). Region and urbanicity distributions were fairly similar to the overall sample. This class had students of slightly above SES index (M = 0.04, SD = 0.34) and standardized test scores (M = 52.7, SD = 8.8).

The second class was characterized by students whose home language was predominantly English (45.4%) or West/South Asian (Arabic, Farsi, Urdu, Hindi/Tamil/Indian subcontinent language) (37.1%), and whose parents were much more educated. Among mothers and fathers, about 90% had graduated from college or higher, and 60% had graduate degrees (e.g., Masters, Ph.D., M.D., J.D.). All mothers of students in this class had obtained a high school diploma or GED and all of the fathers had completed at least two years of college. Parents also had higher educational aspirations for their children: 43.1% hoped students would obtain advanced degrees (e.g., Ph.D., M.D., J.D.). A smaller percentage of students worked while in high school (20.3%). This class was made up proportionally of more students who live in rural areas in the west. This class had above average SES (M = 1.00, SD = 0.33) and standardized test score composites (M = 59.5, SD = 8.9).

In the first class, the smallest of the three, the most commonly spoken home language among students was West/South Asian (Arabic, Farsi, Urdu, Hindi/Tamil/Indian subcontinent language) (68.0%). Well over half (67.4%) of the mothers and 45.6% of the fathers of students in this class did not finish high school, and

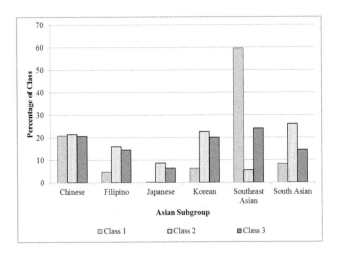

FIGURE 19.2. Racial/Ethnicity Composition of Each Identified Latent Class

TABLE 19.6.   Class-Specific Race/Ethnicity Compositions

Race / Ethnicity	Class 1 (%)	Class 2 (%)	Class 3 (%)
Chinese	20.9	21.4	20.6
Filipino	4.7	16.0	14.5
Japanese	.3	8.6	6.4
Korean	6.3	22.6	20.1
Southeast Asia	59.3	5.4	24.0
South Asia	8.2	26.0	14.5

about half of these parents reported educational aspirations for their child of a four-year degree. The most commonly reported racial/ethnic background of students' first friends was non-Hispanic Asian (68.7%). Only 21.5% of students in this class worked while in high school. Over half (57%) of these students live in urban areas, and about half of the students live in the western region of the United States. The SES (M = -1.01, SD = 0.36) and test score (M = 48.1, SD = 9.0) composites for students in this class were well below average and were clearly the lowest of the three classes.

Latent Class and Student Race/Ethnicity

To examine the potential relationship between student race and latent class, two-way contingency tables were constructed and Cramer's V was computed. The estimated Cramer's V, which is a measure of strength of association between two categorical variables, was .36. The contingency tables were interpreted by rows and columns. The third, and largest, class consisted of 24.0% Southeast Asian, 20.1% Korean, and 20.6% Chinese students. The second latent class was 26.0% South Asian, 22.6% Korean, and 21.4% Chinese. The first, and smallest, class was predominantly Southeast Asian (59.3%) and 20.9% Chinese students. When examining the distribution of the races/ethnicities across classes, we found that 93.8% of Southeast Asian students were in the first or third class. Chinese students were fairly evenly distributed across all three classes. Korean students were most likely to be classified in class 2 (43.6%) or class 3 (45.3%). Filipino students were most likely to be classified in class 2 (43.0%) or class 3 (45.3%). Over half (51.7%) of the South Asian students were classified into class 2. Japanese students were most likely to be found in class 2 (52.6%) or class 3 (45.6%), and were almost never classified in class 1 (1.7%). The percentages of students from each racial/ethnic background within each class are presented in Figure 19.2 and Table 19.6.

DISCUSSION

The purpose of this study was to examine restricted-use ELS:2002 data and determine whether there were underlying subgroups of students who shared similar demographic characteristics. The authors discovered that there were three distinguishable patterns among the variables examined.

The first class is primarily made of Southeast Asians (59.3%), those who speak West/South Asian language (Arabic, Farsi, Urdu, Hindi/Tamil/Indian subcontinent language) at home (68%), those whose first friend was Asian (68.7%), and those who typically have poorly educated parents. Those in the second class had very highly educated parents and include a higher proportion of students who speak English at home. Those in class three had more members than class two who speak West/South Asian language at home and whose parents were not as well educated. Figure 19.2 above indicates the proportion of each Asian subgroup in each class.

There are clearly diverse characteristics for each class, which the authors contend problematize the model minority stereotype of Asian Americans. One class tended to have very highly educated parents and tended to speak English at home, while another class had very poorly educated parents and tended to speak an Asian language at home. Given that the analysis is based only on the Asian students in ELS:2002, the authors consider the stereotype to be fairly destabilized. The heterogeneity that was found in the ELS:2002 data formed three classes, which does not support the model minority stereotype given its homogenous nature.

Due to the tremendous amount of diversity found among the Asian American students examined, this study calls into question the idea that high school Asian American students are a model minority group. Moreover, differences lie not just along ethnic lines, but also along lines of socioeconomic class and language. Consequently, disaggregation solely along ethnic lines appears not to be enough. Researchers, whenever possible, should disaggregate their data and analyses along lines of gender, class, immigrant status, and region of the United States.

Study Limitations

One potential limitation of this study was the choice of indicators of latent class membership. First, the inclusion of different class indicators may produce different latent class compositions. The authors chose latent class indicators of substantive interest in relation to the model minority stereotype (e.g., see Crystal, 1989; Hall, 2001; Qin, Way, & Mukherjee, 2008; Rangaswamy, 1995). Second, the authors used mixture modeling in this study in an exploratory fashion, which allowed them to identify the three latent classes discussed here. Although mixture modeling offers significant benefits over distance-based cluster procedures, it still may not be the best method for classification across all research scenarios. For the purpose of this investigation, mixture modeling was determined to be the most appropriate method for disaggregation and subgroup analysis.

A second potential limitation is the level of specificity of student ethnicities and home languages available in the data. For example, grouping students who self-identified as Southeast Asian was not preferable (but the authors did disaggregate to the extent that was possible given the data). This study provided an initial examination of these variables using an innovative methodological approach. Additional research is recommended with data that further disaggregates student characteristics.

CONCLUSION

This study contributes to the literature on the methodological approaches to critiquing the model minority stereotype. To our knowledge, this is the first study to carry out FMM in order to destabilize the model minority stereotype. This study also contributes to the literature on studies that have used the restricted-use ELS:2002 dataset to carryout subgroup analyses of the Asian American student population.

For example, according to an analysis performed by the authors, the ELS:2002 dataset has been sorely underutilized by model minority stereotype scholars. According to their analysis of NCES (2013), from 2001 until 2013 there have been a total of 142 research studies using the ELS:02 data. Of these 142 studies, the majority of documents have been published in the form of peer-reviewed articles (53), followed by dissertations or theses (26), conference papers (21), book chapters (3), and conference proceedings (2). Most striking is that only 5 of these 142 total studies have examined Asian Americans broadly as a population of interest, and only 1 of these 5 studies—a dissertation—examined Asian Americans by subgroup specifically.

The theoretical, methodological, and practical implications of this study are significant. Disaggregating Asian American high school students and their parents by subgroups, and analyzing them with FMM, reduced the likelihood of committing inferential errors. Another strength of FMM is that it allows readers to see real subgroup differences among the diverse and heterogeneous Asian American population.

Questions for Reflection

1. What was the purpose of this study? How did this study contribute to the literature on the model minority stereotype?
2. What are the benefits of using FMM in disaggregating subpopulations?
3. What are the strengths and weaknesses of this study (refer back to Chapters 16 and 17)?
4. How can future research extend the work of this study?

NOTES

1. The model minority stereotype is not geographically bound to North America (e.g., see Chung & Walkey, 1988; Dechamma, 2012; Fang, 2008, 2009a, 2009b, 2009c, 2010a, 2010b; Hannis, 2009; Ip & Pang, 2005); however, space here does not allow for the model minority stereotype in other locations outside the United States to be addressed.

2. Specific to education, the authors thank Dr. Yoon Pak, who pointed out that Asian American youth were excluded from public schooling altogether in California in the 1800s and racially (*de jure*) segregated in public education until 1949 in California. See *Tape vs. Hurley* (1885), *Gong Lum vs. Rice* (1927), and *Méndez vs. Westminster* (1946) (see Hartlep, 2014).

3. We are thankful to a reviewer who reminded us that another example of exclusion would be the fact that although Chinese indentured workers contributed significantly to the completion of the transcontinental railroad, when the "Golden Spike" picture was taken at Promontory Point, Utah upon completion of the work in 1869, only white workers were photographed. Chinese workers were not allowed to be in the picture.

4. "The Model Minority Stereotype Project" lists 501 model minority stereotype citations and can be accessed here: http://www.my.illinoisstate.edu/blogs/ndhartl

5. Available here: www.nces.ed.gov/surveys/els2002

6. The reason these variables were selected is because research points to the importance of considering sex, home language, mother's education, father's education, composite SES index, parent educational aspirations for student, and work history (Hartlep, 2012) when examining Asian American outcomes. The race of first friend was included since the model minority stereotype implies that Asian Americans are assimilating into white culture. If it is true that Asian Americans are assimilating into dominant European American society, then it would be interesting to see if this is truly reflected in the racial make-up of Asian Americans' friends. Demographic research asserts that Asian Americans are concentrated in certain regions of the United States; hence, region was examined as well as urbanicity. If Asian Americans are academically successful, it would seem reasonable that they should not receive test accommodations in school; hence, test accommodations were explored. Lastly, composite standardized test scores were included in order to test the thesis that Asian American students perform extremely well on academic tests.

REFERENCES

Baker, B. D., Keller-Wolff, C., & Wolf-Wendel, L. (2000). Two steps forward, one step back: Race/ethnicity and student achievement in education policy research. *Educational Policy, 14*(4), 511–529.

CARE. (2013). *iCount: A data quality movement for Asian Americans and Pacific Islanders in higher education.* Retrieved December 1, 2014, from http://aapip.org/files/publication/files/2013_icount_report.pdf

Chae, Y. (2008). Cultural economies of model minority creation. In Y. Chae, *Politicizing Asian American literature: Towards a critical multiculturalism* (pp. 19–30). New York, NY: Routledge.

Chang, M. J. (2011). Battle hymn of the model minority myth. *Amerasia Journal, 37*(2), 137–143.

Chao, M. M., Chiu, C., Chan, W., Mendoza-Denton, R., & Kwok, C. (2013). The model minority as a shared reality and its implication for interracial perceptions. *Asian American Journal of Psychology, 4*(2), 84–92. doi: 10.1037/a0028769

Chu, L. T. (1991). Who are the model minorities among the junior college Asian-American subgroups? Retrieved on March 23, 2012 from http://www.eric.ed.gov/PDFS/ED363362.pdf

Chung, R. C., & Walkey, F. H. (1988). From undesirable immigrant to model minority: The success story of Chinese in New Zealand. *Immigrants & Minorities, 7*(3), 308–313.

Coalition for Asian American Children and Families (CACF). (2011). "We're not even allowed to ask for help": Debunking the myth of the model minority. New York, NY: Pumphouse Projects. Retrieved December 1, 2014, from http://cerc.rutgers.edu/sites/cerc/files/were-not-even-allowed-to-ask-for-help.pdf

Crystal, D. (1989). Asian Americans and the myth of the model minority. *Social Casework: The Journal of Contemporary Social Work, 70*(7), 405–413.

Cunanan, V., Guerrero, A., & Minamoto, L. (2006). Filipinos and the myth of model minority in Hawai'i: A pilot study. *Journal of Ethnic and Cultural Diversity in Social Work, 15*(1/2),167–192.

Davé, S. (2013). Animating Gandhi: Historical figures, Asian American masculinity, and model-minority Accents in *Clone High*. In S. S. Davie (Ed.), *Indian accents: Brown voice and racial performance in American television and film* (pp. 60–84). Urbana, IL: University of Illinois Press.

Dechamma, S. (2012). The model minority: Problematizing the representation of Kodavas in Kannada cinema. *Inter-Asia Cultural Studies, 13*(1), 5–21.

Delucchi, M., & Do, H. D. (1996). The model minority myth and perceptions of Asian-Americans as victims of racial harassment. *College Student Journal, 30*(3), 411–414.

Fang, G. (2008). What it means to be a model minority: Voices of ethnic Koreans in northeast China. *Asian Ethnicity, 9*(1), 55–67.

Fang, G. (2009a). Challenges of discourses on "model minority" and "South Korean wind" for ethnic Koreans' schooling in northeast China. *Diaspora, Indigenous, and Minority Education, 3*(2), 119–130.

Fang, G. (2009b). Model minority, self-perception and schooling: Multiple voices of Korean students in China. *Asia Pacific Journal of Education, 29*(1), 17–27.

Fang, G. (2009c). Researching Korean children's schooling experience behind the model minority stereotype in China: An ethnographic approach. In C. Kwok-Bun, K. S.

Agnes, C. Yin-Wah, & C. Wai-Wan (Eds.), *Social Stratification in Chinese Societies* (pp. 225–245). Leiden, Netherlands: Brill.

Fang, G. (2010a). A comparative analysis of the meaning of model minority among ethnic Koreans in China and the United States. *Comparative Education, 46*(2), 207–222.

Fang, G. (2010b). *Becoming a model minority: Schooling experiences of ethnic Koreans in China.* Lanham, MD: Rowman & Littlefield Publishers.

Galindo, C., & Pong, S. (2011). Tenth grade math achievement of Asian students: Are Asian students still the "model minority"?—A comparison of two educational cohorts. In X. L. Rong & R. Endo (Eds.), *Asian American education—Identities, racial issues, and languages* (pp. 1–29). Charlotte, NC: Information Age.

Hall, R. E. (2001). "Model minority" as Eurocentric stereotype: Southeast Asian gangs. *Loyola Journal of Social Sciences, 15*(2), 135–146.

Hannis, G. (2009). From yellow peril to model minority? A comparative analysis of a newspaper's depiction of the Chinese in New Zealand at the 20th and 21st centuries. *Asia Pacific Media Educator, 19,* 85–98.

Hartlep, N. D. (2012). A segmented assimilation theoretical study of the 2002 Asian American student population. Unpublished doctoral dissertation. University of Wisconsin, Milwaukee. Milwaukee, WI.

Hartlep, N. D. (2013). *The model minority stereotype: Demystifying Asian American success.* Charlotte, NC: Information Age.

Hartlep, N. D. (Ed.). (2014). *The model minority stereotype reader: Critical and challenging readings for the 21st century.* San Diego, CA: Cognella Publishing.

Hartlep, N. D., & Morgan, G. B. (2013). An exploratory study of the restricted-use ELS:2002 dataset: Using finite mixture modeling as a way to problematize the "model minority" stereotype. *International Journal of Research in Methodology, 3*(3), 295–304. Retrieved from http://www.cirworld.com/index.php/IJREM/article/view/1880/pdf_16

Hawkins, N. (2009). Becoming a model minority: The depiction of Japanese Canadians in the globe and mail, 1946–2000. *Canadian Ethnic Studies, 41*(1–2), 137–154.

Hune, S., & Takeuchi, D. (2008). *Asian Americans in Washington State: Closing their hidden achievement gaps.* Retrieved from http://www.capaa.wa.gov

Ip, M., & Pang, D. (2005). New Zealand Chinese identity: Sojourners, model minority and multiple identities. In M. Ip & D. Pang (Eds.), *New Zealand identities: Departures and destinations* (pp. 174–190). Victoria, New Zealand: Victoria University Press.

Kagawa-Singer, M., & Hune, S. (Eds.). (2011). Forging the future: The role of new research, data, and policies for Asian Americans, Native Hawaiians, and Pacific Islanders. *AAPI Nexus Journal, 9*(1&2), iii–268. Retrieved from http://www.aasc.ucla.edu/aascpress/nexu s9_1_2_full.pdf

Kalman-Lamb, N. (2013). The athlete as model minority subject: Jose Bautista and Canadian multiculturalism. *Social Identities: Journal for the Study of Race, Nation, and Culture, 19*(2), 1–16. DOI:10.1080/13504630.2013.789219

Kang, M. (2010). I just put Koreans and nails together: Nail spas and the model minority. In M. Kang, *The managed hand: Race, gender, and the body in beauty service work* (pp. 133–164). Berkeley, CA: University of California Press.

Kao, G. (1995). Asian Americans as model minorities? A look at their academic performance. *American Journal of Education, 103*(2), 121–159.

Kao, G., & Tienda, M. (1998). Educational aspirations of minority youth. *American Journal of Education, 106*(3), 349–384.

Kim, C. J. (1999). The racial triangulation of Asian Americans. *Politics & Society, 27*(1), 105–138.

Kim, K. C., & Hurh, W. M. (1983). Korean Americans and the "success" image: A critique. *Amerasia Journal, 10*(2), 3–21.

Kim, P. Y., & Lee, D. (2013, August 5). Internalized model minority myth, Asian values, and help-seeking attitudes among Asian American students. *Cultural Diversity and Ethnic Minority Psychology*. Advance online publication. doi: 10.1037/a0033351 Accessed here: http://psycnet.apa.org/psycinfo/2013–27668–001/

Kitano, H. L. (1997). *Race relations*. Upper Saddle River, NJ: Prentice Hall.

Kitano, H., & Sue, S. (1973). The model minorities. *Journal of Social Issues, 29*(2), 1–9.

Koo, D. J., Peguero, A. A., & Shekarkhar, Z. (2012). The "model minority" victim: Immigration, gender, and Asian American vulnerabilities to violence at school. *Journal of Ethnicity in Criminal Justice, 10*(2), 129–147.

Lee, S. J. (1994). Behind the model minority stereotype: Voices of high- and low-achieving Asian American students. *Anthropology & Education Quarterly, 25*(4), 413–29.

Lee, S. J. (2001). More than "model minorities" or "delinquents": A look at Hmong American high school students. *Harvard Educational Review, 71*(3), 505–528.

Lee, S. J. (2003). Model minorities and perpetual foreigners: The impact of stereotyping on Asian American students. In M. Sadowski (Ed.), *Adolescents at school: Perspectives on youth, identity, and education* (pp. 41–49). Cambridge, MA: Harvard Education Press.

Lee, S. J. (2005). *Up against whiteness: Race, school, and immigrant youth*. New York: Teachers College Press.

Lee, S. J., & Kumashiro, K. (2005). *A Report on the status of Asian Americans and Pacific Islanders in education: Beyond the "Model Minority" stereotype*. Washington, DC: National Education Association. Retrieved December 1, 2014, from http://www.capsmer.org/assets/Files /Acheiment-Gaps/Status-Asian-American.pdf

Leong, F. T. L., Leach, M. M., & Yeh, C. (2007). Suicide among Asian Americans: What do we know? What do we need to know? *Death Studies, 31*(5), 417–434.

Leung, M. (2013). Jeremy Lin's model minority problem. *Contexts, 12*(3), 52–56. DOI:10.1177/1536504213499879

Lew, J. (2002, May). The truth behind the model minority. *YWCA Newsletter of the City of New York Flushing Branch, 163*, 1–2.

Lew, J. (2004). The "other" story of the model minorities: Korean American high school dropouts in an urban context. *Anthropology of Education Quarterly, 35*(3), 297–311.

Lew, J. (2011). Keeping the American dream alive: Model minority discourse of Asian American children. In S. Tozer (Ed.), *Handbook of research in the social foundations of education* (pp. 614–620). New York: Routledge.

Li, G. (2005). Other people's success: Impact of the "model minority" myth on underachieving Asian students in North America. *KEDI Journal of Educational Policy, 2*(1), 69–86.

Li, G., & Wang, L. (Eds.). (2008). *Model minority myth revisited: An interdisciplinary approach to demystifying Asian American educational experiences*. Charlotte, NC: Information Age.

Mahmud, T. (2001). Genealogy of a state-engineered "model minority" "not quite/not white" South Asian Americans. *Denver University Law, 78*(4), 657–686.

Maramba, D. C. (2011). The importance of critically disaggregating data: The case of Southeast Asian American college students. *AAPI Nexus, 9*(1&2), 127–133.

Martinelli, P. C., & Nagasawa, R. (1987). A further test of the model minority thesis: Japanese Americans in a sunbelt state. *Sociological Perspectives, 30*(3), 266–288.

Miyamoto, S. F. (1984). *Social solidarity among the Japanese in Seattle.* Seattle, WA: University of Washington Press.

McLachlan, G. J., & Peel, D. (2000). *Finite mixture models.* New York: John Wiley & Sons.

Morgan, G. B. (2015). Mixed mode latent class analysis: An examination of fit index performance for classification. *Structural Equation Modeling, 22*, 76–86.

Moynihan, D. P. (1965, March) *The Negro family: The case for national action.* Washington, DC: Office of Policy Planning and Research. Retrieved December 1, 2014, from http://web.stanford.edu/~mrosenfe/Moynihan's%20The%20Negro%20Family.pdf

Museus, S. D., & Kiang, P. N. (2009). Deconstructing the model minority myth and how it contributes to the invisible minority reality in higher education research. *New Directions for Institutional Research, 142*, 5–15.

Muthén, B. O., & Muthén, L. K. (2012). *Mplus: User's guide* (6th ed.). Los Angeles, CA: Muthén & Muthén.

Nadal, K. L., Pituc, S. T., Johnston, M. P., & Esparrago, T. (2010). Overcoming the model minority myth: Experiences of Filipino American graduate students. *Journal of College Student Development, 51*(6), 694–706.

National Center for Education Statistics (NCES). (2013). Bibliography for the educational longitudinal study of 2002. Retrieved on April 3, 2013 from http://nces.ed.gov/surveys/els2002/pdf/ELS2002annotated_biblio.pdf

Ng, J. C., Lee, S. S., & Pak, Y. K. (2007). Contesting the model minority and perpetual foreigner stereotypes: A critical review of literature on Asian Americans. *Review of Research in Education, 31*(1), 95–130.

Ngo, B., & Lee, S. J. (2007). Complicating the image of model minority success: A review of Southeast Asian American education. *Review of Educational Research, 77*(4), 415–453.

Noh, E. (2007). Asian American women and suicide: Problems of responsibility and healing. *Women & Therapy, 30*(3–4), 87–107.

Noh, M. S. (2013). From model minority to second-gen stereotypes: Korean Canadian and Korean American accounts. In M. W. Karraker (Ed.), *The other people: Interdisciplinary perspectives on migration* (pp. 107–118). New York: Palgrave MacMillan.

Nylund, K. L., Asparouhov, T., & Muthén, B. O. (2007). Deciding on the number of classes in latent class analysis and growth mixture modeling: A Monte Carlo simulation study. *Structural Equation Modeling, 14*, 535–569.

Osajima, K. (2005). Asian Americans as the model minority: An analysis of the popular press image in the 1960s and 1980s. In K. A. Ono (Ed.), *A companion to Asian American studies* (pp. 215–225). Malden, MA: Blackwell.

Pak, Y. K. (2001). Unraveling the "model minority" stereotype: Listening to Asian American youth. [book review]. *Urban Education, 36*(1), 152–158.

Park, E. J. W., & Park, J. S. W. (2005). Engineering the model minority. In E. J. W. Park & J. S. W. Park (Eds.), *Probationary Americans: Contemporary immigration policies and the shaping of Asian American communities* (pp. 97–106). New York: Routledge.

Petersen, W. (1966, January 6). Success story: Japanese American style. *The New York Times Magazine, 20–21*, 33, 36, 38, 40.

Poon, O. A., & Hune, S. (2009). Countering master narratives of the "perpetual foreigner" and "model minority": The hidden injuries of race and Asian American doctoral students. In M. F. Howard-Hamilton, C. L. Morelon-Quainoo, S. D. Johnson, R. Winkle-Wagner, & L. Santiague (Eds.), *Standing on the outside looking In: underrepresented students' experiences in advanced-degree programs* (pp. 82–102). Sterling, VA: Stylus.

Qin, D. B., Way, N., & Mukherjee, P. (2008). The other side of the model minority story: The familial and peer challenges faced by Chinese American adolescents. *Youth & Society, 39*(4), 480–506.

Qin, D. B., Way, N., & Rana, M. (2008). The "model minority" and their discontent: Examining peer discrimination and harassment of Chinese American immigrant youth. In H. Yoshikawa & N. Way (Eds.), *Beyond the family: Contexts of immigrant children's development* (pp. 27–42). Hoboken, NJ: Jossey-Bass.

Rangaswamy, P. (1995). Asian Indians in Chicago: Growth and change in a model minority. In M. G. Holli & P. A. Jones (Eds.), *Ethnic Chicago: A multicultural portrait* (4th ed) (pp. 438–462). Grand Rapids, MI: Eerdmans.

Srinivasan, S. (2000). Toward improved health: Disaggregating Asian American and Native Hawaiin/Pacific Islander data. *American Journal of Public Health, 90*(11), 1731–1734.

Sue, S., & Wagner, N. (Eds.). (1973). *Asian-Americans: Psychological perspectives*. Palo, Alto, CA: Science and Behavior Books.

Suzuki, B. H. (1980). Education and the socialization of Asian Americans: A revisionist analysis of the "model minority" thesis. In R. Endo, S. Sue, & N. N. Wagner (Eds.), *Asian-Americans: Social and psychological perspectives, Vol. II* (pp. 155–175). Ben Lomond, CA: Science and Behavior Books.

Suzuki, B. H. (1989). Asian Americans as the "model minority": Outdoing whites? Or media hype? *Change, 21*(6), 13–19.

Suzuki, B. H. (2002). Revisiting the model minority stereotype: Implications for student affairs practice and higher education. In M. K. McEwen, C. M. Kodama, A. N. Alvarez, S. Lee, & C. T. H. Liang (Eds.), *Working with Asian American college students: New directions for student services* (vol. 97, pp. 21–32). San Francisco, CA: Jossey-Bass.

Teranishi, R. T. (2002). The myth of the super minority: Misconceptions about Asian Americans. *The College Board Review, 195,* 17–21.

Teranishi, R. T. (2010). *Asians in the ivory tower: Dilemmas of racial inequality in American higher education*. New York: Teachers College Press.

Um, K. (2003). *A dream denied: Educational experiences of Southeast Asian American youth, issues and recommendations*. Washington, DC: Southeast Asia Resource Action Center. Retrieved December 1, 2014, from http://www.ocf.berkeley.edu/~sasc/wp-content/uploads/2012/01/A-Dream-Denied.pdf

U.S. Census. (2010). *The Asian population*. Retrieved December 1, 2014, from http://www.census.gov/prod/cen2010/briefs/c2010br-11.pdf

U.S. Department of Education. (2004). Educational Longitudinal Study of 2002. Retrieved December 1, 2014, from http://nces.ed.gov/surveys/els2002/avail_data.asp

Whaley, A. L., & Noel, L. T. (2013). Academic achievement and behavioral health among Asian American and African American adolescents: Testing the model minority and inferior minority assumptions. *Social Psychology of Education, 16*(1), 23–43.

Wong, E. F. (1985). Asian American middleman minority theory: The framework of an American myth. *Journal of Ethnic Studies, 13*(1), 51–88.

Wong, L. (1976). The Chinese experience: From yellow peril to model minority. *Civil Rights Digest, 9*(1), 33–35.

Xiong, S., & Joubert, C. (2012). *Demystifying the model minority: The importance of disaggregating subgroup data to promote success for Southeast Asian youth.* Fresno, CA: California State University, Fresno. Retrieved December 1, 2014, from http://www.fresnostate.edu/chhs/ccci/documents/Demystifying%20the%20Model%20Minority.pdf

Yamanaka, K., & McClelland, K. (1994). Earning the model-minority image: Diverse strategies of economic adaptation by Asian-American women. *Ethnic and Racial Studies, 17*(1), 79–114.

Yang, K. (2004). Southeast Asian American children: Not the "model minority." *Future of Children, 14*(2), 127–133.

Ying, Y., Lee, P. A., Tsai, J. L., Hung, Y., Lin, M., & Wan, C. T. (2001). Asian American college students as model minorities: An examination of their overall competence. *Cultural Diversity & Ethnic Minority Psychology, 7*(1), 59–74. Retrieved December 1, 2014, from http://www-psych.stanford.edu/~tsailab/PDF/AA%20College%20Students.pdf

Yoshihama, M. (2001). Model minority demystified: Emotional costs of multiple victimizations in the lives of women of Japanese descent. In N. G. Choi (Ed.), *Psychosocial aspects of the Asian-American experience: Diversity within diversity* (pp. 201–224). New York: Haworth Press.

AFTERWORD

Greg Tanaka

Generations. This volume marks by my reckoning the third generation of work in modern Asian American Studies (see e.g., Aguilar-San Juan, 1994; San Juan, 1972). From the complexity and nuance of this text, I quickly learned that we have come a long, long way from when I first became conscious of an urge to know who I was and what my purpose in life might be. As a student then at an all-white college in New England in the late 1960s, I could not even begin to imagine that the analysis shown in this book would one day be possible. At the same time, these writings surface a number of avenues for future work, and I will attempt to develop some of those here. Stated in another way, I feel the maturation of work in this subfield begs the question of what should come next, *after* the model minority myth. My greatest wish is that this not just be a recrudescence of hurtfulness in another form.

Race. First, I find the oversimplifying and homogenizing operation of a socially constructed "whiteness," in my own limited research, in stark contrast to the rich, nuanced, and complex analytics of identities and cultural meanings of Asian Americans and Asians presented here. Distilled and blended very persuasively through such tools as intersectionality, fluidity, storytelling, irony, and seeming contradiction—the ever-inchoate quality of the Asian American and Asian positionality seen here demonstrates to my sensibility that whiteness may be starting to meet its demise at last, enacting a rigidity and a nostalgia that together hint at

Killing the Model Minority Stereotype: Asian American Counterstories and Complicity,
pages 381–385.

panic. Dependent in part on seeing the Asian as "monolithic," "essentialized," "a model" (even "inauthentic"), whiteness as a racializing force is increasingly strained, a *tired* operation. In the end, it is the great weight of the variegated and evolving nature of Asian and Asian American identities and language ideologies developed so richly in this text that, in comparison, leaves a presumed superiority of whiteness so colorless, thin and brittle, and acted out through ever more frantic contortions to, in some vague sense, prove itself—like in the desperate need to always be at war, perhaps, or a continuing belief that Western science will always trump the pushback of the environment. In my view, this grand weakening raises the stakes on the future viability of whiteness considerably higher. For if not race, then what will yield a sense of worth for the European American tomorrow? *Future research on Asian American and Asian blended identities might benefit from comparative work performed at the same time on whiteness and its declining strength as a subjectivity.*

For instance, if European Americans can no longer rely on essentializing and binary comparisons to people of color in the U.S., then what would whiteness be then? And if whiteness is *already* an empty shell, then how else might European Americans come to know meaning, make judgments about self and others, and find moments of inner quiet, calm, and joy that come from being anchored in time and space? (Absent new meaning, the default is always back to whiteness.) And so again, as the illusory notion of the model minority myth loses legitimacy, where to next for the European American?

Meaning. Each time a chapter in this volume revealed the sense of worth (and yes, the challenges) that come from having one's own cultural meanings—whether from "duty" or "obligation" or "the importance of storytelling"—I registered a very powerful message *that it is not okay not to have meaning.* Stated in a different way, the positionalities discussed in this book show, first, that it is rewarding and meaning*ful* to be able to know and celebrate one's norms, duties, obligations, and rituals (even when those meaning systems put us at odds with the mainstream culture!) and, second, that without those meanings it becomes all the more difficult to have a sense of self in the world or a convincing personal belief in one's purpose in life. For example, how could a person reach out to engage others on the planet on equal footing—or begin to perform as a citizen in a diverse and participatory democracy—when she or he does not feel secure in her or his own meanings?

When we as researchers, thinkers, and performers have purpose and believe that purpose brings honor (even in imagined ways) to one's family and ancestors, then I would say that purpose is automatically *not* binary, automatically *not* reductionistic, and instead as rich and uplifting as there are so many roles that might please the forbearers of our imaginations. It is for this reason that I have come to believe that *having cultural meaning is the antidote to binary and simplistic operations like race, its whiteness, and its model minority myth.* So in my view, *the production of a book like this contributes in a major way to a larger dismantling of binary thinking altogether—and by implication begs the question of what the future meanings of white people will be after the binary construction of whiteness collapses, and how we might research that.* For example, where will the meanings for white people come from then, long after the death of the model minority myth?

Language and Culture Revitalization. Here I will draw from wonderful work in educational anthropology and attempt to apply what researchers in Alaska have come to refer to as "language and culture revitalization" (Dementi-Leonard & Gillmore, 1999). This notion holds that education will be more successful with children from non-Western cultures whose meanings have dissipated if that education is presented through the lenses of those very cultural meanings and language forms. This superb work parallels similar projects with young native Hawaiian children in the Kamehemeha Early Education Program (KEEP) (Tharp & Gallimore, 1982) and Mexican-American youth and their "community cultural wealth" (Yosso, 2005). It might not be too early to suggest a bold extension of that line of work to European Americans now.

What Dementi-Leonard and Gillmore learned is that by first listening to the community members and elders of a village, it is possible to work up an approach to language and culture revitalization that makes sense to the people of that village. Here, it might be a stretch, but possible, to imagine a European American child choosing an ethnic culture in her or his family tree—and then going off on an adventure through the library and internet, and even one day by visiting in person, to (re) discover the shared meanings of the people from whence she or he came.

Could we now venture the proposition that it would be a positive development for educators to begin to teach European American children to appreciate and inculcate the meanings of at least *one* of their own families' cultural backgrounds? This would not only be a grounding experience for these youth (with high value as they go on to interact with others in a culturally rich global human society), but also of strategic value to people of color in the U.S. who would be secondary beneficiaries of a transition by white Americans from a race-based to an ethnic culture-based identity system. When a European American child comes to know the norms, duties, obligations, beliefs, rituals, and myths of forbearers, I am suggesting that those meanings will help this individual to navigate a strange and increasingly diverse world precisely because she or he will have meanings of her or his own—and without relying on race.

In other words, if a volume like this can demonstrate so persuasively just how rich and personally validating (and annoying) one's cultural meanings might be for Asian Americans—and by implication, how very stark and hollow the identity of whiteness may be in comparison to that—then why would we not want to promote a curriculum of "language and culture revitalization" for European American children in the U.S. today? This could conceivably serve as a far superior substitute for a race-based identity and yet provide clarity and direction in much the same way, but without the negative and hurtful effects on others who are not white.

If we know that reclaiming the language and cultural meanings of one's ancestors can enhance learning for (and socially anchor) the Athabascan, the native Hawaiian, the Mexican-American, then why wouldn't this achieve the same result for European American children? Stated in another way, the chapters in this book suggest to me that *doing applied work to (re)develop the cultural meanings, and thus culture, of European American children may be one way of socially anchoring them while also removing the dysfunctionality for them of a race-based identity*. My further hunch is that this would have the added benefit of making a return of the model minority myth (in another form perhaps) far less likely to occur in the future. In other words, the constant, invisible pull toward racialization would be *replaced* by having one's own ethnic cultural meanings.

In addition, we know it is useful for the citizen in a diverse world to have more than one identity by which to guide one's conduct, depending on whom you are associating with at the time. By learning a "repertoire of identities" (Kroskrity, 1993, p. 208; Volosinov, 1973), each child would acquire a capacity to conduct her or himself in one way with children of the same ethnic cultural background, in another way with U.S. adults who are of color, and in yet another way with students from Africa, etc. It is this child who will have the skill set to adapt well and be successful in a shrinking and increasingly global human society—but it is by first learning who you are that you have a more stable base for that. In this way, "new identity formation could potentially compensate for 'erasure'" of a race-based identity (Tanaka, 2002, citing Irvine & Gal 2000, p. 38) hinted at in this text. Conversely, a decision *to turn away from* this kind of reflowering or *re-cueillement* (Baudelaire, 1989, p. 192) of family cultural norms could potentially widen the anomie and soul loss (Ruti, 2006, p. 19, p. 88) as that child reaches adulthood and finds her or himself in a room full of people from other cultures.

How Will We Know When We Have Succeeded? While this may not happen soon, it would seem to make sense now for applied researchers to start preparing for what this book anticipates—a post-model minority myth era. So, more language and culture revitalization for children of color in the U.S. *and* beginning this for European American children. More writings about hyphenated or conflicted or shifting cultural identities. With all this, *I think that we as a diverse nation could one day encounter "a moment of complementarity" where we as individuals with different, evolving, and polyvalent identities will each come to know who we are and what our purpose in life might be—not by putting others down but by helping the others also to discover who they are and what their purposes might be*. Can we let some of our research go in that direction, too?

What I am emboldened to conclude after reading this text is that we will have arrived at a better time and place when there is a mutual coming to be, or "mutual immanence," in which not just Asian Americans but also European Americans come to enjoy deeper sources of meaning and identity not based on race, and do this in a mutually reinforcing way with others. To prepare for that moment, it might be useful to begin now to recontextualize and operationalize such terms as "subjectivity," "intersubjectivity," and "mutual immanence" to aid in the assessment process.

So that is one possible reality after the end of the model minority myth. We would, by then, be in a wholly different universe from my college days when I struggled in my own vacuum to write an empirical research paper on the changing personality needs of Japanese-Americans. Thanks to this volume, I now feel very confident that this better world will one day come; and I urge all the writers here to continue their great work, as it matters much.

REFERENCES

Aguilar-San Juan, K. (Ed.). (1994). *The state of Asian America: Activism and resistance in the 1990s*. Boston, MA: South End Press.

Baudelaire, C. (1989). Recueillement. In M. Mathews & J. Mathews (Eds.), *The flowers of evil* (pp. 192–194). New York: New Directions. (Original work published in 1955).

Dementi-Leonard, B., & Gillmore, P. (1999). Language revitalization and identity in social context: A community-based Athabascan language presentation project in interior Alaska. *Anthropology & Education Quarterly, 30*(1), 37–55.

Irvine, J. T., & Gal, S. (2000). Language ideology and linguistic differentiation. In P. V. Kroskrity (Ed.), *Regimes of language: Ideologies, polities, and identities* (pp. 35–84). Santa Fe, AZ: School of American Research Press. Retrieved October 15, 2014, from http://web.stanford.edu/~eckert/PDF/IrvineGal2000.pdf

Kroskrity, P. V. (1993). *Language, history and identity.* Tucson, AZ: University of Arizona Press.

Ruti, M. (2006). *Reinventing the soul: Posthumanist theory and psychic life.* New York: Other Press.

San Juan, E. (1972). *Carlos Bulosan and the imagination of the class struggle.* Quezon City, Philippines: University of the Philippines Press.

Tanaka, G. K. (1970). "'Enryo' and the changing personality needs of Japanese-Americans." Unpublished manuscript, Williams College, Williamstown, MA.

Tanaka, G. K. (2002). *Remaking the subject for anthropological discourse.* Unpublished dissertation manuscript, Department of Anthropology, University of California, Los Angeles, CA.

Tharp, R. G., & Gallimore, R. (1982). Inquiry process in program development. *Journal of Community Psychology, 10*(2), 103–118.

Volosinov, V. N. (1973). *Marxism and the philosophy of language.* Cambridge, MA: Harvard University Press. (Original work published in 1929).

Yosso, T. (2005). Whose culture has capital? A critical race theory discussion of community cultural wealth. *Race, Ethnicity & Education, 8*(1), 69–91.

BIOGRAPHIES

ABOUT THE EDITORS

Nicholas D. Hartlep is Assistant Professor of Educational Foundations at Illinois State University in Normal, IL. He teaches courses on multicultural education, social and cultural foundations of education, and the model minority stereotype. Hartlep received his Ph.D. in Urban Education (Social Foundations of Education) in 2012 at the University of Wisconsin-Milwaukee from the Urban Education Doctoral Program (UEDP). During his doctoral studies, he was awarded several awards and an Advanced Opportunity Program (AOP) Fellowship. He has published numerous peer-reviewed articles, books, book chapters, edited volumes, and conference papers on the topics of urban education, Asian/Americans, the "model minority stereotype," and critiques of whiteness and neoliberalism. He has published three books on the "model minority" stereotype: *The Model Minority Stereotype: Demystifying Asian American Success* (Information Age), *The Model Minority Stereotype Reader: Critical and Challenging Readings for the 21st Century* (Cognella), and *Modern Societal Impacts of the Model Minority Stereotype* (IGI). He is the co-editor of *Unhooking from Whiteness: The Key to Dismantling Racism in the United States* (Sense). In 2015 he received the University Research Initiative (URI) Award from Illinois State University.

Killing the Model Minority Stereotype: Asian American Counterstories and Complicity,
pages 387–395.

Brad J. Porfilio is the Director of the Doctorate in Educational Leadership for Social Justice at California State University, East Bay. His research interests and expertise include urban education, gender and technology, cultural studies, neoliberalism and schooling, and transformative education. Several of his recent books have received the American Educational Studies Association's (AESA's) Critics' Choice Award. Dr. Porfilio has recently been appointed as co-editor of *Issues in Teacher Education,* a scholarly publication focused on the education of teachers from initial preparation through induction and ongoing professional growth. Over his past fifteen years in higher education he has been a faculty member of educational studies and of pedagogy and teacher education, a Director of Social Studies Education, and a University Supervisor of pre-service and in-service teachers.

ABOUT THE COMMISSIONED COVER ARTIST

Tak Toyoshima is the creative director at the award-winning alternative news-weekly newspaper *DigBoston*. He is also the creator and illustrator of *Secret Asian Man*, a comic strip that started in 1999 that focuses on the divisive issues of race, gender, religion, politics, and anything else that causes us to be placed into identifiable groups.

ABOUT THE CHAPTER CONTRIBUTORS

Daisy Ball is an Assistant Professor of Sociology at Framingham State University (FSU). She is the Coordinator of the Criminology Program at FSU, and teaches a number of courses for the program including "The Culture of Punishment" and "White-Collar Crime, and Criminological Theory." She also teaches an "Inside-Out Prison Exchange Program" course at MCI-Framingham, the nation's oldest female correctional institution in operation. In this course, traditional college students study as peers alongside incarcerated individuals. Her research interests include crime and deviance, race and ethnicity, and culture.

Alice Bradbury is a member of the Centre for Critical Education Policy Studies at the UCL Institute of Education, University College London, United Kingdom. After teaching in inner city London schools, she completed her doctoral studies at the Institute of Education. She currently teaches and supervises on a range of programs at the Institute, from undergraduate to doctoral level study. Dr Brad-bury's research explores the relationships between education policy and issues of equality, with a particular focus on early childhood education. Her book *Understanding Early Years Inequality* details the first major research project on this sector in the U.K. for a decade. She is on the editorial board of the *British Journal of Sociology of Education* and *Race, Ethnicity and Education* and is a member of the Academic Forum of the Runnymede Trust, the United Kingdom's leading race equality organization.

Yoonjung Choi is an Assistant Professor of Social Studies Education at Ewha Womans University in Seoul, South Korea. She previously taught courses in social studies methods, diversity/social justice education, and curriculum studies at University of Maine at Farmington in the United States. Her research interests include social studies curriculum and instruction, global teacher education, culturally relevant pedagogy for newcomer English language learners, and Asian American teacher and student identities. Her scholarship has been published in a variety of journals including *Multicultural Perspectives* and *Journal of Social Studies Research*, and books on educational issues on diversity and global citizenship in Korea.

Jocelyn Chu is a staff consultant at John Snow, Inc., a public health research and consulting organization headquartered in Boston, Massachusetts. Primary to her research work is the active engagement of diverse communities through capacity building and participatory processes. She serves as evaluator and technical advisor on multiple projects ranging from teen pregnancy prevention, maternal and child health issues to healthy aging initiatives. Jocelyn's research interests have focused on the plight of Asian immigrants and their second-generation children, and she has taught and co-authored on health of immigrants. Prior to joining JSI, Jocelyn was a Research Associate at the Institute for Community Health in Cambridge, Massachusetts where she worked primarily on community-academic engagement efforts for participatory research. Jocelyn received her doctorate from the Harvard School of Public Health and her MPH from Boston University School of Public Health.

Edward R. Curammeng is a Ph.D. student in the Social Science and Comparative Education Division (Race and Ethnic Studies Specialization), Graduate School of Education and Information Studies, University of California Los Angeles. His research interests are at the nexus of critical race theory, community colleges, access, and retention of Filipina/o Americans. He earned his M.A. in Asian American Studies from San Francisco State University, where he studied the educational experiences of suburban Filipina/o American youth. While in San Francisco, he taught Filipina/o American studies and Ethnic Studies with Pin@y Educational Partnerships (PEP).

Antonio L. Ellis is an Adjunct Professor at the College of Charleston School of Education, Health, and Human Performance, where he teaches Educational Foundations. He earned a doctoral degree in Educational Leadership and Policy Studies from the Howard University School of Education. Dr. Ellis's individual and joint scholarship has been published by a variety of journals and book publishers including *Education Review, Journal of Negro Education, Diverse: Issues in Higher Education*, Sage, and Peter Lang. His research centers on theoretical frameworks such as Critical Race Theory, Social Theory, Path-Goal Theory,

Synergistic Leadership Theory, Facilitative Leadership Theory, and other widely known theories that guide teacher education and educational leadership alike. Dr. Ellis is widely known for his scholarship and advocacy towards African American males who are speech and language impaired. He has presented his research at multiple academic conferences. Most recently, Dr. Ellis received the Howard University School of Education 2013 Outstanding Alumni Award in the category Leader of Change.

Marybeth Gasman is a Professor of Higher Education in the Graduate School of Education at the University of Pennsylvania. She is also director of the Penn Center for Minority Serving Institutions. Marybeth's expertise pertains to Minority Serving Institutions, Students and Faculty of Color, and Fundraising and Philanthropy in communities of color.

Grant Hannis heads the graduate journalism program at Massey University in Wellington, New Zealand. He teaches journalism history, media law and ethics, news writing, business journalism, and statistics for journalists. He is the editor of the standard journalism textbook used in New Zealand journalism schools. His research interests include reporting on diversity and the place of research in university journalism programs. As a Fulbright Senior Scholar, he spent six months at San Francisco State University teaching business journalism and researching the depiction of Chinese gold miners in the 19th-century U.S. press. Prior to becoming an academic, he spent 14 years as a senior financial journalist and research manager at *Consumer* magazine, the New Zealand equivalent of *Consumer Reports*.

Chia S. Her is a doctoral student in the San Diego State University and Claremont Graduate University Joint Ph.D. program in Education. She received her M.Ed. in Education with an emphasis in Counseling in Student Affairs from the University of California, Los Angeles and her B.A. in Political Science/Public Policy from the University of California, San Diego. She is also currently a counselor for the Educational Opportunity Programs/Ethnic Affairs at San Diego State University, which supports low-income, first generation college students in attaining a college degree. Her research interests are in the educational trajectories and experiences of racial and ethnic low-income, first-generation college students, specifically in the areas of access, persistence, and degree attainment.

Rob Ho is a Ph.D. candidate in the Graduate School of Education & Information Studies at the University of California, Los Angeles (UCLA). His dissertation focuses on comparing Asian Canadian and Asian American student experiences at higher education institutions in North America. Rob also teaches Asian Canadian Studies in the Asia-Canada Program at Simon Fraser University.

Kari J. Hodge is currently a Ph.D. student in Educational Psychology at Baylor University with a focus in measurement and quantitative methods. She holds a Masters of Arts in Education Curriculum and Instruction with a focus on teacher leadership, and a Bachelors of Arts in Elementary Education. She is currently an Instructor for Baylor University where she teaches instructional technology courses and teacher education and co-teaches Experimental Design. Her research interests include cross-country studies in teacher education, technology implementation, assessment validity, and research methodology. Hodge has published in the areas of educational technology, gifted education, and the effects of the model minority stereotype in education.

Amardeep Kahlon serves as the Dean of Academics at BML Munjal University in New Delhi, India, where she is responsible for curriculum development and academic policies for an emerging university. Dr. Kahlon earned her Ph.D. in Higher Education Administration from The University of Texas at Austin. Her research interests include the model minority stereotype, South Asian Indian students, and the use of technology to aid students' success. Dr. Kahlon also earned her Masters of Computer Science from Binghamton University in Binghamton, New York and has taught Computer Science at the post-secondary level in New York and Texas for over two decades.

Nathan Kalman-Lamb is a Ph.D. candidate in Social and Political Thought at York University in Toronto. He received an M.A. from the same institution and program for his project entitled *"The only religion without atheists:" Sport as Spectacle in the Contemporary North* (2007). He is the co-author with Gamal Abdel-Shehid of the book *Out of Left Field: Social Inequality and Sports* (2011) and has additionally been published on the topics of whiteness, multiculturalism, and high-performance athletics in the journals *Topia* and *Social Identities*. His current research focuses on labor and injury, race, gender, and spectatorship in the realms of professional hockey and basketball.

Jae Hoon Lim is an Associate Professor of Research Methods at the University of North Carolina, Charlotte, and she teaches introductory and advanced research method courses in the College of Education. Her research explores the intersection of gender, race, and class in mathematics and STEM education. Having served as president of Korean-American Educational Researchers Association (KAERA), she has an extensive record of research on Korean transnational students, and has led multiple international and comparative educational research projects. Her research has been published in numerous scholarly journals including *Journal of Educational Psychology* and *Equity & Excellence in Education*. She is a contributing author to several books published by Oxford University Press, University of California Press, and Springer.

Amy Miller serves as the Director of Global Immersion Programs and Associate Director of Academic Affairs for the Wharton School at the University of Pennsylvania, where she is responsible for managing a portfolio of international programs and advising over 400 M.B.A. students. Additionally, Ms. Miller is currently pursuing her Ed.D. in Higher Education at the University of Pennsylvania's Graduate School of Education (GSE), where she also earned a Master of Science in Education in 2008. Her research interests include multiracial college students and the intersection of college environments and identity development. She also holds a B.S. in Strategic Communications from Ithaca College and worked as a publicist in the fashion and beauty industries in New York City prior to beginning her graduate studies at UPENN.

Grant Morgan is an Assistant Professor in Educational Psychology with specialization in Advanced Quantitative Methods at Baylor University. Having earned a Ph.D. in Educational Research and Measurement from the University of South Carolina, his methodological research interests include mixture modeling, latent variable modeling, classification/clustering, and nonparametric statistics. At Baylor University, Dr. Morgan teaches doctoral-level courses in research methods, experimental design, psychometric theory, item response theory, and latent variable modeling. He also enjoys collaborating with colleagues on applications of advanced quantitative methods. To date, he has collaborated with colleagues in such areas as music education, student success in higher education, literacy among elementary aged children, secondary teacher effectiveness, dispelling the model minority stereotype, and job satisfaction among home health care workers. Dr. Morgan has authored or coauthored numerous publications in peer-reviewed methodological and applied academic journals, has presented over 50 studies at national or international conferences, and has received numerous awards from professional organizations for his methodological and applied research.

Annie Nguyen is a second-generation Vietnamese American and a first-generation college student. She earned her M.A. in Education with an emphasis in multicultural counseling and social justice at San Diego State University. Nguyen works with high school students as an academic and career guidance counselor. She is currently completing her doctorate in the San Diego State University and Claremont Graduate University Joint Ph.D. program in Education. Her research interests include multicultural education, resiliency, and the impact of race and ethnic issues on achievement and cross-cultural/cross-ethnic interactions.

Thai-Huy Nguyen is a Ph.D. candidate at the University of Pennsylvania's Graduate School of Education. His dissertation focuses on underrepresented racial minorities (URM) and the effects of attending a Minority Serving Institution (MSI) on medical school admissions. Nguyen serves as the project manager for the national study on MSIs, as well as a national study funded by the Robert Wood

Johnson Foundation on diversity in nursing. Additional research interests include healthcare workforce policy and the promotion of URM students and professionals within STEM fields.

Valerie Ooka Pang is a Professor in the School of Teacher Education at San Diego State University. She has published books such as *Multicultural Education: A Caring-centered, Reflective Approach* (2nd ed., 2010) and was series editor with E. Wayne Ross of *Race, Ethnicity, and Education*, a four-volume collection. She was senior editor of a resource for the National Council for the Social Studies on the intersection of human rights and natural disasters, which produced the text *The Human Impact of Natural Disasters: Issues for the Inquiry-Based Classroom* published in 2010. She has published in a variety of journals including *Educational Researcher, Harvard Educational Review, The Kappan, The Journal of Teacher Education, Asian American and Pacific Islander Nexus, Action in Teacher Education, Social Education, Theory and Research in Social Education, Educational Forum, and Multicultural Education*. Pang has been a consultant for organizations such as Sesame Street, Fox Children's Network, Family Communications (producers of *Mr. Rogers Neighborhood*), and Scott Foresman. Pang was a senior Fellow for the Annenberg Institute for School Reform at Brown University and has been honored by organizations such as the American Educational Research Association's Standing Committee on the Role and Status of Minorities in Education, National Association for Multicultural Education, and the University of Washington's College of Education.

Vijay Pendakur currently serves as the Associate Vice President for Student Retention at California State University-Fullerton. Prior to this role, he was the Director for the Office of Multicultural Student Success, a department charged with increasing the retention and persistence of low-income students, first generation students, and students of color at DePaul University. He holds a B.A. in History and East Asian Studies from the University of Wisconsin-Madison, an M.A. in U.S. History from the University of California-San Diego, and a doctorate in education from DePaul University. Vijay is also an experienced trainer and facilitator on issues of social justice and diversity education and has worked with colleges and universities throughout the country. He is currently working on editing a new book from Stylus Publishing, *Identity Conscious Approaches to Student Success and Retention,* which will be available September 2015. You can reach him at www.vijaypendakur.com.

Thomas M. Philip is an Assistant Professor in the Urban Schooling Division, Graduate School of Education & Information Studies, UCLA. Thomas's scholarship leverages theoretical and methodological approaches from the learning sciences to explore questions of ideology. His research focuses on how teachers understand the purpose and nature of their work within a society stratified by power, particularly how they make sense of race, racism, and racial justice. His work also explores the unique strengths, needs, and trajectories of teachers of color. A second strand in Thomas's research focuses on the ideological contexts that shape the work of teachers and how these contexts enable and constrain teachers' ability to engage in social justice oriented work. Through this strand of research, Thomas teases apart common assumptions about new digital technologies as a motivator for learning in schools, their troubling intersection with market-based solutions for school-reform, and their real and significant effects on the work of teachers. Thomas's scholarship has appeared in journals such as *Harvard Educational Review, Cognition and Instruction, Journal of Teacher Education,* and *Educational Policy.*

Gordon Pon is an Associate Professor in the School of Social Work at Ryerson University. His research and teaching interests include anti-racism, anti-colonialism, child welfare, and Asian Canadian Studies. He is a current collaborator on a national research project titled "Building and Mobilizing Knowledge on Race and Colonialism in Canada." He is a social worker by training and has worked as a front line worker in child welfare.

Shalini A. Tendulkar is a Research and Evaluation Scientist at the Institute for Community Health (ICH) and an Instructor in Medicine at the Harvard Medical School. Dr. Tendulkar's work spans multiple content areas and utilizes diverse approaches to understanding and addressing population health issues. Dr. Tendulkar is particularly committed to community based participatory research and has extensive experience conducting research and evaluation in collaboration with community and academic partners. She is also committed to working with partners to address racial, ethnic, and other health disparities. In this effort she works collaboratively with her partners to develop research and evaluation capacity as they seek to build the evidence for their community-based programming to improve the health and mental health of racial and ethnic minorities. Dr. Tendulkar's work has privileged her with the opportunity to work on a range of topics, and she has a particular interest in understanding and addressing mental health disparities with Asian communities. Dr. Tendulkar has published her research and evaluation work in peer-reviewed journals, presented in local and national settings, often in collaboration with her community partners, and teaches both graduate and undergraduate students in these areas. Dr. Tendulkar received her undergraduate degree from Wellesley College and her Masters and Doctorate in Maternal and Child Health from the Harvard School of Public Health.

Tien Ung is an Assistant Professor at Simmons School of Social Work and director of the Urban Leadership Program. Dr. Ung teaches courses on research, leadership, trauma, and social work practice. As a practitioner-scholar, Dr. Ung works with clients, trains practitioners, and provides organizational consultation in child and family settings with specific expertise in child protection, adoption, forensic social work, child and family trauma, and immigrant and refugee mental health. Consequently, Dr. Ung's research is broadly focused in the field of transnationalism, with particular attention to the effects of culture and intercultural dynamics on identity, mental health, and family well-being. Dr. Ung anchors her practice experience in her research by drawing on the principles of community-engaged scholarship. Inspired by a translational approach to research, she draws on a unique framework developed during her doctoral studies informed by social capital, human capital, and cultural capital to examine relationships between client, practitioner, and community capacity and individual and family well-being.

Marissa S. Yenpasook is a first-generation, multi-ethnic member of the Asian American Pacific Islander community. Her mother is Pilipino and her father is Thai-Chinese. Yenpasook is completing her doctoral studies in multicultural education in the San Diego State University and Claremont Graduate University Joint Ph.D. program. She completed her Master of Arts in Education with an emphasis in multicultural counseling and social justice education at San Diego State University. Her areas of interest and research are in multicultural counseling, mixed-race and mixed-ethnicity issues, as well as marginalized populations, particularly foster youth and the LGBTQIA community. Presently Yenpasook is working on research in the areas of counseling and interracial families. Additionally, she is a part-time practicum supervisor and lecturer at San Diego State University, and she serves as a Court Appointed Special Advocate (CASA) for foster youth in San Diego County.